Advancing Crisis Communication Effectiveness

Advancing Crisis Communication Effectiveness shows how crisis communication plans and efforts for complex and challenging issues benefit when academic perspectives are connected with practitioner experiences. The book brings crisis and public relations scholars together with practicing professionals to integrate academic theories and research with the knowledge and lessons learned on the frontlines of crisis communication and management.

This book illustrates how having insights and observations from both leading crisis communication scholars and professionals strengthens crisis management and communication strategies, plans, and coordination. Chapters co-authored by leading scholars and professionals highlight how academic theories and research can inform crisis management and response – and how practitioners can utilize, inform, and strengthen academic theories and research. For each topic area covered, examples and applications are provided that show how integrating public relations scholarship with practice can advance crisis communication effectiveness.

This book represents a unique and timely contribution to the field of crisis management and communication. It will be an important resource for public relations and crisis management and communication scholars, educators, professionals, consultants, and graduate students.

Yan Jin (PhD, University of Missouri) is the Georgia Athletic Association Professor and a Professor of Public Relations at the Grady College of Journalism and Mass Communication, University of Georgia. Dr. Jin has authored more than 85 peer-reviewed journal articles and over 20 book chapters. She is co-editor of the Routledge book *Social Media and Crisis Communication*. In 2019, Dr. Jin received the Kitty O. Locker Outstanding Researcher Award from the Association for Business Communication, which recognizes her research excellence and contribution to the business communication discipline. She is a member of the Arthur W. Page Society.

Bryan H. Reber (PhD, University of Missouri) is C. Richard Yarbrough Professor in Crisis Communication Leadership and Head of the Department of Advertising and Public Relations at the Grady College of Journalism and Mass Communication, University of Georgia. Dr. Reber has published over 50 journal articles, book chapters, and encyclopedia entries. He is co-author of the book *Gaining Influence in Public Relations: The Role of Resistance in Practice* and three top-selling public relations textbooks. Dr. Reber is a member of the Arthur W. Page Society and serves as Research Director of the Plank Center for Leadership in Public Relations.

Glen J. Nowak (PhD, University of Wisconsin-Madison) is a Professor of Advertising and Public Relations at the University of Georgia Grady College of Journalism and Mass Communication, and Director of its Center for Health and Risk Communication. Dr. Nowak spent 14 years at the US Centers for Disease Control and Prevention, including six years as the Communications Director for the National Immunization Program and six years as the agency's Director of Media Relations.

Routledge Research in Public Relations

Bringing together theories and thought from a variety of perspectives, this series features cutting-edge research addressing all the major issues in public relations today, helping to define and advance the field.

4 **The Bauhaus and Public Relations**
Communication in a Permanent State of Crisis
Patrick Rössler

5 **Public Relations and Religion in American History**
Evangelism, Temperance, and Business
Margot Opdycke Lamme

6 **Public Relations in the Nonprofit Sector**
Theory and Practice
Edited by Richard D. Waters

7 **Public Relations and the Public Interest**
Jane Johnston

8 **The Moral Compass of Public Relations**
Edited by Brigitta R. Brunner

9 **Relationship Building in Public Relations**
Petra Theunissen and Helen Sissons

10 **Advancing Crisis Communication Effectiveness**
Integrating Public Relations Scholarship with Practice
Edited by Yan Jin, Bryan H. Reber, and Glen J. Nowak

For more information about this series, please visit: https://www.routledge.com/Routledge-Research-in-Public-Relations/book-series/RRPR

Advancing Crisis Communication Effectiveness

Integrating Public Relations Scholarship with Practice

Edited by
Yan Jin, PhD,
Bryan H. Reber, PhD, and
Glen J. Nowak, PhD

Routledge
Taylor & Francis Group
NEW YORK AND LONDON

First published 2021
by Routledge
52 Vanderbilt Avenue, New York, NY 10017

and by Routledge
2 Park Square, Milton Park, Abingdon, Oxon, OX14 4RN

Routledge is an imprint of the Taylor & Francis Group, an informa business

Library of Congress Cataloging-in-Publication Data
A catalog record for this title has been requested

ISBN: 978-0-367-35317-9 (hbk)
ISBN: 978-0-429-33065-0 (ebk)

Typeset in Times New Roman
by codeMantra

Dedicated to the crisis communicators and crisis communication scholars, one whose work informs the other's; to the encouragement of greater collaboration between and among these individuals; and to the more effective crisis communication that results.

Contents

Illustrations

Figures

Tables

Textbox

Foreword

For a profession that has a lot to do with image, public relations has not always had the best image. Too many times, the discipline has not been at the decision-making table when a crisis occurs. It has been relegated to communicating decisions made by others, rather than being a part of the decision itself.

This observation comes from a person who labored at the highest level of two complex organizations, won a couple of Silver Anvils from the Public Relations Society of America, and was recognized by an industry publication as one of the "100 Most Influential Public Relations People of the 20th Century." And who never took a PR course in college.

My introduction to public relations was accidental and providential. I was working for a local radio station when I was offered an opportunity to join Southern Bell Telephone Company in Atlanta and become the company's contact person with the local media. I knew nothing about the company and even less about public relations but jumped at the opportunity because it paid $10 a week more. Thus began my on-the-job training that continued for the next 40-plus years.

The first thing I learned was that, in an engineering-oriented business like Southern Bell, public relations was considered a necessary evil but not relevant to its operations. One of the first directives I received was to "get good things in the paper and keep the bad stuff out," and to write a news release whenever told to, whether it made sense or not.

I am not sure at what point it dawned on me that, while the role of public relations was to present my company in the best light possible to the outside world, it was also incumbent to inform management of what the various publics we served were thinking about us. Management in any organization can become myopic in their decision-making, and that is when a crisis is most likely to occur.

I became a true believer in the role that my adopted profession could and should play in the company's decision-making process. I wasn't hesitant to let my peers know that I considered myself and the public relations discipline an equal among equals, and when a crisis did happen, I wanted to be in on the discussions. Waiting until a crisis occurs is too late to be having that conversation.

That carried on to the top of the business. When I became Vice President of Public Relations at BellSouth Corporation, I was tasked with reorganizing the department. My CEO wanted to know what I would need to get that accomplished. He later told me he was thinking about budget and personnel, so my answer surprised him. My response was simple. I wanted to be at the head table when he was making the decisions only the CEO can make, particularly at the time of crisis. Obviously, he would be getting legal counsel. I wanted him to get external counsel at the same time. He agreed.

Then came the hard part: making sure the counsel was sound and that it would be accepted. Many times, the advice ran counter to what others were suggesting—theirs was usually "Don't say anything." I was not always the most popular person in the room, but I was right enough of the time that I earned my way to the table and stayed there until my retirement.

Then came an opportunity to serve as managing director of communications and government relations for the Atlanta Committee for the Olympic Games (ACOG). ACOG was responsible for staging the 1996 Centennial Olympic Games in Atlanta, and I was to get a crash course in crisis management, unlike anything I had experienced in my previous career.

From collapsing light stanchions during construction of the main stadium to convincing management to open our records to the media as if we were a public agency, even though we were privately funded, to gay rights issues to controversies over a state flag that represented the Confederate battle flag to the most high-profile crisis of the Games—the bombing in Centennial Olympic Park—I was there for all of them and a part of the final decision.

I consider myself fortunate to have had the career I did and proud that I was able to make the public relations discipline relevant in crisis communications. But I was self-taught, and much of my advice and counsel was instinctive. In today's rapidly changing world, that won't suffice.

The fundamentals of a crisis have remained pretty much unchanged since those long-ago days when I began my career in public relations. It is the environment that is drastically different. Much of that is due to the impact of social media, the communications equivalent of a wildfire. Organizations must be able to respond rapidly and accurately to a crisis. If there was ever a time to have public relations at the decision-making table, it is now.

It has been my privilege to work with the faculty at the Grady College of Journalism and Mass Communications at the University of Georgia in establishing a professorship in Crisis Communications Leadership under the direction of Dr. Bryan Reber. One of outgrowths of that effort has been the Crisis Communications Think Tank, bringing together practitioners and academics to discuss crisis issues and to share experiences and research with one another. The Think Tank is also an invaluable resource for the students.

This book is a result of discussions emanating from Crisis Communications Think Tank sessions. It is intended for both academics and professionals, and ultimately to produce a new generation of professionals with all the tools necessary to be an effective voice at the table when a crisis arrives.

We have come a long way from the days of public relations being just a communicator of someone else's decisions in a time of crisis to having a part in those decisions. In doing so, we accept the fact that trying to gauge public reaction in many cases is like walking a high-wire. It is risky. But the more we understand what to do and how to do it, the more valuable we will be to our organization. That is why I consider *Advancing Crisis Communication Effectiveness* such an important addition to our never-ending learning curve.

C. RICHARD YARBROUGH

Acknowledgments

The editors would like to thank Taylor S. Voges and Caitlin Oh for their excellent assistance with the book project.

Part I

Overview and Context

1 Complex and Challenging Crises

A Call for Solutions

Bryan H. Reber, C. Richard Yarbrough, Glen Nowak, and Yan Jin

This book is the product of collaboration between university scholars whose research focus is on crisis communication and professionals who practice crisis communication. In this chapter, we begin with a discussion of definitional issues of crises. We introduce theories that will be more fully examined later in the book. We examine the definitions of crisis and crisis response and how those are rapidly changing, often becoming what we call "sticky" crises. Sticky crises are those that are particularly difficult to deal with or solve. Sticky crises are complex and challenging. We end the chapter by examining the benefits of collaboration between the academy and profession.

The Evolving Definition of Crisis

Traditional definitions of crisis often include words like "difficulty" or "danger" or "turning point." But traditional definitions are evolving as the breadth of crises and needs for crisis communication have also expanded.

The Institute for Public Relations defines a crisis as "a significant threat to operations that can have negative consequences if not handled properly" (Institute for Public Relations, 2018). In their textbook, *Effective Crisis Communication*, Ulmer et al. (2019) define an organizational crisis as a "specific, unexpected, and nonroutine event or series of events that create high levels of uncertainty and simultaneously present an organization with both opportunities for and threats to its high-priority goals" (p. 7). Crisis scholar Timothy Coombs defines crisis as "the perception of an unpredictable event that threatens important expectancies of stakeholders and can seriously impact an organization's performance and generate negative outcomes" (Coombs, 2019). Consultant Steven Fink's book, *Crisis Communication: The Definitive Guide to Managing the Message*, states "A crisis is a fluid and dynamic state of affairs containing equal parts danger and opportunity. It is a turning point; for better or worse" (2013, p. 7).

So, crises are not only difficult and dangerous turning points but also can be "significant," potentially "negative," and "unexpected." They create "uncertainty" and "perceived reality," which can affect stakeholders and "an organization's performance." And the causes of crises seem to be ever-changing and growing. Crises are also increasingly difficult, demanding, and complex. They can threaten not only an organization's public image, but also its reputation long-term. For example, in Chapter 3 of this book, Coombs and colleagues define sticky corporate crises as "crises that are made complex and challenging due to some combination of the situation increasing susceptibility, extending over an extended period of time, evoking moral outrage, spreading across an industry, and/or affecting multiple industries and geographic areas." Finally, while "crisis" is a word that usually strikes fear in business communicators, it entails both danger and opportunity for a crisis-stricken organization (Fink, 2013).

Like definitions, theories or ways of understanding crises are evolving. Among the early academic efforts to understand, describe, and test effective crisis communication was the Situational Crisis Communication Theory (SCCT). Coombs's SCCT is discussed in detail in Chapter 11 of this book. But briefly, Coombs and colleagues suggest that crisis response by an organization should be influenced both by crisis responsibility and potential for reputational damage. Evidence of the effectiveness of SCCT via experimental testing is summarized and further discussed in light of crisis communication practice.

Another normative theory is the contingency theory of strategic conflict management (known as the contingency theory in public relations research), developed by Glen T. Cameron and colleagues. The contingency theory is examined in Chapter 12 of this book. In sum, the contingency theory describes the dynamism of crisis situations and how organizational stances and situational variables affect whether an organization primarily accommodates any affected publics or primarily advocates solely for the organization.

The internalization, distribution, explanation, and action (IDEA) model has been developed by Timothy Sellnow and Deanna Sellnow. It is the focus of Chapter 13 of this book. The IDEA model was created to provide an easy and empirically tested way to develop instructional messages meant to alleviate risk or mitigate crises. Messages should help recipients "Internalize" the problem (i.e., how will/could I be affected). "Distribution" of messages depends on communicating via credible sources. "Explanation" describes what is happening and how it is being addressed. The "Action" in IDEA is the goal of moving message recipients to the desired behavior.

The social-mediated crisis communication (SMCC) model, which is covered in Chapter 14 of this book, was first developed by Yan Jin and Brooke Liu. In Chapter 14, Liu and their colleagues argue that existing crisis communication models do not account for the complexity that social media enter into the equation. The model identifies three types of SMCC publics: influential social media creators, social media followers, and social media inactives. It also describes how crisis information flows both directly and indirectly among online and offline communication channels and between the organization and its publics.

There are other crisis communication theories and models but these four illustrate the possibilities among the tested and validated scholarship in crisis communication theory building. Understanding these theories enables crisis communicators to apply tested and actionable insights to their work. The theories address persuading publics to avoid risks, communicating in an effective way that both satisfies stakeholders and manages risks to organizational reputation, and managing relationships between publics and organizations during and after a crisis.

Listening to Crisis Communicators

If the public relations professional is not relevant in their organization before a crisis occurs, they won't be when it does. In practice, public relations serves as an organization's ombudsman. While public relations pros represent their organization to the various publics they serve (inside out), they also must accurately represent the public's perceptions back into the organization (outside in), sometimes telling management what they do not wish to hear. That is not always a comfortable situation in which to find oneself. A lot of public relations practitioners are not willing to run that risk and content themselves with carrying out decisions made without their input.

Professional Insights: C. Richard Yarbrough

At both BellSouth Corporation and the Atlanta Committee for the Olympic Games, I spent much of my time with my colleagues in other departments talking about the role public relations had within the organization and how we could assist them.

Paramount in those discussions was that they consult with us on their issues and let us work with them on solutions. Said another way, don't come into our department saying there is a problem and we need you to put out a news release. Responses needed to be a collective determination.

Lest all of this sounds adversarial, it was just the opposite. The departments welcomed our help and we worked as partners. It also raised the level of expectation on us to come up with satisfactory solutions and in turn earn their respect.

One important point that crisis managers need to get ingrained into their management's thinking is that there is no general, singular "public." There are, instead, "publics" and they interact with each other. How one group reacts to an organizational crisis can differ dramatically from another (e.g., media vs. customers vs. competitors vs. public officials). The publics can be defined by race, age, gender, income, etc. and may look at a crisis from their own unique perspective.

It is important that an organization not wait for a crisis to occur before communicating with these many publics. Communications must be proactive. And clear, concise messaging is critical as is proactively conveying those messages to the various publics.

Distinguishing Characteristics of Crises

Crises are not simply a bad news day for an organization. They threaten the organization's ability to meet stakeholder needs and demands. Crises also have the potential to threaten the organization's very existence. Crises cross organization types and can be caused by natural disasters, such as Hurricane Sandy in the Northeastern United States in 2012, or health challenges, such as the COVID-19 pandemic in 2020. Crises can arise from corporate malfeasance, as exemplified in the 2001 Enron Energy case of creative accounting or employees' and consumer relations' demand for accountability in diversity and inclusion programs. Industrial accidents such as the Pacific Gas & Electric power lines causing the Camp fire in 2018 can be crisis creators. Nonprofit crises are often linked to donors, like the extreme case of Jeffrey Epstein, a sex offender who gave millions of dollars to the nonprofit MIT Media Lab as revealed in 2019. The list could go on almost endlessly. Data breaches, consumer and shareholder activism, consumer product recalls, and food-borne illnesses are all additional sources of sticky organizational crises. The breadth and speed of mass media has affected the nature of crises and accentuated the necessity of seemingly instant crisis communication.

There is a longstanding crisis communication dictum that any initial communication following a crisis must occur within the first hour, the "golden hour." In 2017, the blog *Crisis Response* updated that axiom: "those in command of the immediate response to a crisis no longer have the comfort of a 'golden hour' – today it is routinely not even a 'golden minute'" ("The Demise of the Golden Hour," 2017). The timeframe has only condensed since 2017. The need for speed arises because of the increase in particularly complex and challenging crises. Such crises make it more difficult to respond quickly because knowledge of the crisis doesn't yet exist. One doesn't typically know at the start of a financial embezzlement, chemical exposure, food or waterborne illness, or infectious disease outbreak that something is amiss. Additionally, it is news to no one involved in crisis communication that in a world where everyone has cameras in their phones and events can be livestreamed on a variety of platforms, knowing about and responding to a crisis is expected to be nearly instantaneous.

Adding to the challenge of the speed and breadth of the communication environment is the omnipresence of these demanding crises. A 2019 global crisis survey by professional services firm PricewaterhouseCoopers (PwC) found that of the more than 2,000 respondents to its survey, 24% had one crisis in the past five years, 38% had between two and five crises in that timeframe, and 7% had more than five crises in five years—more than one crisis a year. The PwC report noted, "But crises often travel in packs. And a crisis is never more dangerous than when it spins off one or several ancillary crises – each of which can create its own feedback loop of consequences" (Rivera & Stainback, 2019). These challenging or ancillary crises are part of what we call sticky crises. All the challenges and the diversity of crisis causes discussed thus far are the fodder for this book.

Sticky crises demand not only a near-instant response, but they may require crisis communicators to see possibilities, understand the potential breadth and scope of an emerging crisis, and be ready to change strategy and tactics quickly. As the PwC study noted, what we call sticky crises can spawn a host of additional crises, each which can bring it additional complexities and communication demands. PwC identified "three bedrock elements to successful crisis management: preparedness, a fact-based approach, and effectiveness of (all!) stakeholder communications."

Dealing with Sticky Crises

Preparedness, facts, and effective communications to all stakeholders are, indeed, the hallmarks of successful crisis management and successful crisis communication. But for sticky crises, which are complex and challenging, we offer some additional specificity.

The first and perhaps the most important element for successful crisis communication, sticky or otherwise, is being sure that the communicator is in the decision-making hierarchy. In the book, *Excellence in Public Relations and Communication Management* (Grunig, 1992), Jon White and David Dozier wrote:

> The general theory of public relations [the Excellence Theory] maintains that the senior public relations practitioner must be part of the dominant coalition, function at a high level of decision making, and participate in strategic management if public relations is to be excellent and is to make the organization more effective.
>
> (p. 91)

This seminal book introduced "dominant coalition" into the public relations lexicon. The dominant coalition, according to White and Dozier (1992), is the "group of managers who hold the most power in an organization" (p. 91). For successful crisis communication in every situation, an organization's top communications person should be a member of the dominant coalition.

Second, elements of an effective response to sticky crises are a combination of classic crisis communication tactics, including those linked specifically to social media. As with all crisis communication, sticky crisis communication relies first on crisis preparedness, that is, having a plan and having practiced or reviewed the plan enough that it is internalized and fixed to muscle memory among the key players in the organization. It is important to recognize that an effective crisis response depends not only on the CEO and management team being well versed in the crisis communication, but that planning efforts encompass employee communication as well. The key aspects of a crisis plan should be drilled and rehearsed on a regular basis. Producing a crisis communication plan with everything from lists of key personnel to templates for tweets is no good unless those who will be asked to participate in its implementation know the plan's elements and their responsibilities like the back of their hands. Software platforms and applications aid in both planning and rehearsing.

Third, experts suggest that regardless of the type of crisis, truth-telling is essential. Nathan Miller of Miller Ink, told *Forbes*, "Acknowledge responsibility, explain how you are going to move forward, frame the issue as positively as possible, and be prepared for follow-on coverage and questions" (Council Post, 2020). Of course, telling the truth and taking responsibility when the responsibility is yours are not advice unique to sticky crisis communication. It is foundational to successful crisis communication. Period.

Fourth, organizations should have a crisis social media policy as part of their guidelines and rules for staff to follow when communicating with external publics. When facing a crisis that has elements of social media (and what crisis doesn't today?), companies must hit pause on their scheduled social media posts. When facing a crisis that is being discussed or fanned via social media, continuing with routine posts can be seen as disrespectful to those affected by the crisis.

Fifth, sticky crisis communicators should make sure their messages are relevant and responsive, with a focus on the concerns and questions of affected populations and stakeholders. As previously noted, speed of response, relevance, and accuracy in messaging are vital. Furthermore, whether the crisis is internal or external or both, maintain consistency in key message points and themes across publics. Telling employees something that is in conflict with what you are telling consumers can create a spin-off crisis. A good example is the conflicting messages attributed to United Airlines' former CEO Oscar Muñoz during a 2017 incident involving a passenger. After a United Airlines customer was forcibly dragged off a plane for refusing to give up his seat, Muñoz described the customer as "disruptive and belligerent" in an internal message that soon became external. In labeling the customer, Muñoz broke a cardinal rule of crisis communication—avoid blaming the victim, even if some could perceive that person contributed to the adverse situation. The statement Muñoz issued to employees in an effort to demonstrate he supported them was contrary to the message that needed to be delivered to customers and the broader public. As a result, he needed to address a second self-created crisis. He soon issued a statement that said, "I deeply apologize to the customer who was forcibly removed... No one should ever be mistreated this way." The dissonance of the statements was immediately noted on social media and Muñoz was accused of hypocrisy (Czarnecki, 2017).

Finally, in sticky crises, the affected organizations should engage with key publics both during the crisis but also in calmer times. Positive relationships and reputation serve as protection against crisis blowback.

Among the challenges of sticky crises are their complexity, uncertainties involved, lack of information, competing priorities and needs between the organization and stakeholders, conflicting values, partisanship, and lack of consensus regarding best responses. Publics affected by complex and challenging crises may suffer from message wear out; that is, they grow weary and/or wary of messages that tell them time and again how to keep themselves safe or how an organization is taking corrective actions. Publics may be conflicted about which messenger to trust. The challenge for the crisis communicator is to maintain a steady stream of new and responsive messages to avoid wear out. Ongoing issues related to security of consumer data, employee grievances, product recalls, or food-borne illness outbreaks are examples of sticky crises that could be susceptible to these problems.

Professional Insights: C. Richard Yarbrough

Crisis management and communication must be a collaborative effort within an organization. It is incumbent on the public relations professionals to help foster a climate of cooperation before a crisis occurs. Public relations professionals have to earn their seat at the decision-making table long before a crisis occurs; otherwise, they won't be there when it does.

In the early morning hours following a bomb going off in Centennial Olympic Park during the 1996 Centennial Games, representatives from the International Olympic Committee, the White House, the Georgia governor's office, and Atlanta City Hall gathered with members of the Atlanta Committee for the Olympic Games (ACOG), which I served as managing director—communications and government relations.

Two decisions were made quickly. The first was that while the source of the bombing had not been identified, the Games would nevertheless continue. The second was that a clear line would be drawn between what the committee's responsibilities were in staging the Games and all the ancillary activities, such as transportation, ticket sales, food service, etc., and those of law enforcement in their efforts to investigate the bombing. Both sides agreed that neither of us would comment or speculate on the other's efforts. With that determined, ACOG's CEO Billy Payne turned to me and said, "Dick, go get us back in business." No one told me what to say or how to say it and no one asked to see what I intended to say. Looking back on that time, it was a validation that the public relations discipline was at the decision-making table and that I had earned the right and respect to be there.

Benefits of Collaboration

Collaboration between crisis communication scholars and practitioners can have benefits for both parties, particularly when it comes to complex, multifaceted, and difficult crises. For example, such collaboration can benefit academic theory-building and research as well as strengthen crisis communication practice. Most current academic research focuses on a single crisis as the unit of analysis. But as the PwC study showed, increasingly crises are traveling in "packs" and are growing in their difficulty, complexity, and uncertainty. Academics need to move beyond studying relatively simple image and reputational crises and moving toward efforts that involve complex, multi-faceted, and dynamic crises. They should be working to identify, describe, and understand how these crises are different and how they unfold. They should be developing theories and frameworks that recognize the challenges brought about by uncertainties and competing stakeholder and affected public needs, priorities, and values.

What does collaboration between academics and professionals look like? There are many ways to undertake collaboration. One model is the Crisis Communication Think Tank at the University of Georgia (UGA). Each year about 15 crisis communicators and about 15 crisis communication scholars meet for a day to discuss themed, current issues related to crisis communication. The end-of-day deliverable is a research agenda for the coming year. Teams are formed with practitioners and scholars on each team. This book is the deliverable for the 2019 UGA Crisis Communication Think Tank.

Another collaboration model brings these two groups together to answer either industry or proprietary questions relevant to practice. This may be done through industry support of graduate student researchers, or a university research group of diverse industries, or through specific relationships between a practitioner and a researcher. While the bulk of the research findings may be proprietary, such a collaboration allows universities to grow graduate programs and bring practical questions to research labs that often focus on more esoteric problems.

Crisis communicators can collaborate with crisis scholars by providing access to the workplace as a research "lab." The access may be for ethnographic research in which the scholar embeds herself. It may be to allow a scholar to survey employees and perhaps report findings to the communication team after survey data is collected and results are tabulated. It may be to facilitate in-depth interviews with senior leaders about their notion of best practices in crisis communication. This collaboration may take the form of allowing scholars access to proprietary data to conduct secondary analysis and answer questions the organization may not have had time to examine. For example, at the UGA, we have worked with a global public relations agency to conduct secondary analysis of data. We tackled questions the agency was interested in but that did not fit into its overall theme for the year. The team developed research questions, analyzed data from a series of worldwide surveys, published journal articles, and led panels at the Public Relations Society of America (PRSA)'s annual conferences.

The opportunities for collaboration are limited only by the imagination of the people involved. Building collaborations is difficult, there are many hurdles that need to be cleared—but we need to find ways to overcome the difficulties and hurdles because collaborations will benefit both parties. The key is for crisis managers and crisis communication scholars to find ways to meet each other and find common interests and concerns. That may be through attendance at professional conferences, but these are quite limited. However, organizations such as PRSA are quite encouraging of panels that bring together professors and professionals. Practitioners can contact the communication or public relations or strategic communication department at a nearby university to identify potential leaders for team-building activities or research-driven workshops. Academics can invite professionals from area companies and nonprofits to speak to their students about case studies or simply trends in crisis communication practice. Collaboration does take active intent. It is uncommon that collaboration between industry and academia happens organically.

Challenges of Crisis Communication and Scholarship

As noted, long-lasting crises are increasingly common. Add to earlier lists in the chapter: racial tensions, sexual harassment, mismanagement of personal data, and economic collapse. These and other situations may arise again and again. For example,

- In 2020, the Federal Communication Commission (FCC) proposed fining T-Mobile, AT&T, Verizon, and Sprint a combined $200 million for sale of personal tracking data. This occurred after multiple investigations into the sale of personal data and industry pledges to be more transparent with consumers.
- Facebook seems to be a chronic offender of allowing misappropriation of users' personal data with episodes reaching well before the Cambridge Analytica case of 2016.
- Disinfectant producers, including Lysol, had to clarify in an April 2020 statement that social media-circulated rumors suggesting ingested or injected disinfectants were effective deterrents to the deadly COVID-19 were not true. The statement noted, "under no circumstance should our disinfectant products be administered into the human body."

These and other types of crises are recurrent. Like the arcade game Whac-a-Mole, an organization or individual just deals with one crisis and another pops its head up. But together, crisis communicators and crisis communication scholars can move toward solutions.

During the 2019 Crisis Communication Think Tank at the UGA, "sticky crisis" was defined broadly as "complex and challenging crisis issues." One goal of this book is to bring more specificity to that definition.

Evidence of Mutual Benefit

The increasingly complex and changing nature of today's crises means that professional crisis communicators are constantly meeting new challenges that demand new strategies, approaches, considerations, and tools. This is where the demand for knowledge development begins. "From the work of practitioners, researchers then seek to validate what factors actually work and do not work for addressing the problem. The goal is to build an evidence-based approach to problem solving" (Coombs, 2014, citing Pfeffer & Sutton, 2006).

Real-world problems lead to research that, in turn, develops effective solutions to these problems, providing benefit to both practitioners and scholars. In a 2014 article, Coombs laid out six recommendations for crisis communicators based on published research findings. In sum, he noted that research shows that self-revelation of a crisis is best; use of social media to distribute news provides the opportunity to self-reveal on the organization's schedule; tell people how to protect themselves, if necessary; provide victims with information about psychological coping resources; communicate aggressively rather than passively; and use denial as a strategy only when the organization is subject of a rumor or misinformation (2014).

Mats Ericksson identified 104 published research studies that provide scientifically tested solutions to the effective use of social media in crisis communication. Ericksson found "157 explicit but thematic pieces of advice from scholars to practitioners" (2018, p. 529). The findings, in their simplest form were stated by Ericksson:

> The study finds that effective crisis communication is about using social media's potential to create dialogue and to choose the right message, source and timing; performing precrisis work and developing an understanding of social media logic; using social media monitoring; and continuing to prioritize traditional media in crisis situations… the recommendation about using social media for monitoring has increased significantly during the last year.
>
> (Ericksson, 2018, p. 540)

While academics, especially those in applied disciplines such as public relations, strive to make sure their research matters to the field of practice, it is hard to get those research findings into the hands of crisis communication professionals. One common source where this marriage of research and practice may be evident is trade publications and websites. For example, Elizabeth Cholis wrote in *O'Dwyer's*: "Recent analysis published in *World Psychiatry* reveals that Internet and technology use has shortened the average person's attention span and even taken a toll on memory processes" (2020, p. 16). Jenn Deering Davis cited USC Annenberg's 2019 *Global Communications Report* in *O'Dwyer's 2020 Guide to Crisis Communications*. In each edition of *Crisis Insider*, a publication of *PR News*, there is a "data vault" article that features research pertinent to crisis communicators. References to Pew Research reports are also common in trade publications.

Academic research seems to gain more attention when a current or former crisis communication professional is associated with the study.

When corporate communicators become professionals-in-residence in university programs, they bring their crisis communication street credentials with them. This is one motivation for the founding of the UGA Crisis Communication Think Tank: to bring street cred to campus.

Research about Sticky Crises

Scholars have noted that research of crisis communication has heavily relied on case studies as a means of illustrating good and bad practices (e.g., Manias-Muñoz et al., 2019). With the advent of theory-building in crisis communication, more experimental testing has been forthcoming. In the *Journal of International Crisis and Risk Communication*, Liu and Viens (2020) urged what they called "Multiphase Scholarship." They wrote,

> Crises do not occur as isolated incidents in a vacuum, soon to be forgotten by those who experience them… [S]cholarship needs to include the long-term impact of crises and further explore the influence of repeated instances. How do memory and recall of a crisis affect communication…?
>
> (p. 10)

Complex and challenging crises can recur over time, which may change the effectiveness of crisis communication as linked to the concept of sticky crises.

Solutions to any crisis, sticky or not, are based on cooperation as well as the aforementioned internalization of the crisis communication plan among organization leaders and staff.

Learning from Past Successes and Failures

There are few organizations that lack a crisis communications plan. But as the myriad crises generated by COVID-19 illustrated, it is likely few organizations had crisis communication plans that enabled swift, appropriate, and continual responsive communication strategies and efforts to a complex, dynamic crisis replete with uncertainties and unforeseeable challenges. That is because the department responsible for the plan—usually public relations—does little or nothing to make it a relevant document. Consequently, a well-intentioned effort usually ends up on a bookshelf collecting dust. Conditions change. Personnel change. Contact numbers change. The crisis plan must reflect those changes and be top of the mind with management.

Professional Insights: C. Richard Yarbrough

At BellSouth, we had the prerequisite crises identified, who in what department would be the contact person and what their role would be. The person in the public relations department responsible for the administration of the crisis plan would call randomly to see if their contact was available and would know what to do should a crisis situation be occurring. It was not unusual that the individual would be out of the office—perhaps at lunch—with the secretary unaware of how to find the person. When the sought-after crisis communication link did return the call, they would be reminded of the necessity of being available immediately had a crisis occurred and to always leave a contact number. Also, it was incumbent on the manager of the crisis plan to ensure that we knew when there were personnel changes in other departments that we needed to be made aware in order to brief the new person on the crisis plan role they had inherited from their predecessor.

Key Takeaways

Crisis communication is complex and becoming more so. However, the tools to distribute messages and knowledge about what messages are most effective are substantial and growing.

This book aims to advance crisis communication practice by introducing research-vetted tools to public relations professionals tasked with managing crisis communication. The book explores four specific risk and crisis communication theories. These theories provide empirically tested methods and message types for crisis communication practitioners. The book also examines the challenges of crisis communication in a variety of settings from corporate to nonprofit to government affairs.

The book strives to advance and improve academic crisis communication theory and research by introducing theories and research techniques and findings that generate unexplored research questions. Questions that might be asked include whether or how to communicate differently to maintain effectiveness when a public is affected by a sticky crisis that may recur; do publics become inured to crisis communication over time; or how, if at all, do crisis communication messages change given the same sticky crisis (e.g., data breaches) in different settings (e.g., corporate vs. nonprofit vs. government).

Perhaps most importantly, each chapter in this book is imbued with the perspectives and expertise of active crisis communication researchers and practicing crisis communicators.

In this chapter specifically, we discussed common elements of definitions of crisis communication and introduced theories that will be further explored in the remainder of the book. The changing faces of mass social media and crises mean adaptation is not an option, but a mandate. For example, understanding that crises travel in "packs" or become sticky is increasingly relevant. We believe collaboration between crisis communication scholars and practitioners is the fastest route to adaptation and understanding. This chapter and book have the goals of serving to ignite conversations about how these two groups with common objectives can more frequently and meaningfully interact.

There are challenges to developing research questions and programs that are mutually beneficial. Applied research exists, as evidenced by Coombs,

Ericksson, and others, but there is a dearth of research about sticky crises—perhaps the most prevalent problem for crisis communicators. But whether crises are one-and-done or sticky, there are still some universal truths. The golden hour has been reduced to what seems like golden nanoseconds. Taken literally, that is one-billionth of a second; a very short time to respond.

Preparation and practice are required and move crisis communication plans from dust collectors to responsive actions seared into muscle memory. Crisis communicators need to be part of almost all high-level conversations. A crisis communicator who is only recognized when the proverbial stuff hits the fan will have a hard time being effective. Likewise, a crisis communicator needs to be a constant organizational networker and bridge builder. When a crisis occurs, it is good to have positive and productive working relationships with internal legal counsel and operations managers and human resources executives. And best practice is to have those relationships from the C-Suite to the receptionist, because you will likely need help from all levels of the organization.

Finally, this book is a clarion call for the practitioners and researchers of best crisis communication practices to actively search for ways to get together so practitioners work from empirically tested toolboxes and researchers are exploring the most current and pertinent questions and problems.

References

Cholis, E. (2020, January). How technology redefines crisis readiness. Retrieved July 28, 2020. https://www.odwyerpr.com/story/public/13626/2020-01-13/how-technology-redefines-crisis-readiness.html

Coombs, W. T. (2014, Summer). State of crisis communication: Evidence and the bleeding edge. https://instituteforpr.org/state-crisis-communication-evidence-bleeding-edge/

Coombs, W. T. (2019). *Ongoing crisis communication: Planning, managing, and responding.* SAGE Publications.

Council Post: 10 Crisis Management Tactics For... – Forbes. (2020, April 3). https://www.forbes.com/sites/forbesagencycouncil/2020/04/03/10-crisis-management-tactics-for-managing-internal-problems/

Czarnecki, S. (2017, June 6). *Timeline of a crisis: United airlines.* PR Week. https://www.prweek.com/article/1435619/timeline-crisis-united-airlines

Ericksson, M. (2018). Lessons for crisis communication on social media: A systematic review of what research tells the practice. *International Journal of Strategic Communication, 12*(5), 526–551. http://doi.org/10.1080/1553118x.2018.1510405

Fink, Steven, (2013). *Crisis communications: The definitive guide to managing the message*, McGraw-Hill Education.

Grunig, J. E. (1992). *Excellence in public relations and communication management.* Hillsdale, NJ: Erlbaum Associates.

Institute for Public Relations. (2018, February 20). Crisis management and communications. Retrieved July 26, 2020. https://instituteforpr.org/crisis-management-and-communications/

Liu, B., & Viens, J. (2020). Crisis and risk communication scholarship of the future: Reflections on research gaps. *Journal of International Crisis and Risk Communication Research, 3*(1), 7–13. http://doi.org/10.30658/jicrcr.3.1.1

Manias-Muñoz, I., Jin, Y., & Reber, B. H. (2019). The state of crisis communication research and education through the lens of crisis scholars: An international Delphi study. *Public Relations Review, 45*(4), 101797. http://doi.org/10.1016/j.pubrev.2019.101797

Pfeffer, J., & Sutton, R. I. (2006). Evidence-based management. *Harvard Business Review, 84*(1), 62.

Rivera, K., & Stainback, D. (2019). PwC's Global Crisis Survey 2019. Retrieved July 27, 2020. https://www.pwc.com/gx/en/forensics/global-crisis-survey/pdf/pwc-global-crisis-survey-2019.pdf

The demise of the Golden Hour. (2017, November 28). Retrieved July 27, 2020, from https://www.crisis-response.com/comment/blogpost.php?post=364

Ulmer, R. R., Sellnow, T. L., & Seeger, M. W. (2019). *Effective crisis communication: Moving from crisis to opportunity*. SAGE.

White, J., & Dozier, D. M. (1992). Public relations and management decision making. In J. E. Grunig (Ed.), *Excellence in public relations and communication management* (pp. 91–108). Routledge, Taylor & Francis Group.

2 The Evolving Complexity of Crisis Issues

The Role of Crisis History

LaShonda L. Eaddy and Shelley Spector

Corporate history has the potential to provide fertile ground for communication scholarship and practice. However, this can only be accomplished if organizations are committed to providing authentic and accurate accounts of their actual crisis management (Watson, 2015). Moreover, archival documents and historical insights can provide illustrations of strategies and tactics that have been used previously. In turn, scholars and professionals can use this information to inform their research and practice.

The Birth of Contemporary Crisis Management

According to Mitroff and Harrington (1996), the crisis management field was born in 1984 after the Tylenol tampering crisis and gained traction as more crises occurred. There were corporate crises long before the Tylenol incident, but *crisis management* as an area of study or practice was not formalized until then. Johnson & Johnson (J&J) was able to successfully manage the crisis and regain market share and reputation in spite of the crisis that could have proven to be disastrous for the company. Practitioners were inspired by this demonstration and began to reverse engineer Johnson & Johnson's process to see how it could be replicated to manage other crises. As the crisis management field has evolved, it has gone through several phases where emphasis shifted. During the 1980s, the field was focused on tactical advice that provided checklists and plans. During the 1990s, more attention was focused on strategic issues with considerations of contingency impacts, uncertainty, and possible multiple outcomes. Both phases have helped define the dominant paradigm of crisis management and now open-endedness, multiple stakeholder roles, and interactions between internal and external crisis drivers. Although Johnson & Johnson's tampering crisis gave "birth" to the crisis management field, public relations professionals had long been managing crises, many decades before the field was formally named. Even around the turn of the 20th century, public relations professionals understood that the manner in which a crisis was handled could make or break a company's reputation. This chapter uses case studies to offer insight into crisis history, both theoretically and literally, shedding light on its contributions to crisis management. The pairing of these perspectives offers valuable information for crisis managers and scholars alike.

Crisis History's Theoretical Underpinnings

One of the crisis communication scholarship's prevailing theories is the Situational Crisis Communication Theory (SCCT). SCCT suggests that people attribute more or less responsibility to organizations that are experiencing crises based on the crisis type that occurs (Coombs, 1995; Coombs & Holladay, 1996, 2002). Each crisis type/cluster differs based on the amount of control the organization had over the crisis. Victim crises are those that the organization did not have control over such as acts of terrorism or natural disasters, accident crises refer to those resulting from incidents such as technical malfunction or faulty products, and preventable crises result from intentional misdeeds and human error. Perceptions of crisis responsibility increase with each crisis type/cluster. SCCT also prescribes crisis response strategies based on the crisis typology. Moreover, SCCT offers performance history as an intensifier of attribution of responsibility. Performance history includes relationship history, which refers to the rapport that organizations have or are perceived to have with stakeholders, while crisis history refers to organizations previous crises (Coombs, 1995, 2004).

Empirical Research Surrounding Crisis History

Few studies have examined crisis history empirically, and crisis history has not gained traction among crisis professionals. Coombs (2004) examines crisis history's impact on perceived organizational reputation and suggests both a direct and indirect effect. In addition to examining how the presence of crisis history impacts reputational threats, crisis history valence has also been shown to have significant impacts (Eaddy et al., 2017; Eaddy & Jin, 2018; Seo et al., 2013). Despite this initial support of crisis history and its significant impacts, further exploration of this concept is needed.

Crisis History Framework

The Crisis History Framework offers seven influential crisis history factors: proximity, stability, valence, crisis type, prominence/visibility, influential perspectives, and crisis emotions. The influential factors impact publics' perceptions of crisis history and how they rely on those perceptions to make evaluations of organizations that are currently experiencing crises. Salience refers to a striking feature of prominence that stands out noticeably (Merriam-Webster, 2020). The proposed framework and influential factors identify crisis aspects that make previous crises more or less salient to publics and possibly impact their interpretation of crisis history. The insight provided can inform crisis communication strategy and messaging, and can offer new avenues for crisis scholarship.

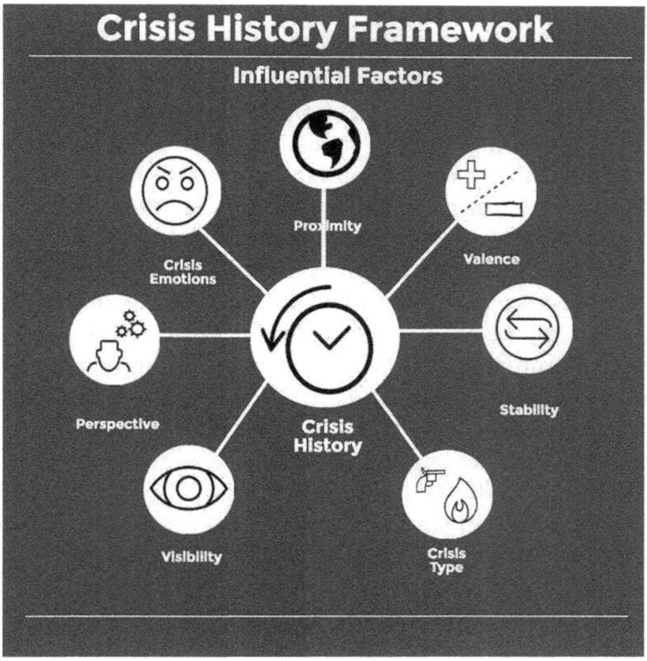

Figure 2.1: Crisis History Framework (Eaddy, 2017).

Empirical examinations of crisis history have defined it as when an organization experiences a crisis similar to one it had experienced in the past. However, Eaddy (2017) used a multi-disciplinary lens to offer an encompassing Crisis History Framework with utility for various disciplines (see Figure 2.1). The proposed framework uses conceptualizations from several disciplines such as business, corporate social responsibility (CSR), disaster/risk, finance, and organizational science to offer key crisis history insights. Time is central to the framework as it is the essence of literal and theoretical crisis history. Therefore, time must be considered in any investigation of crisis history.

Proximity. Proximity, both temporal and geographical, shape publics' and stakeholders' perceptions regarding crisis history. Crises are catastrophic, unexpected, and terrible, thus creating the perfect combination to also be memorable (Centers for Disease Control and Prevention [CDC], 2002). Crises that occurred in the recent past are easier to recall. Similarly, crises are most memorable when they occur in geographical regions close to or familiar to stakeholders and publics.

Valence. Crisis history valence refers to whether the previous crisis is perceived positively or negatively. Crisis history valence can be a double-edged sword because a positive crisis history can create a halo effect in current crises that helps weather crisis storms. At the same time, a negative crisis history can create a Velcro effect that exacerbates reputational damage (Coombs & Holladay, 2002, 2006).

Stability. Stability considerations examine if the cause of a crisis is changing over time or constant. As stakeholders and publics perceive the stability of crises, they will view organizations as repeat offenders and attribute more crisis responsibility. When crises are perceived as unstable, publics and stakeholders will not expect similar crises to recur.

Crisis Type. As publics make current evaluations of organizations' crises, they will likely attribute the most crisis responsibility and control to organizations that experience preventable crises. Their recall of these negative characteristics can influence their current perceptions of the organization that is experiencing the crisis. Conversely, if an organization has previously experienced a victim crisis, publics do not perceive any crisis responsibility nor control, so when they may evaluate the organization more leniently during a current crisis.

Visibility. Research shows that residents of disaster-prone areas are more likely to take heed to disaster/risk messaging if they have had similar experiences or are aware of similar disasters that have occurred (Rød et al., 2012). Residents have implicit visibility when they have experienced similar disasters, either by firsthand accounts or seeing news reports, video footage, photographs, or other artifacts from the previous disaster. Media depictions contribute to crisis history visibility because they can provide details of current and previous crises regardless of publics' direct or indirect involvement. Media depictions can also supersede direct experience when publics are evaluating organizations that are experiencing current crises.

Influential Perspectives. Although crisis history is the focus of this chapter, it is evident that the concept is intertwined with relationship history. Therefore, the framework includes three influential crisis history perspectives that also can commence inquiry of relationship history's impact.

Stakeholder Perspective. There are three types of stakeholders: real stakeholders, stakewatchers, and stakeseekers (Fassin, 2010). Each stakeholder type differs based on their connections to the organization. Therefore, stakeholders' crisis history considerations may also differ. Each group's perspective of previous crises would probably vary based upon their relationship with the organization and their involvement with the organization when the previous crisis occurred. More recently, the term stakeseeker has been offered to provide a better characterization of social movements that may disrupt organizations (Holzer, 2007). Stakeseekers are those who seek to put new, social advocacy issues on corporate agendas.

Public Perspective. Oftentimes, crises are tried in the courtroom of public opinion (Haggerty, 2003). Therefore, it is crucial to consider the public perspective. When the public considers the effect of crisis history, people rely on their own recall or influential community leaders can remind them of what transpired. A minority of the public could also impact the majority by diffusing ideas related to the previous crisis. An organization's actual performance as well as the public's perception of it can also impact crisis history acuities. Brand equity, industry reputation, and track records are crucial in crises and can influence future behaviors and competitive advantage (Barnett, 2007; Standop & Grunwald, 2009; Zou et al., 2015). Additionally, organizations' CSR initiatives are visible to the public and can impact organizations' crisis reputation and publics' evaluations of organizational blame during current crises (Klein & Dawar, 2004). Furthermore, organizations' CSR claims are more effective when the organizations have a long and credible CSR history, suggesting that public-facing CSR can influence publics' evaluations of organizations experiencing crises (Vanhamme & Grobben, 2009).

Industry Perspective. It is imperative for organizations to consider the perspectives of their industry or sectors. Barnett (2007) discusses the interdependence of rival firms and suggests that trade associations and industry self-regulation may ultimately benefit both participating and non-participating firms. Similarly, organizations can also have reputational interdependence that creates crisis susceptibility when other organizations experience crises within their industry. Companies can also be forced to change their reputation and performance strategies due to their industry's actions (Barnett, 2007; Barnett & Hoffman, 2008). Thus, it is crucial for organizations to be mindful of their industries' and competitors' actions because of the potential impact they can have on reputation and performance. When organizations consider crisis history, they should pay close attention to previous crises within their industry regardless of their involvement in or connection to the crisis.

Crisis Emotions. Crisis emotion research is an emerging body of crisis scholarship and identifies the discrete emotions most likely experienced during crises (Jin, 2009, 2010; Jin & Cameron, 2007). Jin and colleagues (2007) suggest that anger, fright, anxiety, and sadness are the most dominant emotions during crises while guilt are and shame are secondary. Crisis emotion research indicates that crisis responsibility can significantly predict anger, fear, surprise, worry, contempt, and relief (Choi & Lin, 2009). Furthermore, there is evidence of a significant negative relationship between organizational reputation, anger, and alert. Therefore, crisis emotions elicited by crisis history can impact publics' current evaluations of organizations experiencing crises.

Yesteryear's Crisis Pioneers

The previous section highlights crisis history theoretically and offers insight for crisis managers regarding contemporary previous crises. However, crises of yesteryear also provide valuable insight for crisis management today. While these crisis case studies cannot be retrofitted using contemporary theories and models like SCCT and the Crisis History Framework, parallels can be made to show how some crisis management tenets have existed in public relations' infancy and have stood the test of time.

Jin and colleagues (2016) allude to the notion of public relations being often overlooked from a historical perspective: "We fail to examine the foundational wisdom of those who created our discipline. The mastery of these pioneers remains a source of fascination and inspiration for practitioners and academics alike" (para. 1). Although organizations like Johnson & Johnson are credited with the founding of crisis management, it was being practiced before the term was ever coined. When using a public relations lens to examine how crises were handled in the field's early days, many of the pioneers' efforts would easily qualify. Public relations pioneers and historical figures such as Ivy Lee, Doris Fleischman, Edward Bernays, and Franklin Delano Roosevelt achieved tremendous feats with few communications technologies available, or business precedents to apply—making their successes all the more remarkable. Their work was innovative and groundbreaking, and laid the foundation for generations of future public relations professionals who would one day council chief executive officers through a variety of crises, whether of their own making or those out of their immediate control. While they did not call it "crisis management" nor "crisis communications," these pioneers knew how to mitigate a crisis or prevent one altogether. There is much to be mined from early pioneers' case studies, especially those which took place in the first three decades of the 20th century. An examination of those case studies reveals that crisis management strategies of today—transparency, empathy, and accountability—all were first successfully employed decades ago. The following sections provide historical case studies that spotlight successful strategies and show how similar contemporary crises could have benefited from considerations of historical crises. Perhaps today's professionals will see value in using early examples of crisis management efforts to inform current planning and incorporate their learnings into the guidance they give to clients or CEOs. The case studies that follow are more fully understood by providing historical and cultural context.

Ivy Lee and The Ludlow Massacre of 1913

Many financiers of the robber baron era were despised by the public, including the infamous John D. and his son John D. Rockefeller, Jr. Their reputation especially suffered from unrest during a worker strike at a coal mine owned by John D. Rockefeller, Jr. in Ludlow, Colorado. In 1913, employers were hardly interested in workers' welfare. Working conditions were perilous and miners were expected to work long hours for little pay. Local management told Rockefeller that all was well at his Ludlow mine: "The workers were thoroughly satisfied with conditions in the mine..." (Hiebert, 2017, p. 142). However, to Rockefeller's surprise, more than 9,000 workers had gone on strike on September 23, 1913. Workers and their families moved out of their company homes to nearby tents owned by the union. One day, the mine operators drove past the tent colony and used machine guns to shoot at the miners and their families, commencing a battle with the displaced miners known as The Ludlow Massacre.

Newspaper coverage of the Ludlow Massacre was stark and tragic, painting Rockefeller as the villain. The *Cleveland Press* reported, "the charred bodies of two dozen women and children show that Rockefeller knows how to win." Protesters thousands of miles away in New York City chanted, "shoot [Rockefeller] like a dog" (Hiebert, 2017, p. 143).

Rockefeller called in Ivy Lee for advice. Lee outlined a plan to ease the tensions between the workers and management and bring the mine back to full operation. Lee interviewed the miners and their families and discovered the source of their discontent was not pay or working conditions but the inability to communicate their grievances to management. The workers felt they were not being heard and their opinions did not matter. Lee wrote to Rockefeller, "The men are afraid to complain or appeal. There is distinctly a missing link here. There is no safety valve for the men to get petty grievances out of their system" (Hiebert, 2017, p. 148).

Lee's solution was revolutionary for the era: a campaign enabling two-way communications between management and miners, with a goal of both sides feeling understood. Once the strike ended, Lee issued a series of posters expressing management's appreciation for the workers, desire to treat them fairly, and inviting them to share their complaints. Lee also was aware that the miners' families were integral, so he wrote leaflets demonstrating the company's respect for workers' wives. One leaflet reads, "women are voters in the state, and their influence is important in every way" (Hiebert, 2017, p. 148). Perhaps the most notable strategy Lee introduced was putting a "human face" to the problem.

Upon Lee's urging, Rockefeller took the long train ride to Ludlow, where he spent two weeks getting to know the miners firsthand. He toured the mines and visited with families at their homes. But one act made the strongest impression of all: at a miners' social event, Rockefeller insisted on dancing with every wife in the room. In the days that followed, photos of a waltzing Rockefeller appeared in newspapers around the country, presenting Ludlow in a positive light for the first time. Most importantly, the workers unanimously agreed to a new employee representation plan that would open lines of communications with mine operators. Following Ludlow, Rockefeller became known as an advocate for industrial relations. He even wrote articles about creating better relationships between capital and labor. According to Rockefeller, "The Colorado strike was one of the most important things that ever happened to the Rockefeller family" (Hiebert, 2017, p. 154).

Classic Case in Recent Decades: Uber's Crisis-Prone Pandemonium

Ivy Lee's work to recreate Rockefeller's image by "humanizing" him is a great example of how individuals, organizations, and brands can change their trajectory by reshaping the narrative. Ride-hailing company, Uber, is a present-day example of an organization working to change its notoriety by transforming its core business principles and reshaping its image. Uber Technologies, Inc., referred to as Uber, is a startup founded in 2009 by Garrett Camp and Travis Kalanick. The company quickly gained success as it disrupted the market with innovation. Silicon Valley investors viewed this disruption positively, while most others regarded it with contempt (The Economist, 2017). Silicon Valley and the finance industry welcomed Uber to the "unicorn club"—an elite group of startups valued at $1 billion or more (Rodriguez, 2015). However, the startup's notoriety was augmented by allegations of a toxic organizational culture and evidence of the company intentionally breaking the law.

Crisis History Learning for Uber. Ivy Lee was able to consider the influential perspectives of proximity and visibility to reshape John D. Rockefeller Jr.'s image. More than 100 years later, Uber could have benefitted from these considerations before situations reached a climax. Unfortunately, Uber was slow to implement sound crisis strategies as it faced backlash for its misdeeds, resulting in the organization changing its public face with the hiring of a new CEO, Dara Khosrowshahi in 2017. Khosrowshahi's appointment supposedly signified a new era to reform Uber's organizational culture and business practices. The new CEO led Uber into its initial public offering (IPO) and more recently an acquisition of Postmates. Despite Uber's financial successes, old habits have seemed to die hard as the company still faces similar accusations to those from Kalanick's tenure. Uber could learn a lesson from John D. Rockefeller Jr. by righting its wrongs in action and deed, especially considering the organization's recent crises.

Edward Bernays & Doris Fleishman Alleviate Brewing Tensions in the Deep South

In 1920, Edward Bernays was asked to handle publicity for the 11th annual National Association for the Advancement of Colored People (NAACP) Convention. The Convention had been held in the North for decades, but Bernays and the NAACP decided to hold it in the South for the first time. Their goal was to generate positive national press. To make their point, they chose to hold it in Atlanta, the heart of the deep South, where racism was pervasive. It was a risky idea that could incite violence or result in a visit from the Ku Klux Klan.

For the Bernays team, the execution had minimal importance compared to bringing attention to Black peoples' plight in the post-war era. After all, Black people had just fought side by side with White soldiers in the Great War. They were promised educational and business opportunities when they returned to the States—promises that never materialized. The South's climate had stayed the same even after the war, where lynching, police brutality, and massive discrimination persisted. The White population needed to know that Black people were in an earnest battle for civil rights after the war, having valiantly fought beside Whites. They had progressed in literacy, college attendance, property ownership, transitioned from plantation labor, and wanted equal rights and peaceful coexistence. Thousands of Black people also fled the South for better opportunities in northern cities like New York, Detroit, and Chicago, and by doing so, hurting the South's economy. Thus, one of the NAACP's goals was to improve economic and educational conditions for Black people so they would remain in the South and be able to live good lives.

There had been little, if any, coverage of Black peoples' perspectives in the mainstream Southern press. Therefore, the White population and the government had few opportunities to hear firsthand about the African American community's suffering. The NAACP convention could enable Bernays's team to communicate those messages via newspapers the White population found credible, and Georgia's mainstream media could give a voice to the Black community, reaching and hopefully influencing the Southern White audience directly.

Edward Bernays sent his colleague, Doris Fleischman (who later became his wife), to Atlanta prior to the event to survey the city's mood. She saw signs around the city prohibiting Black people from entering stores or using water fountains. Fleischman heard shoppers making disparaging comments about Black people and saw the poverty-stricken neighborhoods in which they lived. Fleischman was introduced to state officials prior to her Atlanta trip and met with as many as she could during the visit to explain the conference's objectives and why the NAACP was taking the risk of holding it in Atlanta. Fleischman also visited Atlanta newspaper editors and other editors in the region, spending time detailing the purpose of the conference—raising awareness for racial equality and humane treatment of Black people. Most editors, except the *Atlanta Constitution* editor, told her they were not inclined to carry such a story because it was not one that resonated with their readers. The *Atlanta Constitution*'s city editor asked perplexedly, "How would you advise me to handle this story?" Fleischman answered, "most meetings like this would be handled on the front page in the left-hand column. Why don't you treat it as a straight news story?" The editor looked at her and said, "Yes, that's right. That's what I'll do" (Bernays, 1965, p. 212).

Bernays arranged a *New York Times* advance editorial that said in part:

> A conference under the auspices of the National Association for the Advancement of Colored People should be held in Atlanta this year—the first of 11 annual conferences ever held in a Southern city—is startling to say the least.
>
> (Bernays, 1965)

Bernays joined Fleischman in Atlanta before the event. Word of the conference had spread, and the prevalent mood was dreadfully quiet. They were told the mood was atypical and akin to quiet preceding violence. Bernays could overhear bellboys, taxi drivers, and room clerks suggesting that violence might ensue at any moment.

Therefore, the Bernays team wrote three strategic and newsworthy themes the conference would now cover: (1) Black people were vital to the economy, and them going North jeopardized the southern economy; (2) A growing number of Southern business and political leaders now supported civil rights and equal opportunity—and both races were seeking new status for Black people; and (3) Northern business leaders viewed the NAACP increasingly positive. The NAACP convention went off without a hitch and was covered by the state's and nation's mainstream newspapers. For the first time in history, news was published under the dateline of a southern city proposing that both White and Black populations were seeking new status for Black citizens. The Bernays team turned a potential disaster into a turning point for race relations by positioning southerners—the ones who perceived Black people as—as modern, progressive thinkers, who were advocating for a New South.

Classic Case in Recent Decades: The University of Georgia's Integration Crisis

Bernays' and Fleishman's work with the NAACP vividly illustrates considerations of the Crisis History Framework's influential perspectives of visibility, influential perspectives, and crisis emotion. Although they did not mention these factors explicitly, their strategy displayed how important they are in crisis planning. While this dynamic duo provides a great example of preventing crises and bridging racial gaps in the Deep South, over 40 years later, The University of Georgia (UGA) failed to prevent and mitigate its integration crisis and ensuing riot.

The Supreme Court's (1954) Brown vs. Board of Education of Topeka ruling sent shockwaves through the US, especially in states that upheld the white preeminence notion viewing the ruling as an attack on their lives and future wealth. Georgia Governor Herman Talmadge, politicians, and citizens expressed their displeasure publicly (Pratt, 2002). Much of the discontent stemmed from the ruling's impact on the state's prized institution, The University of Georgia (UGA), and led to legislation being passed to prevent the University's integration. The Atlanta Committee for Cooperative Action (ACCA), a civil rights group of young Black professionals displeased with the "old guard's" handling of the movement, handpicked two Atlanta-area seniors, Hamilton Holmes and Charlayne Hunter, to apply to the University. University administrators, students, and Georgia citizens tried to impede their university acceptance and jeopardize their safety, culminating with a student riot on campus. By most historical accounts, the University was aware of its administrators' misdeeds as well as the volatile climate surrounding the integration that ultimately led to the crisis (Eaddy, 2016; Hunter-Gault, 1993; Pratt, 2002; Trillin, 1964).

Crisis History Learning for UGA. While it seems University officials could have gained insight from the crisis prevention of the NAACP's 1920 convention, apparently they did not consider previous racially charged crises. Instead, they focused solely on preserving the status quo. During the University's integration, administrators did not consider the influential factors of proximity, valence, stability, visibility, influential perspectives, nor crisis emotions. These considerations could have improved their crisis preparation, planning, prevention, and mitigation.

The Great Depression

Perhaps the greatest crisis management campaign of all time was not considered a "campaign" at all, but an authentic, natural effort to ease the public's fear in the worst economic collapse the US had ever faced, The Great Depression. It was in a climate of pervasive hopelessness that Democrat Franklin Delano Roosevelt (FDR) handily won the 1932 election with a great advantage over the incumbent President Herbert Hoover. The proceeding decades featured the competing interests of the government's executive branch and "big business"/manufacturers. Both factions shared a goal of reassuring citizens the country would survive the Great Depression, but had differing strategies for progressing.

Big Business: Ushering the Nation into Prosperity through Free Enterprise and Innovation. Immediately following the Great Depression, the National Association of Manufacturers (NAM) launched a massive nationwide public relations campaign, the first of its kind in scope and ambition. NAM's strategy presented business and free enterprise as solutions to the country's economic suffering (as opposed to the federal government, specifically, the New Deal). Using the tagline, *It's the American Way*, their message equated the freedoms embedded in America's democracy—speech, religion, and assembly—with the private sector's freedoms to operate without government intervention as "free enterprises" (Eaddy et al., 2018).

The campaign used every communications channel available—from news columns to newsreels to sponsored radio dramas. *The American Family Robinson* was a NAM-sponsored family drama radio series spanning 40 episodes and broadcast by networks reaching every corner of the country. Pro-business and anti-New Deal messages were inside every script, creating storylines extolling capitalism and free enterprise, and warning about the dangers of government interference. Citizens could also read a syndicated newspaper column, *You and Your Nation's Affairs*, that supported NAM's agenda. Paul Garrett launched a series of groundbreaking campaigns designed not to sell cars to the public but to rebuild public trust in the economy. One campaign, *The Parade of Progress*, featured caravans of Futurliner vehicles, setting out to win the hearts and minds of small town America. These roving science museums showcased futuristic technologies, capturing the public's imagination. More importantly, they helped distraught Americans believe in the American Dream again. While big business advocated for innovation, the government attempted to sway the American public the opposite direction (Eaddy et al., 2018).

FDR: Rebuilding the Nation through Restored Faith and Trust. Throughout the 1930s, FDR fought to restore trust and faith—not only in the economic system—but in the country's future. He created federal programs, referred to as the "New Deal," focused on supporting the health and welfare of people, something no previous president had done. FDR and the New Deal agencies used a variety of communication strategies and tactics to gain political support to implement the social welfare reform needed to propel the country out of the Depression. He was the first president to use radio, a technology now becoming affordable for most families and a medium perfect for speaking directly to a public needing reassurance.

After his inauguration on March 4, 1933, FDR faced the forced closing of banks across the nation after another wave of panic and the consequent loss of trust in the financial system. After a massive run on the banks, FDR declared a four-day bank holiday in order to allow Congress to pass the Emergency Banking Act, a bill allowing the president to reopen solvent banks and aid indebted banks. The day before reopening the banks, FDR launched a program that would become a trademark of his persona and administration: the Fireside Chats.

FDR's Fireside Chats. At a time when home radios were becoming commonplace, FDR used Fireside Chats—more than 30 total—to address the nation's most pressing issues in a calming, confident way that helped rebuild trust in the government and belief in FDR's New Deal. With every Fireside Chat, FDR addressed millions, providing practical information as well as guidance, wisdom, and hope.

He won loyalty by praising listeners' contributions to the recovery, stating he owed them an explanation "because of the fortitude and good temper with which everybody [had] accepted the inconvenience and hardships of the banking holiday" (Roosevelt, 1933). A tactic that made his talks believable was his use of disclaimers, often leading to a positive, hopeful twist: "I do not promise you that every bank will be reopened or that individual losses will not be suffered, but there will be no losses that possibly could be avoided..." (Roosevelt, 1933). FDR personalized his talks, tying them back to listeners, emphasizing citizens' responsibilities, and explaining how they themselves could help alleviate some of the pain.

The Fireside Chats were part of a strategy to win Americans' hearts and trust. He also used them to influence Congress to pass his New Deal bills. The public's trust in its leader ultimately allowed FDR to introduce and implement a series of revolutionary reforms.

Resettlement Administration. Congress had to be convinced to provide help to the thousands of poverty-stricken families in the rural Midwest. In order to do this, FDR arranged for some of the nation's best-known photographers to visit these families and vividly document their urgent plight.

Newspapers throughout the nation published these dramatic photographs, enabling the public—and the Congress—to witness for themselves the suffering experienced by these families. This effort proved highly persuasive, managing to shift public opinion in favor of providing relief programs to the impacted families. The campaign also propelled the careers of such photographers as Jack Delano, Arthur Rothstein, Russell Lee, and Dorothea Lange.

Classic Case in Recent Decades: The Great Recession

The Great Depression was an unprecedented crisis of epic proportions. "Big business" and FDR employed communications strategies they believed were fitting for the circumstances and would deliver the country from the Great Depression's economic ruin. Although neither party used contemporary crisis history terms, it is evident that several of crisis history's influential factors underscored their strategy. Nearly 80 years later, the US experienced The Great Recession, that was the first financial crisis to cause disruption comparable to the Great Depression.

The 2008 financial crisis, commonly referred to as The Great Recession, had a global impact that touched business, governments, and the public and private sectors alike. The Great Recession led to economic downturn, reputational threats for organizations and industries, and financial ruin of many investors. Thousands of Americans also lost their homes and retirement savings and corporate communicators faced unseen challenges: "growing (dis)trust on the part of the public became more pivotal than ever. But those businesses practicing effective and ethical communication were able to withstand the crisis better than most" (Jin et al., 2018, p. 2).

Crisis History Learning for The Great Recession of 2008. One might struggle to draw parallels between crises beyond their financial impact, but the financial industry and government could have used inspiration from the Great Depression. However, similar to the Great Depression, there were two key players during the crisis: the government and finance industry. Both parties worked in their best interests and competed for the American public's favor. While crisis counselors and the government failed to realize how strategies employed during the Great Depression could inform their strategies, it is apparent that several influential factors endured (Jin et al., 2018). In hindsight, crisis counselors could have benefited most from careful consideration of influential perspectives. While the finance industry was villainized on one hand, it was also the victim of the crisis. Although systems and fail safes were in place to prevent such crises from occurring, preceding events created the perfect environment for the crisis to occur. The conflicted message of industry being both the villain and victim was difficult, if not impossible, for crisis counselors to convey. If the finance industry had rallied together, similarly to the NAM, perhaps the American public could have understood the events that transpired better.

Key Takeaways

Crisis communication scholarship is ripe with opportunities to refine research frameworks that explore the processes and outcomes of organizational and interorganizational crisis learning specifically related to crisis history (Jin et al., 2018). Concurrently, it is essential for industry professionals to consider crisis history's contributions to organizational learning. While crisis communication professionals may consider previous crises anecdotally, few make a conscious and concerted effort to include crisis history considerations in their crisis planning. The Crisis History Framework can serve as a guide to professionals who recognize the importance of gleaning insight from crisis history so their organizations can learn from the past.

This chapter highlights the evolving complexity of crisis history by exploring the Crisis History Framework and revisiting historical crisis case studies along with their contemporary counterparts, to provide practical insights for crisis communications professionals and scholars. The historical and contemporary cases illustrate how integral crisis history considerations can be for weathering crisis storms. Scholars' and professionals' collaborative efforts are key to bridging this gap and ultimately enhancing crisis communication strategy and tactics with valuable insight from crisis history's annals and inspiring crisis history research exploration. Crisis managers should challenge the notion of hindsight; instead recognizing and acknowledging the role crisis history plays in organizational learning and crisis management strategy. Those who fail to consider the past could be destined to repeat it.

References

Barnett, M. L. (2007). Tarred and untarred by the same brush: Exploring interdependence in the volatility of stock returns. *Corporate Reputation Review, 10*(1), 3–21. https://doi.org/10.1057/palgrave.crr.1550035

Barnett, M. L., & Hoffman, A. (2008). Beyond corporate reputation: Managing reputational interdependence. *Corporate Reputation Review, 11*(1). https://doi.org/10.1057/crr.2008.2

Bernays, E. L. (1965). *Biography of an idea: Memoirs of public relations counsel Edward L. Bernays*. Simon and Schuster, Inc.

Centers for Disease Control and Prevention. (2002). *Crisis and emergency risk communication manual*. pp. 1–194. U.S. Department of Health and Human Services.

Choi, Y., & Lin, Y.-H. (2009). Consumer responses to Mattel product recalls posted on online bulletin boards: Exploring two types of emotion. *Journal of Public Relations Research, 21*(2), 198–207. https://doi.org/10.1080/10627260802557506

Coombs, W. T. (1995). Choosing the right words: The development of guidelines for the selection of the "appropriate" crisis response strategies. *Management Communication Quarterly, 8*(4), 447–476. https://doi.org/10.1177/0893318995008004003

Coombs, W. T. (2004). Impact of past crises on current crisis communication. *Journal of Business Communication, 41*(3), 265–289. https://doi.org/10.1177/0021943604265607

Coombs, W. T., & Holladay, S. J. (1996). Communication and attributions in a crisis: An experiment study in crisis communication. *Journal of Public Relations Research*, *8*(4), 279–295. https://doi.org/10.1207/s1532754xjprr0804_04

Coombs, W. T., & Holladay, S. J. (2002). Helping crisis managers protect reputational assets: Initial tests of the situational crisis communication theory. *Management Communication Quarterly*, *16*(2), 21. https://doi.org/10.1177/089331802237233

Coombs, W. T., & Holladay, S. J. (2006). Unpacking the halo effect: Reputation and crisis management. *Journal of Communication Management*, *10*(2), 123–137. https://doi.org/10.1108/13632540610664698

Eaddy, L. L. (2016, August). *Saving face: How the University of Georgia survived the integration crisis and maintained its image through stakeholder management.* Association for Education in Journalism and Mass Communication (AEJMC), Minneapolis, MN.

Eaddy, L. L. (2017). *Unearthing the facets of crisis history in crisis communication: Testing a conceptual framework* [Doctoral dissertation, University of Georgia]. UGA Electronic Theses and Dissertations Database.

Eaddy, L. L., Brummette, J., & Jin, Y. (March, 2017). *Repeat crises: How crisis history affects stakeholder attributions and coping.* Paper presented at the International Public Relations Research Conference, Orlando, FL.

Eaddy, L. L., & Jin, Y. (2018). Crisis history tellers matter: The effects of crisis history and crisis information source on publics' cognitive and affective responses to organizational crisis. *Corporate Communication: An International Journal*, *23*(2), 226–241. http://doi.org/10.1108/CCIJ-04-2017-0039

Eaddy, L. L., Spector, S., Austin, L., Jin, Y., Reber, B., Espina, C., Plascencia, R., & Morales, M. (2018, July). *Public relations during financial crises: How lessons from the great depression informed responses to the great recession.* Paper accepted for presentation at the International History of Public Relations Conference, July 11–12, 2018, Bournemouth.

Fassin, Y. (2010). A dynamic perspective in Freeman's stakeholder model. *Journal of Business Ethics*, *96*, 39–49. https://doi.org/10.1007/S10551-011-0942-6

Haggerty, J. F. (2003). *In the courtroom of public opinion: Winning your case with public relations.* Wiley.

Hiebert, R. E. (2017). *Courtier to the crowd: Ivy Lee and the development of public relations in America.* PR Museum Press.

Holzer, B. (2007). Turning stakeseekers into stakeholders: A political coalition perspective on the politics of stakeholder influence. *Business & Society*, *47*(1), 50–67. https://doi.org/10.1177/0007650307306341

Hunter-Gault, C. (1993). *In my place.* Vintage Books.

Jin, Y. (2009). The effects of public's cognitive appraisal of emotions in crises on crisis coping and strategy assessment. *Public Relations Review*, *35*(3), 310–313. https://doi.org/10.1016/j.pubrev.2009.02.003

Jin, Y. (2010). Making sense sensibly in crisis communication: How publics' crisis appraisals influence their negative emotions, coping strategy preferences, and crisis response acceptance. *Communication Research*, *37*(4), 522–552. https://doi.org/10.1177/0093650210368256

Jin, Y., Austin, L., Eaddy, L. L., Spector, S., Reber, B., & Espina, C. (2018). How financial crisis history informs ethical corporate communication: Insights from public relations leaders. *Public Relations Review*, *44*(4), 574–584. https://doi.org/10.1016/j.pubrev.2018.06.003

Jin, Y., & Cameron, G. T. (2007). The effects of threat type and duration on public relations practitioner's cognitive, affective, and cognitive responses in crisis situations. *Journal of Public Relations Research, 19*(3), 255–281. https://doi.org/10.1080/10627260701331762

Jin, Y., Pang, A., & Cameron, G. T. (2007). Integrated crisis mapping: Towards a publics-based, emotion-driven conceptualization in crisis communication. *Sphera Publica, 7*(1), 81–96. Research Collection Lee Kong Chian School of Business.

Jin, Y., Spector, S., Reber, B., & Austin, L. (2016, August 30). *Standing on the shoulders of past communicators.* https://www.bellisario.psu.edu/page-center/article/standing-on-the-shoulders-of-past-communicators

Klein, J., & Dawar, N. (2004). Corporate social responsibility and consumers' attributions and brand evaluations in a product–harm crisis. *International Journal of Research in Marketing, 21*(3), 203–217. http://dx.doi.org/10.1016/j.ijresmar.2003.12.003

Merriam-Webster. (n.d.). *Salience.* Retrieved April 29, 2020, https://www.merriam webster.com/dictionary/salience

Mitroff, I. I., & Harrington, L. K. (1996). Thinking about the unthinkable. *Across the Board, 33*(8), 44–48.

Pratt, R. A. (2002) *We shall not be moved: The desegregation of the University of Georgia.* University of Georgia Press.

Rød, S. K., Botan, C., & Holen, A. (2012). Risk communication and the willingness to follow evacuation instructions in a natural disaster. *Health, Risk & Society, 14*(1), 87–99. https://doi.org/10.1080/13698575.2011.641522

Rodriguez, S. (2015, September 15). *The real reason everyone calls billion-dollar startups 'Unicorns'.* International Business Times. https://www.ibtimes.com/real-reason-everyone-calls-billion-dollar-startups-unicorns-2079596

Roosevelt, F. D. (1933, March 12). On the bank crisis [Speech transcript], Marist University FDR Library, http://docs.fdrlibrary.marist.edu/031233.html

Seo, S., Jang, S., Miao, L., Almanza, B., & Behnke, C. (2013). The impact of food safety events on the value of food-related firms: An event study approach. *International Journal of Hospitality Management, 33*, 153–165. https://doi.org/10.1016/j.ijhm.2012.07.008

Standop, D., & Grunwald, G. (2009). How to solve product-harm crises in retailing? *International Journal of Retail & Distribution Management, 37*(11), 915–932. https://doi.org/10.1108/09590550910999352

The Economist. (2017, March 25). *Uber is facing the biggest crisis in its short history.* https://www.economist.com/business/2017/03/25/uber-is-facing-the-biggest-crisis-in-its-short-history

Trillin, C. (1964). *An education in Georgia: Charlayne Hunter, Hamilton Holmes, and the integration of the University of Georgia.* University of Georgia Press.

Vanhamme, J., & Grobben, B. (2009). "Too good to be true!" The effectiveness of CSR history in countering negative publicity. *Journal of Business Ethics, 85*, 273–283. https://doi.org/10.1007/s10551-008-9731-2

Watson, T. (2015). "Crisis, credibility and corporate history." Book review. *Corporate Communications: An International Journal, 20*(4), 518–520. https://doi.org/10.1108/CCIJ-02–2015–0007

Zou, H. L., Zeng, R. C., Zeng, S. X., & Shi, J. J. (2015). How do environmental violation events harm corporate reputation? *Business Strategy & the Environment (John Wiley & Sons, Inc), 24*(8), 836–854. https://doi.org/10.1002/bse.1849

Part II

Most Challenging Organizational Crises

3 Corporate Crises

Sticky Crises and Corporations

W. Timothy Coombs, Sherry J. Holladay, and Rick White

By definition, a crisis is a serious situation for an organization. The designation "crisis" is a signal that the situation warrants attention and resources, including the activation of a crisis management plan and the assembly of the crisis management team. However, not all crises are created equal, which means some are more challenging to manage than others. For instance, the first time a food producer handles a product harm requiring a recall is likely to be much more challenging than the second or third product harm crisis. An industrial accident caused by management's disregard for safety is more challenging than an industrial accident caused by a lightning strike. All crises are serious, but the challenges each creates can be variable.

The rising use of digital channels, highlighted by social media platforms, creates new challenges for crisis communication. Public relations, for example, has adapted to challenges presented by the digital age and integrated social and other digital channels into the practice (e.g., Wright & Hinson, 2017). Similarly, crisis communication has integrated digital channels into its practice, but that integration is not without complications for crisis managers (Coombs, 2019; Frandsen & Johansen, 2017). The digital age contributes to sticky crises but is not the reason for them. The Crisis Communication Think Tank broadly defines *sticky crises* as "complex and challenging crisis issues." Sticky crises existed prior to the Internet, but digital channels facilitate the development and occurrence of sticky crises. Crisis communication becomes more complex and complicated when digital channels are used to add new voices to the crisis communication effort (Frandsen & Johansen, 2017) or the power of digital channels leveraged to create a potential crisis for an organization (Coombs & Holladay, 2015).

Sticky crises are unique due to the challenges these crises create, especially for crisis communication. This chapter focuses on the ramifications of sticky crises for corporations. The analysis of sticky crises and corporations covers two points. First, the challenges of sticky crises for corporations are detailed by exploring various types of sticky crises and the contextual factors that help to make a crisis sticky. Second, preliminary guidance for communicating during a sticky crisis is presented by focusing on the concerns that arise during sticky crises and how crisis communication can be used to address those concerns.

Challenges of Sticky Crises to Corporate Communications

In this section, we explore the challenges a sticky crisis can present for managers. After decades of practice and research, we have a solid knowledge base for understanding how to utilize communication during "typical" crises (Coombs, 2019). However, sticky crises take managers outside of the normal crisis communication knowledge base by creating unique demands. The Crisis Communication Think Tank broadly defines *sticky crises* as "complex and challenging crisis issues." We build upon this definition by exploring different types of sticky crises corporations encounter and articulating complicating contextual factors related to sticky crises. The end result of this analysis is a richer and more nuanced understanding of the unique communicative demands sticky crises place upon crisis managers and a more nuanced definition of the concept.

Types of Sticky Crises

To understand the unique demands of sticky crises, it is important to consider a range of sticky crises. Different factors can make a crisis sticky, therefore, there are various types of sticky crises. These different types of sticky crises each can create unique exigencies for crisis communication. That is why it is important to explore some common types of sticky crises. We will focus on five types of sticky crises that emerged from the 2019 Crisis Communication Think Tank discussions and one emerging from the COVID-19 pandemic: data breaches, longitudinal crises, scansis, industry-wide crises, and public health crises. We will consider characteristics that make each of these crises "sticky." Textbox 3.1 presents a list of the corporate sticky crises.

Textbox 3.1: Types of Sticky Corporate Crises and Contextual Factors

Types of Sticky Corporate Crises

Data breaches: create strong perceptions of susceptibility of harm for victims
Longitudinal crises: extend over a prolonged period of time
Scansis: fusion of a scandal and crisis that evokes moral outrage
Industry-wide crises: spillover effect of a crisis to others within the same industry
Public health crises: effects multiple industries and geographic locations

Contextual Factors

Misinformation: harmful and wrong information circulates about an organization
Social issues: polarizing effect on stakeholders
Race and Gender: social issues that are politicized adding to the polarizing effects

Data breaches are rapidly becoming one of the most common forms of sticky crises. Between 2010 and 2019, there were over 8,000 data breaches in the US (Annual, 2020). On the surface, a data breach appears to be a simple form of crisis to manage. Data breaches are the result of external attacks. Other crises that are a result of external attacks, such as product tampering, create low levels of crisis responsibility, making the crisis less threatening and easier to manage. Even though data breaches are external attacks, stakeholders shift attributions of data breaches from external attackers to the actual organizations being breached. The internal attributions for data breaches are found in the polling data that definitively shows most stakeholders hold the organization responsible/accountable for the data breach (Whitelegg, 2019). Moreover, stakeholders perceive a strong threat to their own well-being from a data breach—there is a strong perception of susceptibility. Potential vulnerabilities produce the immediate need to take actions such as replacing credit cards, locking accounts, and monitoring credit for indicators of identity theft. Data breaches create a very real threat for all customers. This is in stark contrast to most "typical" crises that usually place only a limited subset of customers or other stakeholders at risk. An example would be a product harm crisis involving a food product. Companies that offer multiple food products recall only a subset of their products. Hence, not all customers are at risk. Another example would be a chemical release that would require certain community members to evacuate or shelter-in-place. The susceptibility to harm from the crisis felt by most if not all stakeholders helps to make data breaches sticky.

Longitudinal crises are crises that last for an extended period of time. An extended period of time means months or even years. Typical crises might last a few hours or days and crisis managers seek to shorten crises as much as possible (Coombs, 2019). One way to shorten a crisis is to use communication to end media interest in the crisis—establish an ending for the crisis (Barton, 2001). The reputational and potential financial damages from negative media coverage are serious concerns for managers (Ni et al., 2014). When the media stops reporting on the crisis, the negative stories about the organization end. Sometimes, the crisis is extended because of legal or regulatory timelines that impede a swift resolution to the crisis. A longitudinal crisis not only persists for an extended period of time but also may garner recurring media interest in the negative aspects of the crisis. The point is that some crises disrupt operations for an extended time period but do not attract recurring, negative media coverage. For example, when Blue Bell Ice Cream experienced its first product harm crisis due to Listeria, the product was off the market for five months. During that time, the media stories concentrated on the efforts to remedy the problems and return to the market—positive stories (Elkind, 2015). Contrast this with Boeing the 737 Max. The plane was removed from service after two deadly crashes. The Boeing 737 Max grounding will exceed 12 months. In addition, there are regular negative stories about the inability to address the problem, the identification of potential new problems, and the damage of the crisis to Boeing stock and personnel (German, 2020).

The Boeing 737 Max grounding is a longitudinal crisis, but the Blue Bell Listeria product harm is not. The negative media coverage that ebbs and flows over an extended period of time is what makes a longitudinal crisis sticky.

A *scansis* is when a crisis situation also becomes a scandal (Coombs et al., 2018). Both crises and scandals are the result of perceptions. In a crisis, stakeholders perceive a violation of their expectations that can have negative consequences for other stakeholders and/or the organization. Scandals involve perceptions of a moral violation (Fine, 1997; Nichols, 1997). Scandals require media attention and people have a sense of moral outrage. Moral outrage is the perception that the organization acted in a way that was both unjust to stakeholders and motivated by greed (Antonetti & Maklan, 2016). A crisis transmogrifies into a scansis when media coverage raises awareness of the situation and cues in the situation lead to perceptions of injustice and greed (Coombs et al., 2018). Moral outrage was evoked when Mylan dramatically increased the price of EpiPens 400% in 2016 and Wells Fargo charged customers for new accounts Wells Fargo opened without customers even knowing the accounts existed (Egan, 2016; Willingham, 2016). The moral outrage associated with a scansis is what makes it sticky (Coombs & Tachkova, 2019).

An *industry-wide crisis* is one that impacts all or most of an industry. There are two variations of an industry-wide crisis. *Spillover* is the first type. Spillover can occur when stakeholders perceive others in an industry are affected by the crisis in one organization when that is not the case. An entire industry becomes tainted as stakeholders perceive the crisis in one organization applies to other organizations. Product harm crises in the food industry frequently have a spillover effect. Examples include romaine lettuce and cantaloupe growers finding a recall from one area or farm lead people to believe all lettuce and cantaloupes are dangerous to eat. In the case of cantaloupe, even a top US official told people to avoid all cantaloupe even though the problem was traced to a single farm in Colorado (Coombs, 2014). Another example is the way that the crisis at the Fukushima Daiichi Nuclear Plant in Japan negatively affected the nuclear power industry globally.

Intrinsic is the second type of industry-wide crisis and occurs when a large number of organizations within an industry are affected by the same crisis. Honda, Toyota, and other automobile manufacturers all had to recall vehicles due to unsafe airbags. The companies used the same airbag manufacturer, which resulted in the intrinsic industry-wide crisis (Associated Press, 2020). A similar problem occurred with laptop lithium-ion batteries in 2018 and 2019 (Newman, 2019; St. John, 2018). Intrinsic industry-wide crises really do pose a problem for a variety of companies in the same industry. Anxiety about a product category helps to make industry-wide crises sticky. The product anxiety can result in suppressed sales and an economic slump for an industry. The ability of a crisis to have an industry-wide effect helps to make it sticky.

The year 2020 demonstrates how public health crises can extend across multiple industries and geographic locations. COVID-19 is a public health crisis driven by a pandemic. Part of the governmental response to the public health crisis was the use of social distancing and lockdowns to prevent the spread of the virus by keeping people physically isolated from one another. The effects of the governmental actions created crises for organizations. Could an organization still function either as an essential service or as a virtual organization? The situation highlights the need for corporations to be prepared to communicate with stakeholders during a public health crisis. *Public health crises* can create unique crisis communication situations for organizations as government restrictions can reshape the corporate landscape helping to create a sticky crisis.

Complicating Contextual Factors

Stickiness is not simply a product of certain types of crises but also can be enhanced by contextual factors. We examine three contextual factors that emerged from the 2019 Crisis Communication Think Tank discussions: disinformation, social issues, and race and gender concerns. The purpose is to explain how these contextual factors contribute to the stickiness of a crisis.

Disinformation is a widely discussed topic in the digital age (Barfar, 2019). *Disinformation* is incorrect information about an organization that has the potential to disrupt the stakeholder-organization relationship. Often the spread of the incorrect information is purposeful and intended to harm an organization (Hodge, 2020). But we should remember the need for organizations to address disinformation predates the emergence of the digital environment. For instance, Procter & Gamble has been addressing disinformation that links the company to support of the Church of Satan since the disinformation first appeared in the 1980s. The disinformation centers on reports that the CEO stated on television that the founder of P&G sold his soul to the devil for business success. Evidence included the man in the moon logo (Mikkelson, n.d.). P&G seemed to be winning the battle of disinformation until the Internet provided new life for the misinformation. Eventually, P&G dropped the man in the moon symbol, a logo they had used for over 100 years. P&G was concerned about the disinformation because links to Satan can hurt reputations, sales, and stock prices (Stampler, 2013). Disinformation damages stakeholder-organization relations by eroding the organizational reputation and weakening identification with an organization.

Disinformation is sticky because it is difficult to dispel. Rumor research, one version of disinformation, finds that rumors are compelling when they seem plausible. Once people believe the disinformation, it is hard to displace that initial erroneous view even when the "truth" is revealed. There are actually two broad categories of disinformation: unintentionally spread misinformation and intentionally spread misinformation. Unintentionally spread misinformation emerges spontaneously as people seek to share information with friends and family. Intentionally spread information originates with a malicious source that seeks some gain or wants to harm another entity (Wu et al., 2016). Both forms can stick in people's minds and damage the stakeholder-organization relationship.

Social issues are controversial by nature and create at least two sides that debate the issue. The social aspect is that the issue is an undesirable condition that harms society and should be corrected. Controversy arises over what issues are really social issues (undesirable) and how to correct the condition. Common social issues include public health, immigration, climate change, and poverty. Managers are finding it increasingly difficult to avoid social issues. The need for organizations to be socially responsible coupled with an emphasis on being purpose driven creates expectations among stakeholders that organizations will take a stand on issues (Global, 2019; Horst, 2018). Managers realize, no matter which side the organization takes, some faction of its stakeholders will vehemently oppose them. In 2019, the Hallmark Channel experienced the complexity of social issues. The first concern was a protest by the conservative group One Million Moms over the Hallmark Channel running an advertisement from the wedding planning site Zola that contained same-sex couples. One Million Moms did not approve of a commercial that advanced the LGBTQ agenda. Management at the Hallmark Channel limited which Zola advertisements were aired, and Zola canceled their advertising. Then #BoycottHallmark began to trend on Twitter as people were upset by the censoring of the Zola advertisements. Three days later, the Hallmark Channel reversed its decision (Mullen, 2019). In the end, the Hallmark Channel seemed to have angered both sides of the same-sex marriage issue. The controversial nature of social issues can complicate an already sticky situation.

Racial concerns add a unique dimension to a crisis situation. While race is a social issue, it is highly politicized creating a socio-political issue. An issue is politicized when it is viewed through a political lens and linked to public policy. Politicization increases the polarizing effects of an issue (McCright & Dunlap, 2011). When the crisis is linked to racism, there often is increased media interest and tensions created by this powerful socio-political issue. Consider how the brands of Uncle Ben's, Aunt Jemima, and Mrs. Butterworth's all decided to change what many considered racist logos during the early 2020s in the US when anti-racism concerns were prominent in the media (Ward & Wiley, 2020). We see racial concerns manifest in crises when some element of the crisis reflects racial discrimination or bias. This might involve how a particular group is represented in a message or mistreatment of a particular group. Racial concerns have the potential to offend various stakeholder segments. It is the offensiveness of racial concerns that serves to complicate a situation. A similar dynamic holds true for crises that center on gender concerns such those related to #MeToo (the Me Too movement).

Creating Guidance for Sticky Crisis

In this section, we consider what guidance we can offer crisis managers confronting a sticky crisis. The optimal crisis communication response will vary by the nature of the stickiness of a crisis. We begin by isolating the concerns that arise during a sticky crisis that must be navigated by crisis communicators and then translate this information into tentative crisis communication guidance. We refer to these as "tentative" because many of the ideas presented here are grounded in theory but are as yet untested.

Concerns Arising during Sticky Crises: Empathy, Trust, and Emotions

An important aspect of crisis communication that emerges from the professional and academic literature is the need for empathy. More specifically, managers need to have empathy for those affected by the crisis—crisis victims and potential victims. Empathy is reflected in the crisis responses, the words and actions offered after a crisis occurs. Any crisis response must convey empathy to the crisis victims. Empathy is one means of building trust between crisis managers and stakeholders.

The Crisis Communication Think Tank discussion of sticky crises frequently returned to the topic of trust. A crisis damages the level of trust between the organization in crisis and its stakeholders. Crises are a violation of trust because crises violate how stakeholders expect an organization to behave (Coombs, 1999). We expect food to not make us sick, for an airbag to help not hurt us, and for executives to not discriminate or harass employees. Part of the crisis response must acknowledge the need to rebuild this trust. Though trust repair may entail apologies, there are limits to apologies. We must consider what other elements in the crisis response can address trust.

We appreciate that all crises can engender emotional reactions. Anxiety, anger, and even sympathy can accompany a crisis. Sticky crises seem to heighten the emotions and magnify negative affect toward the organization in crisis. Scansis, for example, evokes the very negative emotion of moral outrage. Crises with racial elements create feelings of being offended. These are serious emotions that can have a negative and long-term effect on the stakeholder-organization relationship (Antonetti & Maklan, 2016). Public health crises raise anxiety levels (WHO, 2009) as do many other crisis types (Jin et al., 2012).

One consequence of the digital environment is the exposure of organizations to social issues. Stakeholders expect organizations to engage with social issues that are important to the stakeholders (Global, 2019). However, social issues can be divisive and evoke a variety of emotions. Stakeholders will disagree on which social issues are important, how they feel about the social issues, and how or if an organization should address the social issue. The digital environment makes it easier to observe if and how organizations are engaging with social issues. It also provides platforms for questioning an organization's commitment or lack thereof to social issues. This environment places greater demands on organizations to live their values, articulate their purpose, and explain their relationships to various social issues.

Acting in accordance with one's proclaimed values helps an organization to present a consistent stance on various social issues.

Preliminary Communicative Guidance for Sticky Crises

Research has documented the limits of apology, expressions of sympathy, and even curative actions having a positive effect on common crisis outcomes (Coombs & Tachkova, 2019; Ma & Zhan, 2016). Scansis and data breaches require us to rethink the optimal crisis response, and recognition of emotional reactions can help us reconsider responses. Moral outrage raises the question of value incongruence. The moral violation signals the organization does not share the same values as its stakeholders. Thus, it is critical that the crisis response acknowledges the specific moral violation. Managers must specify what they have done wrong, not simply declare they will fix the problem. The response must directly address the moral violation. Similarly, the data breach response must focus on how the problem impacts the stakeholders, and racially tinged crises must address the offensiveness of the crisis. It is not enough to apologize, express sympathy, or promise a better future; managers must demonstrate to stakeholders that the managers know why the stakeholders are so upset about the crisis. Such recognition of the violation helps to express empathy and to rebuild trust (Coombs & Tachkova, 2019).

Moreover, research demonstrates the value of stealing thunder in a data breach crisis. Shaikh and Joseph (2019) found that voluntary disclosure of a data breach by the organization reduced the negative effects of a data breach on stock prices. Stealing thunder, when the organization is the first source to disclose a crisis, could prove extremely valuable in sticky crises (Claeys, 2017). However, managers are often hesitant to steal thunder because releasing crisis-related information results in immediate loss for an organization (Claeys & Coombs, 2019; Claeys & Opgenhaffen, 2016). Additional training may be needed to convince managers that stealing thunder is a desirable option during a sticky crisis.

Social issues place a premium on pre-crisis communication. It is advantageous to articulate or at least consider internally your organization's position on a social issue before, and not during, a sticky crisis. Crisis preparation is about saving time during a crisis because wasting time can harm stakeholders and the organization. Managers should monitor social issues that are likely to be connected with their sector. Moreover, as part of risk management, managers should draft the organization's position on the salient social issues. The 2017 Harris Poll on Reputation Quotient emphasized the need for corporations to understand their own values (Harris Poll, 2018). Management may or may not share those positions publicly, that is an internal decision. But articulating positions allows managers to respond quickly and consistently during a crisis, two hallmarks of effective crisis communication (Coombs, 2019).

Frandsen and Johansen (2018) examined the spillover effect in industry-wide crises by applying Rhetorical Arena Theory (RAT) to explore how trade associations respond to such sticky crises. They found tensions arise when deciding how to respond to crises that threaten the industry's reputation. Does the trade association speak with one voice or does it express multiple voices and multiple interests? The trade association represents the entire industry. Does that mean the trade association seeks to protect all members or does the trade association focus on the one or few organizations responsible for the crisis? Industry-wide crises can create a need for competitors to work together or provide an opportunity for an organization to articulate its advantage over rivals in crisis (Paruchuri et al., 2019).

Disinformation illustrates RAT's concept of multiple voices during a crisis. Crisis managers need to map the various voices and the effects of those voices when deciding on a response to disinformation. The extant research on false rumors provides the best guidance for responding to disinformation. The two response options tend to be (1) passively ignore/minimize the disinformation and (2) actively correct the disinformation. The choice is driven by the degree of threat posed by the disinformation. Managers are passive when they see little or no threat from the disinformation. Consider how managers at Corona beer claimed their customers were aware the disinformation linking Corona beer to the 2020 novel coronavirus was false (Kotoky, 2020). The managers did not identify the disinformation as a threat and only responded when questioned by reporters. This situation stands in contrast to the response of peanut butter producers who aggressively denied their products were linked to the peanut butter paste recall in 2009. Over 70% of American consumers believed peanut butter was included in the peanut paste recall. In reality, peanut butter was not part of the recall and the peanut butter companies communicated that message aggressively to stakeholders (Coombs, 2014). Tensions arise from fears that choosing to not address the disinformation allows it to be accepted as "fact" and that refuting the disinformation attracts attention and may prompt the spread of the disinformation. Managers must decide if refuting the disinformation poses a greater risk than ignoring it. As more research emerges on the topic of disinformation, especially on how to combat disinformation, we can develop more nuanced crisis responses to sticky crises involving disinformation.

Longitudinal crises create a unique dynamic where crises act much like issues. The crisis/issue will ebb and wane in terms of media and public interest. Issues have life cycles that reflect various levels of interest in the issue (Crable & Vibbert, 1985). The issue development graph is an early attempt to articulate how managers could monitor changes in the attention and public salience of issues (Crable & Faulkner, 1988). Many media monitoring companies offer dashboards that allow managers to "see" the rise and fall of crisis attention and interest. Longitudinal crises demand a shift in thinking from crisis mode to issues management. The crisis is not about an immediate response but about the ability to monitor crisis attention and develop responses that mesh with the rise and fall of interest in the crisis. To better understand longitudinal sticky crises, we can look to Southern California Gas Company's methane gas leak at one of the largest natural gas storage facilities in the Western United States. Located in the San Fernando Valley, about 20 miles from downtown Los Angeles and one mile from the affluent residential community of Porter Ranch, SoCal Gas's Aliso Canyon facility included an aging oil well completed in the 1950s that had been converted to natural gas storage in 1973. Though the initial revelation of the leak at well SS-25 and its numerous attempts to seal the well generated media attention from October 2015 to February 2016, SoCal Gas operations continue to be scrutinized to this day (Blade Energy Partners, 2019; Save Porter Ranch, nd Torres & Shyong, 2016).

An independent investigation of SoCal's Aliso Canyon activities dating back into the 1970s uncovered more than 60 casing leaks that were not investigated before the well leak in 2015 (Blade Energy Partners, 2019). In response to the highly critical report, SoCal insisted its Aliso Canyon activities complied with regulations governing gas storage at the time of the leak. A year prior to the leak, SoCal had reported plans to the California Public Utilities Commission (CPUC) for upgrading the facility to address the types of well failures and leaks that already had occurred (Abram, 2015). As early as 1992, company documents revealed it was aware of a possible leak in the storage tank. However, SoCal failed to assess this risk and other risks (engage in crisis prevention) that eventually materialized into the 111-day crisis (Blade Energy Partners, 2019; Tabibzadeh et al., 2017). SoCal's release of more than 100,000 tons of methane (hydrocarbon gas) is among one of the longest-running methane leaks in US history (Blade Energy Partners, 2019). The Environmental Defense Fund's dramatic infrared photos of SoCal's massive methane leak frequently resurface in debates surrounding the need for increased regulation of and decreased dependence on fossil fuels (O'Connor, 2015).

A \$119.5 million settlement between SoCal Gas and the city, county, and state officials was finally reached in August 2018 (Barboza, 2018). However, news of additional unsettled lawsuits, including a class-action case, as well as ongoing concerns over the safety of SoCal's operations have prolonged interest in the Aliso Canyon crisis (Varian, 2019). Although SoCal apologized and offered temporary relocation opportunities for over 8,000 Porter Ranch residents (CPUC, 2020), the persistence of stories concerning negative health effects, its failure to conduct adequate safety inspections and engage in record-keeping, multiple failures to cooperate with Safety and Enforcement Division (SED) investigations (Blade Energy Partners, 2019), and a multitude of pending lawsuits continue to evoke sympathy for victims and generate anger toward the company. For instance, by 2019, over 50 lawsuits had been filed by LA city firefighters who had assisted evacuees without wearing personal protective gear. SoCal had failed to warn firefighters about possible exposure to toxic chemicals and many developed symptoms similar to those of residents, including migraine headaches, dizziness, nosebleeds, sleeping and breathing difficulties, and cancer (Grigoryants, 2019). The 2019 independent third-party investigation reported a litany of questionable safety-related decisions and violations by SoCal, including attempts to conceal information from investigators (Blade Energy Partners, 2019). In June 2020, SoCal Gas reminded people of its crisis by garnering unfavorable media attention for requesting an extension for required testing of wells at the Alison Canyon facility due to the COVID-19 pandemic (Roth, 2020).

Despite potential risks posed by the aging storage facility, independent investigations demonstrated SoCal Gas had no comprehensive risk management plan, no testing programs, and no plans to remediate substandard wells (Blade Energy Partners, 2019; Tabibzadeh et al., 2017). Exactly when the Aliso Canyon leak began is unknown. It was discovered by a SoCal crew on October 23, 2015 and its own crews immediately began to investigate the leak. On October 24, Save Porter Ranch (SPR), a community organization formed in 2014 and dedicated to environmental protection of the area by "building community awareness through education, advocacy, organizing and strategic partnerships" (Our Mission, 2016), used social media to notify residents of the strong mercaptan odor. The unpleasant odor is deliberately created by adding mercaptan to natural gas to produce a rotten egg smell that can alert people to a problem (Abram, 2015). SPR also contacted the Air Quality Management District (AQMD) and the fire department. Air samples confirmed the leak on October 24, and the following day AQMD announced the leak to residents.

The standard kill procedures used by SoCal were unable to stop the leak and outside well experts were brought to the scene on October 25. After subsequent attempts also proved unsuccessful, construction of a relief well began on December 4, a process projected to take three to four months to complete (Blade Energy Partners, 2019).

To address concerns about the leak, SoCal Gas held its first "open house" for residents on October 26 (Save Porter Ranch Advocacy, n.d.). On October 28, SoCal sent a letter to area residents, apologized for creating concern and inconvenience, and provided a website where residents could secure additional information about work to seal the leak. Though the company claimed the odor did not pose a health hazard, residents were understandably concerned about the smell, and some experienced symptoms, including bad headaches, dizziness, nose bleeds, and nausea (Wilcox, 2015). Throughout the four-month crisis, SoCal initiated regular public outreach through customer letters, updates at its website, community awareness documents, an informational booth at Porter Ranch, 24/7 phone and email responses, and press releases. Community bulletins apologized for the inconvenience and frustration, thanked residents for their patience, contained diagrams depicting the well, and reported information about its progress, safety concerns, and online and physical community resources.

On October 28, the Office of Emergency Management reported resident complaints to the Los Angeles County Department of Public Health (LACDPH) and requested it assess potential health effects of exposure to the leak. Based on its analysis of health complaints, on November 19, the LACDPH responded with a Public Health Directive ordering SoCal Gas to pay for the relocation of residents (LACDPH, 2015). On December 7, Los Angeles City and County sued the company, accusing it of violating health and safety codes and hazardous material reporting requirements. SoCal was sued again on December 22 to increase the speed of resident relocations. About two months after the leak was identified, California Governor Jerry Brown finally met with Porter Ranch residents and declared a state of emergency on January 6. The lengthy delay generated controversy because the Governor was accused of putting family, financial, and political ties before the interests of his constituents. Sempra Energy, SoCal's parent company, is a long-time donor to Brown's campaigns and Brown's sister serves on the board of Sempra Energy (Koerner, 2016). The visibility of the Governor's declaration afforded residents the opportunity to participate in interviews with regional and national media. Erin Brockovich, the well-known consumer advocate and environmental activist, lives about 30 minutes from Porter Ranch. In conjunction with legal work, Brockovich met with residents to hear their accounts (Stuart, 2016). By the beginning of February 2016, 11 local, state, and federal agencies were investigating or suing SoCalGas.

Finally, on February 18, the California Department of Conservation's Department of Oil, Gas and Geothermal Resources (DOGGR) announced the well was permanently sealed. Initially, residents were given eight days to return from their temporary housing. However, an LA county judge ordered SoCalGas to continue to cover relocation costs for several more weeks. Ultimately, SoCal reported it met with over 30,000 residents at its Community Resource Center at Porter Ranch, processed about $78 million in reimbursements, installed air filtration systems, and cleaned parks, schools, and playgrounds. It also promised to mitigate the natural gas released by the leak (SoCalGas, 2016). Save Porter Ranch continues to operate and will observe the fifth anniversary of the leak.

The prolonged industrial crisis was sticky as it offered ample opportunities for local, regional, and national news to report a range of negative events associated with the company. These included multiple failed attempts to stop the leaks, company claims the leak posed no risk to public safety, reluctance to acknowledge residents' concerns over the effects of exposure to natural gas and mercaptan, delayed responses to resident requests for relocation and assistance, local and state lawsuits against the company, dramatic infrared images of the magnitude of the leak, and comparisons to the devastating Deepwater Horizon spill in the Gulf of Mexico. Table 3.1 provides a summary of the theory-driven communicative advice being offered for sticky corporate crises.

Key Takeaways

Sticky crises arise in part due to the digital environment but that is a small part of the process. It is critical to understand the challenges sticky crisis

Table 3.1 Response to Sticky Corporate Crises

Nature of the Sticky Corporate Crisis	*Optimal Response*
When management recognizes the crisis before it is known by external actors	Steal thunder by being the first source to disclose the crisis
When a crisis appears to reflect injustice and exploitation by the organization and evokes moral outrage	Acknowledge the moral violation as part of the effort to re-establish shared values
When a social issue or socio-political issue is raising in salience	Create and share a position statement on the issue
When the crisis has potential for spillover	Seek to facilitate an industry-wide response
When potentially harmful disinformation is emerging about the organization	Aggressively seek to combat the misinformation
When a crisis extends over weeks or months	Fuse your crisis communication approach with issues management by monitoring the changing salience of the crisis situation and responding as the crisis re-gains public interest

situations create for crisis managers. The challenges provide insight for creating communicative responses to sticky crises. Our analysis of the challenges focused on the types of sticky crises and the complicating contextual factors related to sticky crises. We identified five primary types of sticky crises: (1) data breaches, (2) longitudinal, (3) scansis, and (4) industry-wide (spillover and intrinsic), and (5) public health crises. Each crisis type can present unique communicative demands for crisis managers. The complicating contextual factors include disinformation, social issues, and race and gender. These provide additional insights into the unique demands sticky crises place upon managers. We can then refine the definition of sticky corporate crises to be crises that are made complex and challenging due to some combination of the situation increasing susceptibility, extending over an extended period of time, evoking moral outrage, spreading across an industry, and/or affecting multiple industries and geographic areas.

The complex nature of sticky crises renders the use of "best practices" moot. Best practices are oversimplifications that tend toward a one-size-fits-all mentality. Sticky crises demand a more thoughtful approach that is contingent in nature (Ambler, 2011). The discussion of communicative guidance for sticky crises emphasizes the need to understand the key concerns that emerge in a sticky crisis and how to address those concerns through communication. The types of sticky crises and complicating contextual factors provide insights into concerns that can be used to create communicative guidance for sticky crises that takes a contingent approach. It is by seeking to illuminate the nature of sticky crises that we can gain communicative insights that can help managers facing such complicated crisis situations.

References

Abram, S. (2015, December 19). Two months in, Porter Ranch gas leak compared to BP Gulf oil spill. *LA Daily News*. https://www.dailynews.com/2015/12/19/two-months-in-porter-ranch-gas-leak-compared-to-bp-gulf-oil-spill/

Ambler, S. (2011). *Questioning the "best practices" for software development*. Ambysoft. http://www.ambysoft.com/essays/bestPractices.html

Annual number of data breaches and exposure records in the United States from 2005 to 2019. (2020). Statista. https://www.statista.com/statistics/273550/data-breaches-recorded-in-the-united-states-by-number-of-breaches-and-records-exposed/

Antonetti, P., & Maklan, S. (2016). An extended model of moral outrage at corporate social irresponsibility. *Journal of Business Ethics*, *135*(3), 429–444. http://dx.doi.org/10.1007/s10551-014-2487-y

Associated Press. (2020, January 22). *Toyota and Honda recall 6 million vehicles over airbag dangers* (2020). *LA Times*. https://www.latimes.com/world-nation/story/2020-01-22/air-bag-woes-force-honda-toyota-to-recall-6m-vehicles

Barboza, T. (2018, August 8). SoCal gas agrees to $119.5-million settlement for Aliso Canyon methane leak—biggest in U.S. history. *LA Times*. https://www.latimes.com/local/lanow/la-me-aliso-canyon-settlement-20180808-story.html

Barfar, A. (2019). Cognitive and affective responses to political disinformation in Facebook. *Computers in Human Behavior*, *101*, 173–179. https://doi.org/10.1016/j.chb.2019.07.026

Barton, L. (2001). *Crisis in organizations II* (2nd ed.). College Divisions South-Western.

Blade Energy Partners. (2019). Informational webinar for the parties regarding the Blade RCA report. https://www.blade-energy.com/press-releases/

California Public Utilities Commission (CPUC). (2020). *Aliso Canyon well failure*. https://www.cpuc.ca.gov/aliso/

Claeys, A. S. (2017). Better safe than sorry: Why organizations in crisis should never hesitate to steal thunder. *Business Horizons*, *60*(3), 305–311. http://dx.doi.org/10.1016/j.bushor.2017.01.003

Claeys, A. S., & Coombs, W. T. (2019). Organizational crisis communication: Suboptimal crisis response selection decisions and behavioral economics. *Communication Theory*, qtz002. https://doi.org/10.1093/ct/qtz002

Claeys, A. S., & Opgenhaffen, M. (2016). Why practitioners do (not) apply crisis communication theory in practice. *Journal of Public Relations Research*, *28*(5–6), 232–247. http://dx.doi.org/10.1080/1062726X.2016.1261703

Coombs, W. T. (2014). *Applied crisis communication and crisis management: Cases and exercis*es. Sage Publications.

Coombs, W. T. (2019). *Ongoing crisis communication: Planning, managing, and responding* (5th ed.). Sage Publications.

Coombs, W. T., & Holladay, S. J. (2015). Digital naturals and crisis communication: significant shifts in focus. In W. T. Coombs, J. Falkheimer, M. Heide, & P. Young (Eds.), *Strategic communication, social media and democracy: The challenge of the digital naturals* (pp. 54–62). New York: Routledge.

Coombs, W. T., Holladay, S. J., & Tachkova, E. R. (2018). When a scandal and a crisis fuse: Exploring the communicative implications of scansis. In A. Haller, H. Michael, & M. Kraus (Eds.), *Scandology: An interdisciplinary field* (pp. 172–190). Herbert Von Verlag.

Coombs, W. T., & Tachkova, E. R. (2019). Scansis as a unique crisis type: Theoretical and practical implications. *Journal of Communication Management*, 23(1), 72–88. https://doi.org/10.1108/JCOM-08-2018-0078

Crable, R. E., & Faulkner, M. M. (1988). The issue development graph: A tool for research and analysis. *Communication Studies*, *39*(2), 110–120.

Crable, R. E., & Vibbert, S. L. (1985). Managing issues and influencing public policy. *Public Relations Review*, *11*(2), 3–16. http://dx.doi.org/10.1016/S0363-8111(82)80114-8

Egan, M. (2016). 5,300 Wells Fargo employees forged over 2 million phony accounts. *CNN*. https://money.cnn.com/2016/09/08/investing/wells-fargo-created-phony-accounts-bank-fees/

Elkind, P. (2015). *How ice cream maker blue bell blew it*. Fortune. https://fortune.com/2015/09/25/blue-bell-listeria-recall/

Fine, G. (1997). Scandal, social conditions, and the creation of public attention: Fatty Arbuckle and the problem of Hollywood. *Social Problems*, *44*(3), 297–323. http://dx.doi.org/10.2307/3097179

Frandsen, F. and Johansen, W. (2017). *Organizational Crisis Communication*. Thousand Oaks, CA: Sage.

Frandsen, F., & Johansen, W. (2018). Voices in conflict? The crisis communication of meta-organizations. *Management Communication Quarterly*, *32*(1), 90–120. http://dx.doi.org/10.1177/0893318917705734

German, K. (2020). Boeing 737 Max could stay grounded until late 2020. *CNET*. https://www.cnet.com/news/boeing-737-max-8-all-about-the-aircraft-flight-ban-and-investigations/

Global Strategy Group (2019). *Doing business in an activist world*. GSG. https://www.globalstrategygroup.com/wp-content/uploads/2019/02/GSG-2019_Doing-Business-in-an-Activist-World_Business-and-Politics.pdf

Grigoryants, O. (2019, February 5). Firefighters sue SoCal Gas over big gas leak near Porter Ranch. *LA Daily News*. https://www.dailynews.com/2019/02/05/more-l-a-firefighters-sue-socal-gas-over-big-gas-leak-near-porter-ranch/

Harris Poll (2018). *IBM survey reveals consumers want businesses to do more to actively protect their data*. Stagewell. https://theharrispoll.com/ibm-survey-reveals-consumers-want-businesses-to-do-more-to-actively-protect-their-data/

Hodge, N. (2020). Fake facts: What the rise of disinformation campaigns mean for business. *RM Magazine*. http://www.rmmagazine.com/2020/04/01/fake-facts-what-the-rise-of-disinformation-campaigns-means-for-businesses/

Horst, P. (2018). New research encourages brands to weigh in on the big social issues. *Forbes*. https://www.forbes.com/sites/peterhorst/2018/06/06/new-research-encourages-brands-to-weigh-in-on-the-big-social-issues/#3dd1d2741a12

Jin, Y., Pang, A., & Cameron, G. T. (2012). Toward a publics-driven, emotion-based conceptualization in crisis communication: Unearthing dominant emotions in multi-staged testing of the integrated crisis mapping (ICM) model. *Journal of Public Relations Research*, *24*(3), 266–298. http://dx.doi.org/10.1080/1062726X.2012.676747

Koerner, C. (2016, January 6). State of emergency declared as huge gas leak forces Californians to flee. *BuzzFeed*. https://www.buzzfeednews.com/article/claudiakoerner/california-governor-declares-state-emergency-over-massive-gas

Kotoky, A. (2020). 'Corona Beer virus?' The global epidemic is taking a real-life toll on the beverage. *Time*. https://time.com/5792470/corona-beer-virus/

Los Angeles County Department of Public Health. (2015, November 19). http://www.lapublichealth.org/EH/docs/AlisoCanyonBoard.pdf

Ma, L., & Zhan, M. (2016). Effects of attributed responsibility and response strategies on organizational reputation: A meta-analysis of situational crisis communication theory research. *Journal of Public Relations Research*, *28*(2), 102–119.

McCright, A. M., & Dunlap, R. E. (2011). The politicization of climate change and polarization in the American public's views of global warming, 2001–2010. *The Sociological Quarterly*, *52*(2), 155–194. http://dx.doi.org/10.1111/j.1533-8525.2011.01198.x

Mikkelson, D. (n.d.). Proctor and Gamble and satanism rumor. *Snopes*. https://www.snopes.com/fact-check/trademark-of-the-devil/

Mullen, C. (2019). Hallmark reverses its ban on LGBTQ commercial. *Biz Journals*. https://www.bizjournals.com/bizwomen/news/latest-news/2019/12/hallmark-reverses-its-ban-on-lgbtq-commercial.html?page=all

Newman, J. (2019). MacBook pro recall: How to find out if your 15-inch Apple laptop is a fire hazard. *Fast Company*. https://www.fastcompany.com/90367624/apple-macbook-pros-recalled-for-fire-risk-how-to-check-yours

Ni, J. Z., Flynn, B. B., & Jacobs, F. R. (2014). Impact of product recall announcements on retailers' financial value. *International Journal of Production Economics*, *15*(3), 309–322. http://doi.org/10.1016/j.ijpe.2014.03.014

Nichols, L. (1997). Social problems as landmark narratives: Bank of Boston, mass media, and money laundering. *Social Problems*, *44*(3), 324–341. http://dx.doi.org/10.1525/sp.1997.44.3.03x0118n

O'Connor, T. (2015, December 10). Infrared camera reveals huge, wafting cloud of methane over California's Aliso Canyon. *EDF*. http://blogs.edf.org/energyexchange/2015/12/10/infrared-camera-reveals-huge-wafting-cloud-of-methane-over-californias-aliso-canyon/

Our Mission. (2016). https://www.saveporterranch.org/

Paruchuri, S., Pollock, T. G., & Kumar, N. (2019). On the tip of the brain: Understanding when negative reputational events can have positive reputation spillovers, and for how long. *Strategic Management Journal*, *40*(12), 1965–1983. http://dx.doi.org/10.1002/smj.3043

Roth, S. (2020). Remember the Aliso Canyon disaster? SoCalGAs just tried to delay safety testing. *LA Times*. https://www.latimes.com/environment/story/2020-06-30/remember-the-aliso-canyon-disaster-socalgas-just-tried-to-delay-safety-tests

Save Porter Ranch Advocacy and Community Leadership. (n.d.). https://3943fe07-fafa-456b-b52d-8b30035ef94a.filesusr.com/ugd/3d1481_81e9bbe2703840798cd144e739309871.pdf

Shaikh, F. A., & Joseph, D. (2019, June). Effects of information security legitimacy on data breach consequences: Moderating effect of impression management. In *Proceedings of the 2019 on Computers and People Research Conference* (pp. 118–121).

SoCalGas. (2016, May 20). *SoCalGas responds to court decision ending relocation program*. https://www.socalgas.com/1443739502582/news-release-court-hearing-52016.pdf

St. John, A. (2018). *HP recalls 50,000 lithium-ion laptop batteries over fire risk*. Consumer Reports. https://www.consumerreports.org/hp/hp-recalls-50-000-laptops-over-li-ion-battery-fires-/

Stampler, L. (2013). In spite of old, false satanism accusations, P&G put a moon back into its logo. *Business Insider*. https://www.businessinsider.com/pg-puts-moon-in-new-logo-despite-satanist-accusations-2013-5

Stuart, T. (2016). The BO oil spill on land: Erin Brockovich on LA's gas leak. *Rolling Stone*. https://www.rollingstone.com/politics/politics-news/the-bp-oil-spill-on-land-erin-brockovich-on-las-gas-leak-235342/

Tabibzadeh, M., Stavros, S., Ashtekar, M. S., & Meshkati, N. (2017). A systematic framework for root-cause analysis of the Aliso Canyon gas leak using the AcciMap methodology: Implication for underground gas storage facilities. *Journal of Sustainable Energy Engineering*, *5*(3), 212–242. https://doi.org/10.7569/jsee.2017.629515

Torres, Z., & Shyong, F. (2016, January 3). Leaking gas well in Porter Ranch area lacked a working safety valve. *LA Times*. https://www.latimes.com/local/california/la-me-0104-gas-leak-20160104-story.html

Varian, E. (2019, May 20). Attorneys, plaintiffs say "root cause" report sheds new light on SoCalGas actions after Aliso Canyon blowout. *Los Angeles Daily News*. https://www.dailynews.com/2019/05/20/attorneys-plaintiffs-with-claims-against-socalgas-say-aliso-canyon-root-cause-report-sheds-new-light-on-blowout-aftermath/

Ward, M., & Wiley, M. (2020). 14 racist brands, mascots, and logos that were considered just another part of American life. *Business Insider*. https://www.businessinsider.com/15-racist-brand-mascots-and-logos-2014-6.

Whitelegg, D. (2019). Customers blame companies not hackers for data breaches. *Security Boulevard*. https://securityboulevard.com/2019/02/customers-blame-companies-not-hackers-for-data-breaches/

Wilcox, G. J. (2015, October 29). Gas leak near Porter Ranch lingers nearly one week later. *Los Angeles Daily News*. https://www.dailynews.com/2015/10/29/gas-leak-near-porter-ranch-lingers-nearly-one-week-later/

Willingham, E. (2016). Why did Mylan hike epipen prices 400%? Because they could. *Forbes*. https://www.forbes.com/sites/emilywillingham/2016/08/21/why-did-mylan-hike-epipen-prices-400-because-they-could/#389feb79280c

World Health Organization. (2009). *Cities and public health crises: Report of the international consultation*. https://www.who.int/ihr/lyon/FRWHO_HSE_IHR_LYON_2009.5.pdf?ua=1

Wright, D., & Hinson, M. (2017). Tracking how social and other digital media are being used in public relations practice: A twelve-year study. *Public Relations Journal*, *11*(1), 1–30.

Wu, L., Morstatter, F., Hu, X., & Liu, H. (2016). Mining misinformation in social media. In *Big data in complex and social networks* (pp. 135–162). Boca Raton, FL: CRC Press

4 Connected in Crisis

How Nonprofit Organizations Can Respond and Refocus

Hilary Fussell Sisco and Mark McMullen

Every organization is susceptible to crisis. Crisis communication is inherently needed both proactively in issues management (Dougall, 2008) and in reputational repair in a post-crisis situation (Coombs, 2007). The scope of crisis communication both professionally and academically has primarily focused on those organizations that have brand power and bandwidth as a for-profit entity. In these sectors, crisis communication is able to utilize internal and external resources, paid media, and other privileged platforms to spread their message. On the contrary, in the nonprofit sector, crisis communication has hurdles and challenges both in methods of communication and also in leveraging the reputational impact on an organization (Sisco, 2010). This chapter will outline some of the challenges and issues that nonprofit organizations face in a crisis, provide scholarly insights into those crisis theories that are applicable to nonprofits, outline an example of a nonprofit organizational crisis, and define key takeaways for the future of nonprofit crisis communication from this scholarly and practical perspective.

Challenges

To understand the specific challenges to nonprofit crisis communication, it is first important to understand the variances within the sector for different types of organizations. According to Feinglass (2005), a nonprofit organization has a collective "mind-set of supporters and professionals alike that are engaged in fulfilling a significant mission, as opposed to increasing a corporate bottom line"; this influences "the choices that are made and how those choices are implemented" (p. 7). There are also differences in the scope of nonprofit organizations, their reporting structure, and financial protocols that can impact their overall communications strategies. In the United States, the common thread that defines many nonprofit organizations is their tax-exempt status. Under this threshold, the sector is built by "religious, educational, charitable, scientific, literary, testing for public safety, to foster national or international amateur sports competition, or prevention of cruelty to children or animals' organization" (IRS, 2019, p. 2), all of which need to report their financial activities in the same manner. The financial reporting of these organizations builds an identity of accountability that should be apparent in their communication strategies. Organizations that have to be open and honest about their donations, funds, and other activities must also communicate with the same obligations and expectations from their various constituents. Nonprofit organizations are distinctly different in their dependence on a voluntary network of participants, their zero-revenue status, and their lack of identified "ownership and accountability" (Frumkin, 2002, p. 3).

Lack of Resources

Overall, nonprofit organizations tend to operate with much more limited resources than their counterparts in the for-profit sector and often those resources are donation based. Therefore, the intricacies of communication are vitally important once a crisis occurs. Organizations reveal their true character and intentions in a crisis situation (Sisco, 2012) so their regular activities are put on display and are critical to their reputational and operational success post-crisis. They are also dependent on a network of volunteers that can shepherd them through the day-to-day but also hinder their ability to communicate a consistent message. Williams and Buttle (2013) found that negative word-of-mouth communication during a crisis can not only impact the reputation of a nonprofit organization but can have lasting damage to the sector as well. Unfortunately, very little attention has been paid to understanding the theoretical underpinnings of why crisis communication is quite critical for nonprofit organizations.

In their 2013 analysis, Sisco et al. found that there was an overall "paucity of research specifically about nonprofit public relations" (p. 282). It seems that not much has changed overall in the public relations literature since 2013, and there is even more limited information on how nonprofit organizations theoretically navigate crises. Furthermore, the expectation of nonprofit transparency in their organizational structure, finances, and communication has led to substantial research studies, but many of those studies do not specifically highlight the differences or challenges that nonprofit organizations face but rather use them as a methodological tool for theoretical understanding. As theory is developed, it is important to consider the identity of an organization and how that might impact the perceptions surrounding its reputation.

Reputation

Nonprofit organizations have historically been regularly impacted by crises, which can lead to reputational damage and a loss of donors (Sisco et al., 2010). The American Red Cross has a consistent record of scandal, including the misappropriation of funds during the Haiti Earthquake and delaying donations for the Australian wildfire victims. But they are not alone in their efforts to remain transparent and accountable; other nonprofits have also come under fire. The Senate Finance Committee has had to step in several times to better understand how donations can be used for direct relief rather than overhead costs and nonessentials. As Kinsky et al. (2015) explained, "donations are the lifeblood of any nonprofit deserving of the protection of effective crisis communication" (p. 152). For nonprofit organizations, crises can be natural disasters and human-made disasters (Gilstrap et al., 2016). Research has found that a nonprofit in crisis requires a specific style of leadership to measure the scope, duration, and impact a crisis can have on an organization (Pauchant & Mitroff, 1992).

Networked Organizations

The internal structure of a nonprofit organization varies greatly by size and distribution of volunteers and staff. Research has shown that trust and distrust between board members and staff (Reid & Turbide, 2012), staff and volunteers (Bortree, 2014) and the public (Sisco, 2012) can cause an internal crisis for a nonprofit. Externally, nonprofit organizations are typically intrinsically networked with a group of publics, a community, and other organizations. This can lead to a substantial domino effect when one organization suffers a scandal and the impact is felt throughout that organization's network. Sundstrom et al. (2013) note that nonprofit crisis communication is complex and can come from several organizations at once, which can either improve or damage a single organization's reputation. Some scholars have argued that nonprofit organizations must operate with dynamic capabilities (Kaltenbrunner & Reichel, 2018, p. 999), meaning they are able to communicate on behalf of many different interests to provide clarity in their internal processing and communication. This can be very difficult to do when there is a crisis at one central unit yet the local chapters and or affiliate organizations are reputationally impacted.

Stakeholders are able to make informed decisions when an organization remains open with their community. The literature on nonprofit organization divides terminology, which also inhibits progress. In scholarship, transparency has been promoted as a theoretical term for the intimate look inside an organization by public relations scholars. In practice, organizations are often criticized if they do not have transparent communication. For nonprofit organizations, transparency becomes a much more significant conversation about finances and reporting transactions.

Transparency adds credibility to an organization's communication efforts. Rawlins (2008) has found that organizational transparency can build public trust. This is especially important for nonprofits as they are required by the Internal Revenue Service (IRS) to be financially transparent, but their communication transparency is able to build community as well. These efforts for disclosure can impact an organization's reputation and its perception of fostering goodwill.

Stewardship

Stewardship is the heart of the reciprocal relationship between a nonprofit organization and its publics. Stewardship is a relationship management strategy defined by four distinct dimensions: reciprocity, responsibility, reporting, and relationship nurturing (Kelly, 1998). These dimensions help solidify the support of the public and organizational stakeholders and keep them engaged in a nonprofit organization's activities. The outcome of successful stewardship is primarily measured in monetary support through donations. O'Neil (2007) found that "the strongest indicators of a strong, positive relationship were between the relationship scores and donors' happiness to continue giving and happiness to recommend others to donate" (p. 102). Therefore, nonprofit organizations should focus their attention on those closest to the organization as research has shown that this relationship is the most rewarding both in reputational benefits and in financial support. This financial support from donors is a critical thread that links an organization to its public and any infraction that puts that relationship in jeopardy can result in dire consequences.

Further, research has expanded the application of stewardship beyond primarily donor support. Waters et al. (2013) found that stewardship strategies can strengthen the organization-volunteer relationship. Volunteers feel more connected to the organization and are able to reciprocate through support, which leads to a stronger impact for the nonprofit organization. These strategies to communicate more to increase involvement have positively impacted both external publics and internal publics like employees (Waters et al., 2013).

Case Study: Wounded Warrior Project

The Wounded Warrior Project (WWP) is the largest veteran's charity in the United States. In its first ten years, the WWP grew to 22 locations with roughly 500 employees and raised at least $1 billion—largely through small donations from people over 65 (Philips, 2016). John Melia, a Somalia-wounded Marine veteran, initiated the WWP when he started giving backpacks full of items to returning Iraq war veterans in 2003. WWP "provides vital programs and services to severely wounded service members and veterans to support their transition to civilian life as well-adjusted citizens, both physically and mentally" (WWP, "Who We Are", n.d.). The organization is one of very few devoted to this distinctive and well-respected population.

In 2016, reports surfaced that the nonprofit had been misspending its donations on lavish conferences and unnecessary business trips for employees (Philips, 2016). Several former employees claimed that the organization was spending millions every year on lavish travel, dinners, hotels, and conferences rather than the mission it served. Charity Navigator, a group that monitors and rates charities stated that WWP spent about $124 million on overhead in 2014, which is roughly 40% of donations (Charity Navigator, 2014). It was reported later that spending on conferences and meetings rose from $1.7 million in 2010 to around $26 million in 2014.

In response to these reports, the WWP responded to the crisis through a letter posted on Facebook. The letter was addressed to Al Ortiz, Executive Director at CBS demanding that *CBS* make retractions to its original story. The WWP claimed that *CBS* misrepresented its financial information and that the WWP actually spends 80.6% of its donations on programs for veterans, and that 94% of the previously mentioned $26 million figure related to conferences and meetings was really spent on programs for veterans and their families (Renfree, 2016).

The denial was short-lived as the media scrutiny only increased for the WWP. They soon started their own investigation resulting in the dismissal of several key leaders. On March 9, 2016, the WWP Board of Directors terminated Chief Executive Officer Steve Nardizzi and Chief Operations Officer Al Giordano. Termination of Nardizzi and Giordano occurred after multiple news reports highlighted lavish spending, including extravagant parties and events, and cited dozens of former team members describing a toxic leadership culture (Cahn, 2016). As the organization continued to struggle, donations went into steep decline.

The Senate Judiciary and Finance Committee began to investigate the misdeeds of the WWP based on the scale of the impact and the public that it served. In their report, they cited several issues that illustrated problems from the very beginning of the organization. The report found that there were not appropriate policies and procedures and that management was left with too much power and not enough oversight. It also found that excessive amounts of money were spent on employee travel. Additionally, administrative and fundraising events were too lavish (Grassley, 2017).

In 2018, the WWP began to rebuild under new leadership. Mike Lennington stepped in as CEO and set his own salary to well-below those of his predecessors and put a stop to lavish travel, expenses, and events (Seck, 2019). The WWP also cut back on all-staff outings; moved away from pricey ticketed events in favor of addressing complex quality-of-life issues for veterans; made efforts to be more collaborative in the veterans' organization community; and even tweaked its advertising strategy to tell a more positive story about veterans, an effort the WWP said was calculated not to bring in the most advertising dollars but to do the most good for the community (Seck, 2019).

At the end of the Senate's investigation, they issued a recommendation that aligns with the theoretical foundations of stewardship and transparency. Senator Chuck Grassley concluded that

> moving forward, the WWP needs to improve and restore the public trust and it can begin to do so by being transparent and honest about the use of donor contributions and program activities that provide real benefits to veterans. In turn, transparency will bring accountability and lead to a better fulfillment of its mission.
>
> (2017, p. 60)

Many praised the rebrand of the organization and the accountability the WWP demonstrated in their efforts to rebuild after the crisis. The impact of the crisis was severe as donations were significantly impacted. But through the actions and communication strategies implemented by the organization, donations stabilized by 2018 (NPQ). The turnaround has been used as a positive example of how to use transparency to rebuild trust in an organization with a very strong base of supporters.

Theory Recommendations

The issues of the WWP reflect how organizations with internal conflict will soon have external problems. The internal culture of an organization can soar as donations and their dominance in the industry grows, but if this expansion infringes upon the mission of the organization, there can be repercussions from publics and stakeholders. The WWP experienced great success in their reputation and activities, but their tactics ultimately failed because of their lack of focus and commitment to the communities they claimed to serve.

Many nonprofits are structured in a way where power, decisions, and communication stems predominantly from the top of the organization but research (O'Neil, 2007) has shown that empowering those throughout the organization can help to maintain transparency and trust during a crisis. Nonprofit organizations must leverage their communication to serve their community and fulfil their mission and if not managed strategically can have dire consequences for nonprofit organizations (Archambeault & Webber, 2018). Nonprofit organizations should be systematic and diligent about their communication with those that they are most closely associated. Bortree and Waters (2008) found that building strong relationships with these kinds of publics requires a two-way dialogue to build trust and increase reputation repair.

Discourse of Renewal

As an organization under fire, the WWP and other nonprofits facing turmoil must refocus their efforts on the future and re-establish their actions moving forward. The discourse of renewal theory originated from the idea that we seek forgiveness for transgressions so that we can experience a spiritual rebirth and a return to a state of grace (Seeger & Griffin Padgett, 2010). The premise of the theory is, after a crisis has occurred, the organization should recommit their focus to atonement and an optimistic outlook toward the future. If done sincerely, an organization can transcend the crisis and even rebuild as a better and more solid organization overall (Seeger & Griffin Padgett, 2010). For many organizations that suffer a crisis from their headquarters and yet must build back trust at the local level, the discourse from an altruistic leader and well-known community member can help to bridge the divide between external publics and the internal conflict.

There are four dominant features of post-crisis discourse: "prospective focus; the opportunities inherent in the crisis; provisional rather than strategic responses; and ethical communication grounded in core values" (Seeger & Griffin Padgett, 2010, p. 136). In order to attract new members after a crisis, nonprofit organizations must build "a vision of the future designed to create consensus and commitment among a diverse group of stakeholders" (p. 136). Although previous research on the discourse of renewal has focused primarily on for-profit entities that are able to take advantage of losses through the rebuilding of new facilities or retraining of existing employees, nonprofit organizations must focus their opportunities around the reapplication of their mission and values in their communities. In a well-led organization, crisis provides the opportunity to re-evaluate and rebuild into a more transparent and open organization. If the organization has committed to an optimistic future, then their communication should move to a prospective tone "driven by value systems and patterns of conduct and relationships" (Seeger & Griffin Padgett, 2010, p. 137). This will help to build authenticity as well as the immediacy in their actions and the hope is that communication is attractive to new members, volunteers, and potential donors that may want to become involved with an organization.

Finally, the foundation of discourse of renewal is in the use of ethical communication and a value-based approach. Authentic and honest communication helps to open the door to those that feel uncertain and are not sure about the intentions of the organization because of the larger issues. Research has shown that discourse of renewal has been transformative for several organizations from the auto industry to technology and even national branding after the terrorist attacks of 9/11 (Ulmer et al., 2017). Crisis communication for an organization not directly experiencing a crisis should not be retrospective but instead should build an open dialogue for the chapter or local level to reinforce the trust and commitment. Hopefully, over time, this goodwill can build back into the affiliated organizations. Practitioners can embrace and recognize these theoretical elements and incorporate them into their work. By so doing, they can help to lessen the reputational burden that their network may have endured.

Key Takeaways

Crisis communication literature in both practice and scholarship has overlooked the nonprofit sector despite the need. Nonprofit organizations have complex systems both internally and externally where they are dependent on others for their success. This connection to others can spur even more reputational damage when the organization is impacted by an internal crisis. This situation is unique to the sector as those in for-profit entities are usually able to operate without external impact. Both practitioners and scholars can benefit from a renewed focus on these differences and the specific strategies that would enable a nonprofit to endure a crisis situation. In this case, while nonprofits have limited resources and dependent constituents, they can also use their inherent mission and values to rebuild and refocus their communities to instill trust.

Scholars can also use the insights and experience from nonprofit practitioners to better understand the structures and relationship management strategies used every day in the sector. Often, scholars use a nonprofit in a case study or as a easily accessible sample for study, but the findings of that research have not explicitly been tailored to the nonprofit sector but have instead been applied as a finding for broad application. Research specific to the field and those working to manage those expectations would help to bridge the divide between scholarship and practice.

Academic-Professional Collaborations: Needs and Possibilities

Overall, more attention should be paid to understand the intrinsic nature of nonprofits and their wide typology of missions, structures, and stakeholders. The insights of practitioners and scholars together help to shape the narrative of how nonprofits need to address crisis communication and the factors that can help drive their success. Practitioners working in nonprofit organizations have many a tale to tell about their own organizational mistakes and achievements, but these are often not shared broadly as resources for organizational learning. Similarly, scholars often study nonprofits without specifically highlighting the unique positions and qualities that nonprofit organizations hold in comparison to other for-profit organizations. As we move forward into a world in which social justice and equity is necessary for our continued success, it is vitally important to recognize organizations for what they are and what their abilities can achieve. The collaborations for better understanding how a case study compares or emulates a crisis theory are beneficial for both parties in its exploration of new ideas and new evidence of communication strategies. As we study the best and the brightest campaigns in industry, scholars need to enhance and deepen theoretical assumptions in crisis communication that have rarely dissected organizations by their structure. The combination of factors working together will strengthen the resources but also the interest from various publics and future professionals in the specific callings of nonprofit communication. As noted in this chapter, if nonprofit organizations can reflect on their own challenges and prioritize ways in which communication can help to overcome the lack of resources, they are able to be nimbler and more innovative than many other organizations. Their commitment to transparency through the financial declaration system should be met with transparency in their actions as well in order to reduce the impact of a crisis situation. If volunteers and donors understand the inner workings of the organization, then if a situation of questionable actions occurs, it is much easier to explain and rebuild any trust that may be lost. Scholars must also recognize that crisis communication is not a one-size-fits-all model, and the message must be tailored to be authentic and reasonable to the source. The literature on crisis communication that presents best practices is inherently not inclusive to every organization and that needs to be recognized in both the research and the scholarship for the profession.

Reputation and financial success for a nonprofit is highly dependent on the level of trust from the public. Nonprofit organizations and practitioners understand that their work is measured not only by what they do but also by what they say. The level of trust is more complicated because of these two, sometimes contrary, strategies. If scholars can identify how crisis communication is unique in terms of sector, it will strengthen the importance and the diligence of professionals to remain committed to transparency and openness in their communication strategies.

References

Archambeault, D. S., & Webber, S. (2018) Fraud survival in nonprofit organizations: Empirical evidence. *Nonprofit Management and Leadership, 29*, 29–46. https://doi.org/10.1002/nml.21313

Bortree, D. (2014). New dimensions in relationship management: Exploring gender and inclusion in the nonprofit organization–volunteer relationship. In R. Waters (ed.), *Public relations in the nonprofit sector: Theory and practice*, pp. 21–46. Routledge.

Bortree, D., & Waters, R. (2008) Admiring the organization: A study of the relational quality outcomes of the nonprofit organization-volunteer relationship? *Public Relations Journal, 2*(3), 1–17. https://prjournal.instituteforpr.org/wp-content/uploads/Admiring-the-Organization.pdf

Cahn, D. (2018, April 20). *Wounded Warrior Project on the rebound financially following dismal 2017.* Stars and Stripes. https://www.stripes.com/news/wounded-warrior-project-on-the-rebound-financially-following-dismal-2017-1.523167

Charity Navigator. (2014). www.charitynavigator.org.

Coombs, W. T. (2007). Crisis and risk communication special section introduction. *Public Relations Review, 33*(2), 113. http://doi.org/10.1016/j.pubrev.2006.11.022

Dougall, E. (2008). "Issues Management" institute for public relations. https://instituteforpr.org/issues-management/

Feinglass, A. (2005). *The public relations handbook for nonprofits: A comprehensive and practical guide* (1st ed.). Jossey-Bass.

Frumkin, P. (2002). *On being nonprofit: A conceptual and policy primer.* Harvard University Press.

Gilstrap, C. A., Gilstrap, C. M., Holderby, K. N., Holderby, K. N., Valera, K. M. (2016). Sensegiving, leadership, and nonprofit crises: How nonprofit leaders make and give sense to organizational crisis. *VOLUNTAS: International Journal of Voluntary and Nonprofit Organizations, 27*(6), 2787–2806. http://doi.org/10.1007/s11266-015-9648-1

Grassley, C. (2017, March 24) Wounded warrior project makes reforms after media coverage, Grassley oversight inquiry. https://www.grassley.senate.gov/news/

news-releases/grassley-wounded-warrior-project-makes-reforms-after-media-coverage-grassley

Kaltenbrunner, K., & Reichel, A. (2018). Crisis response via dynamic capabilities: A necessity in NPOs' capability building: Insights from a study in the European refugee aid. *Voluntas, 29*(5), 994–1007. http://doi.org/10.1007/s11266-017-9940-3

Kelly, K. S. (1998), *Effective fund-raising management*. Mahwah, NJ: Lawrence Erlbaum Associates.

Kinsky, E. S., Drumheller, K., Gerlich, R. N., Brock-Baskin, M. E., & Sollosy, M. (2015). The effect of socially mediated public relations crises on planned behavior: How TPB can help both corporations and nonprofits. *Journal of Public Relations Research, 27*(2), 136–157. http://doi.org/10.1080/1062726X.2014.976826

O'Neil, J. (2007). The link between strong public relationships and donor support. *Public Relations Review, 33*(1), 99–102 https://doi.org/10.1016/j.pubrev.2006.11.021

Pauchant, T. C., & Mitroff, I. I. (1992). Management by nosing around: Exposing the dangerous invisibility of technologies. *Journal of Management Inquiry, 1*(1), 70–78. http://doi.org/10.1177/105649269211012

Philipps, D. (2016, January 27). *Wounded Warrior Project Spends Lavishly on Itself, Insiders Say*. Https://Www.Nytimes.Com/#publisher. https://www.nytimes.com/2016/01/28/us/wounded-warrior-project-spends-lavishly-on-itself-ex-employees-say.html

Rawlins, B. (2008). Measuring the relationship between organizational transparency and employee trust. *Public Relations Journal, 2*(2), 1–21.

Reid, W., & Turbide, J. (2012). Board/staff relationships in a growth crisis: Implications for nonprofit governance. *Nonprofit and Voluntary Sector Quarterly, 41*(1), 82–99. http://doi.org/10.1177/0899764011398296

Renfree, M. (2016, January 28) Wounded warriors project in crisis after claims of improper spending. *PR News*. https://www.prnewsonline.com/wounded-warriors-project-in-crisis-after-claims-of-improper-spending/

Seck, H. H. (2019, August 9). After public crisis and Fall from grace, wounded warrior project quietly regains ground. *Military*. https://www.military.com/daily-news/2019/08/09/after-public-crisis-and-fall-grace-wounded-warrior-project-quietly-regains-ground.html

Seeger, M. W., & Griffin Padgett, D. R. (2010). From image restoration to renewal: Approaches to understanding postcrisis communication. *Review of Communication, 10*(2), 127–141. http://doi.org/10.1080/15358590903354526

Sisco, H. F. (2010). Crisis definition and response: Understanding non-profit practitioner perspectives. *PRism Online PR Journal*. http://praxis.massey.ac.nz/prism_on-line_journ.html

Sisco, H. F. (2012). The ACORN story: An analysis of crisis response strategies in a nonprofit organization. *Public Relations Review, 38*(1), 89–96. http://doi.org/10.1016/j.pubrev.2011.11.001

Sisco, H. F., Collins, E. L., & Zoch, L. M. (2010). Through the looking glass: A decade of red cross crisis response and situational crisis communication theory. *Public Relations Review, 36*(1), 21–27. http://doi.org/10.1016/j.pubrev.2009.08.018

Sisco, H. F., Pressgrove, G., & Collins, E. L. (2013). Paralleling the practice: An analysis of the scholarly literature in nonprofit public relations. *Journal of Public Relations Research: Public Relations and Nonprofit Organizations, 25*(4), 282–306. http://doi.org/10.1080/1062726X.2013.806869

Sundstrom, B., Briones, R. L., & Janoske, M. (2013). Expecting the unexpected: Non-profit women's organizations' media responses to anti-abortion terrorism. *Journal of Communication Management*, *17*(4), 341–363. http://doi.org/10.1108/JCOM-08-2012-0069

Ulmer, R. R., Sellnow, T. L., & Seeger, M. W. (2017). *Effective crisis communication*. Sage.

U.S. Department of the Treasury. Internal Revenue Service. (2019). *Exempt purposes—Internal Revenue Code Section 501(c)(3)*. https://www.irs.gov/charities-non-profits/charitable-organizations/exempt-purposes-internal-revenue-code-section-501c3

Waters, R., Bortree, D., & Tindall, N. (2013). Can public relations improve the workplace? Measuring the impact of stewardship on the employer-employee relationship. *Employee Relations*, *35*(6), 613–629. http://doi.org/10.1108/ER-12-2012-0095

Williams, M., & Buttle, F. (2013). Managing word-of-mouth: A nonprofit case study. *Journal of Nonprofit & Public Sector Marketing*, *25*(3), 284–308. http://doi.org/10.1080/10495142.2013.81619

Wounded Warrior Project. (n.d.). Who We Are. https://www.woundedwarriorproject.org/

5 Media Relations for Government/Public Affairs Crises

Ethical and Unethical Components of Scandal and Spin

David E. Clementson, Joseph Watson Jr., and Michael Greenwell

When crises erupt in government and public affairs, the decision-makers tasked with formulating media responses should not need to proverbially "reinvent the wheel" and employ tactics "from scratch." Political communication, public relations, and related fields offer a corpus of empirical research that helps practitioners diagnose and combat public affairs crises that address the public's needs and remedy the scandal while bolstering the entity's reputation. A collaboration of scholars and researchers in academia as well as professionals working in government and public affairs industries provide an optimal melding of practical, theory-driven insight. In this chapter, a team of authors who have held leadership positions in this domain share experiential knowledge and summarize relevant theories. The chapter's theme is drawn around "spin" and the pertinent ethical vs. unethical components of spin that inevitably enter the equation.

Defining characteristics of crises in government/public affairs generally include five key features, which this chapter examines. First, a scandal arises in which some segment of the public has been victimized and/or an entity (e.g., a politician) sustains unearthed information jeopardizing the entity's credibility and reputation. Second, the public demands answers and stakeholders seek restitution. Third, the media clamor for those answers by soliciting responses in the form of interviews or prepared remarks. Fourth, the alleged wrongdoer, typically through a media relations department or spokesperson, prepares a response. Fifth, the entity's response inevitably is cast as "spin." This chapter argues that the crisis communicator's response can be based on normative theory and "good" spin, prescribed by ethical standards and best practices, despite a pervasive motivation to peddle "talking points" and quotations that deflect and divert from salacious and damaging information. This chapter provides an overview of the challenging and complex demands of crises in this high-profile field of study. The aim is to both offer actionable insight for practitioners and also to advance the literature, with summaries of pertinent theories and empirical research, in the dynamic and minefield-strewn realm of government and public affairs.

The Unpredictability of Crisis Communication in Government/Public Affairs

Best practices for the management of crises in public relations suggest planning for foreseeable crises. However, many of the crises that vex public affairs communicators are especially difficult to predict. In the public affairs context, public relations crises are often regarded as political scandals. Political scandals are actions or events that are perceived by the public and/or media as inconsistent with governing laws or contemporary morals and norms that yield some form of public outrage (King, 1984). Consider the political scandals that most often impact candidates for public office and public officials. Such scandals generally revolve around personal and/or sexual behaviors, corruption or other criminal activity, as well as racial and cultural insensitivity to name a few manifestations. The information that a communicator needs to plan for a potential crisis here is rarely given because the subject matter is so sensitive that it is unlikely that the principles in question would confide in communicators.

Professional communicators who serve as the spokespeople and representatives of governmental organizations are often on the frontlines of addressing the public and fielding questions from journalists. Public officials and candidates for office tend to be evasive when questioned under fire (Clementson, 2016; Clementson & Eveland, 2016). News coverage of public affairs crises will tend to feature journalistic questioning that catches officials and their spokespeople off guard (Clementson, 2019b). Often, the crises could not have been anticipated, or the spokespeople were misled by their superior, and thus the communicators are caught "flat footed" or unknowingly spread messaging that turns out to be untrue.

The case of Democratic Virginia Governor Ralph Northam's blackface and Ku Klux Klan (KKK) scandal is a classic example of the kind of crisis that challenges public affairs communicators. On February 1, 2019, a right-wing political website, Big League Politics, published images taken from Northam's page in his medical school yearbook that included a photo of two individuals, one in blackface and another in KKK hood and robes. The reaction on social media, as well as from the traditional media, and other public officials, both Republican and his fellow Democratic colleagues, was immediate and not surprisingly severe. There were almost immediate bipartisan calls for his resignation and his communications team was with little doubt caught unaware. However, Northam apologized the same day stating:

> Earlier today, a website published a photograph of me from my 1984 medical school yearbook in a costume that is clearly racist and offensive. I am deeply sorry for the decision I made to appear as I did in this photo and for the hurt that decision caused then and now. This behavior is not in keeping with who I am today and the values I have fought for throughout my career in the military, in medicine, and in public service.

> But I want to be clear, I understand how this decision shakes Virginians' faith in that commitment. I recognize that it will take time and serious effort to heal the damage this conduct has caused. I am ready to do that important work. The first step is to offer my sincerest apology and to state my absolute commitment to living up to the expectations Virginians set for me when they elected me to be their Governor.
>
> (Mirshahi, 2019)

Northam's response was a veritable textbook example of how not to respond to a crisis. He largely recanted the apology that he made on Friday evening with an awkward press conference the following day in which he denied that he was depicted in the photograph. Northam weathered the storm largely due to the fact that both the Democratic Lieutenant Governor and Attorney General of Virginia were also in the midst of their own controversies and crises, so the party lacked a readily available successor should Northam have in fact resigned. Interestingly, the publication of the yearbook photo came on the heels of an earlier controversy in which Northam made comments defending legislation in the state that would legalize what the bill referred to as "third-trimester abortion" and its opponents derided as post-birth abortion and infanticide. Some commentators suggested that the publication of the yearbook photo was in response to these comments, demonstrating how even political figures who wade into these controversial issues can face public relations consequences from them (Mark, 2019).

The challenges of managing public affairs crises also extend to corporations, nonprofits, and other organizations that are engaged in public issue advocacy. For those organizations, crises that touch on particularly divisive public policy issues such as abortion or gun control can prove difficult for even the most seasoned corporate communications executives to manage. In February 2018, in the wake of the Parkland High School shooting, social media calls to boycott the National Rifle Association's corporate partners trended on Twitter. In response to these calls, United Airlines and Delta Airlines announced that they would cut ties to the organization. Delta issued the following statement:

> Delta informed the National Rifle Association Saturday that the airline will end its contract for discounted fares for travel to the association's 2018 annual meeting. The company requested that the NRA remove Delta's information from its meeting website. Delta's decision reflects the airline's neutral status in the current national debate over gun control amid recent school shootings. Out of respect for our customers and employees on both sides, Delta has taken this action to refrain from entering this debate and focus on its business. Delta continues to support the 2nd Amendment.
>
> This is not the first time Delta has withdrawn support over a politically and emotionally charged issue. Last year, Delta withdrew its

> sponsorship of a theater that staged a graphic interpretation of "Julius Caesar" depicting the assassination of President Trump. Delta supports all of its customers but will not support organizations on any side of any highly charged political issue that divides our nation.
>
> (Galluccio, 2018)

In the wake of this statement, Georgia-based Delta Airlines faced a backlash led by Republican gubernatorial candidates who chided the company for not supporting Second Amendment rights. This ultimately led the state legislature to abandon plans to consider favorable tax legislation for the airlines during the 2018 legislative session in Atlanta.

So, what do you do when you are not expecting a crisis in political communication? Crisis communication in public affairs communication entails the messaging that the alleged wrongdoer composes and disseminates, typically through the media, in order to assuage a distraught public, rectify the wrongdoer's standing with stakeholders, and mitigate fallout in a competitive marketplace of ideas. Unlike private companies that answer to their customers and employees but do not necessarily have allegiance to the general public or policy makers, government and public affairs entities answer directly to the public in the form of taxpayer and voter accountability (e.g., office-holding politicians, government agencies) or otherwise relying on government regulatory facets and tax write-offs or incentives, as in the case of Delta noted above. Accordingly, public affairs messaging can embrace general insights of crisis communication norms and tactics but—as discussed throughout this chapter—entails its own unique sets of demands and encounters scrutiny unlike other fields of crisis communication in the public and media realm. The messaging can be straightforward and honest, or, all too often, can feature diversionary maneuvering to deflect scandalous inquiries from a scrutinizing but capricious press corps. By their nature, crises are unplanned, and the extent to which crises could have been prevented is debatable, especially from the standpoint of the practitioners, such as a press secretary or other media relations operative, thrown into the pressure cooker of crisis response strategizing. The next section covers a unique feature of government/public affairs crises: the public's partisanship skewing perceptions of scandals. The partisan lens through which public affairs crises are processed by the media and general audiences is a particularly "sticky" component of media relations that presents its own set of demands and challenges, and heightens the rhetorical (and behavioral) rancor.

The Partisan Lens

Communicators today face a landscape shaped increasingly by strident partisan political views. Crises concerning policy issues and candidates for elective office, government/public affairs are often seen through a partisan lens which makes them challenging to navigate. Public opinion polls indicate that the American electorate has grown to a new apex in polarization and ideological division (Jones, 2020). For example, a 2013 Public Policy Polling survey found that 38% of respondents that identified themselves as conservative believed that President Barack Obama was the Antichrist, as compared to 17% of respondents that identified as liberal. The partisanship dividing the country has even resulted in violence in some instances. For example, a construction worker murdered his boss after a political argument in which the boss expressed support for President Trump (Dahm, 2020), and an anti-Trump man opened fire with a rifle on Republican members of Congress (Campbell et al., 2017). Experiments indicate that partisanship clouds people's judgment of whether a politician is producing deceptive or honest discourse (Clementson, 2018a). For example, voters consider a politician who is evasive to be significantly more trustworthy when the politician shares the voter's party identification than a politician who is not evasive but holds the voter's opposing party label (Clementson, 2018b).

The aforementioned case of Governor Ralph Northam demonstrates how partisan views can impact a public affairs communications crisis. In the aftermath of the publication of the blackface and KKK photographs and his subsequent apology, a Washington Post-Schar School poll posed the question "Considering everything, do you think Northam should step down as governor of Virginia or not?" Given the nature of the controversy, one might expect African Americans would largely support resignation. However, 58% of African Americans polled opposed resignation, a figure that is virtually identical to the percentage of Democrats opposed to resignation—57%. This is in contrast to 56% of Republicans who believed that he should in fact resign. A contemporaneous Quinnipiac University poll produced similar results with 56% of black voters opposing resignation and 57% of Democrats opposing resignation. In that poll, a majority of Republicans, 60%, believed that he should resign. The fact that Northam had such strong support among both Democrats and black voters, a key Democratic constituency, was a significant factor in his ability to survive the crisis.

The Perils of Political "Spin"

Whether a government/public affairs spokesperson can anticipate the crisis or gets "caught off guard" by scandalous lines of questioning, the messaging that the professional communicator produces for the public is typically considered "spin." Spinning may be defined as "manipulating information disclosures that put the client, issue, or situation in a positive light, withholding negative facts, and outright deception" (Clementson, 2019a, p. 52; see also McNair, 2004; Sumpter & Tankard, 1994; Tsetsura et al., 2015). Spin will attempt to shift the public's attention and change the subject from damaging information, by reframing issues toward positive terrain (Potter, 2010). "Bad" spin is a tactic whereby media relations operatives, such as governmental spokespersons and politicians, intentionally mislead reporters and mass-mediated audiences (Jackson & Jamieson, 2007). Public relations practitioners are pejoratively called "spinmeisters" and "spin doctors" who unethically advocate for clients (Jo, 2003), using "trickery or deceit to capture unsuspecting audiences" (L'Etang, 2011, p. 16). According to Potter (2010),

> This art form often called 'spin' has become as much a part of our culture as the media we depend upon to connect and inform us. The 'spin doctors' who shape much of what we see and read are often shadowy figures in the multibillion dollar industry we call public relations. The most successful of them hobnob with royalty and presidents, CEOs and movie stars.
>
> (p. 45)

Some define public relations itself as "the art of *stealthy manipulation* of public opinion, the manipulation of opinions of consumers and politicians. It is viewed as *spinning the truth* to the selfish interest of some organization" (Heath, 2005, p. 679, emphasis added). Mass media representations, societal stereotypes, and popular literature depict public relations as practically synonymous with deceptive spin (Coombs & Holladay, 2014; Heath, 2005). TV shows and films portray public relations as a profession of manipulative and dishonest spin doctors (Tsetsura et al., 2015). In their reporting, journalists derogate crisis communicators for spin (Jo, 2003; Spicer, 1993). A spokesperson deceiving the public on behalf of his or her entity is a primary depiction of public relations and crisis communication by which critics derogate the fields (Coombs & Holladay, 2014). Journalists claim to battle an industry of unethical spin doctors (Macnamara, 2016; Sumpter & Tankard, 1994).

Theorizing about Ideal vs. Pragmatic Crisis Response

Most crisis communication research explores how response strategies, such as apologies and denials, affect an organization's reputation (De Waele & Claeys, 2017). The theory of image restoration discourse (Benoit, 1997) regards the design of messages by public relations practitioners when handling crises. The theory has particularly gained prominence in the literature for its typology of strategies whereby entities may respond to threats. Strategies frequently elaborated upon include: denying allegations, evading responsibility (e.g., "It was an accident"), taking corrective action, and apologizing. Drawn from Kenneth Burke's rhetorical work, image repair theory refers to proper apology during a crisis as "mortification"—dying to yourself—confessing your sins and begging for forgiveness (Benoit, 1997). An apology is presumably considered most sincere and believable, and most efficient in resulting in the public pardoning an indiscretion. Conversely, dodging responsibility, or other forms of denial, is less advisable for bolstering one's image and emerging from a crisis with reputation and credibility intact. The theory also posits a less-noticed message option detached from the strategy typology: avoiding the charges by not responding. As Benoit (1997) noted, an entity's attorneys may have their spokesperson avoid saying anything that could risk litigation. According to the theory of image restoration discourse, the accused does not always need to respond to the charges. The organization "may attempt to refocus attention on other issues" (Benoit, 1997, p. 183). A company's spokesperson may try to evade questions and change the subject.

Governmental spokespeople and other public affairs figures submit to media interviews amidst crises in which the facts may not all be known to the public and thus the speaker wants to appear to be telling the truth (Benoit & Hanczor, 1994). Public relations practitioners aspire to have their messages perceived as being truthful, among other measures of favorability (Callison, 2004). For instance, Queen Elizabeth spoke directly to the public, in response to allegations that the royal family did not care about Princess Diana's death. Presumably, she wanted to be perceived as direct and transparent with a grieving public, and presumably, her directness helped bolster her credibility (Benoit & Brinson, 1999).

Conventional wisdom holds—theoretically and practically—that crisis communicators should truthfully and directly answer questions in order to help their entities emerge from scandals. According to the descriptive theory of behavioral crisis communication (Claeys & Coombs, 2019), however, crisis managers tend to avoid optimal response strategies, because entities pursue short-term benefits without thoughtfully considering long-range goals. The theory draws upon behavioral economics, in which people claim to embrace rational and contemplative behavior in principle; meanwhile, people's actual behavior is overly reactive, intuitive, and suboptimal. The descriptive theory of behavioral crisis communication also draws upon prospect theory (Kahneman & Tversky, 1979), which emphasizes that people are risk-averse and uncertainty-averse to the point of irrationality. That is, people are concerned with avoiding losses to the detriment of maximizing gains. By taking a myopic approach to crisis communication and caving under time constraints and pressure, a rushed and substandard strategy ultimately harms an entity (Claeys & Coombs, 2019). Based on the descriptive theory of behavioral crisis communication, an entity's supervisors and legal counsel may espouse spinning as a strategy that succeeds in the short-term. Instead of accepting responsibility and exhibiting transparency and openness with the public—which should promote long-term success—entities in crisis more often choose evasive maneuvers (Claeys & Coombs, 2019). And the most common evasive maneuver allegedly employed in crisis is "spinning" (Coombs & Holladay, 2014).

Image repair theory (Benoit, 2015) specifies the cognitive process by which optimal answering should bolster an organization's reputation more effectively than suboptimal spinning. According to image repair theory, a spokesperson coming clean with the public and answering questions should instill more favorable attitudes from the public than by spinning.

The attitudinal effect ultimately should translate to a favorable reputation for the represented entity.

Surveys of public relations professionals have long indicated that they denounce deceptive practitioners (Aronoff, 1975), and most public relations practitioners are embarrassed by unethical practitioners besmirching their industry (Macnamara, 2014). Interviews with practitioners indicate that they generally reject the spin doctor label (Macnamara, 2016). Practitioners express that their unethical colleagues need "remedial intervention" in ethics (Macnamara, 2016, p. 136). Survey research has long indicated that practitioners report an opposition to those in their profession who engage in deceptive spin (e.g., Aronoff, 1975; Clementson, 2019a; Macnamara, 2016). In the only experiment testing how practitioners (and journalists) react to deceptive spin, the two professions shared distrust toward a spin doctor as well as toward an organization represented by a spin doctor (Clementson, 2019a). In line with the psychological "black sheep effect," practitioners liked a spokesperson less than a journalist when the journalist was on the receiving end of spin, and liked the spokesperson more when the spokesperson truthfully answered questions. Media response approaches discussed by the theory of image restoration discourse and image repair theory, coalesced with the descriptive theory of behavioral crisis communication, may be summarized as follows.

Suboptimal	***Optimal***
Deny allegations	Apologize
Evade responsibility	Take corrective action
Dodge questions	Answer truthfully and directly
Shift attention to other issues	Display transparency and openness
Limit disclosures	Disclose facts as solicited

The Necessity of "Good" Spin

If an entity is accused of wrongdoing and may bear responsibility, the organization may choose between apologizing or attempting to shift attention from the misdeed (Fuoli et al., 2017). Reports of an entity harming, offending, or otherwise injuring its constituents can devastate the entity (Griffin et al., 1992). Organizations are scared of legal liabilities and constituent complaints that can shatter their image, electability, bank account, and validity in government and public affairs. When accused of mishaps, admitting fault is oftentimes a preferred last resort (Griffin et al., 1992). After all, an entity can control the extent to which its messaging admits fault or evades lines of inquiry. Legal counsel may propose that a spokesperson engage in covert evasion under questioning, as a form of ethical advocacy for one's client organization, if the practitioner is limited in what can be fully disclosed during a crisis with litigious ramifications (Edgett, 2002). Entities must never lie, but their crisis response strategies sometimes challenge ethical boundaries with their efforts to evade responsibility (Fuoli et al., 2017). During crises, the preferred ideal response of crisis communicators is fully informative disclosures; the sooner an entity opens up with audiences and answers their questions, the sooner crises tend to diminish (Arpan & Roskos-Ewoldsen, 2005). But legal counsel usually extols limiting disclosures (Kim & Wertz, 2013), and legal strategy often overrides crisis communication strategy (Fitzpatrick & Rubin, 1995).

A divide has emerged in the literature contesting whether practitioners should cede to legal counsel and employ diversionary tactics, or retain public relations idealism and apologize when confronted with crisis (Fuoli et al., 2017). Recent experimental research in organizational trust repair suggests that forms of "obfuscating the truth" may help an organization recover from allegations of wrongdoing more effectively than if the organization apologizes (Fuoli et al., 2017, p. 646). The reason a deflection may be more efficacious than an apology could be because overtly commenting on improprieties may stand out in audiences' minds and cast a stronger impression than diversionary responses, which allow negative impressions to dissipate sooner—especially when stakeholders may give an accused bad actor "the benefit of the doubt" (Fuoli et al., 2017).

Codes of ethics emphasize sharing factual and truthful information with the public, but practitioner codes also emphasize the professional duty of loyal service to the employer or client. Thus, practitioners may share factual and truthful information—just not the information solicited by the journalist. An entity's representative may diverge from the solicited information and evade the question topic, steering their answer to more favorable domains. After all, Public Relations Society of America (PRSA) advises that spokespeople need to control the journalist's topical agenda (Jacobs, 2009).

In practice, public relations spokespeople often covertly dodge journalists' questions in interviews (Lieberman, 2004). Edward Bernays "fathered the science of spin" (Tye, 1998, p. viii) as "the father of spinmeisters who manipulate our perceptions" (p. 249). Ivy Lee advised clients on how to dodge reporters' questions (Cutlip, 1994). Press agent Benjamin Sonnenberg would flatter reporters during interviews and change the subject to conversational topics cajoling the journalists (Cutlip, 1994). Sometimes, public relations practitioners employ forms of deception in the performance of their obligatory duties to the client or employer. For example, spokespeople might evade questions covertly while exuding truthful impressions (De Waele & Claeys, 2017). Morality and ethical practice become blurred when utterances are not falsehoods, yet they are not "the whole truth and nothing but the truth" either and intend to manipulate through misleading the audience (Edgett, 2002). Features and determinants of ethical vs. unethical spin may be summarized as follows.

"Good" Spin	"Bad" Spin
Ethical disclosures that positively frame the alleged wrongdoer.	Changing the subject from damaging details and ignoring inquiries concerning improprieties.
Emphasizing corrective action being taken, if indeed the charges of impropriety are true.	Casting blame on others in an attempt to avoid responsibility for malfeasance.
Transparently disclosing truthful information responsive to media inquiries that places the alleged wrongdoer in a favorable light.	Limiting disclosures to the point of "lies of omission" (e.g., "paltering") and employing diversionary maneuvers to shift attention.
If the entity is truly at fault: apologizing in an effort to move beyond the crisis. (Ideally offering rhetorical "mortification" deemed as fully expressing remorse for misdeeds.)	Answering questions through linguistic evasion (e.g., equivocation, obfuscation, "double speak," "coach-speak") that sounds responsive to questioning but actually avoids culpability.

A Case Study of the Collapse of the Product Safety Net

In this section, we provide a case study from our own experience in the field, exemplifying how government agencies can be challenged with an unforeseen crisis facing mass scrutiny and the choices that a crisis communicator faces in disclosing information under media pressure. In 2007, the year that *Consumer Reports* (2007) called "the Year of the Recall," a wave of dangerous, and even deadly, children's products flooded the US marketplace from China. One relatively small federal regulatory agency was tasked with monitoring the safety of imports, setting product safety standards, and enforcing safety laws. The US Consumer Product Safety Commission (CPSC) was charged with managing the crisis—and the public response. The CPSC is an independent agency that oversees more than 15,000 types of consumer products—more than the Food and Drug Administration oversees. The CPSC had 420 employees and a $63 million budget in 2007. Years of policymaker inattention challenged the agency when tens of millions of defective baby cribs, lead-laden children's toys and jewelry, and defective magnetic toys poured through US ports. The result: dozens of vulnerable babies suffocated to death in broken cribs; children were rushed into surgery after swallowing loose, powerful magnets; and countless children were exposed to lead paint on popular toys like Thomas the Train.

A crisis erupted at CPSC and the leadership was ill-prepared to manage the situation operationally and also maladroit in their communications. No surrogates on Capitol Hill or academia were willing to defend the agency. The Acting Chairman pleaded for more funding and authority, which was met by largely deaf ears across the media and oversight committees in Congress. With just a handful of investigators at the nation's ports and no presence in mainland China, CPSC was hamstrung to stop the source of the problem. Mornings brought new scandalous stories from the *Washington Post* and the *New York Times*, and the evenings were filled with damaging coverage across the 24/7 TV news networks. The public was confused, hysterical, and in pandemonium.

The messaging from the agency was dominated by new recall announcements—a million defective cribs and 180 million pieces of cheap vending machine jewelry. Recalls were necessary, of course, but the public clamored for far more than learning about the millions of potentially fatal toys lurking around town. The public needed to hear that the CPSC was formulating and activating an action plan. The CPSC needed to inform the public about how risk was being mitigated in the short-term and how tougher testing and enforcement regimes would be implemented long-term. Congressional hearings were contentious, with the Acting Chairman of the agency being criticized by Senators of her own party. The Speaker of the House called for the chair's resignation. A tension-filled US-China Summit resulted in small concessions from the Chinese government to impose stronger lead standards for toys.

Staff morale at the CPSC plummeted. Internal communications were sparse and top-down. Best practices in crisis communications—such as transparency and sympathy toward victims—seemed to be forgotten. The public's lack of awareness of CPSC's mission and a lack of understanding of how regulatory agencies function compounded the government's challenges. In short, the agency attempted to engage in forms of "bad" spin. There were instances of evading responsibility, trying to pivot away from accountability, and changing the subject from past malfeasance to future recall details. However, attempts to dodge questions and deflect scrutiny were unsuccessful in the court of public opinion, as well as the chambers of Congress.

It was not until both chambers of Congress voted nearly unanimously in August 2008 to pass the Consumer Product Safety Improvement Act, the most sweeping reform of the nation's product safety regime in nearly 30 years, that the public's opinion of the CPSC started to change. In summary, a practical lesson may be gleaned from this experience. Crisis communicators working in public affairs and government relations can spare themselves years of national and international frustration if they are quick to come clean with the public, execute an action plan, and avoid the urge to engage in "bad" spin. Positively framing your work through "good" spin may be fine, if you are truthfully informing the public about dangers and taking corrective action to remedy a scandal. In some cases, as with the unfortunate experience of the Consumer Product Safety Commission's recall scandal and agency overhaul, we know in hindsight that the work of avoiding "bad" spin even helps save lives.

Key Takeaways

Crisis communicators navigate an ethical "minefield" in which any misstep can quench loyalties to either the employer or society (p. 310, Gabrielsen, 2004). During a crisis, an entity's spokesperson performs a balancing act between serving the public through immediate transparency, while speaking for a boss and legal counsel who may prefer withholding information and evading media questions (Tyler, 1997). But, as Heath and Coombs (2006) exhort, "Remember that it is your obligation as a public relations professional to protect your organization and to not reinforce the negative stereotype of the profession as mere spin" (p. 85).

Increased partisanship further complicates a communicator's mission in the midst of a crisis. Audiences that are politically aligned with the party in a public affairs crisis are more likely to support that individual or organization, as contrasted to those unaligned with them. Awareness of these realities paired with the ability of the practitioner to conduct "good" or effective spin are keys to successfully managing public affairs crises that often are unpredictable.

References

Aronoff, C. (1975). Credibility of public relations for journalists. *Public Relations Review, 1*, 45–56. http://doi.org/10.1016/S0363-8111(75)80023-3

Arpan, L. M., & Roskos-Ewoldsen, D. R. (2005). Stealing thunder: Analysis of the effects of proactive disclosure of crisis information. *Public Relations Review, 31*, 425–433. http://doi.org/10.1016/j.pubrev.2005.05.003

Benoit, W. L. (1997). Image repair discourse and crisis communication. *Public Relations Review, 23*(2), 177–186. https://doi.org/10.1016/S0363-8111(97)90023-0

Benoit, W. L. (2015). *Accounts, excuses, and apologies: Image repair theory and research* (2nd ed.). State University of New York Press.

Benoit, W. L., & Brinson, S. L. (1999). Queen Elizabeth's image repair discourse: Insensitive royal or compassionate queen? *Public Relations Review, 25*(2), 145–156. http://doi.org/10.1016/S0363-8111(99)80159-3

Benoit, W. L., & Hanczor, R. S. (1994). The Tonya Harding controversy: An analysis of image restoration strategies. *Communication Quarterly, 42*(4), 416–433. http://doi.org/10.1080/01463379409369947

Callison, C. (2004). The good, the bad, and the ugly: Perceptions of public relations practitioners. *Journal of Public Relations Research, 16*(4), 371–389. https://doi.org/10.1207/s1532754xjprr1604_3

Campbell, B., Chappell, B., & Wamsley, L. (2017, June 14). Wounded congressman in critical condition, will require additional surgery. *NPR*. https://www.npr.org/sections/thetwo-way/2017/06/14/532894023/gunman-opens-fire-as-members-of-congress-practice-baseball

Claeys, A.-S., & Coombs, W. T. (2019). Organizational crisis communication: Suboptimal crisis response selection decisions and behavioral economics. *Communication Theory*. Advance online publication. http://doi.org/10.1093/ct/qtz002

Clementson, D. E. (2016). Why do we think politicians are so evasive? Insight from theories of equivocation and deception, with a content analysis of U.S. presidential debates, 1996–2012. *Journal of Language and Social Psychology, 35*, 247–267. http://doi.org/10.1177/0261927X15600732

Clementson, D. E. (2018a). Susceptibility to deception in a political news interview: Effects of identification, perceived cooperativeness, and ingroup vulnerability. *Communication Studies, 69*, 522–544. http://doi.org/10.1080/10510974.2018.1454486

Clementson, D. E. (2018b). Truth bias and partisan bias in political deception detection. *Journal of Language and Social Psychology, 37*, 407–430. http://doi.org/10.1177/0261927X17744004

Clementson, D. E. (2019a). Do public relations practitioners perceptually share in-group affiliation with journalists? *Public Relations Review, 45*, 49–63. http://doi.org/10.1016/j.pubrev.2018.12.008

Clementson, D. E. (2019b). Why won't you answer the question? Mass-mediated deception detection after journalists' accusations of politicians' evasion. *Journal of Communication, 69*, 674–695. http:/doi.10.1093/joc/jqz036

Clementson, D. E., & Eveland, W. P., Jr. (2016). When politicians dodge questions: An analysis of presidential press conferences and debates. *Mass Communication and Society, 19*, 411–429. http://doi.org/10.1080/15205436.2015.1120876

Consumer Reports. (2007, October 30). 2007: The year of the recall. https://advocacy.consumerreports.org/press_release/2007-the-year-of-the-recall/

Coombs, W. T., & Holladay, S. J. (2014). *It's not just PR: Public relations in society* (2nd ed.). Wiley Blackwell.

Cutlip, S. M. (1994). *The unseen power: Public relations. A history*. Lawrence Erlbaum Associates.

Dahm, D. (2020, January 21). *Man stabs, kills pro-Trump boss, drapes American flag over him, deputies say*. WKMG. https://www.clickorlando.com/news/local/2020/01/21/man-stabs-kills-pro-trump-boss-drapes-american-flag-over-him-deputies-say/

De Waele, A., & Claeys, A-S. (2017). Nonverbal cues of deception in audiovisual crisis communication. *Public Relations Review, 43*, 680–689. http://doi.org/10.1016/j.pubrev.2017.06.004

Edgett, R. (2002). Toward an ethical framework for advocacy in public relations. *Journal of Public Relations Research, 14*(1), 1–26. https://doi.org/10.1207/S1532754XJPRR1401_1

Fitzpatrick, K. R., & Rubin, M. S. (1995). Public relations vs. legal strategies in organizational crisis decisions. *Public Relations Review, 21*(1), 21–33. http://doi.org/10.1016/0363-8111(95)90037-3

Fuoli, M., van de Weijer, J., & Paradis, C. (2017). Denial outperforms apology in repairing organizational trust despite strong evidence of guilt. *Public Relations Review, 43*, 645–660. http://doi.org/10.1016/j.pubrev.2017.07.007

Gabrielsen, K. (2004). Loyalty versus conflict in Norwegian practitioners. *Public Relations Review, 30*, 303–311. doi:10.1016/j.pubrev.2004.05.003

Galluccio, B. (2018, February 26). Georgia senate blocks Delta tax break after company cuts ties with NRA. *KCJB*. https://kcjb910.iheart.com/featured/political-junkie/content/2018-02-26-georgia-senate-blocks-delta-tax-break-after-company-cuts-ties-with-nra/

Griffin, M., Babin, B. J., & Darden, W. R. (1992). Consumer assessments of responsibility for product-related injuries: The impact of regulations, warnings, and promotional policies. *Advances in Consumer Research, 19*, 870–878.

Heath, R. L. (2005). *Encyclopedia of public relations*. Sage.

Heath, R. L., & Coombs, W. T. (2006). *Today's public relations: An introduction*. Sage.

Jackson, B., & Jamieson, K. H. (2007). *UnSpun: Finding facts in a world of disinformation*. Random House.

Jacobs, C. (2009, December) *How to prepare spokespeople for interviews*. Public Relations Tactics. http://apps.prsa.org/Intelligence/Tactics/Articles/view/8459/1005/How_to_prepare_spokespeople_for_interviews#.Wck8D6hSzIU

Jo, S. (2003). The portrayal of public relations in the news media. *Mass Communication and Society, 6*, 397–411. http://doi.org/10.1207/S15327825MCS0604_4

Jones, J. M. (2020, Jan. 21). *Trump third year sets new standard for party polarization.* Gallup. https://news.gallup.com/poll/283910/trump-third-year-sets-new-standard-party-polarization.aspx

Kahneman, D., & Tversky, A. (1979). Prospect theory: An analysis of decisions under risk. *Econometrica: Journal of the Econometric Society, 47*, 263–292. http://doi.org/10.2307/1914185

Kim, S., & Wertz, E. K. (2013). Predictors of organizations' crisis communication approaches: Full versus limited disclosure. *Public Relations Review, 29*, 238–240. http://doi.org/10.1016/j.pubrev.2013.03.004

King, A. (1984). *Sex, money and power: Political scandals in Great Britain and the United States. University of Essex, Dept. of Government.*

L'Etang, J. (2011). Imagining public relations anthropology. In L. Edwards & C. E. M. Hodges (Eds.), *Public relations, society & culture: Theoretical and empirical explorations (pp. 15–32). Routledge.*

Lieberman, T. (2004). Answer the &%$#* question! *Columbia Journalism Review, 42*(5), 40–44.

Macnamara, J. (2014). Journalism-PR relations revisited: The good news, the bad news, and insights into tomorrow's news. *Public Relations Review, 40*, 739–750. http://doi.org/10.1016/j.pubrev.2014.07.002

Macnamara, J. (2016). The continuing convergence of journalism and PR: New insights for ethical practice from a three-country study of senior practitioners. *Journalism & Mass Communication Quarterly, 93*, 118–141. http://doi.org/10.1177/1077699015605803

Mark, M. (2019, February 3). The tip about the racist photo in Gov. Ralph Northam's yearbook reportedly came from an ex-classmate angry about his abortion comments. *Business Insider.* https://www.businessinsider.com/ralph-northam-racist-yearbook-photo-tip-concerned-citizen-2019-2

McNair, B. (2004). PR must die: Spin, anti-spin and political public relations in the UK, 1997–2004. *Journalism Studies, 5*, 325–338. doi:10.1080/1461670042000246089

Mirshahi, D. (2019, February 4). Gov. Northam addresses 'clearly racist and offensive' yearbook photo. *WRIC.* https://www.wric.com/news/virginia-news/gov-northam-addresses-clearly-racist-and-offensive-yearbook-photo/

Potter, W. (2010). *Deadly spin: An insurance company insider speaks out on how corporate PR is killing health care and deceiving Americans.* New York, NY: Bloomsbury.

Spicer, C. H. (1993). Images of public relations in the print media. *Journal of Public Relations Research, 5*, 47–61. doi:10.1207/s1532754xjprr0501_03

Sumpter, R., & Tankard, J. W., Jr. (1994). The spin doctor: An alternative model of public relations. *Public Relations Review, 20*, 19–27. doi:10.1016/0363-8111(94)90111-2

Tsetsura, K., Bentley, J., & Newcomb, T. (2015). Idealistic and conflicted: New portrayals of public relations practitioners in film. *Public Relations Review, 41*, 652–661. doi:10.1016/j.pubrev.2014.02.018 0363-8111

Tye, L. (1998). *The father of spin: Edward L. Bernays and the birth of public relations.* Crown Publishers.

Tyler, L. (1997). Liability means never being able to say you're sorry: Corporate guilt, legal constraints, and defensiveness in corporate communication. *Management Communication Quarterly, 11*(1), 51–73. https://doi.org/10.1177/0893318997111003

Part III

Most Challenging Public Crises

6 A Promising but Difficult Domain

Complex Health-related Crises and Academic-Professional Collaboration

Glen Nowak and Michael Greenwell

In Winter of 2020, a novel coronavirus that would soon be named SARS-CoV-2 brought about one of the largest and most complex health-related crises ever seen in modern history. Initial confirmed cases of an illness that would become called COVID-19 were identified in Wuhan, China, in mid-December 2019, and by January 26, 2020, the novel coronavirus had caused 2,794 laboratory-confirmed infections, including 80 deaths in the Hubei province (Zhou et al., 2020). On March 11, the World Health Organization (WHO), noting that there were over 118,000 confirmed COVID-19 illnesses and 4,291 deaths across 114 countries and territories around the world and expected sustained spread, declared COVID-19 a global pandemic (WHO, 2020a). In making the declaration, Dr. Tedros Adhanom Ghebreyesus, WHO director-general, at a media briefing stated:

> This is not just a public health crisis. It is a crisis that will touch every sector – so every sector and every individual must be involved in the fights. . . I remind all countries that we are calling on you to activate and scale up your emergency response mechanisms. Communicate with your people about the risks and how they can protect themselves – this is everybody's business.
>
> (WHO, 2020b)

In the months following the WHO pandemic declaration, the spread of a virus for which no proven effective medical treatments or vaccines to prevent infections existed prompted most countries to implement strict public health infection control measures. The primary measures—strict physical distancing that closed schools and businesses, the closing of country borders, extensive travel restrictions, and urging most people to stay home as much as possible for several weeks—significantly impeded the spread of COVID-19 (Chu et al., 2020). According to one statistical model, the public health actions taken in six countries—China, South Korea, Italy, Iran, France, and the United States (US)—prevented or delayed an estimated 62 million confirmed cases, corresponding to averting an estimated 530 million total infections (Hsiang et al., 2020).

However, it also quickly became apparent at multiple levels that the scope and duration of broad and restrictive public health measures came with highly visible, significant, and inequitably distributed economic and social costs. These included high unemployment, temporary and permanent business closures, disruption of formal education and instruction at all levels, declines in childhood immunization and other needed health services, more people struggling with mental health issues, and large negative effects on many industries from travel to manufacturing (Continetti, 2020; Dua et al., 2020; Maani & Galea, 2020; Olson, 2020; Wilkinson, 2020). Ultimately, COVID-19 infections, outbreaks, and the overall pandemic generated multiple, often extensive, crises for national governments, public health agencies at all levels, health care systems and providers, most industries and businesses, educational systems and institutions, and a host of other organizations.

The evolution of COVID-19 from multiple infectious disease outbreaks in many countries to an extended global pandemic meant crisis communication was essential. All the organizations affected, particularly government agencies, public health departments, and health care providers and facilities, needed to communicate promptly and accurately to citizens, affected publics, key stakeholders, and the news media about the actions they were considering, taking, and recommending in response to COVID-19. As would be expected, use of crisis communication principles and practices were widely recommended and promoted. In January 2020, the US Centers for Disease Control and Prevention was providing updates in line with its six crisis and emergency response (CERC) principles: Be First, Be Right, Be Credible, Express Empathy, Promote Action, and Show Respect (CDC, 2018; Reynolds, 2008) as well as foreshadowing the likely effects of COVID-19 in the US internationally, WHO issued an interim guidance on "Risk Communication and Community Engagement (RCCE) Readiness and Response to the 2019 novel coronavirus" on January 26, 2020 (WHO, 2020c), followed days later with a draft 2019 "Novel Coronavirus (2019-nCoV): Strategic Preparedness and Response Plan" (WHO, 2020d). Both documents urged countries and public health authorities to use crisis and risk communication principles, including regular and proactive updates, being transparent about uncertainties and risk, and involving communities in response efforts. As such, the COVID-19 pandemic, in concert with the communication needs and efforts it generated, provides an instructive foundation for considering how greater integration of academic perspectives with practitioner experiences could advance crisis communication theories and efforts involving complex health-related issues.

Complex Health-related Crises—The Challenges

Much about the COVID-19 pandemic was vastly different than any previous health-related crisis, including its scope and duration. However, from a crisis communication standpoint, much of what happened is commonplace in a complex health-related crisis. The crisis begins with a cluster of people who are severely ill, but there is initial uncertainty as to the cause. If there is rapid and unpredictable spread of the serious health threat, social and economic disruptions on multiple fronts and in multiple places will result. Prior to COVID-19, many complex health-related crises had already challenged crisis communication practitioners and scholars, including HIV/AIDS, pandemic influenza (e.g., 2009 H1N1A), avian flu viruses, Ebola, severe acute respiratory syndrome (SARS 2003), outbreaks of measles and other vaccine-preventable diseases, opioid misuse and addiction, environmental contamination (e.g., high levels of lead in public water systems), food-borne illness outbreaks, and chemical or radiation exposures (e.g., the Fukushima Daiichi nuclear power plant accident; Coombs, 2014; Lundgren & McMakin, 2018; Rasmussen & Goodman, 2019; Reynolds, 2008; Ulmer et al., 2019). When it comes to advancing crisis communication practice and scholarship, it is essential for all parties to understand that complex health-related crises encompass much more than threats to an organization's image or reputation (CDC, 2020; Tumpey et al. 2019). These types of crises pose or bring actual and significant harm to individuals, communities, and potentially countries, with the harm ranging from illnesses and deaths to immediate and extended economic and social disruption (CDC, 2018; Sandman, 2003).

Complex health-related crises differ from image or reputation crises in at least two important respects. First, many image and reputation crises, including in the health care domain, stem from a single event, such as financial or operational mismanagement (e.g., product defects or recall), sexual harassment, discrimination, failure to comply with state or federal laws and regulations, or bad decision-making by someone in an organization (Coombs, 2014; Institute for Crisis Management, 2020; Ulmer, et al. 2019). In most cases, the single event precipitates a relatively well-defined singular crisis, such as a health-related product recall. However, as the COVID-19 pandemic illustrated, complex health issues simultaneously prompt public health, economic, and social crises as well as a variety of crises for multiple firms and organizations.

Further complicating the crisis communication situation, the origin and locations of a complex health crisis are often initially unclear, and the effects—such as many people becoming severely ill or dying—surface without warning and continue long after the cause is identified (Rasmussen & Goodman, 2019). Thus, as in the case of infectious or food-borne disease outbreaks, little may be initially known about where or how widespread the pathogen is, the actual and potential scope of the outbreak, or how to discern illness and harm caused by the pathogen from other potential or actual causes (e.g., many adverse health-related illnesses involve "flu-like" symptoms). These challenges are present even when a single event is discernible, such as incidents involving an intentional or unintentional release of radiation, chemicals, or other potentially harmful substances into the environment. While the presence of a crisis is known, information about the actual and potential extent of harm, as well as who was exposed and the type of exposures, is usually lacking (e.g., dose, duration of exposure) and may be unknown or unknowable. This greatly reduces the ability to communicate specific guidance regarding the scope of the crisis or protective actions that should be taken.

A second major way that complex health-related crises differ from image and reputation crises involves uncertainty and attention. In the case of health-related organization image and reputation crises, uncertainty often has a smaller presence and public relations efforts focus on reducing attention (Sandman, 2003, 2020b). When harm to an individual or organization's image or reputation is the "crisis," the uncertainties usually revolve around identifying the cause and contributing factors, the major events and their timeline, and credible third-party influencers who can provide supportive messages. As Sandman (2020b) noted, image-oriented crisis communication is designed to manage a threat to a client's reputation. In a complex health-related crisis, uncertainties abound and persist—and the threat is to the health and safety of publics and stakeholders (Sandman, 2020b). The entities affected by the crisis will be receiving much and extended public, media, and stakeholder attention. Uncertainties about severity, susceptibility, spread, and the best measures to stem or stop the crisis will frustrate the public, affected and potentially at-risk individuals, health care providers, and policymakers, especially in the initial response stage. Initial and ongoing uncertainties will necessitate crisis communication strategies grounded in risk communication principles and focused on setting, guiding, and managing the varied expectations and desires of multiple publics, policymakers (i.e., politicians), and stakeholders over an extended period versus quickly restoring an entity's reputation among investors and consumers (Tumpey et al., 2019).

Further, unlike image and reputation crises where negative outcomes are quickly and visibly apparent, in complex health-related crises, uncertainties make it challenging to discern whether, when, and where negative outcomes are happening. For example, crises involving infectious diseases, substance use or misuse, food-borne illnesses, and radiation or chemical exposures entail (1) incubation or latency periods between exposure to a possible health threat and onset of symptoms; (2) initial symptoms that are so nondescript and common (e.g., fever, headache, fatigue) that an individual or health care provider may not associate them with a specific exposure; (3) differential effects and outcomes, including some exposed people not becoming infected or ill (with infection and illness being two related, but different outcomes) while others experience severe illness or death; (4) limited, and perhaps no, ability to detect, diagnose, or confirm individuals' exposure to an infectious organism or harmful substance, particularly early on; and (5) difficulty in rapidly determining whether initial cases represent a broader and likely ongoing health-related crisis, a threat that particularly affects some individuals more so than others (e.g., are there high-risk or at-risk groups), or a limited, localized health threat. These complexities are difficult to easily communicate, foster skepticism and misunderstanding, and make reputation or image-based crisis communication strategies less useful.

The uncertainties regarding what is truly happening, in turn, give rise to broader uncertainties that affect whether, when, and what to communicate about a health threat or risk. In some cases, it may not be possible to discern that a health-related crisis exists or is about to unfold. In a 2012 outbreak of hantavirus in Yosemite National Park, months passed before it could be discerned that the exposures that involved ten confirmed infections and three deaths happened in the park (Barcott, 2012). The initially confirmed cases of an infectious disease thus may not provide a basis for a publicly visible crisis communication response. Crisis communicators also need to be mindful that strong warnings and broad health-related recommendations, in the absence of an apparent strong need, credible evidence, and specifics regarding the health threat, can be met with suspicion or doubt. This does not mean prompt crisis messaging should be avoided, but that they may fail to draw attention or prompt action unless journalists and potentially affected audiences perceive a true and significant health threat (i.e., there is a discernible cause and a notable level of harm). At the beginning of a complex health-related crisis, both are often lacking (Tumpey et al., 2019). Such uncertainties frequently frustrate affected publics, communities, and key stakeholders—with those frustrations, in turn, providing a compelling news angle for journalists. As such, organizational leaders and outside observers (e.g., crisis communication scholars) should expect much second-guessing about the actions and communications undertaken in the initial and ongoing response stages of a complex health-related crisis (Nowak et al., 2020).

Barriers to Crisis Communication Collaborations

Complex health-related crises require a strong and state-of-the art communication foundation, with that need recognized by leading public health agencies. Internationally, WHO has undertaken several initiatives to advance scholarship and practice in risk and emergency/crisis communication. These include publishing "Communicating Risk in Public Health Emergencies," an evidence-based 2018 guidance developed using a scholar-practitioner collaboration and based on published research on key issues in emergency risk communication practice (WHO, 2017); supporting the Vaccine Safety Net (VSN), an active international network of scholars, health communication professionals, and vaccine-related websites, that advances research and practice involving digital and social media to disseminate vaccine safety-related information (WHO, 2018); and convening meetings of university-based experts and health communication experts to identify knowledge gaps and best practices related to crisis communication challenges, such as the "infodemics" (i.e., the overabundance of information and misinformation) that arise with significant health threats (WHO, 2020e). The CDC has supported similar scholar-professional collaborations, including in the development of its Crisis and Emergency Risk Communication (CERC) manual and trainings (CDC CERC, 2020); outbreak communications guidance for epidemiologists (Tumpey et al., 2019); research to inform risk and crisis communication efforts (e.g., Frost et al., 2019; Winters et al., 2018); and support for an annual conference on Health Communication, Marketing, and Media, which encompasses identifying learnings, advances, and needs in crisis communication scholarship and practice (https://www.cdc.gov/nchcmm/index.html).

Recent efforts by WHO, CDC, and others to foster crisis communication collaborations between university experts and the professional frontline communicators have advanced research and practice, but there remains a need for continued and greater engagement. There are, however, significant challenges that need to be recognized and addressed when it comes to (1) establishing scholar-practitioner collaborations and (2) advancing crisis communication scholarship and practice in the domain of complex health-related crises. At least three significant challenges exist when it comes to academic-practitioner collaborations on health-related crises, elements of which have been described by others (Claeys & Opgenhaffen, 2016; Kieser & Leiner, 2012). They are:

Subject-matter Knowledge in the Health-related Domain Matters

In addition to knowledge of effective crisis communication practices and principles found in textbooks (e.g., Coombs, 2014; Ulmer et al., 2019), it is often necessary for university-based scholars and researchers to have some knowledge or expertise in the specific health-related topic. Crisis communication theories, advice, or research have little value if the university researcher is unfamiliar with the complexities that exist when communicating about infectious and food-borne diseases, chemicals and radiation, or biological products (e.g., the importance of case definitions in diagnosis health conditions, why it is often not possible to determine exposure or amount of exposure to a potential harm). The complexities will determine whether potential communication strategies are appropriate as well as whether proposed messages are accurate. Similarly, it is also of limited value if a communication scholar has little or no knowledge or understanding of the health-related domain (e.g., influenza, opioids, coronaviruses, radiation) and what is currently known regarding communication in that domain (e.g., how lay people currently understand influenza or opioids). Not surprisingly, much of the crisis and risk communication collaboration that takes place in public health is with academics who have much knowledge and experience in the health-related domain, such as vaccines and vaccine safety, influenza, Ebola, or medical countermeasures (e.g., Schoch-Spana et al., 2018). In general, university-based scholars and researchers seeking to collaborate with government agencies or other organizations on projects to advance crisis communication theory or practice are more likely to succeed if their expertise and experience encompass the health-related subject matter.

Scholars and Practitioners have Different Needs and Priorities

In the academic world, regularly and frequently publishing in high-impact, peer-reviewed journals are typically needed for career success. Successful publishing, in turn, commonly involves grounding research studies and measures in published work and existing theories, and then collecting data that enables strengthening theories or developing new ones. In the world of complex health-related crises, swift, transparent, responsive, and nimble communication on multiple fronts is needed for both crisis and career success (Fink, 2013; Nowak et al., 2020; Tumpey et al., 2019). Academic theories and research must have timely, practical value and evidence of effectiveness to be useful to a crisis communication professional (Coombs, 2015). Even better, in the case of a complex health-related crisis, the theory or research needs to (1) reflect the communication complexities present in an extended crisis communication response and (2) actually help address the concerns or issues present in a serious health crisis. Those are high bars—and often not necessary to attain if one's primary goal is publishing in peer-reviewed journals. Not surprisingly, the different needs and priorities of scholars and practitioners produce limited opportunities for collaborations to advance either scholarship or practice. Practitioners generally do not have time to bring academic-based experts up to speed on a crisis (particularly if the university-based expert does not have knowledge in the health-related subject matter) nor a willingness to assess the effectiveness of an academic theory or framework in a crisis response. In addition, as Claeys and Opgenhaffen (2016) found, a common starting point for many practitioners is that crisis communication theories are too abstract and not readily applicable to specific real-world crisis situations.

True Collaborations Need Formal Agreements

Informal collaborations between university-based experts and crisis communication professionals can and have helped to advance theory, research, or practice (e.g., Jin et al., 2019; Tumpey et al., 2019), but reliance on such efforts is quite limiting. As helpful as informal collaborations can be, they are often ad hoc, sporadic, and difficult to sustain. In addition, it is likely that significant advances in crisis communication theory, research, or practice will require efforts that extend over the course of a complex health-related crisis, assess two or more complex health-related crisis communication responses, or utilize multi-disciplinary teams. These types of collaborations will need significant funding support, and as such, formal agreements. The roles and responsibilities of each party will need to be specified, along with how data, findings, and conclusions will be made available. In the case of US government agencies, grants, cooperative agreements, and contracts are the primary funding mechanisms. Grants give university experts the greatest latitude, contracts the least, with cooperative agreements in the middle.

Collaborations with private sector or non-government organizations provide university-based experts access to perspectives and experiences that can advance theory, research, and practice, but may also involve agreements that prevent disclosure of much of what was learned.

Opportunities and Possibilities

Despite the challenges, recent complex health-related crises like the COVID-19 pandemic indicate a need for advances in crisis communication theories, research, and practice. At present, for instance, crisis communication theories and research rarely recognize or encompass the complexities, dynamic nature, or realities of complex health-related crises. On the practice side, most communication professionals are continually seeking new insights and approaches for preventing, addressing, and mitigating crises, with constantly changing consumer, media, and social environments powerful motivators. For advances to happen—and to happen sooner rather than later—collaborations between academics and practitioners will be essential. As Fischhoff (2015) noted with respect to achieving advances in the science and application of risk-cost-benefit analyses, the pace and amount of advancement in a field often depends on the degree of collaboration, including between academic experts and industry decision-makers.

In the case of complex health-related crises, four general domains that would benefit from greater collaboration are: (1) developing better communication theories and frameworks regarding individuals' beliefs and behaviors in a health-related crisis situation, including as it evolves over time (e.g., ones that recognize and account for race and cultural perspectives and priorities, political ideology and values, generational differences, and variations in risk acceptance as well as risk perceptions); (2) more consistent and extensive efforts to elicit frontline crisis communication practitioner experiences, assumptions, and judgments; (3) developing and evaluating real or near real-time efficient and effective methods for obtaining insights into the knowledge, beliefs, concerns, and preferences of affected or potentially affected publics or sub-populations; and (4) understanding how to use and assess the effects and effectiveness of social and digital media, including the specific and actual influence of these platforms and channels on support for crisis response measures and compliance with public health measures (versus primarily doing content analyses to document and describe content).

In addition to the four general categories, specific possibilities suggested by recent published studies and the crisis communication challenges and issues seen in complex health-related crises include:

Collaborations that identify and describe the lessons learned from CERC strategies, tactics, and messaging used in the COVID-19 response. The COVID-19 response encompassed all countries, different phases and stages of crisis response and communication, a wide variety of communication strategies and plans (e.g., from denial to active engagement with affected communities and individuals), collection of qualitative and quantitative data in many countries regarding public and stakeholder perceptions and behaviors, and a variety of crisis communication messages and activities. Multiple possibilities exist in this space, particularly with government agencies and other organizations interested in learning from and improving their infectious disease and new vaccine-related crisis and risk communications strategies and messages. Toppenberg-Pejcic et al.'s (2018) review of the lessons learned from a rapid review of gray literature on Ebola, Zika, and Yellow emergency risk communication efforts provides a helpful example.

Collaborations that more generally identify, describe, and summarize the experiences and efforts of frontline crisis communication professionals during complex health-related crises. Both scholars and practitioners would benefit from greater knowledge of the major and emerging communication issues in recent health-related crises. For example, partisan divides with respect to communication objectives and messages were highly visible over the course of the COVID-19 pandemic and likely challenged crisis communication plans and activities that did not take political values and ideology into account. Sandman's (2020a) distillation of how the public health risk communicators take political values into account is one approach that could be assessed via a research collaboration. More generally, Liu et al.'s (2016) review found the concept of uncertainty—despite being a key factor in crisis communication practice—was not often acknowledged or included in existing academic crisis communication research and theories. Collaborative research would seem to be a useful way to address this significant knowledge gap.

Collaborations that identify new or highly effective crisis communication tools, approaches, or persuasive strategies for achieving needed behavior change. It is highly likely many frontline CERC professionals gained new insights into effective and not so effective crisis communication strategies and activities over the course of responding to recent highly visible health threats. Documenting what they have learned can help strengthen or update existing crisis communication theories, obtain insights that can generate new theories and frameworks, and equip practitioners with new and better ways to achieve crisis communication objectives. This would include developing and evaluating technologies that enable gaining real or near-real time insights into the knowledge, beliefs, concerns, and preferences of affected or potentially affected publics or sub-populations. It would also include collaborations that use academic theories and research to formulate operational guidance for practitioners. Christiano and Neimand's (2018) "The Science of What Makes People Care" is an instructive example of how academic insights and research can serve as a foundation for creating a set of persuasive communication principles for frontline communicators.

Collaborations that identify current and emerging crisis communication-related needs. While it is difficult for university-based crisis communication scholars to be actively engaged by frontline crisis communicators as part of a real-time response, collaborations involving needs assessments would be helpful and viable. Needs assessments are often an essential part of the crisis communication planning and preparation phase, and use of external experts can help organizations better identify their crisis communication strengths and deficits. This includes identifying communication research needs, such as studies that address gaps that could impede the effectiveness of future crisis communication plans and activities. The collaborative research undertaken by Greven et al. (2018) that used a mental models' approach to assess and compare what experts and laypeople knew and believed about the risks associated with large fires involving hazardous materials is an instructive example. Findings from that study were used to improve crisis communications related to large chemical fires. Additionally, studies have found race, ethnicity, and cultural differences in how information is obtained and accessed in a public health emergency, as was evidenced in the 2009 H1N1A pandemic (Lin et al., 2014). The need to recognize and understand these differences was affirmed during the COVID-19 pandemic, where Black Americans had a significantly higher risk of COVID-19 infection compared with other racial groups (CDC, COVID-NET, March–June 13, 2020). Collaborations that advance crisis communication scholarship, research, and practice with respect to cultural differences, understanding, inclusiveness, and messaging should be a priority.

Key Takeaways

- The COVID-19 pandemic, the ever-present possibility of pandemic influenza, and the daily likelihood of significant health crises emanating from one or more possible sources highlight the importance of continued advancement in crisis communication scholarship and practice.
- University-based experts need high awareness and understanding of the issues, strategies, and challenges facing crisis communication professionals involved in health-related crises. That awareness and understanding is essential for preparing students pursuing degrees in public relations, risk and health communication, and crisis communication. It is also essential for shaping research efforts and informing research priorities.
- For frontline practitioners, it may be that most crisis communications theories and scholarship are too abstract and/or general to apply to the situations they encounter. However, improvements are harder to achieve without their active involvement with academics. Collaborations, whether informal or formal, are one of the best ways they can inform and shape academic scholarship and research.
- Active collaborations enable different perspectives and types of expertise to be strategically focused on important crisis communication questions and issues. Collaborations also help strengthen research designs, improve research measures, and increase the generalizability—and thus

operational value—of research results and findings. The end outcome is a win-win. Academics' crisis communication theories and research are more reflective of reality, and crisis communication practice is informed by more than instinct and one's personal experiences.

References

Barcott, B. (2012, December 18). The story behind the hantavirus outbreak at Yosemite. *Outside Magazine*. https://www.outsideonline.com/1930876/death-yosemite-story-behind-last-summers-hantavirus-outbreak

Centers for Disease Control and Prevention (CDC). (2018). *Crisis plus emergency risk communication manual, Chapter 1*. CDC. https://emergency.cdc.gov/cerc/ppt/CERC_Introduction.pdf

Centers for Disease Control and Prevention (2020). *CERC manual and tools*. Accessed July, 2020. https://emergency.cdc.gov/cerc/resources/index.asp

Christiano, A., & Neimand, A. (2018). The science of what makes people care. *Stanford Social Innovation Review, 16*(4), 26–33.

Chu, D. K., Akl, E. A., Duda, S., Solo, K., Yaacoub, S., & Schünemann, H. J. (2020). Physical distancing, face masks, and eye protection to prevent person-to-person transmission of SARS-CoV-2 and COVID-19: A systematic review and meta-analysis. *Lancet, 395*(10242), 1973–1987. https://doi.org/10.1016/S0140-6736(20)31142-9

Claeys, A-S., & Opgenhaffen, M. (2016). Why practitioners do (not) apply crisis communication theory in practice. *Journal of Public Relations Research, 28*(5–6), 232–247. https://doi.org/10.1080/1062726X.2016.1261703

Continetti, M. (2020, April 4). The social costs of COVID-19. *National Review*. https://www.nationalreview.com/magazine/2020/04/20/the-social-costs-of-covid-19%e2%80%88/#slide-1

Coombs, W. T. (2014). *Applied crisis communication and crisis management: Cases and exercises*. SAGE Publications.

Coombs, W. T. (2015). The value of communication during a crisis: Insights from strategic communication research. *Business Horizons, 58*(2), 141–148. https//doi.org/10.1016/j.bushor.2014.10.003

Dua, A., Mahajan, D., Millan, I., & Stewart, S. (2020, May 27). *COVID-19's effect on minority-owned small businesses in the United States*. McKinsey & Company Report. https://www.mckinsey.com/industries/social-sector/our-insights/covid-19s-effect-on-minority-owned-small-businesses-in-the-united-states

Fink, S. (2013). *Crisis communication: The definitive guide to managing the message*. McGraw Hill Education.

Fischhoff, B. (2015). The realities of risk-cost-benefit analysis. *Science, 350*(6260). https://science.sciencemag.org/content/350/6260/aaa6516

Frost, M., Li, R., Moolenaar, R., Mao, Q., & Xie, R. (2019). Progress in public health risk communication in China: lessons learned from SARS to H7H9. *BMC Public Health, 19*(3). http://doi.org.10.1186/s12889-019-6778-1

Greven, F. E., Claassen, L., Woudenberg, F., Duijm, F., & Timmermans, D. (2018). Where there's smoke, there's fire: Focal points for risk communication. *International Journal of Environmental Health Research, 28*(3), 240–252. https://doi.org/10.1080/09603123.2018.1468422

Hsiang, S. et al. (2020). The effect of large-scale anti-contagion policies on the COVID-19 pandemic. *Nature*, https://doi.org/10.1038/s41586-020-2404-8.

Institute for Crisis Management. (2020). Annual crisis report: Global news coverage of business crises in 2019. https://crisisconsultant.com/icm-annual-crisis-report/

Jin, Y., Austin, L., Vijaykumar, S., Jun, H., & Nowak, G. (2019). Communicating about infectious disease threats: Insights from public health information officers. *Public Relations Review, 45*(1), 167–177. https://doi.org/10.1016/j.pubrev.2018.12.003

Kieser, A., & Leiner, L. (2012). Collaborate with practitioners: But beware of collaborative research. *Journal of Management Inquiry, 21*(1), 14–28. https://doi.org/10.1177/1056492611411923

Lin, L., Jung, M., McCloud, R. F., & Viswanath, K. (2014). Media use and communication inequalities in a public health emergency: A case study of 2009–2010 pandemic influenza A virus subtype H1N1. *Public Health Reports, 129*(4), 49–60. https://doi.org/10.1177/00333549141296S408

Liu, B. F., Bartz, L., & Duke, N. (2016). Communicating crisis uncertainty: A review of the knowledge gaps. *Public Relations Review, 42*, 479–487. https://doi.org/10.1016/j.pubrev.2016.03.003

Lundgren, R. E., & McMakin, A. H. (2018). *Risk communication: A handbook for communicating environmental, safety, and health risks* (6th ed.). John Wiley & Sons.

Maani, N., & Galea, S. (2020, April 13). The true costs of the COVID-19 pandemic. *Scientific American*. https://blogs.scientificamerican.com/observations/the-true-costs-of-the-covid-19-pandemic/

Nowak, G. J., Karafillakis, E., & Larson, H. (2020). Pandemic influenza vaccines: Communication of benefits, risks and uncertainties. In P. Bhari (Ed.), *Communicating about risks and safe use of medicines: Real life and applied research*, 163–178.

Olson, H. (2020, June 11). We can't keep the economy closed forever. *The Washington Post*. https://www.washingtonpost.com/opinions/2020/06/11/we-cant-keep-economy-closed-forever/

Rasmussen, S. A., & Goodman, R. A. (2019). *The CDC field epidemiology manual*. Oxford University Press.

Reynolds, B. (2008). Effective communication during an influenza pandemic: The value of using a crisis and emergency risk communication framework. *Health Promotion Practice, 9*(4), 13–17. https://doi.org/10.1177/1524839908325267

Sandman, P. (2003, April). Four kinds of crisis communication. *The Synergist*. https://psandman.com/col/4kind-1.htm

Sandman, P. (2020a, June 8). *Public health professionals should be saying this about the public's COVID-19 risk choices*. The Peter Sandman Risk Communication Website. http://psandman.com/col/Corona21.htm

Sandman, P. (2020b). *Why so much COVID-19 crisis communication has failed: An expert explains*. The Peter Sandman Risk Communication Website. http://www.psandman.com/articles/Corona24.pdf#search=%22COVID-19%20crisis%22

Schoch-Spana, M., Brunson, E., Chandler, H., Gronvall, G. K., Ravi, S., Sell, T. K., & Shearer, M. P. (2018). Recommendations on how to manage anticipated communication dilemmas involving medical countermeasures in an emergency. *Public Health Reports, 133*(4), 366–378. https://doi.org/10.1177/0033354918773069

Toppenberg-Pejcic, D., Noyes, J., Allen, T., Alexander, N., Vanderford, M., & Gamhewage, G. (2018). Emergency risk communication: Lessons learned from a rapid review of recent gray literature on Ebola, Zika, and Yellow Fever. *Health Communication, 34*(4), 437–455. https://doi.org/10.1080/10410236.2017.1405488

Tumpey, A. J., Daigle, D., & Nowak, G. (2019). Communicating during an outbreak or public health investigation, In S. A. Rasmussen & R. A. Goodman (Eds.), *The CDC field epidemiology manual* (pp. 243–259). Oxford University Press.

Ulmer, R. R. Sellnow, T. L., &Seeger, M. W. (2019). *Effective crisis communication: Moving from crisis to opportunity* (4th ed.). SAGE Publications.

Wilkinson, A. (2020, June 15). How the coronavirus outbreak is roiling the film and entertainment industries. *VOX*. https://www.vox.com/culture/2020/3/10/21173376/coronavirus-cancel-tenet-disney-mulan-french-dispatch-avatar-star-wars-quiet-place-top-gun

Winters, M., Jalloh, M. F., Sengeh, P., Jalloh, M. B., Conteh, L., Bunnell, B., Li, W., Zeebari, Z., & Nordenstedt, H. (2018). Risk communication and Ebola-specific knowledge and behavior during 2014–2015 outbreak, Sierra Leone. *Emerging Infectious Diseases, 24*(2), 336–344. https://doi.org/10.3201/eid2402.171028

WHO. (2017). *Communicating risk in public health emergencies: A WHO guideline for emergency risk communication (ERC) policy and practice*. Geneva: World Health Organization. https://www.who.int/publications/i/item/communicating-risk-in-public-health-emergencies

WHO. (2018). Vaccine safety communication in the digital age: Vaccine Safety Net 2018 Annual Report. https://www.who.int/vaccine_safety/publications/Vaccine-safety-communication-in-the-digital-age-report.pdf?ua=1

WHO. (2020a, March 11). Coronavirus disease 2019 (COVID-19) Situation Report 51. https://www.who.int/docs/default-source/coronaviruse/situation-reports/20200311-sitrep-51-covid-19.pdf?sfvrsn=1ba62e57_10

WHO. (2020b, March 11). Director-general's opening remarks at the media briefing on COVID-19. https://www.who.int/dg/speeches/detail/who-director-general-s-opening-remarks-at-the-media-briefing-on-covid-19---11-march-2020.

WHO. (2020c). Risk communication and community engagement readiness and response to coronavirus disease (COVID-19): Interim guidance, 19 March 2020. https://www.who.int/publications/i/item/risk-communication-and-community-engagement-readiness-and-initial-response-for-novel-coronaviruses

WHO. (2020d, February 3). 2019 Novel Coronavirus (2019-nCoV): Strategic Preparedness and Response Plan. https://www.who.int/docs/default-source/coronaviruse/srp-04022020.pdf

WHO. (2020e, April 7–8). WHO consultation on infodemic management framework 7–8 April. https://www.who.int/docs/default-source/epi-win/final-recap-of-meeting.pdf?sfvrsn=42f71c42_2&download=true

Zhou, P., Yang, X. L., Wang, X. G., Hu, B., Zhang, L., Zhang, W., Si, H. R., Zhu, Y., Li, B., Huang, C. L., Chen, H. D., Chen, J., Luo, Y., Guo, H., Jiang, R. D., Liu, M. Q., Chen, Y., Shen, X. R., Wang, X., Zheng, X. S., … Shi, Z. L. (2020). A pneumonia outbreak associated with a new coronavirus of probable bat origin. *Nature, 579*(7798), 270–273. https://doi.org/10.1038/s41586-020-2012-7

7 Disaster and Emergency Crisis Management Communication

Robert L. Heath, J. Suzanne Horsley, Greg Guest, and Chris Glazier

Although relatively benign in conception, the implications of both emergency (situational) and disaster (damage/harm) are powerful; they point to sticky crises with serious consequences if not responsibly managed and communicated properly. Situational evidence of that claim abounds, including the recent disastrous brushfires in Australia (2019–2020) or the global novel coronavirus pandemic (2020).

Disaster and emergency crisis management communication (DECMC) does not relate primarily to ostensible or actual management, operational and communication missteps by businesses, or the traditional focus of crisis management and communication studies. Rather DECMC focuses primarily on government agencies' managerial and communication responsibilities to keep citizens as safe as possible whether alone or through collaboration with businesses and nonprofits (such as the American Red Cross). DECMC is studied and deployed to keep citizens healthy and safe in the event, for instance, of hurricanes, tornadoes, massive brushfires of the kind that happened in California (2018), or health effects from organisms that produce disease (e.g., tropical storm Dorian that slammed the Bahamas in 2019). As demonstrated during the massive brushfire in Australia, the focus on citizens is very broad, including structures, habitats, and wild and domestic animals. With the COVID-19 pandemic, the scope of concern extended beyond the primary threat to human health to the stability of the economies of countries on every continent of the globe.

The scope of this chapter emphasizes pre-crisis management (planning) and communication as the foundation for DECMC. Emergency managers, including communication specialists, bear primary responsibility for disasters at all three crisis stages: pre-crisis, crisis event, and post-crisis. Response protocols to be followed during severe storms (hurricanes and tornadoes, for instance) should be planned and explained before any specific event. These response protocols often require a balance of management (plans and operations to help a community respond during a hurricane, for instance) and how messages need to be communicated by emergency managers to implement the management plan. However dialogic such planning is, eventually it requires information-based, persuasive influence campaigns that help citizens to know what to do and to be motivated to that end when a "crisis" looms and then occurs. Emergency is time-sensitive and contextual; it is fraught with the functional and ethical challenges of community health and safety. Such campaigns direct citizens' actions to make enlightened choices in the face of uncertainty.

In this conceptualization, professional emergency managers don't like to use the term "crisis" but prefer event or emergency. When engaged in emergency management communication (EMC), even when faced with disaster, professionals prefer to avoid the term crisis. They believe that a crisis is what happens if planning and communication fail. Also, along with pre-crisis emphasis, we include brief post-crisis details, such as what needs to be done for restoration, recovery, and even renewal. During that phase, communication is often fairly routine even when recovery management is severely challenged. In that context, the term crisis is reserved for an emergency that cannot be foreseen and for which responses cannot be well managed.

Based on these observations, we emphasize that disaster and emergency crisis response requires professionally expert analysis, planning, and seasoned response to prevent or mitigate severe impact from events that produce serious harm. We emphasize the need to create and implement strategic management response and communication plans relevant to pre-crisis stages when populations can be warned of and prepared to respond in the best-case way should a disaster occur. DECMC is the communicative application of professional, sound science assessment unique to specific types of disasters and carefully developed prevention and mitigation protocols, which are strategically presented to relevant publics to advise them on protocols designed to maximize health and safety response efficacy before, during, and after a disaster creates the need for emergency response. What follows begins by examining DECMC contexts, relevant theories, stages, and protocols/guidelines.

The Nature of Disaster and Responses to It

Most of us encounter DECMC early in life as children when we learn our parents' scripts: "Don't run with scissors." "This water is very hot so don't burn yourself." "Stay out of the deep end of the pool until you can swim." "Don't ride your bike too fast." "Watch out for cars." These statements should sound familiar because they are scripted EMC narratives. Think about scripts school children learn today about active shooter events.

At-risk citizens (and other populations) need to be prepared to implement best-case, sound-science planned responses to mitigate the harm of a disaster and to recover resiliently. At-risk citizen is a generic concept which refers to those persons most likely to be harmed. Citizens living along the Gulf Coast are most at risk for hurricanes, whereas during the COVID 19 pandemic, older citizens and those with preexisting health conditions were most at risk. DECMC requires that strategic response plans (management) be developed to address the situational nature of disasters, including protocols needed to take mitigating actions and communicate before, during, and after such events. Whereas organizations of all types may experience crisis, the disaster-oriented contexts discussed in this chapter are those that result from outside forces, not because of what an organization does/fails internally to do correctly—for the most part. Although in the case of Pacific Gas and Electricity, for instance, their maintenance and operations policies allegedly led to the 2018 brushfires in Paradise, California.

Elected officials may play key roles, but this type of event is more often addressed as a professional staff function of government in alliance with other key organizations. Titles such as emergency manager are evident in the literature, practice, and news coverage. Businesses based on local commercial activity may partner with a local (national or state) government in the face of or following a disaster. Nonprofits (such as the American Red Cross) develop response expertise, raise money, hire paid staff, develop volunteer cadres, and develop abilities (such as shelter locations) to be deployed during and after events (e.g., providing food, water, and electricity).

Disasters result from events that often cannot be prevented but can be mitigated: severe weather (e.g., hurricanes and tornadoes), brush/forest fires, floods, mass shootings, radiation releases, and even viral or bacterial epidemics. As defined in the language of risk, disasters are low frequency (low likelihood) events (ranging from instantaneous to several days duration, even weeks) that have high (extreme) magnitude/impact.

Well-managed analysis of, expert preparation for, and efficacious response (including communication) to an emergency are the gold standards of DECMC; each of these phases requires thoughtful, proactive scientific analysis, strategic response protocols, ability to engage in strategic communication, and a moral commitment to serve lay populations in the face of harm-laden uncertainty (e.g., disaster). Uncertainty refers to the probability that any disaster will occur and if it occurs, uncertainty refers to the probability that any one person, for instance, will become ill and die. One of the characteristics of disaster is that it is fraught with uncertainty, known occurrences and outcomes. Thus, DECMC is a topic examined by experts in risk management and communication and their counterparts in crisis management and communication; both disciplines seek to maximize safety (i.e., humans, animals and other living things) and minimize property damage. Along with event mitigation, DECMC presumes resilience in restoration, recovery, and renewal.

The pragmatics and ethics of DECMC can be matters of life and death. A fully functioning society is one that knows and understands risks, develops plans tailored to community conditions, and communicates effectively with persons who need emergency response advice to make decisions for their safety. Risk is by definition a matter of uncertainty. Disaster is a major, even extraordinary event, or complex of events. DECMC mitigates or prevents these outcomes.

Hurricane Harvey, for instance, hit the Texas coast on August 25, 2017, and became a major rain event. Costing between $125 and $190 billion, it redefined the metrics for predicting rainfall totals and per-hour rainfall. At least 88 people died. Flooding forced 39,000 people from their homes in the counties near and including Houston. The question: did DECMC mitigate death, injury, and damage?

As emphasized above, DECMC should be segmented into three relatively discrete, but interrelated stages: pre-crisis, crisis/event, and post-crisis. The pre-crisis stage is characterized by impact mitigation through emergency response planning; plans are developed and communicated to help protect at-risk publics by preparing them to take appropriate prevention and/or mitigation responses. For instance, motorists are told when they approach a low water crossing during a flash flood warning "Back up, don't drown." That planning logic continues into the event crisis and disaster stage. If pre-crisis is the stage of planning, event is the stage of plan implementation (Olaniran et al., 2012). Finally, during the post-crisis stage, emergency response efforts are implemented to recover, restore, and even to renew and improve. It taps into, restores, and augments a community's resilience. In essence, planning and implementation are judged by their ability to increase concerned publics' sense of control over the extreme risks they believe can affect them. In these and other examples, one should note the narrative quality of DECMC.

Pre-crisis and DECMC Contexts: Situational, Cognitive, and Communicative

The overarching perspective in this chapter is individuals' collective ability to be as safe and healthy as possible given situational conditions (e.g., disasters) of two primary kinds: one is organic/biological and relevant to public health, often occurring as epidemics (such as COVID-19, SARs, malaria, Ebola, Marburg virus, sepsis or septicemia) and organizational health crises (such as *E. coli* and Listeria). Another is an inorganic/atmospheric/geological disaster produced by natural events such as hurricanes/cyclones, tornadoes, rain events, extreme drought (including forest and brushfires), earthquakes, and tsunamis. These can have an organization-centric component, such as lead contamination in drinking water systems, radiation releases from electric generating plants, exposure to asbestos, or exposure to toxic chemicals (such as community exposure to methyl isocyanate released from a chemical plant in Bhopal, India, in 1984). Such threats can occur because of what others do (e.g., reckless driving, driving while intoxicated [DWI], assault, and terrorism) and what people do to themselves (e.g., smoking, irresponsible alcohol consumption, unhealthy diets, needle sharing). Some events result from conjoined decision-making, such as painkillers and addiction/death—assuming patients are fully informed and able to comply. Although this list includes typical organizational crises because of management failure, the rubric of DECMC features the preventive and mitigative responsibilities of government as means for collective safety and health.

Given the complexity of risk assessment and emergency management, systematic and comprehensive analysis has become the hallmark of such processes. For instance, the work of Palmlund (1992) helps frame disaster by using the dramatis personae of risk management: risk bearers, bearers' advocates, generators, researchers, arbiters, and informers. The question is how and whether these personae cooperate to reduce risk bearers' peril or fail to do so. Such analysis has a narrative quality because it helps identify key roles enacted over time.

As conceptualized and implemented, DECMC is a collective search for community and societal control in the face of harm. Dynamics of control are sensitive to (a) personal control by individual members of the community where the risk exists, (b) authorized (authority) control, (c) activists' control, and (d) self-control by the source of the risk, unless the source is natural phenomena.

Situational Contexts: Disaster Assessment

The point of working to understand the likelihood of and potential impact of emergency events is that they can dramatically affect knowable populations, can occur in predictable patterns, and can be mitigated or avoided if appropriate protocols are strategically enacted. Experts study the origins and effects of events whose occurrence and impact often have community, rather than individual, implications. In the face of disaster, key individuals may need special attention, such as the elderly or high-risk persons in the face of a hurricane.

The paradigm of DECMC is to understand how disasters occur, whom they can and do affect, and what can be done (collectively and individually) to avoid or mitigate harm. Prevention and mitigation abilities and protocols assume that sufficient scientific expertise and community health/safety systems are available. For instance, meteorologists and emergency response teams work together to understand types of storms sufficiently so that each affected community can prepare for response and recovery. Planning presumes that individuals can gain information, knowledge, and values that help them understand risk, event causes, mitigations, and recovery. The objective is to inform and motivate risk bearers to take situationally appropriate actions should a disaster become imminent.

Emergency managers recognize situational differences regarding storm damage in relatively unpopulated sections of the US Gulf Coast: New Orleans, which is a bowl below sea level, and Houston/Galveston, a barrier island from which only one major highway leads inland. For residents of that community to evacuate to safety, they have to travel through a congested metropolis of nearly 7,000,000 people, most of whom do not need to evacuate. Meeting such challenges requires a lot of planning, communication, and coordinated, motivated plan development and implementation.

For sound science to inform emergency management assessment, the role of the expert (expert efficacy) is paramount to gain trust and achieve response efficacy. What does sound science tell us and how does that inform how we manage emergencies, through response planning and communication? The mental models approach to risk management and communication presumes that knowledgeable individuals come together to make decisions that inform planning and implementation (Morgan et al., 2002). That view of risk management is cautious and precautionary. It even asks where and how might experts be fallible and the public wise (Otway, 1992). As plans are developed based on expert assessment, such analysis must be vetted in public by hearings, community meetings, and media coverage and commentary. As people attempt to reduce uncertainty, they cannot always rely on their own judgments and may doubt the opinions and conclusions of experts; risk democracy presumes that risk bearers need to be part of decision-making.

To emphasize how situational context affects DECMC, we close this section by asking readers to ponder the differences in assessment, response, and communication if a mass shooting were to occur on a university/college campus, an elementary or secondary school (e.g., pick a grade), at a place of business or governmental activity, or at a church, synagogue, or mosque. Shooters know these are relatively confined spaces with predictable individuals. That was not true of the mass shooting in Las Vegas, Nevada, at the open-air music event on October 1, 2017. Context matters.

Cognitive Factors

Cognitive factors relevant to disaster and emergency situations affect individual and collective assessments of risk based on uncertainty, threat/harm, risk tolerance, efficacy, trust, and fear and denial. Events cause individuals to experience varying levels of uncertainty and evaluation, cognitive involvement, control, knowledge, risk tolerance, harms/benefits ratios, trust, efficacy, and resilience. Cognitive assessment occurs prior to, during, and after crisis events.

Uncertainty results from probabilistic-based doubts and predictions about what will happen, what the effect will be, who will be harmed, and what response options are best to manage the uncertainty (Heath & O'Hair, 2009; Krimsky, 1992).

Threat assessment and *risk tolerance* are two concepts related to uncertainty. One of many relevant studies on those concepts, Floyd et al. (2000) investigated interactions among threat severity, threat vulnerability, response efficacy, and self-efficacy and adaptive intentions or behaviors. Thus, "decreases in maladaptive response rewards and adaptive response costs increased adaptive intentions or behaviors" (p. 407). *Risk tolerance* is an important concept. Just as everyone is not equally aware of specific risks or the emergency response measures required to increase their safety (decrease the risk), members of a community often have different perceptions of the likelihood that a risk exists, whether it is harmful, how harmful it is, and who is likely to be harmed. Women, for instance, tend to be less tolerant of technical risks than are men; they are more likely to be collective or communal in their planning and response.

Trust is a multidimensional construct that results from the amount of control and judgment citizens believe they can exert over sources of risk information and assessment and the conditions of the event. Renn and Levine (1991) emphasized the multi-dimensionality of trust: perceived competence/technical expertise, objectivity/sound science, fairness, consistency (of arguments, messages, and intentions), sincerity (honesty and openness), and faith (perception of good will and caring for others). Trust is affected by vulnerability, predictability, and reward dependability. Party A is vulnerable to party B if A's interests can be harmed or enhanced by what B does. If B can enhance rather than harm A, the trust relationship is different than if no prediction can be made or if B can be predicted to harm A.

Knowledge is one of the most problematic variables in this analysis. One underpinning assumption in risk assessment is that experts can obtain scientific knowledge about the degree to which a risk exists, use that knowledge to properly abate the risk, and supply concerned publics with the details of the risk and means for its abatement. Knowledge shapes attitudes which lead to behavioral intention, which should motivate actions. Each stage in this formulation of response can vary situationally, including by gender, age, risk tolerance, sense of community efficacy, as such.

Such cognitive factors are relevant to the ability to understand and assess risk, as well as to communicate about it, and, in doing so, influence mitigating and recovery behavior.

Communicative Context

As control declines and perception of risk increases, people's cognitive involvement rises if the risk is believed to affect their self-interests or the interests of persons and entities for which the person has concern. In this regard, uncertainty—doubt as to facts and conclusions—and cognitive involvement—belief that self-interests are at stake—motivates increased communication activity. High-involved persons are more likely to access the Internet, watch televised news, listen to radio programs, and read books, magazines, and newspaper stories regarding some disaster. They are more likely to attend meetings and to converse with others (especially friends and family) on the matter. Uncertainty and cognitive involvement motivate a desire to understand the risk, its potential harm and control measures that reduce harm, and the likelihood those controls will be exerted wisely and strategically. In this way, knowledge is sought as the means for control, but knowledge is idiosyncratic, inconsistent, culturally sensitive, and often incomplete. And risks, by definition, are fraught with uncertainty.

That basic paradigm has spawned many related concepts that are valuable not only for situational assessment and response planning but also for communication planning. As much as the paradigm of emergency communication is a flow or transmission from expert to lay public, evidence suggests that media coverage and other commentary socially amplify risk and risk response. Communication infrastructures exhibit social amplification as various players receive, comment on, and pass along information and opinions. Making this point, Kasperson (1992) concluded,

> The concept of social amplification of risk is based on the thesis that events pertaining to hazards interact with psychological, social, institutional, and cultural processes in ways that can heighten or attenuate perceptions of risk and shape risk behavior. Behavioral responses, in turn, generate secondary social or economic consequences. These consequences extend far beyond direct harms to human health or the environment to include significant indirect impact such as liability, insurance costs, loss of confidence in institutions, stigmatization, or alienation from community affairs.
>
> (pp. 157–158)

As Kasperson (1992) observed, "Amplification stations can be individuals, groups, or institutions" (p. 159). If more media coverage occurs and for longer periods of time, people believe that such indicators point to greater seriousness and response necessity. As people receive risk information from experts, they are also likely to ask friends and relatives to vet that information for its efficacy.

Trust predicts what people believe and the sources on which they rely. Precrisis communication can focus attention on science-based indicators (such as weather forecasts) of the risk, its manifestation and effect, and the measures that can and will be taken to mitigate the event's effects and foster the recovery from them. Such protocols seem most efficacious when messages are sensitive to community residents' needs and are supplied by sources that are similar (familiar) to community members (Heath et al., 2009).

Sustained emergency response (management) planning and relevant communication can increase community/social trust and efficacy of various kinds (Kellens et al., 2013; McComas, 2006; Siegrist et al., 2005, 2012; Ter Huurne & Gutteling, 2009; Terpstra, 2011). Trust and efficacy interact with other key variables, especially confidence, procedural fairness, outcome fairness, moral conviction, risk tolerance, and perceived risk. These variables are highly complex and multidimensional. For instance, in the face of an emergency, response efficacy becomes especially relevant (Kellens et al., 2012).

In high-risk emergency situations, fear is likely, but potentially dysfunctional even as a motivator for citizens to attend to and respond to emergency messages. Rather than using fear appeals (Rogers, 1975) as a direct component of emergency communication, communication plans and tracking research should investigate and implement emergency communication in the context of fear as modified by efficacy. Understanding the conceptual nature of emergency management campaigns is important to creating, planning, executing, and assessing them. If planned emergency response action, such as evacuation or shelter-in-place (or inoculation, expedient reaction to symptoms, or damage mitigation), is the desired outcome of a DECMC campaign, one key variable is efficacy. Conceptual grounding for this conclusion draws on Kim Witte's extended parallel process model (EPPM) (Witte, 1992, Witte & Allen, 2000, see especially Roberto et al., 2009). EPPM postulates informed action addresses topics such as fear/threat perception and dread as motivating concepts relevant to attentiveness to messages and cognitive decision-making leading to preferred actions.

Since 1992, Witte has wrestled with the question of which message design is most likely to gain attention and spark engaged information seeking and response planning. She focused on fear appeals, a standard concept in persuasion campaigns (See also, Witte & Allen, 2000). The research question addressed was this: if targeted populations (e.g., risk bearers) are confronted with a fear appeal to increase their willingness to focus on emergency messages, will that produce denial or dread? If people "deny" the implications of explicit warning, as some seem prone to do when confronted with anti-smoking (anti-vaping) messages, they either ignore each message or reshape/reinterpret it to be less threatening. That conclusion was central to decades of research under the theoretical umbrella of cognitive dissonance. Dissonance caused by encountering a "threatening/fear producing message" can be reduced to many factors, including denial.

Witte and her associates would explain such findings by focusing on why fear was not a factor and even dread was low. Efficacy is the key variable. If a communication campaign targets enjoy sufficient efficacy, fear is reconstituted as dread. Rather than reacting by denial, dread can lead to message reception and understanding of and preference for constructive action. Arguably, communities with fully functioning risk communication infrastructures (Heath, 2006) respond to risks as manageable uncertainties (dread rather than fear) based on efficacious advisory relationships between industry and local government (Roberto et al., 2009; see also, Epstein & Votaw, 1978; Heath & Lee. 2016). Roberto et al. (2009) observed how emergency management messages that elicit high self-efficacy, response efficacy, low susceptibility, and manageable severity led to no threat perceived/no response taken (or strategic responses based on expert advice that mitigates event severity). This could account for some high-efficacy individuals not evacuating in the face of apparent threat of severe weather, whereas others see evacuation as efficacious. If "fear" or "threat denial" is elicited from messages/discussion, it can lead to defense motivation and maladaptive choices. The preferred route is no fear response, protection motivation, and adaptive behavior. That cognitive decision route presumes community, collective efficacy as well as self-efficacy.

In addition to expert and self-efficacy, a third kind should be emphasized: community response efficacy. Expert efficacy allows assessment of whether risk bearers trust the advice and recommendations of experts; do they add value to collective efficacy? This set of questions exemplifies such reasoning: if threats arise, then will experts' advice increase individuals' safety? Experts can be risk bearers' advocates, researchers, arbiters, and informers. Community efficacy refers to the ability of an entire community to respond effectively. In the case of hurricanes, do those who need to evacuate do so, and can they accomplish evacuation successfully without others blocking their way? Do those who should shelter-in-place, do so instead of evacuating, which can clog streets? Individual self-efficacy asks can I do what is recommended as it is recommended; how should I respond? If elderly or handicapped people cannot evacuate by their own volition, they likely ask, will the "community" care for me?

Thus, to summarize this section, community members assess emergency response planning, response, and communication based on its attributed impact on their own efficacy (self-efficacy), their trust for experts (expert efficacy), and their sense of community efficacy (trust in others' willingness and ability to respond according to established protocols) (See Heath et al., 2009; Kellens et al., 2013; Roberto et al., 2009, for a discussion of response efficacy and reported findings on various efficacies and their relationships to pre-crisis messages). Ter Huurne and Gutteling (2009) demonstrated that social trust and confidence in self and in agencies contribute positively to constructive risk responses and predict risk information needs and preferences for risk information. Pre-crisis communication should increase response efficacy if it informs and motivates people to act during, in the event of, a crisis—and afterward.

This section has highlighted key variables relevant to DECMC and demonstrated how they interact in a complex web of threat recognition, risk estimation, and source impact. The discussion in this section will be coupled with stages-models of DECMC in the next section to suggest guidelines for creating campaigns to minimize the impact of disaster.

Relevant Theories Supporting Emergency Management and Communication Campaigns

DECMC's sustained risk and crisis communication campaigns require managerial infrastructures to sustain them programmatically in context (Renn, 2009). Several factors are relevant to campaign effectiveness; Rowan et al. (2009) featured five communication elements, which they defined as CAUSE: confidence, awareness, understanding, satisfaction with proposed solutions and procedures, and enactment. The process starts by building trust (**C**onfidence) in community leadership (expert efficacy) as a precursor to building self- and community efficacy. Awareness is multidimensional; experts must become aware of and understand the nature of each type of emergency in context. So too, lay persons need at least a threshold of threat perception: to be aware of the emergency and protocols for responding strategically and efficiently in the event the emergency occurs. Understanding presumes the knowledge acquired by experts through a combination of analytical processes, including engagement with community members and relevant organizations, and key individuals—collectively. Satisfaction is a measure of how readily and positively, even proactively, all parties to an emergency are regarding their understanding of it and the response protocols. **E** stands for enactment: putting plans into place and enacting them through expertise, community coordination, and individual actions. Risk communication practices attempt to inform risk bearers about potential future harm and related dangers so that they can take action to better manage and ideally mitigate the risk to themselves, their families, and friends (e.g., Seeger, 2006).

To address campaign requirements, Lindell and Perry's (2012) protective action decision model (PADM) features threat perception based on environmental cues, social cues, information sources, channel access and preferences, warning messages, and receiver characteristics. Based on the known nature of an emergency, pre-decision processes focus on ambient messages: exposure, attention, and comprehension. As a consequence of pre-decision processes, three factors (threat perception, protective action perceptions, and stakeholder perceptions) combine to predict whether lay publics are likely to engage in protective action decision-making. Supported by principles drawn from the Theory of Reasoned Action, response-decision factors include attitudes (threat perceptions and evaluations), action perceptions (what actions can be taken), and stakeholder perceptions, the actions that individuals perceive that significant others recommend: subjective norms. These decision-making elements predict risk bearers' behavioral intentions: planned actions based on attitudes, known actions, and preferred actions. These predict behavioral response: focused information seeking, protective response, and emotion-focused coping.

As a narrative, recognition of disaster potential sets the stages for time-sensitive, coordinated action, which can be learned and enacted by professional responders to help lay publics (risk bearers) to maximize their health and safety. DECMC communication not only exhibits narrative characteristics, but also requires spokespersons who are similar to relevant populations and whose messages are sensitive to their needs. In such narratives, spokespersons are important and can include animated spokes-characters who inform and nudge compliance with expert recommendations (Heath et al., 2018, 2019).

Narrative Model: DECMC Stages

DECMC requires the development of a management team that knows the nature of relevant disasters, has sufficient personnel and equipment to respond, and is capable of long-and short-term planning and implementation. Teams must know how to bring response capabilities to prepare for, respond to, and recover from disaster. The team needs to understand the strategies, abilities, channels, and challenges of communicating in a timely and sustained manner. Internal to the team, effective communication is needed for the coordination and implementation of the response team's strategic plan. Communicating during a disaster event is like swimming upward in a waterfall. It is rarely capable of being successful based on a single message; it needs sustained and repeated messaging before, during, and after the event occurs.

Expert Efficacy: Analysis and Planning

Pre-event risk analysis requires a solid mix of sound science to fully understand the natures of disasters by type and ability to incorporate seasoned emergency planning into response expertise. At what points in the face of an oncoming hurricane, for instance, should experts motivate certain residents' monitoring and readiness, including their decision-making to evacuate or shelter-in-place as advised? What precautions are necessary for evacuation, such as stocking up food and water, getting gasoline, gathering and protecting pets, securing buildings and possessions (such as outdoor furniture and sailboats in harbor), and knowing evacuation protocols and driving routes (See Lindell et al., 2011)? Trust and confidence on the part of publics at risk depend on perceived procedural fairness, outcome fairness, moral conviction, and risk tolerance/acceptance (Siegrist et al., 2012). In the case of hurricanes, reporters and weather forecasters are primary sources of useful information; they constitute channels through which emergency management messages reach at-risk publics.

Hurricanes require tracking. Monitoring services (weather forecasts) should partner with emergency management and elected officials' planning, communication, and implementation. Basic decisions require knowing whether to advise sheltering or evacuation, and on what timetables by route; expert advice or orders need to conform as much as possible with the response strategies preferred and advocated by friends/neighbors (or vice versa). As much as this occurs in pre-crisis and crisis stages, post-crisis requires return and recovery strategies, often entailing input by disaster recovery teams.

Such planning includes the development and implementation of early warning systems that typically call for combinations of channels: radio, television, telephone, internet, and social media. In special circumstances (interpersonal), these may include personal contact: friends, relatives, and specialized responders. How, for instance, does a community evacuate the blind, disabled, and elderly before a hurricane? Do people who need special medical equipment have personal generators, access to skilled treatment, or carefully developed evacuation plans? Emergency managers have discovered that persons who own and personally stable horses, for instance, require evacuation protocols so that fairgrounds and veterinary clinics become designated evacuation centers. Similarly, floods and major snowstorms may require substantial post-crisis emergency response protocols.

Communication Campaigns

Staged campaigns are likely to feature the following: pre-crisis threat perception and emergency response protocols, trusted sources based on expert efficacy, multiple voices communicating in coordination, and narrative clarity. Weinstein and Sandman's (1992) staged model examined these conditions from risk bearers' decision-making points of view: unaware of issue; unengaged by issue; deciding about acting, including deciding to act or not; deciding to act; acting; and maintenance.

> According to a stage theory, interventions need to be tailored to the status of the intended audience, focusing on the specific barriers that inhibit the transition to the next stage and changing over time as the audience progresses from stage to stage.
>
> (p. 170)

At each stage of a decision-model based campaign, the general public needs to become aware of danger and response protocols; PADM, for instance, presumes that awareness is ambient situationally: environmental cues, social cues, information sources, channel access and preferences, warning messages, and receiver characteristics. Disaster relevant information may be readily available to populations at risk, but if they are inattentive to it and unaware of the potential emergency, it lacks efficacy. Information seeking increases the likelihood that messages reach key publics, but publics need to know how and when to seek information about disasters and relevant response protocols.

The model affirmed by Kellens et al. (2012) emphasized the relevance of demographic characteristics, their perception of risk, and their perceived hazard knowledge. These factors interact to produce information need, which, when predicated on perceived response efficacy, leads to information seeking behavior. Information seeking is predicated on individual characteristics and perceived response efficacy. Information seeking presumes that life experience creates risk perception and hazard knowledge, which creates information needs to increase response efficacy.

Sources are of three kinds: experts; community leaders, including elected officials and emergency response voices; and friends/neighbors (pooled expertise based on experience, knowledge acquired from experts, and personal sense of efficacy, see Lindell & Perry, 2012). As noted above, communication sources can be spokes-characters (e.g., Wally Wise Guy, Smokey Bear, Woodsy Owl, McGruff, Sparky the Dog, and Red Panda). Such characters are tailored to narrative conditions of response efficacy ("only you can prevent forest fires" "take a bite out of crime" or "pack up and go"), have high message impact without suffering high threat (denial) levels, and demonstrate high personal efficacy. Mayors, for instance, have in the face of hurricane threats told area residents who seem unwilling to evacuate to write their social security or driver's license numbers on their arms so they can be identified in the morgue.

As noted in PADM, subjective norms are important predictors of protective action behavioral intentions; citizens ask, what do my friends, neighbors, and relatives want me to do, as well as city officials, news weather forecasters, emergency managers, and when, and how? Messages need to be simple to understand and easy to comply with.

Enactable DECMC Protocols: Planning and Response Guidelines as Narratives

Over the years templated crisis communication plans and implementation protocols have become boiler-plated. In terms of DECMC, some of this standard advice is relevant, and some is not. Specific decisions should be based on the unique, contextual nature of DECMC and assume that if proper planning and execution are in place, pre-crisis efforts can avert and mitigate crisis even in the face of potential disaster.

Organizational Planning and Team Leadership

DECMC presumes that each type of disaster needs idiosyncratic planning and implementation; responding to hurricane conditions is different from tornadoes or floods. Such is the case for an Ebola outbreak, a food-borne hazard, or other health disasters. In all cases, a myth (such as that cats carry severe acute respiratory syndrome [SARs] or that individual actions are better than community programs) is a challenge and may require refutation. Preparation and response factors are worth consideration, however much they need to be tailored to disaster conditions.

Expert Monitoring, Planning, and Response Coordination: Expert Efficacy

Community agencies (governmental, nonprofit, or corporate) are needed (created, funded, and staffed) to understand, prepare for, monitor, and initiate plans in a timely, orderly, science-based fashion. This is a multidisciplinary effort. Communication specialists are needed to help in DECMC planning and implementation. The pre-crisis period requires messages vital to that stage, as well as the event and post-crisis stages. Planning needs to be event comprehensive; the devil is in the detail. Hurricanes vary in nature, and therefore one-size-fits-all planning is unsound. In the case of SARs, unsophisticated implementation of quarantine affected medical personnel and their families in ways that impeded their response efficacy.

Communication Planning and Coordination

DECMC is inherently narrative, enacted over time, with knowable tracking and response plots and characters (coordinated voices). Each hurricane, for instance, is an idiosyncratic, unique, but knowable narrative. Tested protocols become useful but may require adjustment. Trusted sources (e.g., emergency managers, first responders, news media, and community leaders) need to be in place, and the lay public needs to be aware of them and able to recall relevant narratives. Websites are one key means for accomplishing this. (See the site for emergency management, Galveston, TX, gcoem.org or www.facebook.com/GalvestonOEM, or the Centers for Disease Control, www.emergency.cdc.gov, or National Oceanic and Atmospheric Administration [NOAA], noaa.gov.) Standard news outlets, especially meteorologists and public health spokespersons, tailor news reporting to disaster threat perception. Experts need to be visible parts of the reporting/commentary teams. Each hurricane season is likely to begin with an alert and may include informational interviews with county, city, and state emergency managers.

Sources must be familiar to residents, and messages must be sensitive to the community. Jargon may aid DECMC, but also confound its impact and effectiveness. "Turn-around-don't-drown" campaigns are frustrated by drivers who do not believe the protocol or do not understand when a crossing is unsafe. Clarity can be tested by using focus groups. Wise emergency managers ask friends and family to call them if they do not understand the managers' DECMC messages. Urgency is not the same as panic. Repetition is vital, as is consistency. Drivers monitoring an evacuation on the car radio must not get different messages by station. Thus, emergency management command centers become vital to coordinated and updated communication.

DECMC is time sensitive. Updates are important. The concepts of pre-event and post-crisis are important. For instance, as this chapter was being written in the spring of 2020, the COVID-19 pandemic had spread from Asia to every continent on the globe.

DECMC is educational. Lay publics' risk assessment and response depend on their understanding and appreciating risk and the proper mitigation protocols.

Key Takeaways

- Effective DECMC can reduce the likelihood that an emergency becomes a crisis.
- Disaster and emergency crisis response requires professionally expert analysis, planning, and seasoned response to prevent or mitigate severe impact from events that produce serious harm.

- Internal to organizations, such as petrochemical facilities, effective EMC can prevent or mitigate in-plant incidents that otherwise could become community crises.
- As the COVID-19 pandemic grows, reports of numbers of diagnoses and deaths demonstrate the effectiveness or lack thereof of sound science, effective crisis management planning, and effective information by political and community leaders to help citizens be safe.
- Messaging must be tailored to the reality that lay publics are not universally aware of and knowledgeable of threat, nor do they have the same risk tolerance levels.
- DECMC is not over until recovery has occurred, whether there is a return to the status quo or renewal.

References

Epstein, E., & Votaw, D. (Eds.) (1978). *Rationality, legitimacy, responsibility: Search for new directions*. Goodyear Publishing Co.

Floyd, D. L., Prentice-Dunn, S., & Rogers, R. W. (2000). A meta-analysis of research on protection motivation theory. *Journal of Applied Social Psychology, 30*(2), 407–429. https://doi.org/10.1111/j.1559-1816.2000.tb02323.x

Heath, R. L. (2006). Onward into more fog: Thoughts on public relations' research directions. *Journal of Public Relations Research, 18*(2), 93–114. http://doi.org/10.1207/s1532754xjprr1802_2

Heath, R. L., & Lee. J. (2016). Chemical manufacturing and refining industry legitimacy: Reflective management, trust, pre-crisis communication to achieve community efficacy. *Risk Analysis, 36*(6), 1108–1124. http://doi.org/10.1111/risa.12504

Heath, R. L., Lee, J., & Lemon, L. L. (2019) Narratives of risk communication: Nudging community members to shelter-in-place. *Public Relations Review, 45*(1), 128–137. http://doi.org/10.1016/j.pubrev.2018.12.004

Heath, R. L., Lee, J., & Ni, L. (2009). Crisis and risk approaches to emergency management planning and communication: The role of similarity and sensitivity. *Journal of Public Relations Research, 22*(2), 123–141. http://doi.org/10.1080/10627260802557415.

Heath, R. L., & Lee, J., Palenchar, M. J., & Lemon, L. L. (2018). Risk communication emergency response preparedness: Contextual assessment of the protective action decision model. *Risk Analysis, 38*(2), 333–344. http://doi.org/10.1111/risa.12845

Heath, R. L., & O'Hair, H. D. (Eds.) (2009). *Handbook of risk and crisis communication*. Routledge.

Kasperson, R. E. (1992). The social amplification of risk: Progress in developing an integrative framework. In S. Krimsky & D. Golding (Eds.), *Social theories of risk* (pp. 153–178). Praeger.

Kellens, W., Terpstra, T., & De Maeyer, P. (2013). Perception and communication of flood risks: A systematic review of empirical research. *Risk Analysis, 33*(1), 24–49. http://doi.org/10.1111/j.1539-6924.01844.x

Kellens, W., Zaalberg, R., & De Maeyer, P. (2012). The informed society: An analysis of the public's information-seeking behavior regarding coastal flood risks. *Risk Analysis, 32*(8), 1369–1381. http://doi.org/10.1111/j.1539-6924.2011.01743.x

Krimsky, S. (1992). The role of theory in risk studies. In S. Krimsky & D. Golding (Eds.), *Social theories of risk* (pp. 3–22). Praeger.

Lindell, M. K., Kang, J. E., & Prater, C. S. (2011). The logistics of household hurricane evacuation. *Natural Hazards*, *58*(3), 1093–1109. http://doi.org/10.1007/s11069-011-9715-x.

Lindell, M. K., & Perry, R. W. (2012). The protective action decision model: Theoretical modifications and additional evidence. *Risk Analysis*, *32*(4), 616–632. http://doi.org/10.1111/j.1539-6924.2011.01647.x

McComas, K. A. (2006). Defining moments in risk communication research: 1996–2005. *Journal of Health Communication*, *11*, 75–91. http://doi.org/10.1080/10810730500461091

Morgan, M. G., Fischhoff, B., Bostrom, A., & Atman, C. J. (2002). *Risk communication: A mental models approach.* Cambridge University Press.

Olaniran, B. A., Williams, D. E., & Coombs, W. T. (Eds.) (2012). *Pre-crisis planning, communication, and management: Preparing for the inevitable.* Peter Lang.

Otway, H. (1992). Public wisdom, expert fallibility: Toward a contextual theory of risk. In S. Krimsky & D. Golding (Eds.), *Social theories of risk* (pp. 215–228). Praeger.

Palmlund, I. (1992). Social drama and risk evaluation. In S. Krimsky & D. Golding (Eds.), *Social theories of risk* (pp. 197–212). Praeger.

Renn, O. (2009). Risk communication: Insights and requirements for designing successful communication programs on health and environmental hazards. In R. L. Heath and H. D. O'Hair (Eds.), *Handbook of risk and crisis communication* (pp. 80–98). Routledge.

Renn, O., & Levine, D. (1991). Trust and credibility in risk communication. In R. Kasperson & P. J. Stallen (Eds.), *Communicating risk to the public* (pp. 175–218) Kluwer.

Roberto A. J., Goodall, C. E., and Witte, K. (2009). Raising the alarm and calming fears: Perceived threat and efficacy during risk and crisis. In R. L. Heath & H. D. O'Hair (Eds.), *Handbook of risk and crisis communication* (pp. 285–301). Routledge.

Rogers, R. W. (1975). A protection motivation theory of fear appeals and attitude change. *Journal of Psychology*, *91*, 93–14. https://doi.org/10.1080/00223980.1975.9915803

Rowan, K. E. Botan, C. H. Kreps, G. L. Samoilenko, S., & Farnsworth, K. (2009). Risk communication education for local emergency managers: Using the CAUSE model for research, education, and outreach. In R. L. Heath & H. D. O'Hair (Eds.), *Handbook of risk and crisis communication* (pp. 168–192). Routledge.

Seeger, M. W. (2006). Best practices in crisis communication: An expert panel process. *Journal of Applied Communication Research*, *34*(3), 232–244. http://doi.org/10.1080/00909880600769944

Siegrist, M., Connor, M., & Keller, C. (2012). Trust, confidence, procedural fairness, outcome fairness, moral conviction, and the acceptance of GM field experiments. *Risk Analysis*, *32*(8), 1394–1403. http://doi.org/10.1111/j.1539-6924.2011.01739.x

Siegrist, M., Gutscher, H., & Earle, T.C. (2005). Perception of risk: The influence of general trust, and general confidence. *Journal of Risk Research*, *8*(2), 145–156. http://doi.org/10.1080/1366987032000105315

Ter Huurne, E. F. J., & Gutteling, J. M. (2009). How to trust? The importance of self-efficacy and social trust in public responses to industrial risks. *Journal of Risk Research*, *12*(6), 809–824. http://doi.org/10.1080/13669870902726091

Terpstra, T. (2011). Emotions, trust, and perceived risk: Affective and cognitive routes to flood preparedness behavior. *Risk Analysis*, *31*(10), 1658–1675. http://doi.org/org/10.1111/j.1539-6924.2011.01616.x

Weinstein, N. D., & Sandman, P. M. (1992). A model of the precaution adoption process: Evidence from home radon testing. *Health Psychology*, *11*(3), 170–180.

Witte, K. (1992). Putting the fear back into fear appeals: The extended parallel model. *Communication Monographs*, *59*, 329–349. http://doi.org/org/10.1080/03637759209376276

Witte K., & Allen, M. (2000). A meta-analysis of fear appeals: Implications for effective health campaigns. *Health Education & Behavior*, *27*(5), 591–615. https://doi.org/10.1177/109019810002700506

Part IV

Crises Amplified by Media and Aggravated by Misinformation

8 Managing Misinformation and Conflicting Information

A Framework for Understanding Misinformation and Rumor

Lucinda Austin, Toni G.L.A. van der Meer, Yen-I Lee, and Jim Spangler

In a polarizing media environment increasingly fraught with misinformation, disinformation, contradicting information, and rumor, it is tougher than ever for brands and agencies to correct the record or make their voices heard. With the proliferation of social media platforms, information is spread more quickly and more widely than ever before. A rumor can become a crisis in a very short period of time, and this misinformation and rumor can be damaging to a company's reputation and to its profits and stock prices (Atkinson, 2019).

While misinformation has been examined more extensively from the perspective of journalism, information technology, and politics (Anderson & Rainie, 2017), there is a lack of understanding regarding how misinformation disseminated via social media affects brand image and organizational reputation and legitimacy, potentially leading to crisis. These social media crises represent the "bleeding edge" of crisis communication research for organizations (Coombs, 2014, p. 1). While research in this arena has been emerging, it has not been sufficient or fully evidence-based.

Misinformation and rumor, as it relates to crisis, has been studied more extensively in the health communication and political communication realms, and a large trend in journalism includes the study of "fake news" (Egelhofer & Lecheler, 2019). Some of the most widely studied topics regarding misinformation in the health realm include vaccination and novel infectious diseases, such as Ebola and Zika, and misinformation has most commonly been studied through frameworks from psychology and network studies (Wang et al., 2019). According to research from the Pew Internet Center (Mitchell et al., 2019), most Americans believe that fake news is spreading confusion, and around half of Americans believe that they have unknowingly shared fake news with others. And the Institute for Public Relations' report on disinformation highlights that two-thirds of Americans think misinformation and disinformation is a major problem—on par with gun violence and terrorism (McCorkindale, 2019).

So why does fake news or misinformation spread so quickly? Marwick (2018) asserts that, at least in the political realm, fake news fits with partisan narratives and helps people to express their political identity and personal values. Fake news also frequently taps into news values such as negativity, sensationalism, and conflict, which makes it more arousing compared to other news and therefore more likely to be read and shared (Lewandowsky et al., 2017). And, while fact-checking websites, such as Snopes, PolitiFact, and others, have gained momentum within journalism circles, these sites have not been able to stem misinformation, but, instead, in some cases, have caused individuals to "double down" on their beliefs in the rumor (Marwick, 2018), perhaps due to lack of trust in sources, organizations, and authorities.

In this chapter, we will define misinformation and rumor, as it has been discussed in academic and scholarly literature and in practice, describe challenges in dealing with misinformation and rumor in practice, and develop future directions for crisis research and practice.

Challenges in Application

Sources estimate that more than 6.6 million tweets sharing fake news were sent in the months before the 2016 US presidential election with much of this coming from bot or semi-automated accounts and often identifiable as part of a coordinated campaign (Hindman & Barash, 2018). And close to half of the accounts discussing COVID-19 and the reopening of the US, even as COVID-19 cases began to grow, were linked to supposed bot accounts according to researchers from Carnegie Mellon (Young, 2020).

Social media organizations are taking a more active role in monitoring misinformation on select topics, which has been shown to be successful in limited applications. An example from the political realm provides some insight. The Real Strategy, an extreme conspiracy site that shared fake news prior to the 2016 US presidential election and was a prominent actor in the debunked Pizzagate child sex trafficking conspiracy theory hoax, was linked to or referenced by over 700,000 tweets in data collected by the Knight Foundation (Hindman & Barash, 2018). Twitter took action against the account and Reddit blacklisted the site—likely due to issues of libel, rumors shared from The Real Strategy were greatly reduced and their website became defunct.

In addition to addressing the social media company policies that can impact the spread of misinformation, companies are starting to hire firms to employ artificial intelligence to search for misinformation related to their organizations (Atkinson, 2019). Finding and addressing this misinformation before it spreads widely can help to limit the impact on reputation and stock prices. With the rapid spread of misinformation and rumor via social media, a company can quickly be in the position of having to defend itself on social media; as social media has given a voice to every individual with access, false information can be easily constructed and spread among small but active groups of like-minded individuals, which, in turn, can result in misinformation reaching a broader audience. Individuals can publish information of their choosing, instantly acquiring a degree of credibility and more easily reaching a larger audience.

Defining and Situating Rumor in Crisis

The study of rumor is not new, although the focus on "fake news," misinformation, and disinformation has only more recently entered our collective vernacular. Rumor has been studied from a social psychological perspective in a variety of crisis settings. Rumor, which is said to thrive in times of social upheaval, has historically been defined by three characteristics: has a distinct mode of transmission, provides information about a happening or condition, and satisfies some kind of expressive or gratifying need (Knapp, 1944).

Rumor has been defined as a "collective and collaborative transaction" (Oh et al., 2013, p. 409), in which people offer, evaluate, and interpret information to reach a common understanding of uncertain situations, to mitigate social intention, and to solve collective crisis problems (Bordia, 1996; Bordia & DiFonzo,2004; Bordia et al., 1999; Oh et al., 2013; Shibutani, 1966). Furthermore, rumor has been distinguished from "gossip" and "urban myth" by DiFonzo and Bordia (2007), who clarified the construct of rumor as: (1) arising from ambiguous or threatening situations, (2) providing sense-making or threat management functions, and (3) containing unverified (but potentially useful information).

To understand how and why rumor is spread, scholars have conceptualized rumor in different ways. For instance, Allport and Postman (1947) proposed rumor as a multiplicative function of "importance" and "informational ambiguity" (p. 33). Later, Anthony (1973) argued the difficulty of quantifiable importance, and thus claimed rumor involved the relationship between anxiety and informational ambiguity—a similar sentiment to Rosnow (1980), who suggested rumor strength is enhanced by anxiety and uncertainty. In this vein, rumor has been conceptualized as "a verbal outlet to release emotional pressure (anxiety or concern) by rationalizing ambiguous information" (Oh et al., 2010, p. 3). These conceptualizations of rumor imply that the degree of emotional tension, such as anxiety, fear, worry, or concern, is key for spreading rumor when people receive the rumor content with a high degree of ambiguity related to the context surrounding the rumor (i.e., the problem or issue at hand that may already be a crisis or have the potential to become one).

Scholars have also examined the social factors that need to be considered in generating and spreading rumors. Shibutani (1966) stated that rumor is a collective transaction and "improvised news generated in the process of discussion by a group of people" (p. 62). Moreover, rumor is information without any factual basis about current issues that are spread by word of mouth (Morin, 1971). Rosnow (1988) claimed that rumor is a public communication reflecting a private hypothesis about how the world works. These conceptualizations of rumor not only indicate the importance of rumor content on spreading rumor, but also imply the influence of individuals' networks, social pressures, and knowledge on the spread of rumor.

Since crisis situations are often characterized by high information needs contrasted with little available knowledge, rumors commonly prevail during such times. In an attempt to make sense of the emotional and uncertain situation at hand, absence of conclusive information might challenge the public debate on the crisis. Interpretations of frightening ambiguous information might result in statements without factual basis that can form the basis of further communication regarding understanding of the crisis. In this process, rumors might be born in an effort to define the crisis situation, but might only further fuel the complexity of crisis communication and of addressing it. The high demand for information during a crisis can make rumors even more newsworthy and such information might get uncritically accepted as the truth in the absence of other information.

Defining and Situating Misinformation in Crisis

Distinct from the study of rumor, three different types of false information have been defined as: (1) misinformation—false information shared without the intention of harm, (2) disinformation—false information shared with the intention of harm to individuals or organizations, and (3) malinformation—information based on some aspect of reality but shared with the intention of creating harm (Wardle & Derekshan, 2017). For example, malinformation may involve leaking private company information at a time crucial to company support or sharing works from a company spokesperson out of context.

Misinformation often, though, is used as a blanket statement for the presence or belief in "objectively" incorrect or false information (Bode & Vraga, 2015), without considering the original intent of the information (such as in malinformation or disinformation). Scholars further argue that incorrect information is inaccurate, incomplete, vague, or ambiguous information perceived by the recipient in a given moment and in a specific context (Karlova & Lee, 2011; Karlova & Fisher, 2013; Ruokolainen & Widén, 2020). Standing on receivers' perspectives, Ruokolainen and Widén (2020) further proposed two types: perceived misinformation and normative misinformation. Perceived misinformation is defined as "information is understood as information that is perceived as inaccurate, incomplete, vague or ambiguous information by receiver in a context or situation" (p. 3), while normative misinformation "is information in some social contexts generally accepted as inaccurate" (p. 3). This distinction in misinformation definitions is important, as what is "objectively" false may be hard to determine.

Misinformation has also been defined through integrating the message content and sharing outcomes. For instance, Southwell and colleagues (2018) defined misinformation as false information that is "both deliberately promoted and accidentally shared" (p. 1). van der Meer and Jin (2020) further defined crisis misinformation as false information about a crisis that may initially be assumed valid, but that may later be corrected or retracted and lead to factual misperceptions. Misinformation often leads to incorrect belief about crises and the further sharing of misinformation, and can affect companies' reputations and ultimately their stock prices and profits (Atkinson, 2019).

Misinformation and rumor are closely related concepts and often used interchangeably to refer to information that lacks truth. Though not always inaccurate, rumors are used in contemporary media environment to spread falsehoods. Overall, there is some conceptual overlap as well as difference between both terms. On the one hand, rumors can be considered a specific form of misinformation as rumors refer to claims of fact that have not been proved true but are considered credible because other people spread them and therewith seem to believe them (Berinsky, 2017). Thus, rumors relate to misinformation as they are considered an acceptance of unsubstantiated information that are not warranted beliefs and acquire their power through widespread transmission (Berinsky, 2017; Fine & Ellis, 2010). On the other hand, as rumors are largely defined as information that is not confirmed, it may also turn out to be true in the end (DiFonzo & Bordia, 2007). As misinformation broadly refers to false claims, rumors differ as their falsity is unknown and may turn out to be accurate even though they were factually unsubstantiated at the time of circulation (Shin et al., 2018).

Characteristics of Misinformation and Rumor Affecting Spread

Misinformation and rumor that is shared more widely has been shown to share some common features. For example, social media messages that are shared and consumed more widely may share the following characteristics including: a strong narrative, a powerful visual component, repetition, and provoking an emotional response (Wardle & Derekhshan, 2017). Additionally, the polarity of this emotional response and message sentiment affects the speed of message spread, as does the negativity of this emotional response with negative messages spreading more quickly than positive messages (Tsugawa & Ohsaki, 2015). Negative messages also elicit more attention and longer viewing times, particularly when multitasking (Kätsyri et al., 2016). Stories that are coherent (i.e., fits a broader story consistent with human behavior or similar stories) are also more likely to be perceived as credible (Lewandowsky et al., 2012). Messages are perceived as less credible when they appear to have persuasive intent or violate expectancies of receivers (Metzger & Flanagin, 2013).

Related to message characteristics, evaluators of these messages may use the following heuristics, or mental shortcuts, to evaluate the trustworthiness of these messages before deciding whether to share this misinformation.

Messages are increased in perceptions of credibility when they offer self-confirmation (i.e., confirmation of one's existing beliefs), consistency (i.e., consistent with other sources and messages), endorsement (i.e., recommendations from trusted others), and prior reputation (i.e., the reputation of the source is known or the name of the source is at least known) (Metzger & Flanagin, 2013). In addition, debunking misinformation appears to be harder when individuals have thought about their reasons for support of the misinformation or engaged in confirmation bias (Chan et al., 2017).

Sources thought of as mainstream media sources are ranked as more trustworthy than partisan or satirical news sources across the general public, although distrust of mainstream news is higher among conservative audiences in the US (Pennycook & Rand, 2019) and trust of media as a whole is low (Edelman, 2020). Weighing into this, individuals with higher cognitive reflection and greater familiarity of news sources were better able to discern between quality of news source and information (Pennycook & Rand, 2019).

Countering Misinformation and Rumor in Crisis

Challenges in dealing with misinformation and crisis include the correction and countering of misinformation on social media. The study of misinformation has discussed this challenge in terms of the perspectives of the misinformation flow, individual belief and social norms, and trustworthy sources and message content.

Misinformation Flow

First, regarding misinformation flow, scholars have adopted the two-step flow theory to examine how and why individuals spread and stop misinformation (Pang & Ng, 2017; Qin et al., 2015). The opinion climate, the individual's social influence, and costs involved in confirming the information are three factors to impact people's decision-making on spreading or stopping misinformation about crises on social media (Pang & Ng, 2017; Qin et al., 2015). The findings support the two-step flow theory that opinion leaders play a role in stopping the spread of crisis misinformation in public emergencies (Pang & Ng, 2017); however, on social media such as Twitter, crisis misinformation and corrective information may not always flow from opinion leaders (Pang & Ng, 2017). This approach helps researchers understand crisis misinformation flow on social media, but does not consider the influence of emotional tension (e.g., anxiety, fear, worry), media literacy, social factors, and message content on sharing crisis misinformation.

Individual Beliefs and Social Norms

Second, scholars have examined the effect of individual belief and social norms on combating misinformation behavior. For example, a study using the theory of planned behavior (TPB) (i.e., attitude toward combating misinformation behavior, subjective norms, and perceived behavioral control) as well as the norm activation model (i.e., awareness of adverse consequences, ascribed responsibility, and personal norms) examined the formation of social media users' misinformation combating behavior during crises (Zhao et al., 2016). Zhao and colleagues (2016) further operationalized: (1) ***awareness of adverse consequences*** as a signifier for perception of harm stemming from the misinformation, (2) ***ascribed responsibility*** as the perceived responsibility of an entity for any negative consequences resulting from misinformation, and (3) ***personal norms*** as the sense of individuals' obligation to actively combat misinformation during crisis.

Zhao et al.'s (2016) findings showed that awareness of adverse consequences, ascribed responsibility, and personal norms, as well as attitudes toward the behavior, positively correlated to behavioral intentions to combat misinformation on social media. Perceived behavioral control positively predicted actual behavior of combating misinformation on social media (Zhao et al., 2016). This approach helps researchers understand how individual beliefs and social norms impact people's intentions and actual behaviors in combating misinformation on social media; however, questions remain as to how misinformation content on social media impacts people's beliefs and perceived social norms.

Trustworthy Sources and Message Content

Lastly, the trustworthiness of information sources as well as message content has been shown to matter in terms of misinformation spread and correction. This approach focuses on how the features of content of crisis misinformation and corrective strategies for misinformation impact people's accuracy beliefs and preventive actions.

Corrective information—information that directly addresses and corrects the rumor or misinformation—has been recommended as a strategy; however, corrective information as a standalone strategy has received mixed support. For example, a study examining Zika and Yellow Fever misinformation found that corrective information targeting Zika misperceptions not only failed to change inaccurate beliefs, also decreased accurate beliefs that individuals held prior (Carey et al., 2020). While corrective information was slightly more successful for a disease that was less novel and more well-known—Yellow Fever—it still did not increase support for policies or enhance preventive behaviors. Dispute messages to misinformation—or corrective information—have also been shown to possibly strengthen original (and sometimes incorrect) beliefs about environmental issues and simultaneously decrease trust in media (Yang & Overton, 2020). Additionally, exposure to corrective information may cause individuals to lash out at sources sharing the misinformation and at social media platforms as news sources—causing negative effects toward the source, but not lowering agreement with the misinformation (Jang et al., 2019). In addition to debunking (corrective) information, research has also examined pre-bunking information—media literacy training received *in advance of* misinformation—and found this to be more successful than corrective information after the misinformation has spread (Hameleers, 2020).

Other research suggests that the type of corrective information, along with the source, and engaged emotions matter when it comes to addressing misinformation. van der Meer and Jin (2020) argued that the type of source and corrective strategy for misinformation result in different outcomes for perceived severity of public health crises, accuracy of beliefs, and taking preventive actions. van der Meer and Jin (2020) further examined how discrete emotions impact people's decision-making for preventive actions taking, providing evidence that factual elaboration and sources of government agency and news media significantly improved belief accuracy and intention to take protective actions in an infectious disease outbreak scenario (van der Meer, 2020). Results showed that negative emotions (e.g., fear and anxiety) mediated the relationship between corrective misinformation through factual elaboration and individuals' intention to take preventive actions (van der Meer & Jin, 2020). On the other hand, the positive emotion of hope mediated the relationship between corrective information from government agencies or news media and perceptions of health crisis severity (van der Meer & Jin, 2020).

van der Meer and Jin's (2020) approach can help researchers and practitioners to understand how the strategy of correcting misinformation and including credible sources can impact people's beliefs and intentions to take preventive actions in academic and practical ways. Future academic- and practice-based research about misinformation needs to examine different types of corrective strategies with different types of misinformation, such as incomplete, vague, or ambiguous misinformation about crises.

Recommendations for Organizations in Dealing with Misinformation and Rumor

A large question remaining is how businesses and corporations can address misinformation and rumor. Insights from psychology research, health, and political science studies can also be applied here. For organizations and businesses, planning and process can help to address the longer-term issue of rumor and misinformation. A few steps are recommended below, including: building trust, relationships, and reputation in advance; media monitoring, social listening, and assessing issues; planning and communication strategies; and legal action and policy considerations.

Build Trust, Relationships, and Reputation

A big part of the preparation for dealing with misinformation and rumor comes not in thinking about how to deal with the actual false information, but rather the "before work" of building a solid relationship with stakeholders and consumers and engendering trust. As illustrated above, trust is a major theme regarding the spread of misinformation and rumor. As societal inequities expand, trust is low in government, business, non-governmental organization (NGOs), and media (Edelman, 2020). Emotions play a role as fear eclipses hope, but collaboration with other sectors shows potential for increasing trust (Edelman, 2020). For example, businesses that show their focus on ethics and competence can demonstrate how they operate for the good of society by focusing on social issues and working to make broader societal change.

Additionally, reputational history, in particular crisis history, can help to build reputation and trust. Acting ethically in past crises is one way to help build a strong crisis history and demonstrate the character and value of an organization (Coombs, 2007). Connection to concern and commitment to stakeholders, commitment to correcting mistakes, and the organization's core values can help organizations move to renewal after past crises (Ulmer & Sellnow, 2002).

Monitor and Assess

Social listening is a good first step to monitor the conversation surrounding an organization or company, whether in-house or externally sourced (Ferraro, 2019). Having an active and robust social media presence in normal times—and not just times of crisis—is a great start at engaging in dialogue with stakeholders and audiences and listening to how people are talking about an organization. Additionally, monitoring social media, news, and web traffic for company, product, topic, service, and issue mentions and conversation can help organizations to monitor issues and paracrises before they become a full crisis (Coombs & Holladay, 2012). Coombs and Holladay (2012) define paracrises as crisis risks that look like crises, often because they occur online and over social media and receive significant discussion; however, paracrises do not typically warrant a full crisis response from an organization and do not pose significant risk to the organization's reputation or operations. A paracrisis is a crisis risk, however, and should be monitored for potential threat.

Part of this monitoring may include blocking or reporting bad actors on social media platforms, including suspected troll or bot accounts or unknown entities seeking to sow disinformation. For example, after Broadcom announced an acquisition of CA Technologies in 2018, a fake memorandum circulated saying that the Defense Department would review the acquisition (Horowitz, 2018). When the memo was announced as forgery, stock shares fell, and at a time when investors were more attentively weighing investing in the merger (Ferraro, 2019). Proactively reporting bad actors on social media can help to limit the spread and sharing of some misinformation, although not eradicating it entirely.

Prepare and Communicate

Based on knowledge from issues monitoring, organizations can benefit from preparing for response to likely misinformation and rumor, including thinking about how they would respond to a variety of different types of misinformation and rumor they are likely to encounter (Ferraro, 2019). In terms of messaging characteristics, organizations should think about the end goal of communication beyond debunking the rumor alone, including a focus on organizational identity and values, if appropriate.

As shown above, corrective information alone is not always enough to debunk a rumor or misinformation; however, directly addressing a minor rumor may be enough to stop the spread. For example, false ads were created for Starbucks in 2017 in an attempt to lure undocumented Americans to Starbucks on a set day, claiming to offer a promotion for "Dreamer Day" (see Yakowicz, 2017). Starbucks responded directly to accounts sharing this information, asking them to stop spreading misinformation (see Starbucks, 2017).

In polarizing issues, messages can seek to reduce the aspects of correcting information that threaten one's worldview or find ways to simultaneously affirm worldview, as this is often why a rumor or piece of misinformation is more widely spread or acted upon (Lewandowsky et al., 2012). This requires communicators to evaluate and try to understand the worldview of those sharing misinformation and why this misinformation speaks to a gratifying need for them. Additionally, messaging should be simple and clear—and easier to remember than the misinformation, if possible, but that also fills any gaps in explanations that may be left behind by the alternate story (Lewandowsky et al., 2012); repetition of this simple, clear counter communication is also key, as misinformation has a way of sticking around and repetition will help to solidify the counter communication.

Practitioners also caution against overreacting to rumor and misinformation, as sometimes recognizing rumor in a big way may suggest validation of the rumor and draw more attention to it (Crawford, 1999). Starbucks' response above shows a direct and simple way to address misinformation and rumor that is not yet widespread.

Additionally, addressing the misinformation on the platform where it happens is important, as the Starbucks example also illustrates. A press release on a company's news site may not be read by users sharing information on a social media platform; however, a press release linked to a social media post—or better yet an actual social media post—may be.

Legal Action and Policy Considerations

A more drastic and final measure for dealing with misinformation is litigation or policy actions. Where legal issues are at play, such as in cases or defamation, libel, deceptive trade practices, or violation of intellectual property law, organizations may have a case for litigation (Golston, 2019). Litigation can be a lengthy and expensive process, and companies and organizations will need to think carefully about whether to venture here—or if they can, as misinformation and rumor may be protected by free speech laws, if it does not fit into the categories above (Ferraro, 2019).

Policy considerations may be another avenue for organizations, particularly for issues with longstanding rumor problems, as these policy changes can take time to advocate for. The policies of social media companies that allow misinformation and rumor to be shared represent one arena of policy consideration. As an example from the health realm, social media organizations have been more proactively monitoring vaccine misinformation. In academic research, Guidry et al. (2015) found that sites like Pinterest were sharing anti-vaccine information and conspiracy theories, and that most posts on the platform were related to negative mentions of vaccines. User searches for vaccine images mostly returned anti-vaccine messages and images. A profile of this research highlighted that these anti-vaccine posts were "going under the radar" on Pinterest (van Hilten, 2016). Likewise, reports surfaced indicating that Facebook and YouTube were helping the anti-vaxxer movement to "go viral" (Moon, 2019) and California Representative Adam Schiff condemned large social media companies for helping perpetuate this movement.

In response to these calls, Pinterest took an unprecedented step. While other social media giants were considering removing anti-vaccine posts from their platforms, Pinterest made a bold action that went one step further. In response, Pinterest first banned all vaccine content from its platform but later shifted to allow content from public health organizations, including governmental organizations; users who searched for vaccine information on Pinterest would receive official information from public health organizations only (Rutschman, 2019). Facebook took steps to remove anti-vaccine advertising and changed the ranking and recommendation of anti-vaccine information, although this information was not banned (Rutschman, 2019). YouTube, similarly, did not allow advertising on channels with anti-vaccine content and changed the filtering so anti-vaccine information was not presented in top search results, as it previously had been (Rutschman, 2019).

Recommendations for Further Research

Recommendations are made below for future scholarly and practice-based research on the spread of misinformation and rumor, as well as correcting and combating misinformation.

Future Research on the Spread of Misinformation

Building from the scholarship and practical examples shared in this chapter, a framework for characterizing and typologizing misinformation is suggested. To more comprehensively examine sharing of misinformation and rumor, future research is recommended to collect data on: (1) sources of misinformation by platform type (i.e., news, social media platform, blog, forum, etc.), format (e.g., video, photo, link, etc.), location, and influence of those sources (i.e., number of followers, influence score), (2) topics of misinformation (e.g., common misinformation shared for each crisis case), (3) features of misinformation content (e.g., emotional appeals, false legitimacy, worldview alignment, Joyce, 2016; and self-confirmation/ consistency, endorsement, prior reputation, Metzger & Flanagin, 2013), and (4) types of information disorder (e.g., misinformation, disinformation, malinformation; Wardle & Derekhshan, 2017). Attempts should be made to identify bots or fake accounts to assess their influence.

The misinformation characteristics above should be considered in combination with outcomes, including metrics to capture processing and sharing of misinformation (e.g., impressions, likes, and shares), in addition to analysis of the conversation trends on social media. Results from this examination can be used to examine relationships between sources, topics, characteristics, and types of misinformation to identify influential factors in the development and spread of misinformation.

Future Research on Correcting and Combating Misinformation

While Coombs (2014) has suggested denial is the recommended strategy for misinformation crises, future research is recommended to examine specific response strategies based on the characterization of the misinformation, as defined above. Survey and experimental research is recommended to examine how trust in source, relational and reputational history, characteristics of the corrective information (e.g., clarity and simplicity, worldview alignment), repetition, individual beliefs, social norms, and information flow all work together to aid in effectively combating misinformation and offering corrective information.

Key Takeaways

Promising research suggests that sharing of misinformation on some social media platforms, such as Facebook, has gone down from its peak due to measures the platforms have taken to limit the spread of misinformation and rumor (Allcott et al., 2019). However, the sharing of misinformation on Twitter has been shown to be still on the rise (Allcott et al., 2019); clearly more work is needed to be done here in this arena. And as, at this writing, the US enters an election year (i.e., 2020) with COVID-19 still in outbreak, social media companies are grappling with how to deal with the spread of misinformation; rumor and misinformation that interferes with a fair and informed election is where some social media companies are choosing to draw the line (Barrett, 2020), although social media companies have long said they do not wish to police information shared and be the arbiters of truth.

This chapter offers some promising ways forward in terms of scholarly and practitioner research and guidelines for organizations and businesses to think about when addressing and correcting misinformation, and long before, as they plan and prepare for the possibility of rumor and misinformation. As research and literature suggest, there is no easy fix for correcting misinformation, and periods of social tension, uncertainty, and ambiguity will likely only further the potential for rumor. Better understanding why misinformation is likely to spread, and how to make corrective information more likely to also spread and be effective, is one step forward to addressing a large issue for scholarship and practice.

References

Allcott, H., Gentzkow, M., & Yu, C. (2019). Trends in the diffusion of misinformation on social media. *Research & Politics*, *6*(2). https://doi.org/10.1177/2053168019848554

Allport, G. W., & Postman, L. (1947). *The psychology of rumor*. Russell & Russell.

Anderson, J., & Rainie, L. (2017, Oct.). The future of truth and misinformation online. *Pew Research Center*. http://www.pewinternet.org/2017/10/19/the-future-of-truth-and-misinformation-online

Anthony, S. (1973). Anxiety and rumor. *The Journal of Social Psychology*, *89*(1), 91–98. https://doi.org/10.1080/00224545.1973.9922572

Atkinson, C. (2019, April 25). Fake news can cause "irreversible damage" to companies—and sink their stock price. *NBC Business News*. https://www.nbcnews.com/business/business-news/fake-news-can-cause-irreversible-damage-companies-sink-their-stock-n995436

Barrett, B. (2020, May 28). COVID-19 shows how hard it will be for Facebook and Twitter to crack down on voting misinformation. *Slate Magazine*. https://slate.com/technology/2020/05/twitter-facebook-trump-election-misinformation-coronavirus.html

Berinsky, A. J. (2017). Rumors and health care reform: Experiments in political misinformation. *British Journal of Political Science*, *47*(2), 241–262. https://doi.org/10.1017/S0007123415000186

Bode, L., & Vraga, E. K. (2015). In related news, that was wrong: The correction of misinformation through related stories functionality in social media. *Journal of Communication*, *65*(4), 619–638. https://doi.org/10.1111/jcom.12166

Bordia, P. (1996). *Rumor interaction patterns on computer-mediated communication networks*. Unpublished PhD dissertation, Temple University.

Bordia, P., & DiFonzo, N. (2004). Problem solving in social interactions on the internet: Rumor as social cognition. *Social Psychology Quarterly*, *67*(1), 33–49. https://doi.org/10.1177%2F019027250406700105

Bordia, P., DiFonzo, N., & Chang, A. (1999). Rumor as group problem solving: Development patterns in informal computer-mediated groups. *Small Group Research*, *30*(1), 8–28. https://doi.org/10.1177/104649649903000102

Carey, J. M., Chi, V., Flynn, D. J., Nyhan, B., & Zeitzoff, T. (2020). The effects of corrective information about disease epidemics and outbreaks: Evidence from Zika and Yellow Fever in Brazil. *Science Advances*, *6*(5), eaaw7449. https://doi.org/10.1126/sciadv.aaw7449

Chan, M. S., Jones, C. R, Jamieson, K. H., & Albarracín, D. (2017). Debunking: A meta-analysis of the psychological efficacy of messages countering mis-information. *Psychological Science*, *11*, 1531–1546. https://doi.org/10.1177/0956797617714579

Coombs, T. (2014). State of crisis communication: Evidence and the bleeding edge. *Research Journal of the Institute for Public Relations, 1*(1). https://instituteforpr.org/wp-content/uploads/CoombsFinalWES.pdf

Coombs, W. T. (2007). Protecting organization reputations during a crisis: The development and application of situational crisis communication theory. *Corporate Reputation Review, 10*(3), 163–176. https://doi.org/10.1057/palgrave.crr.1550049

Coombs, W. T., & Holladay, J. S. (2012). The paracrisis: The challenges created by publicly managing crisis prevention. *Public Relations Review, 38*(3), 408–415. https://doi.org/10.1016/j.pubrev.2012.04.004

Crawford, A. P. (1999). When those nasty rumors start breeding on the Web, you've got to move fast. *Public Relations Quarterly, 44*(4), 43–45. https://search.proquest.com/docview/222449127?pq-origsite=gscholar

DiFonzo, N., & Bordia, P. (2007). *Rumor psychology: Social and organizational approaches*. American Psychological Association.

DiFonzo, N., & Bordia, P. (2007). Rumor, gossip and urban legends. *Diogenes, 54*(1), 19–35. https://doi.org/10.1177/0392192107073433

Edelman. (2020, January 19). *2020 Edelman trust barometer*. https://www.edelman.com/trustbarometer

Egelhofer, J. L., & Lecheler, S. (2019). Fake news as a two-dimensional phenomenon: A framework and research agenda. *Annals of the International Communication Association, 43*(2), 97–116. https://doi.org/10.1080/23808985.2019.1602782

Ferraro, M. F. (2019, June 10). Perspectives: Disinformation is harming businesses. Here are 6 ways to fight it. *CNN Business*. https://www.cnn.com/2019/06/10/perspectives/disinformation-business/index.html

Fine, G. A., & Ellis, B. (2010). *The global grapevine: Why rumors of terrorism, immigration, and trade matter*. Oxford University Press.

Golston, P. (2019, January 17). Target of disinformation. *Brunswick Review: The Crisis Issue*. https://www.brunswickgroup.com/crisis-cyber-fake-news-i9290/

Guidry, J. P. D., Carlyle, K., Messner, M., & Jin, Y. (2015). On pins and needles: How vaccines are portrayed on Pinterest. *Vaccine, 33*(39), 5051–5056. https://doi.org/10.1016/j.vaccine.2015.08.064

Hameleers, M. (2020). Separating truth from lies: Comparing the effects of news media literacy interventions and fact-checkers in response to political misinformation in the US and Netherlands. *Information, Communication & Society*, 1–17. https://doi.org/10.1080/1369118X.2020.1764603

Hindman, M., & Barash, V. (2018). *Disinformation, "fake news" and influence campaigns on Twitter*. Knight Foundation. https://knightfoundation.org/reports/disinformation-fake-news-and-influence-campaigns-on-twitter/

Horowitz, H. (2018, October 10). Broadcom: Letter calling for review of its CA technologies merger is fake. *CNN*. https://www.cnn.com/2018/10/10/tech/broadcom-ca-technologies-cfius/index.html

Jang, J.-W., Lee, E.-J., & Shin, S. Y. (2019). What debunking of misinformation does and doesn't. *Cyberpsychology, Behavior and Social Networking, 22*(6), 423–427. https://doi.org/10.1089/cyber.2018.0608

Joyce, E. (2016, August). The prevalence of fake news and how misinformation spreads. *Brandwatch*. https://www.brandwatch.com/blog/react-the-prevalence-of-fake-news-and-why-we-are-more-misinformed-than-ever

Karlova, N., & Fisher, K. (2013). A social diffusion model of misinformation and disinformation for understanding human information behaviour. *Information Research, 18*(1), paper 573. http://InformationR.net/ir/18-1/paper573.html

Karlova, N., & Lee, J. (2011). Notes from the underground city of disinformation: A conceptual investigation. *Proceedings of the Association for Information Science and Technology, 48*(1), 1–9. https://doi.org/10.1002/meet.2011.14504801133

Kätsyri, J., Kinnunen, T., Kusumoto, K., Oittinen, P., & Ravaja, N. (2016). Negativity bias in media multitasking: The effects of negative social media messages on attention to television news broadcasts. *PLOS ONE, 11*(5), e0153712. https://doi.org/10.1371/journal.pone.0153712

Knapp, R. H. (1944). A psychology of rumor. *The Public Opinion Quarterly, 8*(1), 22–37. https://doi.org/10.1086/265665

Lewandowsky, S., Ecker, U. K. H., & Cook, J. (2017). Beyond misinformation: Understanding and coping with the "post-truth" era. *Journal of Applied Research in Memory and Cognition, 6*(4), 353–369. https://doi.org/10.1016/j.jarmac.2017.07.008

Lewandowsky, S., Ecker, U. K. H., Seifert, C. M., Schwarz, N., & Cook, J. (2012). Misinformation and its correction: Continued influence and successful debiasing. *Psychological Science in the Public Interest, 13*(3), 106–131. https://doi.org/10.1177/1529100612451018

Marwick, A. (2018). Why do people share fake news? A sociotechnical model of media effects. *Georgetown Law Technology Review, 2*(2), 474–511. https://georgetownlawtechreview.org/why-do-people-share-fake-news-a-sociotechnical-model-of-media-effects/GLTR-07-2018/

McCorkindale, T. (2019). *IPR disinformation in society report: How Americans perceive deliberately misleading news or information.* Institute for Public Relations. https://instituteforpr.org/wp-content/uploads/Disinformation_Study_IPR-6-18-1014.pdf

Metzger, M., & Flanagin, A. J. (2013). Credibility and trust of information in online environments: The use of cognitive heuristics. *Journal of Pragmatics, 59*, 210–220. https://doi.org/10.1016/j.pragma.2013.07.012

Mitchell, A., Gottfried, J., Stocking, G., Walker, M., & Fedeli, S. (2019, June 5). Many Americans say made-up news is a critical problem that needs to be fixed. *Pew Research Center's Journalism Project.* https://www.journalism.org/2019/06/05/many-americans-say-made-up-news-is-a-critical-problem-that-needs-to-be-fixed/

Moon, E. (2019, February 19). How Facebook helped the anti-vaxxer movement go viral. *Pacific Standard.* https://psmag.com/news/how-facebook-helped-the-anti-vaxxer-movement-go-viral

Morin, E. (1971). *Rumor in Orleans.* Pantheon Books.

Oh, O., Agrawal, M., & Rao, H. R. (2013). Community intelligence and social media services: A rumor theoretic analysis of tweets during social crises. *MIS Quarterly, 37*(2), 407–426. https://doi.org/10.25300/MISQ/2013/37.2.05

Oh, O., Kwon, K. H., & Rao, H. R. (2010). An exploration of social media in extreme events: Rumor theory and Twitter during the Haiti Earthquake 2010. *ICIS 2010 Proceedings—Thirty First International Conference on Information Systems, 231*, 7332–7336. https://aisel.aisnet.org/icis2010_submissions/231/

Pang, N., & Ng, J. (2017). Misinformation in a riot: A two-step flow view. *Online Information Review, 41*(4), 438–453. https://doi.org/10.1108/OIR-09-2015-0297

Pennycook, G., & Rand, D. G. (2019). Fighting misinformation on social media using crowdsourced judgments of news source quality. *Proceedings of the National Academy of Sciences of the United States of America, 116*(7), 2521–2526. https://doi.org/10.1073/pnas.1806781116

Qin, Z., Cai, J., & Wangchen, H. Z. (2015). How rumors spread and stop over social media: A multi-layered communication model and empirical analysis.

Communications of the Association for Information Systems, 36(20), 369–391. https://doi.org/10.17705/1CAIS.03620

Rosnow, R. L. (1980). Psychology of rumor reconsidered. *Psychological Bulletin, 87*(3), 578–591. https://doi.org/10.1037/0033-2909.87.3.578

Rosnow, R. L. (1988). Rumor as communication: A contextualist approach. *Journal of Communication, 38*(1), 12–28. https://doi.org/10.1111/j.1460-2466.1988.tb02033.x

Ruokolainen, H., & Widén, G. (2020). Conceptualising misinformation in the context of asylum seekers. *Information Processing & Management, 57*(3). Advance online publication. https://doi.org/10.1016/j.ipm.2019.102127

Rutschman, A. S. (2019, September 18). Malicious bots and trolls spread vaccine misinformation—now social media companies are fighting back. *The Conversation.* http://theconversation.com/malicious-bots-and-trolls-spread-vaccine-misinformation-now-social-media-companies-are-fighting-back-123430

Shibutani, T. (1966). *Improvised news: A sociological study of rumor.* Bobbs-Merrill Company.

Shin, J., Jian, L., Driscoll, K., & Bar, F. (2018). The diffusion of misinformation on social media: Temporal pattern, message, and source. *Computers in Human Behavior, 83*, 278–287. https://doi.org/10.1016/j.chb.2018.02.008

Southwell, B. G., Thorson, E. A., & Sheble, L. (2018). Misinformation among mass audiences as a focus for inquiry. In B. G. Southwell, E. A. Thorson, & L. Sheble (Eds.), *Misinformation and mass audiences* (pp. 1–14). University of Texas Press.

Starbucks Coffee [@Starbucks]. (2017, August 4). *This is completely false. Starbucks is not sponsoring any such event. Please do not spread misinformation.* [Tweet]. Twitter. https://twitter.com/Starbucks/status/893597346436571136

Tsugawa, S., & Ohsaki, H. (2015). Negative messages spread rapidly and widely on social media. *Proceedings of the 2015 ACM on Conference on Online Social Networks*, 151–160. https://doi.org/10.1145/2817946.2817962

Ulmer, R. R., & Sellnow, T. L. (2002). Crisis management and the discourse of renewal: Understanding the potential for positive outcomes of crisis. *Public Relations Review, 28*(4), 361–365. https://doi.org/10.1016/S0363-8111(02)00165-0

van der Meer, T. G., & Jin, Y. (2020). Seeking formula for misinformation treatment in public health crises: The effects of corrective information type and source. *Health Communication, 35*(5), 560–575. https://doi.org/10.1080/10410236.2019.1573295

van Hilten, L. G. (2016). Anti-vaccine posts are going "under the radar" on Pinterest. *Elsevier Connect.* https://www.elsevier.com/connect/anti-vaccine-posts-are-going-under-the-radar-on-pinterest

Wang, Y., McKee, M., Torbica, A., & Stuckler, D. (2019). Systematic literature review on the spread of health-related misinformation on social media. *Social Science & Medicine (1982), 240*, 112552. https://doi.org/10.1016/j.socscimed.2019.112552

Wardle, C., & Derekshan, H. (2017, September). Information disorder: Toward an interdisciplinary framework for research and policy making, *Council of Europe Report*, F-67075 Strasbourg Cedex. https://rm.coe.int/information-disorder-toward-an-interdisciplinary-framework-for-researc/168076277c

Yakowicz, W. (2017, August 8). Fake Starbucks ad tries to lure the undocumented with discounted coffee. *Inc.Com.* https://www.inc.com/will-yakowicz/fake-starbucks-dreamer-day-4chan-meme.html

Yang, F., & Overton, H. (2020, May 28). *Understanding corporate misinformation and the spread of environmental issues on social media.* Arthur W. Page Center for Integrity in Public Communication. https://www.bellisario.psu.edu/page-center/article/understanding-corporate-misinformation-and-the-spread-of-environmental-issu

Young, V. A. (2020, May). *Nearly half of the Twitter accounts discussing 'reopening America' may be bots: CMU researchers say sophisticated, orchestrated bot campaigns aim to sow divide.* Carnegie Mellon University. https://www.scs.cmu.edu/news/nearly-half-twitter-accounts-discussing-%E2%80%98reopening-america%E2%80%99-may-be-bots

Zhao, L., Yin, J., & Song, Y. (2016). An exploration of rumor combating behavior on social media in the context of social crises. *Computers in Human Behavior, 58*, 25–36. https://doi.org/10.1016/j.chb.2015.11.054

9 Technology and Social Media

Challenges and Opportunities for Effective Crisis and Risk Communication

Deanna D. Sellnow, Lucinda Austin, and Ciro Dias Reis

"We don't have a choice on whether we do social media, the question is how well do we do it." This quotation by Erik Qualman, award-winning speaker and author of the bestselling book, *Socialnomics: How social media transforms the way we live and do business* (2009), reminds us just how firmly embedded technology and social media have become in the fabric of the daily lives of individuals and organizations worldwide. Digital media can no longer be dismissed as a fad that will soon disappear. Rather, technology and social media are integral parts of the global society(s) in which we live and work. Given this reality, it is almost unfathomable to realize how relatively short-lived its history is. In fact, the World Wide Web, which is what made the Internet accessible to general publics, was not available until the early 1990s and the first social networking websites did not come to be until the 21st century (e.g., Facebook, 2006; Myspace, 2003). Today, we have access to a plethora of information, products, and services via Google, Amazon, YouTube, WeChat, Instagram, Twitter, LinkedIn, WhatsApp, Snapchat, and Reddit, among others.

Although Internet technology and social media have been around for a relatively short time, research shows that more and more people are using these resources to stay connected and to track information during periods of crisis and risk (Anderson & Vogels, 2020). Even in its infancy, Facebook was such a source for end users during the Virginia Tech mass shooter crisis event in 2007 (e.g., Tyma, 2008; Tyma et al., 2010). In 2009, government agencies began using Twitter to respond to global pandemics (Smith, 2009). Since then, a variety of online media sources have provided rich data sets for myriad crisis communication studies focused on, for example, health pandemics, natural disasters, food security, chemical spills, agricultural biosecurity, and terrorist attacks (e.g., Burke et al., 2010; Lachlan et al., 2014; Liu & Kim, 2011; Liu et al., 2018; Sellnow-Richmond et al., 2018; Spence et al., 2008; Sutton et al., 2015;).

With the proliferation of smartphones, technology and social media use is growing exponentially around the world—not only in personal and family relationships—but also by individuals and organizations in times of risk and crisis (Niles et al., 2019). To clarify, according to a Pew Research Center survey conducted in March 2020, 93% of US adults believe interruptions in Internet or cell phone service are problematic. Moreover, 76% reported using email or social media to communicate with others and 70% searched online for information during the height of the COVID-19 global pandemic (Pew Research Center, 2020). Clearly, given the increase in 24/7 accessibility via smartphones, the role of technology and social media for communicating during crisis and risk events warrants investigation.

In this chapter, we explore some of the opportunities and challenges technology and social media present for communication before, during, and after crisis events. We frame our discussion around such affordances presented by smartphones, social media, artificial intelligence, and the Internet of Things, although we acknowledge that they are not mutually exclusive (e.g., users may access social media through smartphones and the Internet of Things may send messages to vulnerable populations through mobile messaging on smartphones). To develop our argument, we present a sampling of research done to date and point to suggestions for future exploration as a means to develop best practices for risk and crisis communication as we navigate our way through what Qualman (2009) describes as a "far-reaching revolution . . . driven by people and enabled by [technology] and social media" (p. xvii).

Opportunities and Challenges

The following paragraphs focus on four prevalent technological affordances: smartphones, social media, artificial intelligence, and the Internet of Things. We illustrate opportunities as well as challenges to address when communicating during risk situations and crisis events. Although we focus on myriad examples, we also highlight the critical role technology and social media are playing during the global COVID-19 pandemic. In doing so, we hope to incite curiosity for future research and applications.

Smartphones

Smartphones include any mobile phone or device (e.g., Apple watch) that goes beyond voice calls and text messaging to also afford users access to apps, the internet, and social media, as well as the ability to take photos and make audio and video recordings. In fact, reports reveal that there are more than three billion smartphone users worldwide today (O'Dea, 2020). Moreover, the proliferation of smartphones has actually given rise to a new psychological disorder—nomophobia—that describes the fear associated with not having access to one's smartphone (Bhattacharya et al., 2019). Most recently, since the outbreak of Coronavirus, two new words are being added to the Merriam Webster dictionary. These are doomscrolling and doomsurfing to refer to "tendency to continue to surf or scroll through bad news . . . without the ability to stop or step back" (Merriam-Webster, n.d.). Some of the opportunities and challenges for risk and crisis communication transpired by smartphones center around issues of access to information and alerts/warnings.

Smartphone users have instant access to a plethora of information anytime and anywhere. Thus, smartphone technology can afford large populations worldwide the opportunity to access risk and crisis messages across time and space (González-Ibánez et al., 2012). Conversely, since the three billion users represent less than half of the world population (approximately eight billion), it follows that a good number of people also do not have access to information via these devices. As such, smartphone technology poses both a challenge and an opportunity for risk and crisis communication spokespersons. As Sellnow and Sellnow (2019) clarify, "if an impacted person or group does not have access" to a smartphone, they will not have access to messages delivered via text message or app (p. 72). Thus, one cannot assume that messages distributed via smartphones will reach all people impacted during a risk or crisis event. Farmers living in the Bududa District in Uganda, for example, which is prone to deadly mudslides, may be alerted more effectively via warning drums than a smartphone app (Mushengyezi, 2003).

Nevertheless, the utility of smartphone technology has been demonstrated for alerts and warning messages. For example, Sutton et al. (2015) examined the use of terse messages to warn publics during life-threatening floods in Boulder, Colorado. Others have examined SMS texts to alert those in harm's way of a variety of natural disasters, including, for example, earthquakes, forest fires, tornados, and hurricanes (e.g., Drost et al., 2016; Sherman-Morris, 2010; Wald & Eerie, 2020). Based on multiple research studies, similar wireless emergency alerts (WEAs) are also used to communicate during mass shootings on college and university campuses, to report child abductions in real time and space, and even to impart breaking news reports during crisis events (Liu et al., 2017).

One major challenge to overcome is the short response time often allotted to take appropriate actions for self-protection or to mitigate harm (Hermann, 1963; Seeger et al., 2003). The internalization, distribution, explanation, and action (IDEA) model is a method for developing effective instructional risk and crisis messages (Sellnow & Sellnow, 2019) that can be delivered on a smartphone app when response time is 10 seconds or less (Sellnow et al., 2019a). IDEA is an acronym for recalling required message elements quickly and easily during times of crisis (see Figure 9.1). The "I" stands for internalization. The goal here is to motivate receivers to attend to the message by demonstrating relevance and personal impact. In the case of earthquake early warning (EEW) messages, this can be achieved via timeliness (e.g., a countdown to impact), proximity (e.g., map), and intensity (e.g., shaking level) (see Figure 9.2). The "D" stands for distribution channel (e.g., alert on a smartphone app). The "E" stands for explanation, that is, what is happening (e.g., "very strong shaking"), and the "A" stands for specific action steps to take. In the case of EEW on a smartphone app, users should get down under a table to protect themselves from falling debris and hold on to remain steady during the strong shaking (i.e., "drop/cover/hold on").

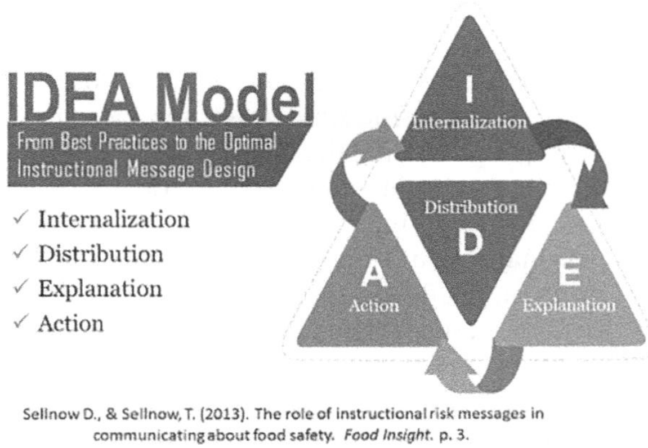

Figure 9.1 IDEA Model (Sellnow & Sellnow, 2019).

Figure 9.2 Earthquake Early Warning (EEW) IDEA App Message.

More recently, smartphones were used to track movement and interactions among people during the COVID-19 global health pandemic in an attempt to stem the spread of the novel coronavirus that was claiming the lives of hundreds of thousands of people worldwide (Roser et al., 2020). In São Paulo, Brazil, for example, the state government used smartphones to monitor obedience of people during the quarantine (see Figure 9.3).

Smartphone movement tracking and contract tracing—which were used in many countries, such as China, Singapore, South Korea, the UK, the US, Italy, Israel, Germany, and Austria—raise concerns about privacy and cybersecurity (Doffman, 2020). Certainly, more research is warranted regarding communication best practices for implementing smartphone location tracking and tracing during major crisis events, particularly when those events reach across the globe and impact many people in significant ways.

With these challenges in mind, however, smartphones remain a prominent device for communicating risk, particularly during the acute stage of crisis events. Thus, future research ought to continue to examine how to use them most effectively for seeking and sharing information, tracking and tracing movement and interactions, distributing alerts and warnings, and instructing disparate publics.

Social Media

Social media are interactive Web 2.0 Internet platforms that afford users the ability to create and share ideas, information, and experiences among virtual communities (Obar & Wildman, 2015). Some of the most popular social media platforms today include Facebook, Twitter, Instagram, and YouTube. Opportunities and challenges for risk and crisis communication posed by social media focus on, for example, information seeking and sharing, as well as both instructional and interpersonal communication.

With regard to information seeking, surveys reveal that most Americans seek news information through social media (Barthel, 2019). They tend to do so even more regularly during crisis events (Austin et al., 2012). Moreover, most do not rely on one singular source when seeking information during crises but rather seek convergence among information drawn from a variety of sources (e.g., Anthony & Sellnow, 2016; Austin et al., 2012; Getchell & Sellnow, 2016; Sellnow et al., 2019c Spence et al., 2008). This is good news given the challenges posed by competing narratives, fake news, misinformation, disinformation, and mal-information often also distributed over social media.

More specifically, research on crisis and disasters shows social media are used by individuals during crises to receive timely updates (e.g., Caplan et al., 2007), to seek unfiltered information (e.g., Liu et al., 2013), to collect preparedness information/instructions (e.g., Houston et al., 2015), to confirm information clarity (e.g., Liu et al., 2013), to discover convergence among sources (e.g., Sellnow et al., 2019), to information check (e.g., Spence et al., 2016), and to take action and mobilize (e.g., Sellnow & Sellnow, 2019). During

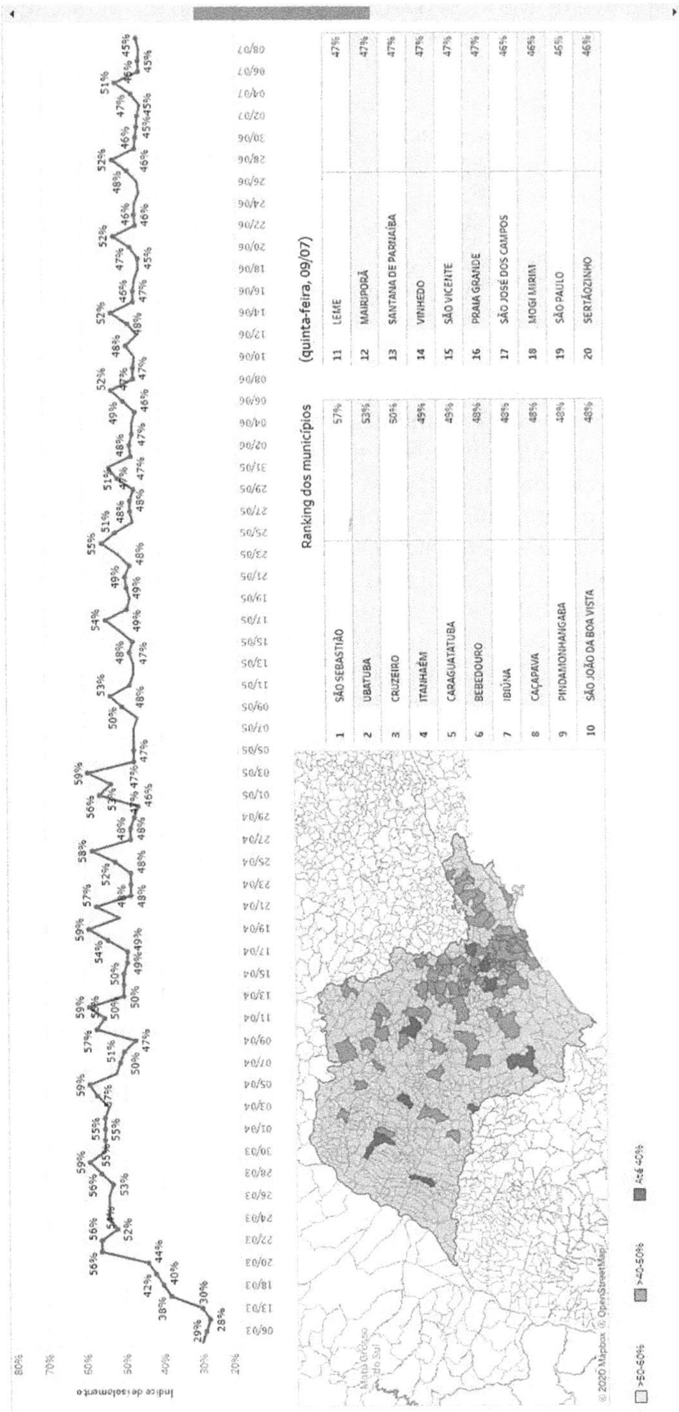

Figure 9.3 Histórico do índice de isolamento [Translation: Isolation Index Series].
Source: saopaulo.sp.gov.br/coronavirus/isolamento/.

lockdowns spurred by the COVID-19 pandemic, social media became a critical means to engage with friends and loved ones, to attend professional meetings, to visit the doctor, to purchase groceries and other supplies, and to teach school. However, some research is beginning to illustrate mental health consequences from so much exposure during a crisis lockdown, such as depression and anxiety (e.g., Dalton et al., 2020; Gao et al., 2020).

Research also reveals that people use social media to communicate among global professional partners and networks and in interpersonal relationships during times of risk and crisis. For instance, social media has been examined as it is used to communicate globally among Communities of Practice (Sellnow et al., 2017), to check in with friends and family (e.g., Fraustino et al., 2017) to build a sense of community (e.g., Houston et al., 2015), to provide humor and levity (Sellnow-Richmond & Sellnow, 2020), and to seek emotional support and healing (e.g., Fraustino et al., 2017).

One area of crisis communication study that emerged with the inception of social media is citizen journalism (a.k.a. participatory journalism), which is essentially when people not trained as journalists use social media platforms to record and distribute news reports (Min, 2016). For more than a decade, citizen journalism has played an increasingly prominent role in crisis and risk communication and poses important opportunities for ongoing research (Allan, 2013; Allan & Thorsen, 2009). Researchers have studied, for example, citizen journalism in crises ranging from mass shootings and terrorist attacks (e.g., Loke & Grimm, 2017) to natural disasters (e.g., Bruns & Burgess, 2014) to what many call "fake news" (e.g., Mayorga et al., 2020; Sellnow et al., 2019; Wall, 2018). Although some research does exist, the growth in citizen journalism, accelerated by "technological convergence and the development of an interactive media environment" (Mythen, 2010, p. 45), is an underdeveloped area of risk and crisis communication research (Carr et al., 2014).

One avenue for future research, for example, is building theory around the dynamic relationships between and among journalists as citizens and citizen journalists during crisis events (e.g., Allan & Peters, 2015). Others include developing frameworks for identifying fake online news stories (e.g., Choy & Chong, 2018; Lee, 2018) and crafting strategies for refuting them (e.g., Ewing & Lambert, 2019; Vafeiadis et al., 2019). The arrest of William Bryan, Jr., for "felony murder and criminal attempt to commit false imprisonment" because he filmed the shooting of Ahmaud Arbery while jogging points to another fruitful area of research for those studying citizen journalism in risk and crisis events (Brice-Saddler, 2020, para. 1). Citizen journalism also helped incite a plethora of Black Lives Matter and police brutality protests around the US and internationally (Dalton et al., 2020). The role of citizen journalism in social movements is certainly another ripe area for future research.

Social media has also been examined as it functions in both personal and professional relationships. However, there is room for myriad research in the future, which was exposed brilliantly during the COVID-19 global pandemic. Professionally, much could be studied about working remotely in telemedicine and education. Similarly, the use of social media to conduct daily personal operations, such as grocery shopping perceptions and interactions among essential workers and consumers. Without doubt, social media was used in these and other ways to manage health and safety during the pandemic; however, little to no empirical research exists to date regarding how they function or the influence they may have on crisis management, food insecurity, health disparities, emotional and economic well-being, etc.

Clearly, social media can be used in myriad positive ways, ranging from information-seeking/-sharing to personal/professional relationships. However, research also points to how these same platforms can be used to distort information (e.g., Shu et al., 2020), spread wrong information (e.g., Coombs & Holladay, 2012), and cause harm to individuals and groups (e.g., Ulmer et al., 2017). With the ever-increasing number of mega-crises and global pandemics occurring across national borders, so too will the power of social media increase. As such, ongoing research on how social media functions and the responsibilities of communicators that use it during times of risk and crisis is imperative.

Artificial Intelligence

Artificial intelligence (AI) refers to machines (i.e., computers) that mimic cognitive functions of the human mind (Russell & Norvig, 2009). As Westerman et al. (2020) note, the study of AI focuses on the "artificiality of the machine and how the machine may appear more human. However, what if we are the 'artificial' part of this equation? At the very least, we sometimes interact in a way that is not really 'human'" (p. 10). Humans also follow scripts, routines, and respond in a default manner to certain cues. AI technology is evolving to likewise follow some of these same scripts and schema to better match human behavior (Westerman et al., 2020). AI poses a number of potentially fruitful opportunities and challenges for risk and crisis communication research.

A key question at play with AI-mediated communication is whether people would trust AI in communication interactions. Authors Jakesch et al. (2019) conducted a multi-part study examining AI and perceptions of trustworthiness using Airbnb profiles as a test. Participants did not know whether the communicator was AI or human. Interestingly, AI was trusted more when it was not interspersed with human communication. However, although participants did not know the source (AI or human), they expressed distrust when they believed a profile to be created by AI (Jakesch et al., 2019). Trust and credibility have long been recognized as central to best practices guidelines for risk and crisis communicators (Seeger, 2006). It follows that research ought to explore perceptions and attitudes various publics may have on AI in risk and crisis situations. One model that could prove useful for such examinations is the Technology Acceptance Model (TAM), which is used to explain how individuals accept and use various technologies (Davis, 1989; Davis et al., 1989).

Additional areas for concern with AI in crisis include misinformation and misrepresentation, transparency, and bias and fairness (Hancock et al., 2020). As AI advances, the potential to use automated methods to spread misinformation increases. For example, researchers at Carnegie Mellon estimate that half of all accounts on Twitter sharing information about COVID-19 are automated bot accounts with their origin still unknown (Allyn, 2020). As bad actors create coordinated campaigns on social media using AI, the potential for paracrises via social media misinformation and rumor also grows (Coombs & Holladay, 2012).

Regarding transparency, AI may not identify itself to users or show full transparency (Hancock et al., 2020). Google Assistant was criticized for sounding too human by including "um" and "uh" and other human vocal patterns to mimic human communication; users expressed that AI should be transparent as such and not feign to be human (Wamsley, 2018). Regarding Google Assistant's language sophistication, Tufecki, a UNC professor studying technology and social movements, expressed, "As digital technologies become better at doing human things, the focus has to be on how to protect humans, how to delineate humans and machines, and how to create reliable signals of each" (Wamsley, 2018).

Virtual reality (VR) computer simulations offer life-saving opportunities as they can be used to encourage risk reduction and preparedness by affording users an opportunity to experience consequences of crisis before the risk actually manifests into an acute crisis event (Heath & O'Hair, 2009). Moreover, these VR games can be developed for computers, smartphones, and other technological affordances as they become available. Kluckner et al. (2014), for example, tested the utility of using virtual simulation software to teach crisis managers about consequences of their words and actions before experiencing the actual event. Such games have demonstrated value in communicating risk prior to an agricultural biosecurity crisis event to foster appropriate actions when the risk manifests into a crisis (e.g., Merrill, Koliba et al., 2019; Merrill, Moegenburg et al., 2019). Robots have also shown promise as crisis responders (Khalil et al., 2009) and in disaster risk communication (Ogie et al., 2018), particularly in reaching audiences who may be in treacherous locations or even unreachable (Lachlan et al., 2016). However, more research is needed to examine the degree to which social presence—that is, the ability to transmit social cues through mediated platforms—influences risk and crisis communication effectiveness (Short et al., 1976).

Right now, research confirms that humans are very much needed for communication responses to crisis; however, by 2023, estimates suggest that approximately 38% of a public relations practitioner's job may be able to be completed via automation (Valin, 2018). Since growing components of the job are risk communication and crisis management, it follows that a part of this may include managing the communication functions in AI. One theoretical framework that could prove useful as public relations professionals grapple with issues of trust and credibility of AI among various publics is the MAIN model, which focuses on how particular aspects of technology may influence different perceptions about its credibility (Sundar, 2008). Each of the letters in the model stand for unique technological affordance. "M" stands for modality and how it is experienced. "A" refers to agency, that is, the perceived "source" of the information. "I" focuses on interactivity affordances, and "N" stands for navigability, that is, ease of use. Ultimately, research can examine user perceptions of each of these AI affordances as they influence perceived trustworthiness of them.

AI poses both challenges and opportunities for risk and crisis communication professionals. Although AI is being used in myriad contexts and ways across risk and crisis types and events, relatively little research is informing such use. Future research ought to build and test theoretical models to develop best practices for integrating AI into the context of risk and crisis communication.

Internet of Things (IoT)

The Internet of Things (IoT) refers to "a huge network of interconnected things" that allow for communication "between things-things, things-people, and people-people" (Lakhwani et al., 2020, p. 1). An interconnected "thing" can range from small devices to large machines to people. IoT is a relatively new technology emerging worldwide and, thus, its utility is just beginning to be examined by government agencies, academic researchers, and industry leaders. It follows that potential opportunities and challenges for communicating in risk and crisis events ought to also be explored.

For example, some research has begun to emerge about how IoT technology may enhance emergency response operations (e.g., Yang et al., 2013), to track sources of insecurities in supply chains (e.g., Kshetri, 2017), for environmental disaster risk and crisis management via early warning systems (e.g., Poslad et al., 2015), as well as for tracing food supply chains and infectious disease migration (e.g., Sundmaeker et al., 2010).

Incorporating the IoT into disaster communications affords the possibility of faster response times and enhanced awareness and planning. As Tremaine and Tuberson (2017) noted, IoT sensor data can provide indicators on environmental surroundings, including temperatures, humidity, air and water quality, smoke, air pressure, and more, to help predict environmental impacts. In wildfires, this sensor data can give an indication about how the fire is and will be spreading to aid communication efforts and crisis management. For flooding, measuring the water rise and indicators can help to predict safe exit routes. This coordination would require that sensors collecting data be linked to a digital command center that emergency managers can access and algorithms that help to detect problems based on this sensor data (Tremaine & Tuberson, 2017). Automated responses and mobile alerts can then be linked to this sensor data to automatically notify vulnerable populations, and sensor data can also aid on the ground response.

What has yet to be explored, however, is specifically how communication functions within them and may be improved to function more strategically in risk situations and crisis events. As with any relatively new technology, much has yet to be discovered about the role of IoT by public relations professionals as they use them in communicating about risk and crisis.

Key Takeaways

The global COVID-19 pandemic has made the critical role of technology and social media extremely transparent. Frankly, each of the best practices that has served us so well in the field needs to be reconsidered in light of this sticky crisis that is plaguing countries around the world, not only in terms of public health, but also in terms of the economy, health disparities, food supply/security, education, and entertainment. Even the stages of crisis are called into question as we experience a global pandemic that reaches each stage differently in different countries and even in different regions of the same country. This global pandemic that also spurred multiple secondary crises (e.g., economic, food security, unemployment, social justice, teaching/learning) certainly points to the need for additional research regarding both opportunities and challenges of technology and social media in risk and crisis communication. Table 9.1 provides a few examples for consideration.

Citizen journalism, for example, is certainly one phenomenon that has established itself firmly in the realm of risk and crisis communication. In 2020 alone, we have watched it used to draw attention to issues of racism and police brutality, causing a ground-swelling of social protests around the world. However, research could further inform practice in how journalists and citizen journalists might work together to share accurate information and counter misinformation, disinformation, and malinformation. In addition, the COVID-19 outbreak in the US affected people of color more widely and severely than white people. How might technological affordances be used to narrow these economic, health, and other social disparity gaps? Since risks and crises—particularly sticky crises—by their very nature tend to put essential workers, first responders, and emergency managers, as well as disparate people and communities in harm's way, more research should be used to create and test software programs that could simulate crises events and provide users an opportunity to explore consequences of what they could say and do in the event of the crisis. For the same reason, more research should test robotic and other artificial intelligence means for communicating about risks and in the event of a crisis. Artificial intelligence and chatbots are proving useful in the realm of marketing and business communications, but have been applied more limitedly in the context of crisis. While marketing research has explored how the use of AI and

Table 9.1 Future Research and Applications

Technological Affordance	*Sticky Topics*	*Sticky Questions*	*Theoretical Perspectives*
Smartphones	Citizen journalism	How might journalists work effectively with citizen journalists in the time of risk or crisis?	Convergence theory
Social media	Fake news	How can communicators counter misinformation, misinformation, disinformation, & malinformation?	SMCC model
Artificial intelligence (AI)	Social disparities	How might technological affordances be used to narrow economic, health, education, and other social disparity gaps in risk preparedness & crisis response?	MAIN model Narrative theory
Internet of Things (IoT)	Global crises	What relationships exist between doomscrolling & efficacy/fatalism?	IDEA model
		How might IoT be used to manage risks & crises across time and space?	Social presence theory
	Chatbots	How do chatbots influence information seeking & vetting during times of risk or crisis?	
		In what ways might virtual reality games influence real-time crisis responses?	
		How might IoT affordances reduce response time for taking protective actions in a crisis?	

chatbots affects consumer interactions and experiences, future research is recommended to explore how AI and chatbots aid or detract from users information seeking and information vetting during crises. Similarly, many questions remain around the potential of using IoT to improve risk preparedness, crisis response, and perhaps also recovery and renewal. These are a few opportunities to combine research and practice as they can mutually inform and benefit each other.

In closing, we pose a challenge to readers. We challenge you to take away from this chapter a desire to explore technology and social media as it is used and may be used more effectively in communication about risks and in the event of a crisis. Research—even research focused on communicating to mitigate harm and potentially save lives—is only useful if we share it beyond academic journals to partner with practicing professionals in discovering issues, conducting research, and proposing solutions. In that way, we hope this chapter and the others presented in this anthology mark a new beginning for risk and crisis communication researchers and professionals.

References

Allan, S. (2013). *Citizen witnessing: Revisioning journalism in times of crisis*. John Wiley & Sons.

Allan, S., & Peters, C. (2015). Visual truths of citizen reportage: Four research problematics. *Information, Communication & Society, 18*(11), 1348–1361. https://www.tandfonline.com/doi/full/10.1080/1369118X.2015.1061576

Allan, S., & Thorsen, E. (Eds.). (2009). *Citizen journalism: Global perspectives*. Peter Lang.

Allyn, B. (2020, May 20). Researchers: Nearly half of accounts Tweeting about coronavirus are likely bots. *NPR*. https://www.npr.org/sections/coronavirus-live-updates/2020/05/20/859814085/researchers-nearly-half-of-accounts-tweeting-about-coronavirus-are-likely-bots

Anderson, M., & Vogels, E. A. (2020, March 31). Americans turn to technology during COVID-19 outbreak: Say an outage would be a problem. *Pew Research Center*. https://www.pewresearch.org/fact-tank/2020/03/31/americans-turn-to-technology-during-covid-19-outbreak-say-an-outage-would-be-a-problem/

Anthony, K. E., & Sellnow, T. L. (2016). The role of the message convergence framework in medical decision-making. *Journal of Health Communication, 21*, 249–256. https://doi.org/10.1080/10810730.2015.1064497

Austin, L. L., Liu, B. F., & Jin, Y. (2012). How audiences seek out crisis information: Exploring the social-mediated crisis communication model. *Journal of Applied Communication Research, 40*, 188–207. https://doi.org/10.1080/00909882.2012.654498

Barthel, M. (2019, July). *5 key takeaways about the state of the news media in 2018*. https://www.pewresearch.org/fact-tank/2019/07/23/key-takeaways-state-of-the-news-media-2018/

Bhattacharya, S., Bashar, M. A., Srivastava, A., & Singh, A. (2019). NOMOPHOBIA: NO mobile phone PhoBIA. *Journal of Family Medicine and Primary Care, 8*(4), 1297–1300. https://doi.org/10.4103/jfmpc_71_19

Brice-Saddler, M. (2020, May 21). Man who filmed Ahmaud Arbery's death arrested on murder charges, Georgia authorities say. *The Washington Post*. https://www.washingtonpost.com/nation/2020/05/21/man-who-filmed-ahmaud-arberys-death-arrested-murder-charges-georgia-authorities-say/

Bruns, A., & Burgess, J. (2014). Crisis communication in natural disasters: The Queensland floods and Christchurch earthquakes. In S. Jones (Ed.), *Twitter and society [digital formations]* (pp. 373–384). Peter Lang.

Burke, J. A., Spence, P. R., & Lachlan, K. A. (2010). Crisis preparation, media use, and information seeking during Hurricane Ike: Lessons learned for emergency communication. *Journal of Emergency Management, 8*(5), 27–37. https://doi.org/10.5055/jem.2010.0030

Caplan, S. E., Perse, E. M., & Gennaria, J. E. (2007). Computer-mediated technology and social interaction. In C. A. Lin & D. J. Atkin (Eds.), *Communication technology and social change: Theory and implication* (pp. 39–57). Lawrence Erlbaum.

Carr, D. J., Barnidge, M., Lee, B. G., & Tsang, S. J. (2014). Cynics and skeptics: Evaluating the credibility of mainstream and citizen journalism. *Journalism and Mass Communication Quarterly, 91*(3), 452–470. https://doi.org/10.1177/1077699014538828

Choy, M., & Chong, M. (2018). Seeing through misinformation: A framework for identifying fake online news. *arXiv*.org. Retrieved from https://arxiv.org/abs/1804.03508

Coombs, W. T., & Holladay, J. S. (2012). The paracrisis: The challenges created by publicly managing crisis prevention. *Public Relations Review, 38*(3), 408–415. https://doi.org/10.1016/j.pubrev.2012.04.004

Dalton, B., Lee, J., & Cahlan, S. (2020, May 30). The death of George Floyd: What video and other records show about his final minutes. *The Washington Post.* https://www.washingtonpost.com/nation/2020/05/30/video-timeline-george-floyd-death/?arc404=true

Dalton, L., Rapa, E., & Stein, A. (2020). Protecting the psychological health of children through effective communication about COVID-19. *The Lancet Child & Adolescent Health, 4*(5), 346–347. https://doi.org/10.1016/S2352-4642(20)30097-3

Davis, F. D. (1989). Perceived usefulness, perceived ease of use, and user acceptance of information technology. *MIS Quarterly, 13*(3), 319–340. https://doi.org/10.2307/249008

Davis, F. D., Bagozzi, R. P., & Warshaw, P. R. (1989). User acceptance of computer technology: A comparison of two theoretical models. *Management Science, 35*(8), 982–1003. https://doi.org/10.1287/mnsc.35.8.982

Doffman, Z. (2020, March 27). COVID-19 phone location tracking: Yes, it's happening now—here's what you should know. *Forbes.* https://www.forbes.com/sites/zakdoffman/2020/03/27/covid-19-phone-location-tracking-its-moving-fast-this-is-whats-happening-now/#5c7c9cd211d3

Drost, R., Casteel, M., Libarkin, J., Thomas, S., & Meister, M. (2016). Severe weather warning communication: Factors impacting audience attention and retention of information during tornado warnings. *Weather, Climate, and Society, 8*(4), 361–372. https://doi.org/10.1175/WCAS-D-15-0035.1

Ewing, M., & Lambert, C. A. (2019). Listening in: Fostering influencer relationships to manage fake news. *Public Relations Journal, 12*(4). https://prjournal.instituteforpr.org/wp-content/uploads/Listening-In-Updated-090519.pdf

Fraustino, J. D., Liu, B. F., & Jin, Y. (2017). Social media use during disasters. In L. Austin and Y. Jin (Eds.), *Social Media and Crisis Communication* (pp. 283–295). Routledge.

Gao, J., Zheng, P., Jia, Y., Chen, H., Mao, Y., Chen, S.,… & Dai, J. (2020). Mental health problems and social media exposure during COVID-19 outbreak. *PLoS ONE, 15*(4), e0231924. https://doi.org/10.1371/journal.pone.0231924

Getchell, M. C., & Sellnow, T. L. (2016). An analysis of social networks and crisis communication: A network analysis of official Twitter accounts during the West Virginia water crisis. *Computers and Human Behavior, 54*, 597–606. https://doi.org/10.1016/j.chb.2015.06.044

González-Ibánez, R., Haseki, M., & Shah, C. (2012). Time and space in collaborative information seeking: The clash of effectiveness and uniqueness. *Asis&t, 49*(1), 1–10. https://doi.org/10.1002/meet.14504901080

Hancock, J. T., Naaman, M., & Levy, K. (2020). AI-mediated communication: Definition, research agenda, and ethical considerations. *Journal of Computer-Mediated Communication, 25*(1), 89–100. https://doi.org/10.1093/jcmc/zmz022

Heath, R. L., & O'Hair, D. (Eds.). (2009). *Handbook of risk and crisis communication*. Routledge.

Hermann, C. F. (1963). Some consequences of crisis which limit the viability of organizations. *Administrative Science Quarterly, 8*, 61–82. https://doi.org/10.2307/2390887

Houston, J. B., Hawthorne, J., Perreault, M. F., Park, E. H., Goldstein Hode, M., Halliwell, M. R.,... & Griffith, S. A. (2015). Social media and disasters: A functional framework for social media use in disaster planning, response, and research. *Disasters, 39*, 1–22. https://doi.org/10.1111/disa.12092

Jakesch, M., French, M., Ma, X., Hancock, J. T., & Naaman, M. (2019). AI-mediated communication: How the perception that profile text was written by AI affects trustworthiness. In *CHI'19: Proceedings of the 2019 CHI Conference on Human Factors in Computing Systems*, 1–13.

Khalil, K. M., Abdel-Aziz, M., Nazmy, T. T., & Salem, A. B. M. (2009). Multi-agent crisis response systems-design requirements and analysis of current systems. *arXiv preprintarXiv:0903.2543.*

Kluckner, S., Heintze, K. E., & Wendt, W. (2014). Designing for the user: Tailoring a simulation software interface to the needs of crisis managers. In S. R. Hiltz, M. S. Pfaff, L. Plotnick, and P. C. Shih (Eds.), *Proceedings of the 2014 International ISCRAM Conference* (pp. 528–532). https://idl.iscram.org/files/kluckner/2014/657_Kluckner_etal2014.pdf

Kshetri, N. (2017). Can blockchain strengthen the Internet of Things? *IT Professional, 19*(4), 68–72. https://doi.org/10.1109/MITP.2017.3051335

Lachlan, K. A., Spence, P. R., Lin, X., & Del Greco, M. (2014). Screaming into the wind: Examining the volume and content of tweets associated with Hurricane Sandy. *Communication Studies, 65*(5), 500–518.

Lachlan, K. A., Spence, P. R., Rainear, A., Fishlock, J., Xu, Z., & Vanco, B. (2016). You're my only hope: An initial exploration of the effectiveness of robotic platforms in engendering earning about crises and risks. *Computers in Human Behavior, 65*, 606–611. https://doi.org/10.1016.05.081

Lakhwani, K., Gianey, H. K., Wireko, J. K., & Hiran, K. K. (2020). *Internet of Things (IoT): Principles, paradigms and applications of IoT.* BPB Publications.

Lee, N. M. (2018). Fake news, phishing, and fraud: A call for research on digital media literacy education beyond the classroom. *Communication Education, 67*(4), 460–466. https://doi.org/10.1080/03634523.2018.1503313

Liu, B. F., Fowler, B. M., Roberts, H. A., & Herovic, E. (2018). Keeping hospitals operating during disasters through crisis communication preparedness. *Public Relations Review, 44*(4), 585–597. https://doi.org/10.1016/j.pubrev.2018.06.002

Liu, B. F., Jin, Y., & Austin, L. L. (2013). The tendency to tell: Understanding publics' communicative responses to crisis information form and source. *Journal of Public Relations Research, 25*(1), 51–67. https://doi.org/10.1080/1062726X.2013.739101

Liu, B. F., & Kim, S. (2011). How organizations framed the 2009 H1N1 pandemic via social and traditional media: Implications for U.S. health communicators. *Public Relations Review, 37*, 233–234. https://doi.org/10.1016/j.pubrev.2011.03.005

Liu, B. F., Wood, M. M., Egnoto, M., Bean, H., Sutton, J., Mileti, D., & Madden, S. (2017). Is a picture worth a thousand words? The effects of maps and warning messages on how publics respond to disaster information. *Public Relations Review, 43*(3), 493–506. https://doi.org/10.1016/j.pubrev.2017.04.004

Loke, J., & Grimm, J. (2017). Cast aside: Journalists' perceptions of citizen journalists' content during the Boston marathon bombings. *Journalism Practice, 11*(1), 101–114. https://doi.org/10.1080/17512786.2015.1076706

Mayorga, M. W., Hester, E. B., Helsel, E., Ivanov, B., Sellnow, T. L., Slovic, P.,... & Frakes, D. (2020). Enhancing public resistance to "fake news": A review of the problem and strategic solutions. In H. D. O'Hair and M. J. O'Hair (Eds.). *The handbook of applied communication research* (Vol 1, pp. 197–212). Wiley Blackwell.

Merriam-Webster. (n.d.). *on "doomsurfing" and "doomscrolling" Can you think of a better way to spend your time?* Retrieved July 11, 2020, from https://www.merriam-webster.com/words-at-play/doomsurfing-doomscrolling-words-were-watching

Merrill, S. C., Koliba, C. J., Moegenburg, S. M., Zia, A., Parker, J., Sellnow, T.,... & Smith, J. M. (2019). Decision-making in livestock biosecurity practices amidst environmental and social uncertainty: Evidence from an experimental game. *PloS one, 14*(4). https://doi.org/10.1371/journal.pone.0214500

Merrill, S. C., Moegenburg, S., Koliba, C. J., Zia, A., Trinity, L., Clark, E.,... & Smith, J. M. (2019). Willingness to comply with biosecurity in livestock facilities: Evidence from experimental simulations. *Frontiers in Veterinary Science, 6*, 156. https://doi.org/10.3389/fvets.2019.00156

Min, S. (2016). Conversation through journalism: Searching for organizing principles of public and citizen journalism. *Journalism, 17*(5), 567–582. https://doi.org/10.1177/1464884915571298

Mythen, G. (2010). Reframing risk? Citizen journalism and the transformation of news. *Journal of Risk Research, 13*(1), 45–58. https://doi.org/10.1080/13669870903136159

Mushengyezi, A. (2003). Rethinking indigenous media: Rituals, "talking" drums and orality as forms of public communication in Uganda. *Journal of African Cultural Studies, 16*(1), 107–177. https://doi.org/10.1080/1369681032000169302

Niles, M. T., Emery, B. F., Reagan, A. J., Dodds, P. S., & Danforth, C. M. (2019). Social media usage patterns during natural hazards. *PloS ONE, 14*(2), e0210484. https://doi.org/10.1371/journal.pone.0210484

Obar, J., & Wildman, S. (2015). Social media definition and the governance challenge: An introduction to the special issue. *Telecommunications Policy, 39*(9), 745–750. https://doi.org/10.1016/j.telpol.2015.07.014

O'Dea, S. (2020, Feb. 28). Number of smartphone users worldwide from 2016 to 2021. *Statista.* https://www.statista.com/statistics/330695/number-of-smartphone-users-worldwide/#statisticContainer

Ogie, R. I., Rho, J. C., & Clarke, R. J. (2018, December). Artificial intelligence in disaster risk communication: A systematic literature review. In *2018 5th International Conference on Information and Communication Technologies for Disaster Management (ICT-DM)* (pp. 1–8). IEEE.

Pew Research Center. (2020*). Most Americans have used email and messaging services to connect with others during the COVID-19 outbreak, while one-in-four have used video calling for work* [Data set]. Pew Research Center. https://www.pewresearch.org/fact-tank/2020/03/31/americans-turn-to-technology-during-covid-19-outbreak-say-an-outage-would-be-a-problem/ft_2020-03-31_techcovid_01/

Poslad, S., Middleton, S. E., Chaves, F., Tao, R., Necmioglu, O., & Bügel, U. (2015). A semantic IoT early warning system for natural environment crisis management. *IEEE Transactions on Emerging Topics in Computing, 3*(2), 246–257. https://doi.org/10.1109/TETC.2015.2432742

Qualman, E. (2009). *Socialnomics: How social media transforms the way we live and do business.* John Wiley & Sons.

Roser, M., Ritchie, H., Ortiz-Ospina, E., & Hasell, J. (2020, April 25). Statistics and research: Coronavirus disease (COVID-19). *Global Change Data Lab of the University of Oxford.* https://ourworldindata.org/coronavirus

Russell, S. J., & Norvig, P. (2009). *Artificial intelligence: A modern approach* (3rd ed.). Prentice Hall.

Seeger, M. W. (2006). Best practices in crisis communication: An expert panel process. *Journal of Applied Communication Research, 34*(3), 232–244. https://doi.org/10.1080/00909880600769944

Seeger, M. W., Sellnow, T. L., & Ulmer, R. R. (2003). *Communication and organizational crisis.* Praeger.

Sellnow-Richmond, George, A. M., & Sellnow, D. D. (2018). An IDEA model analysis of instructional risk communication in the time of Ebola. *Journal of International Crisis and Risk Communication, 1*(1), 135–166. https://doi.org/10.30658/jicrcr.1.1.7

Sellnow, D. D., Iverson, J. O., & Sellnow, T. L. (2017). The evolution of the operational earthquake forecasting (OEF) community of practice: The L'Aquila communication crisis as a triggering event for organizational renewal. *Journal of Applied Communication Research, 45*(2), 121–139. https://doi.org/10.1080/00909882.2017.1288295

Sellnow, D. D., Jones, L. M., Sellnow, T. L., Spence, P., Lane, D. R., & Haarstad, N. (2019a).The IDEA model as a conceptual framework for designing earthquake early warning (EEW) messages distributed via mobile phone apps. In J. Santos-Reyes (Ed.), *Earthquakes—Impact, community vulnerability and resilience.* London. Advanced online publication. https://doi.org/10.5772/intechopen.85557

Sellnow, T. L., Parrish, A., & Semenas, L. (2019b). From hoax as crisis to crisis as hoax: Fake news and information disorder as disruptions to the discourse of renewal. *Journal of International Crisis and Risk Communication Research, 2*(1), 121–142. https://doi.org/10.30658/jicrcr.2.1.6

Sellnow, D. D., & Sellnow, T. L. (2019). The IDEA model for effective instructional risk and crisis communication by emergency managers and other key spokespersons. *Journal of Emergency Management, 17*(1), 67–76. https://doi.org/10.5055/jem.2019.0399

Sellnow, D. D., Sellnow, T. L., & Martin, J. M. (2019c). Strategic message convergence in communicating biosecurity: The case of the 2013 Porcine epidemic diarrhea virus. *Communication Reports, 3*, 125–136. https://doi.org/10.1080/08934215.2019.1634747

Sellnow-Richmond, D. D., & Sellnow, T. L. (2020). The consequences of risk amplification in the evolution of warning messages during slow-moving crises. In H. D. O'Hair & M. J. O'Hair (Eds.), *The handbook of applied communication research* (pp. 443–456). Wiley. https://doi.org/10.1002/9781119399926.ch26

Sherman-Morris, K. (2010). Tornado warning dissemination and response at a university campus. *Natural Hazards, 52*, 623–638. https://doi.org/10.1007/s11069-009-9405-0

Short, J., Williams, E., & Christie, B. (1976). *The social psychology of telecommunications.* John Wiley & Sons.

Shu, K., Wang, S., Lee, D., & Liu, H. (2020). Mining disinformation and fake news: Concepts, methods, and recent advancements. *arXiv preprint arXiv:2001.00623.*

Smith, S. (2009, December 11). New media spread the word on H1N1: Twitter, YouTube messages aimed at public. *Boston Globe*. http://archive.boston.com/news/health/articles/2009/12/11/new_media_spread_the_word_on_h1n1/

Spence, P. R., Lachlan, K. A., & Burke, J. M. (2008). Crisis preparation, media use, and information seeking: Patterns across Katrina evacuees and lessons learned for crisis communication. *Journal of Emergency Management*, *6*, 11–23. https://doi.org/10.5055/jem/2008.0009

Spence, P. R., Sellnow-Richmond, D. D., Sellnow, T. L., & Lachlan, K. A. (2016). Social media and corporate reputation during crises: The viability of video-sharing websites for providing counter-messages to traditional broadcast news. *Journal of Applied Communication Research*, *44*(3), 199–215. https://doi.org/10.1080/00909882.2016.1192289

Sundar, S. S. (2008). The MAIN model: A heuristic approach to understanding technology effects on credibility. In M. J. Metzger & A. J. Flanagin (Eds.), *Digital media, youth, and credibility: The John D. and Catherine T. MacArthur foundation series on digital media and learning* (pp. 73–100). MIT Press. https://doi.org/10.1162/dmal. 9780262562324.073

Sundmaeker, H., Guillemin, P., Friess, P., & Woelfflé, S. (Eds.). (2010). *Vision and challenges for realising the Internet of Things*. European Commission—Information Society and Media DG.

Sutton, J., League, C., Sellnow, T. L., & Sellnow, D. D. (2015). Terse messaging and public health in the midst of natural disasters: The case of the Boulder Floods. *Health Communication*, *30*, 135–143. https://doi.org/10.1080/10410236.2014.974124

Tremaine, K., & Tuberson, K. (2017, December 1). How the Internet of Things can prepare cities for natural disasters. *Harvard Business Review*. https://hbr.org/2017/12/how-the-internet-of-things-can-prepare-cities-for-natural-disasters

Tyma, A. W. (2008). *Expressions of tragedy—Expressions of hope: Facebook, discourse, and the Virginia tech incident*. North Dakota State University.

Tyma, A., Sellnow, D., & Sellnow, T. (2010). Social media use in response to the Virginia Tech crisis: Moving from chaos to understanding. In *Annual meeting of the International Communication Association*. https://citation.allacademic.com/meta/p403670_index. html

Ulmer, R. R., Sellnow, T. L., & Seeger, M. W. (2017). *Effective crisis communication: Moving from crisis to opportunity*. Sage.

Vafeiadis, M., Bortree, D. S., Buckley, C., Diddi, P., & Xiao, A. (2019). Refuting fake news on social media: Nonprofits, crisis response strategies and issue involvement. *Journal of Product & Brand Management*, *29*(2), 209–222. https://doi.org/10.1108/JPBM-12-2018-2146

Valin, J. (2018, May). *"Humans still needed"—Research project reveals impact of artificial intelligence on public relations*. Chartered Institute of Public Relations. https://newsroom.cipr.co.uk/humans-still-needed---research-project-reveals-impact-of-artificial-intelligence-on-public-relations/

Wald, D. J., & Eerie, M. (2020). Practical limitations of earthquake early warning. *Earthquake Spectra*. Early online publication. https://journals.sagepub.com/doi/10.1177/8755293020911388

Wall, M. (2018). *Citizen journalism: Practices, propaganda, pedagogy*. Routledge.

Wamsley, L. (2018, May 9). Google's new voice bot sounds, um, maybe too real. *NPR*. https://www.npr.org/sections/thetwo-way/2018/05/09/609820627/googles-new-voice-bot-sounds-um-maybe-too-real

Westerman, D., Edwards, A. P., Edwards, C., Luo, Z., & Spence, P. R. (2020). I-it, I-]thou, I-robot: The perceived humanness of AI in human-machine communication. *Communication Studies*. Advance online publication. https://doi.org/10.1080/10510974.2020.1749683

Yang, L., Yang, S. H., & Plotnick, L. (2013). How the Internet of Things technology enhances emergency response operations. *Technological Forecasting and Social Change*, *80*(9), 1854–1867. https://doi.org/10.1016/j.techfore.2012.07.011

10 Law and (Lack of) Order in Complex Crises

Joseph Watson, Jr., James D. Firth, and Jonathan Peters

In large organizations, legal and communications professionals work closely on a regular basis, and in times of crisis, the fault lines between them can become all too apparent. They have distinct roles and responsibilities that are mutually reinforcing, and their capacity and willingness to collaborate, particularly in a crisis, is of paramount importance to the organizations that they serve. Fault lines can exacerbate an already sticky crisis, as jostling between communications-prioritized or legal-reliant approaches may extend a crisis by producing unforced errors. Consider Quaker Oats and its languid response to criticism of racial insensitivity in regard to depictions on its Aunt Jemima-branded products (Hsu, 2020). Despite an awareness of concerns about the Aunt Jemima character, the company made only incremental changes over the course of decades, culminating in its 2020 decision to retire the brand. This protracted and tortured response can be attributed, at least in part, to the absence of an integrated approach balancing legal and reputational risks.

Why do lawyers and communicators so often clash when it is most productive for them to come together? Are the conflicts between them insurmountable? This chapter explores these and other problems. We begin by discussing the expressive rights of organizations and the areas of law most likely to present sources of potential liability for organizations in a crisis, such as defamation and misrepresentation. This helps to contextualize how an organization is able to speak publicly and the risks it must manage in doing so. Then we cover the various roles that chief communications officers play in general, such as C-Suite counselor, reputation steward, stakeholder manager, and manager of communications with employees and vendors. After that, we examine the nature and causes of the conflict between legal and communications professionals, highlighting problems in crisis responses that follow legal-reliant or communications-prioritized approaches. And finally, we propose a fully integrated approach.

Legal Roles and Responsibilities

Public relations law is a patchwork of areas, like defamation, privacy, and consumer protection, all applied to the practice of communicating an organization's interests to the public. The roots here extend to the US Constitution, too, because the US Supreme Court ruled in the 1970s that commercial and business expression receive varying levels of First Amendment protection (*First National Bank of Boston v. Bellotti*, 1978). This includes social and political expression, which is of value because it contributes to self-government and to the marketplace of ideas; and it includes purely economic expression about products and services, which is of value because it enables consumers to make informed choices. As the Supreme Court once put it:

> So long as we preserve a predominantly free enterprise economy, the allocation of our resources in large measure will be made through numerous private economic decisions. It is a matter of public interest that those decisions, in the aggregate, be intelligent and well informed.
>
> (Virginia State Board of Pharmacy v. Virginia Citizens Consumer Council, Inc., 1976, p. 765)

All of this means that organizations, in a crisis and beyond, have at least some constitutional rights to communicate their interests to the public. But those rights are variable, not absolute, and numerous areas of law present sources of potential liability. The main ones, in the context of crisis communication, are covered below. It is helpful to keep in mind that lawyers, judges, and scholars often disagree about the meaning and implementation of laws and regulations, whether they were enacted by Congress, for example, or handed down by a state consumer-protection agency.

Trial Publicity

Where there is a crisis, there is often litigation. And an organization might want to shape public perceptions of the claims or the court filings and proceedings. However, the state rules of professional conduct governing lawyers generally include a provision that commands a lawyer participating in the litigation of a matter to show restraint. That means the lawyer must not make any extrajudicial statements that she knows, or reasonably should know, will be disclosed publicly and have a substantial likelihood of materially prejudicing an adjudicative proceeding in the same matter (American Bar Association, Rule 3.6: Trial Publicity).

During a crisis, then, as an organization's lawyers are collaborating with its communications team, the lawyers must take special care to avoid liability under the trial-publicity rules. They were developed to protect the right to a fair trial vis-à-vis the rules of forensic decorum and the exclusionary rules of evidence (they are supposed to govern the basis of any finding of civil or criminal liability), while also recognizing that the public has a legitimate interest in the conduct of judicial proceedings and in the subject matter of individual cases. Importantly, if trial-publicity violations are reported to a state bar disciplinary committee and then established by the appropriate burden of proof, a lawyer can be fined or sanctioned, or even suspended or barred from the practice of law.

Tort Law

The purpose of tort law is to compensate people for harm (physical, mental, reputational, and so on) they have suffered because of the actions of others. Generally, a tort stems from an act of commission or omission that harms another's legal interest in person or property, usually with an accompanying state of mind like recklessness or carelessness (e.g., hastily preparing a news release that contains actionable errors). Some torts are more likely than others to be an issue during a crisis. Consider these:

Defamation. This is a claim for publishing a false statement of fact about another person or organization that causes reputational harm. This is most likely to happen during a crisis if an organization simply makes a fact error while communicating about another's criminal activity, serious moral failings, job-related poor performance, or medical issues. Pursuing or defending against defamation claims is tremendously time-consuming and expensive.

False Light. This is a privacy claim for publishing false or misleading information about a person that would be highly offensive generally. To be clear, defamation protects a person from injury to reputation, while false light protects a person from the offense or embarrassment caused by the publication. This is easier to prove, too, and it is most likely to arise during a crisis if an organization is communicating about a particular person and makes a statement, or uses an illustration in connection with one, that creates an unintended and offensive connotation.

Publication of Private Facts. This is exactly what it sounds like: a claim for publishing private facts about a person, even if they are true. This applies to information about someone's personal life not previously revealed and not of legitimate public concern, the disclosure of which would be offensive to a reasonable person. This is most likely to happen during a crisis if an organization is communicating about an individual's personal finances, drug or alcohol abuse, health issues, school grades, or sexual habits and orientation.

Misrepresentation. This is a claim for making a false statement or omission of material fact (a significant factor in a decision) to induce someone's action or inaction, ultimately causing damages to that person. Such a statement or omission can be made intentionally or negligently, in the latter case where a public relations practitioner acts in his or her professional capacity and fails to use reasonable care to determine a statement's truth while owing a duty to the person who justifiably relied on it. This is a stark reminder that truth and facts do matter.

Administrative Law

Congress and various state legislatures long ago created agencies and empowered them to regulate certain industries and practices. The agencies conduct the actual regulation by making, enforcing, and adjudicating rules within their grants of authority, acting as all three branches of government rolled into one. The agencies are made up of experts in the areas for which they are responsible, and for that reason, among others, the courts typically defer to their expertise when their actions are challenged. Although it is impossible to cover here all of the federal and state agencies that directly affect public relations generally and crisis communications specifically, it is worthwhile to discuss three at the federal level that are especially important: the Securities and Exchange Commission (SEC), the Food and Drug Administration (FDA), and the Federal Trade Commission (FTC). The Federal Communications Commission (FCC) is not covered because its rules, which broadly govern radio, television, wire, satellite, and cable, have a more direct effect on content providers than on public relations professionals who use those providers to distribute their messages.

Securities and Exchange Commission (SEC). The SEC is principally concerned with regulating the buying and selling of stocks and bonds and with corporate communications around that buying and selling. Its rules are voluminous and complex, but they basically boil down to this: publicly traded companies must disclose, in a timely manner, all material information that would affect stock sales or purchase decisions or simply be connected to them, at least where there is a duty to do so (e.g., in cases involving knowledge of insider information or fraudulent schemes). No such information may be knowingly false or misleading, and any erroneous such information must be corrected.

The SEC also enforces rules regarding selective disclosure: providing before public release any positive or negative information to analysts (through conference calls or other non-public forums) that is likely to change perceptions of a company's stock value. The underlying theory is that no person should have that kind of advance notice because a violator would gain an unfair advantage. The SEC monitors trades for unusual patterns, volume, and timing. And like most of its brethren regulatory bodies, the SEC is not a big believer in coincidences.

Notably, too, the SEC stated in a 2013 report that social media can be used to announce "key information" as long as investors "have been alerted" in advance "about which social media will be used to disseminate such information" (Report of Investigation Pursuant to Section 21(a) of the Securities Exchange Act of 1934: Netflix, Inc., and Reed Hastings, 2013). Also, although the SEC has acknowledged the importance of blogs to corporate communications, the agency has urged company bloggers to be mindful that they are acting on their employer's behalf when they blog, in a crisis and beyond.

All of these rules and principles reflect the clear congressional intent that "there cannot be honest markets without honest publicity" and that "manipulation and dishonest practices of the marketplace thrive on mystery and secrecy" (House of Representatives Report No. 1383, 1934). This means a public company's expression should always be conducted in good faith, and its overarching goal, as the Supreme Court once said, "should be to inform, not to challenge, the reader's critical wits" (*Virginia Bankshares, Inc. v. Sandberg*, 1991, p. 1097).

Food and Drug Administration (FDA). The FDA regulates commercial speech related to prescription drugs, medical devices, and tobacco; and it regulates the labels of food, drug, and cosmetic products. (Food, Drug, and Cosmetic Act, 2000, § 343(a); Food, Drug, and Cosmetic Act, 2000, § 321(m)). The purpose of the regulation is broadly to ensure consumer safety, and to that end, the FDA regularly coordinates with the FTC, discussed below in more detail, to enforce FTC restrictions on commercial speech related to cigarettes and smokeless tobacco and to decide whether health and nutrition claims in food advertising are deceptive. In practice, however, the FDA has been most active in the area of prescription drugs, so that is where the agency is most likely to be relevant during a crisis.

The FDA can fine pharmaceutical companies for false or misleading commercial speech. All direct-to-consumer claims must present a fair balance between the risks and benefits of a drug, must reveal facts material to the representations made or the consequences of using a drug, and must disclose any risks. The FDA has issued guidance, too, about commercial speech and social media, saying, "the Internet and various social media platforms have increasingly enabled drug and device manufacturers to more actively engage with consumers and healthcare professionals" (Food and Drug Administration, 2014). Observing, for example, that platforms like Twitter have a limited character count, the FDA suggested communicating benefit and risk information in the same tweet and including a link to more detailed disclosures.

Federal Trade Commission (FTC). The FTC regulates commercial speech to ensure that it is truthful and non-deceptive, and that all claims are substantiated and not unfair. Its portfolio is expansive and covers all but speech about prescription drugs and medical devices (the purview, again, of the FDA), and it regulates any action, method, or device intended to draw the public's attention to services, merchandise, people, or organizations. Companies have tried to challenge the FTC by arguing that a particular expression or claim fell outside those bounds, like an essay or a philosophical statement of principles, but these efforts have rarely been successful.

Against that background, a message is deceptive if it contains or omits information that is important to a consumer's decision to buy or use a product and likely to mislead consumers acting reasonably. A message is unfair if it causes, or is likely to cause, serious injury that is not outweighed by the benefits, and a consumer cannot reasonably avoid them. Finally, a message is deceptive if a typical target consumer would be left with a significant misimpression about it—in view of the message's full context (words, phrases, and pictures). Notably, though, it is permissible to express exaggerated claims about a product's or service's quality, known as puffery, but the exaggerations must be so great that ordinary consumers would not take the claims seriously (e.g., saying that you sell "the world's best coffee").

The FTC has also recognized that social media have supplemented, and in some respects supplanted, traditional media as a venue for strategic messages. But many platforms have space and word limits, so companies initially wondered if the FTC would enforce its various rules on social media. The answer came to be yes, so problematic communications will not find a refuge from the FTC on the Internet generally or on social media.

The FTC enforces these rules through various penalties, such as cease-and-desist letters, civil remedies, and corrective disclosures. For example, in situations where claims are especially egregious or conveyed over a long period of time through substantial public activities, the FTC can bring an action requiring millions of dollars in corrective communications paid for by the offending company. These must be distributed in media similar to those employed to convey the earlier misleading claims. Specific language often must be used to acknowledge those claims, to clarify what is true, and to explain what corrective action has been taken. Even in cases where a company disagrees with the FTC's position, the company may run corrective communications to stem the flow of bad publicity and to limit the cost of litigation. Sometimes, the cost of *winning* is just too high.

Recording Interviews

It is common in a crisis for an organization's leaders and public relations practitioners to engage with the press and to give interviews. Recording them creates not only a helpful record of what was said but also a potential basis to challenge a news outlet's reporting, where there is reason to do so. For example, if an outlet deliberately misquotes an interviewee and materially changes the meaning of what he or she said, ultimately causing reputational harm, the recording could be used later in litigation to prove actual malice—the fault standard required in some libel cases (*Masson v. New Yorker*, 1991).

However, the recording may need to be made with consent. A range of federal and state statutes set out when it is unlawful to record conversations to which you are a party, and some follow a one-party consent rule (meaning any party to a conversation can consent to its recording), while others follow an all-party consent rule (meaning every party to a conversation must consent to its recording). Knowing the applicable requirements is critical to avoid unnecessary litigation. That being said, the greatest cost here can be negative media coverage. Even if a company prevails in an action for improper recording, it might still suffer major damage to its reputation. Accusations can be stronger than denials in the public's eye.

Beware: Errant and Off-the-Record Remarks

Organizations should be mindful that much of what they say during a crisis will be reported on, regardless of whether they want it to be. This underlines the need for careful and intentional engagement with the public and press because the state and federal courts generally have deferred to news outlets on what qualifies as newsworthy and therefore protected by the First Amendment (*Sidis v. F-R Publishing Company*, 1940). An errant remark could end up in the press, and there might be little the organization could do about it under the law.

That said, off-the-record disclosures should remain off-the-record. If a journalist makes a promise and later breaks it, and the organization's representative reasonably relied on it to her detriment, the promise may be enforceable under the principle of promissory estoppel (*Cohen v. Cowles Media*, 1991). It is prudent to be clear, in advance, about the nature of all comments and disclosures to journalists—to establish a shared understanding of whether they are on the record, off the record, and so on, and what those terms mean to the parties involved. One common and indefensible error made by those being interviewed is to make a comment and then claim it was off the record. That is not how it works. Any such agreement must be made *before* the comment; otherwise, a journalist is free to use it.

Communications Roles and Responsibilities

Like their peers in the legal department, communicators within large organizations today perform a plethora of roles and responsibilities that, for our purposes, are best viewed through the lens of chief communications officers (CCOs). CCOs are C-Suite-level executives who are charged with managing the reputations of the organizations that they serve, advising leadership, and maintaining relationships with key stakeholders, among other things (Arthur Page Society, 2016). Before exploring how these functions are performed in a crisis, it will be helpful first to discuss their responsibilities.

C-Suite Counselor

CCOs advise their C-Suite peers on a wide variety of issues and decisions that confront their organizations. Whether they are contemplating a merger or an acquisition, a new product or service offering, entering a new market, building a new facility, or weighing in on public policy, executives will often seek the CCOs counsel on the matter. This stems largely from the accurate view that CCOs typically have the best and most comprehensive understanding of the public relations impact of those and related decisions. Their teams also manage the communications associated with organizational undertakings. When crises arise, CEOs and C-Suite executives look to the CCO to help them understand and approach the communications challenges that come with them.

Reputation Steward

Perhaps the most important role of a modern CCO is serving as the steward of an organization's reputation. There is widespread acceptance of the value of an organization's reputation, not dissimilar from other more tangible assets. Organizational decisions can enhance or diminish the value of that reputation. CCOs are charged with evaluating continually the state of their organization's reputation, along with managing programs designed to maintain or enhance it. Crises, of course, can present large and existential risks to reputation, and how CCOs and their organizations approach such risks is a central issue in this chapter and in other parts of this book.

Stakeholder Manager

CCOs are increasingly called upon to manage relationships with an organization's key stakeholders, which for major nonprofit and corporate organizations can include public officials, news media, advocacy organizations, consumer groups, trade associations, and so on. These stakeholders are critical to the long-term success of an organization. Their allegiance can help secure favorable regulatory, business, or policy outcomes. Conversely, an acrimonious, or even merely a neglectful relationship, can yield the opposite. In a crisis, the standing of these relationships with stakeholders will be put to the test, and organizations look to their CCOs to help engage them constructively.

Employee and Vendor Communications Manager

CCOs are frequently called on to manage communications with employees and vendors and/or consultants. First, strong and positive internal communications to employees often leads to greater cooperation, less confrontation, and increased productivity. These communications strengthen employee relationships within an organization and underscore how they are valued: Are they cogs in a machine or important contributors to a firm's success and profitability?

Second, Henry Ford eventually abandoned his commitment to own and control every aspect of his then-fledgling automotive business. His desire to own coal mines, iron ore, steel production, railroads, tires, wheels, and parts—all needed to produce a simple vehicle—crashed into the reality that he simply could not do it all efficiently and effectively. Extending that to our modern business environment, all manner of companies depend on hundreds, even thousands, of vendors in a global supply chain to meet their organizational goals. A problem with one can stop the production line for days, weeks, or more. CCOs must protect, support, and communicate with these independent, but critical, parts of a company.

Synthesis

These roles merely scratch the surface of what complex organizations expect from their CCOs. They are increasingly called upon to serve as C-Suite integrators, fostering collaborations across functions to achieve strategic objectives. Chief among them is with the general counsel to mitigate risk to the organization. CCOs also help to develop and maintain their organizations' social- and digital-engagement systems, an obvious extension of their roles as managers of stakeholder engagement. In the midst of a crisis, use of social and digital tools is of utmost importance. However, while they offer valuable means of reaching key stakeholders, they can expose organizations to heightened risk, particularly during a crisis.

Conflicts between Legal and Communications Professionals

If both legal and communications professionals are charged with the mitigation of risk, what is the source of conflict between the two? Risk is basically the possibility of loss or injury, but there are different kinds of risk, and organizations are concerned with a wide range of them. Indeed, every function in an organization is concerned with some kind: chief financial officers (CFOs) are concerned with financial risks, chief information officers (CIOs) are concerned with cybersecurity risks—ad infinitum. So, it should come as little surprise that communicators and lawyers are concerned with risks, albeit different ones. Lawyers manage legal risk, and communicators manage reputational risk.

Day to day, lawyers focus on contractual, litigation, regulatory, and structural risks to their organizations. And in the midst of a crisis, they are usually most concerned with the risk of litigation—the risk that an organization will face legal action due to the organization's conduct, product, services, inaction, or other events. This is a very reasonable concern. A 2010 survey of major companies found that US corporations paid out an average of $115 million per year in outside litigation costs (Lawyers for Civil Justice, Civil Justice Reform Group, US Chamber Institute for Legal Reform, 2010).

A frequent charge for in-house corporate lawyers and their outside counsel is to estimate the actual value of litigation risk during a particular circumstance. In fact, major corporations may have attorneys whose jobs are devoted entirely to risk and claims management. This level of specialization can contribute to the perceived rigor that is assigned to estimates of litigation risk in organizations. Measuring legal, and more specifically litigation, risk is of enormous practical importance to C-Suite executives seeking to navigate a crisis, and the lawyers' ability to deliver clear risk calculations gives them considerable credibility in decision-making.

Benjamin Franklin once said that "[i]t takes many good deeds to build a good reputation, and only one bad one to lose it" (Russoniello, 2010). This is the maxim that steadfastly guides professional communicators in their approach to reputational risk. That said, communicators have long struggled to arrive at a consensus on defining such risk, let alone measuring it. Even among sophisticated companies there is only a "fuzzy idea of how to manage reputational risk" (Eccles et al., 2007). Building on Franklin's maxim, reputational risk can be defined as the threat to the good name of an organization or its standing among key stakeholders that may result from the action or inaction of the organization, its employees, or close associates.

Assessing reputational risk has often been a matter of gut reaction for communicators and, regrettably, far more art than science. The corresponding lack of specificity in assessing and measuring risk can have the effect of undermining the credibility of the communicators vis-à-vis the lawyers in managing a crisis. Their significantly different conceptualization of risk, both in substance and in specificity, is the primary driver of conflicts between their teams during a crisis. Lawyers and communicators have been trained to think of risk in unique ways, and that means they tend to view a crisis using different lenses and therefore may advocate for diverging solutions. This can cause good-faith disagreements between general counsels and CCOs about the appropriate approach, ultimately putting the CEO in the undesirable position of making a binary choice between an approach that is legal-reliant and one that prioritizes communication and reputational risk. In the discussion below, we offer some observations of selected crises and their management, based on public news accounts and impressions rather than direct knowledge of actual decision-making or strategies.

Problems of a Legal-Reliant Approach in a Crisis

Lawyers often bring more clear-cut, or at least easier to understand, risk calculations to an organization's decision-making in a crisis. Legal precedents (e.g., demonstrating damages awards) can bring into stark relief the risk of running afoul of legal advice. As a result, it is not uncommon for a legal-reliant approach to be adopted—and indeed we have seen numerous examples in recent years of companies in crisis situations where it appeared that legal risk considerations were driving external messaging and tactics.

Consider aeronautics manufacturer Boeing's 2019 crisis caused by the crashes of two of its newest model passenger airliners within months of each other (Gelles, 2019). Tragically, the crashes killed hundreds of passengers and crew members; they generated headlines around the world. The company initially asserted that its planes were safely designed and manufactured and that the two crashes had to be related to other causal factors. The company also claimed that it was safe for airlines to continue to operate the model in question (it was being promoted at the time as Boeing's new flagship).

During several months of continuing and intense media attention, the company took a foxhole approach to communications, mainly commenting defensively and narrowly. The company stuck to its no-fault position even in light of mounting evidence and speculation that a design flaw had, in fact, led to the disasters. It appeared that the company's public strategy was driven by the goal of avoiding legal liability to the greatest extent possible. Only when presented with government and whistleblower evidence was the company forced to publicly admit its responsibility after a shake-up in senior management and a precipitous decline in stock value.

Problems of a Communications-Prioritized Approach in a Crisis

In the event that a CCO persuades a CEO to discount a general counsel's focus on legal and litigation risk, organizations may approach crises by prioritizing communications. We have seen, in fact, cases in which a company in a crisis has placed so much of its emphasis on communicating to protect reputation that it apparently did not reserve much consideration for legal risk. Consider electric utility companies. They can struggle during widespread power outages caused by major storms, especially in periods of extreme hot or cold weather. There is enormous public and political pressure on the companies to restore power quickly. And sometimes, company communicators have gotten too far out in front of the operational side of the house and publicly predicted unrealistic power-restoration timelines. When those timelines have come and gone, and customers have been left without power for long periods in very difficult circumstances, the companies have quickly lost customer, political, and regulatory trust, all while bringing on significant liabilities.

In 2003, Hurricane Isabel caused power outages throughout the Washington, DC, metro area, leaving hundreds of thousands without power (Becker, 2003). As outages stretched out for more than a week, Pepco, the electric utility serving the area, prematurely issued a statement indicating that power had been restored to all residences and businesses in the city. But after customers notified Pepco, public officials, and the media that they were still without power, a Pepco spokesperson was compelled to walk back the earlier statement. Additionally, Pepco's muffed communications drew media attention to a $10 million system that had been purchased to more effectively manage outages that seemed to fail in this instance. Communications-prioritized approaches like this one can result in heightened legal, regulatory, and political scrutiny of an organization, exposing it to more risk than it might have otherwise encountered.

Synthesis

The irony of these unbalanced approaches is that companies have suffered far greater legal and reputational damage than necessary by adopting them. On the one hand, by trying so hard to avoid liability, companies sometimes have only worsened their legal position. On the other hand, by trying so hard to protect their reputations, they have sometimes caused their favorability ratings to go over the proverbial cliff. Companies that find a way to merge and marry both sets of concerns as they manage communications during a crisis usually come out of it in stronger shape, with fewer legal problems, and with their reputations intact. There is a strong need for integration.

Toward an Integrated Approach to Crises

Choosing between legal and communications is a false choice. It is more prudent to acknowledge the roles and skills of both departments and to leverage them toward a common goal. An integrated approach that includes a comprehensive analysis of risks, and weighs them all on fair and equitable terms, is essential to an effective and sustainable response. Fortunately, there are examples of companies working their way successfully through crises by employing a balanced communications strategy that takes into account both legal and reputational risk.

A well-known case in point involves the fast-casual restaurant chain Chipotle Mexican Grill, which operates restaurants in North America and Europe. In 2015, Chipotle faced a major crisis after a significant number of customers became ill with *E. coli*, the dreaded bacterium that can cause serious health problems, as a result of food served at some of the chain's locations (Ferdman & Bhattarai, 2015). This outbreak brought a great deal of negative media attention to the company, and its response was measured and customer-focused. Rather than deflect and deny, the chain voluntarily closed the restaurants where the problem had occurred and brought in outside food-safety consultants to help assess their operations and recommend improvements. These steps limited their liability from customers and reduced regulatory censure, and they projected a willingness to prioritize customer (and employee) safety over short-term profits, all of which had a positive impact on the company's reputation and bottom line.

As noted above, measurement is an important element of how C-Suite leadership makes decisions in the management of a crisis. While there are well-established measures for litigation risk, such as legal precedents, damage awards, and settlements, communicators must work to establish measures of reputational risk. New and emerging technological solutions like ListenFirst Brand Reputation Index show promise as a potential basis for such consensus in the future. And beyond that, communicators have to begin quantifying that risk in a manner comparable to that which their peers in other functional areas employ. It is a good practice to be accessible, open, concerned, and respectful in the midst of a crisis. However, messaging must be measured against possible legal action, regulatory enforcement, and public opinion.

A classic example of how to manage a crisis is Johnson & Johnson, following a series of murders caused when someone went into Chicago-area stores and replaced Tylenol capsules with others filled with a deadly poison (Latson, 2014). Randomly, consumers bought the bottles and placed them in their medicine chests. Over the next few weeks, several people died after taking just one capsule. Many industry experts announced Tylenol could never again be successfully marketed in the United States. But because of openness, honesty, cooperation, accessibility, and constant communication with consumers, retail outlets, law enforcement, regulators, and media, one year later Tylenol had regained 90 percent of its sales. The company had taken seriously its legal *and* communications responsibilities, among others.

Of course, generally, there can be challenges to achieving such an integrated approach. Some practitioners may be slow to embrace it because of its novelty. When organizations and their principals have become accustomed to doing something in a particular way, even if it is dysfunctional, there can be reticence to trying something different. Additionally, organizations may encounter resistance among current practitioners because of the greater rigor, in terms of data and analytics. Measuring social media trends and mapping stakeholders can quickly become complicated and technical, producing potential barriers to integration. So, a collaborative, cross-functional approach during a crisis can be difficult to sell.

To facilitate changes of this magnitude, organizations should begin sooner than later to change the manner in which they do this work, before a crisis arrives. Once it does, modifying the organization's approach may well be the last thing that leaders are wanting or willing to do, regardless of the benefits that it can bring. This also requires both legal and communications to be represented at the top management level, with direct access to the CEO. Each should routinely attend executive-level meetings and be included meaningfully in discussions and decisions from the start, especially in a crisis situation. Some firms already do this, but others grant more access to lawyers—choosing to consult the communication executive later or in a limited way, too often after key decisions have been made. Limiting access for either party weakens analysis, planning, strategy, tactics, and evaluation. Both must be at the table as respected leaders.

Key Takeaways

When a conflict arises, practitioners have to be aware of the dynamics of the C-Suite and the differing perspectives that parties in an organization bring to the table in assessing risk. Approaching this situation in a judgment-free manner is an important first step in developing the respect and understanding that is necessary to achieve the kind of integrated approach that will be needed to manage the crisis at issue, in an effective and sustainable way.

Crises are largely inevitable: disasters happen, mistakes get made, employees break the law, products fail, and so on. What is not inevitable, however, is adding internal political conflicts to the turmoil of a crisis. By focusing on relationships and shared interests, and on bringing a realistic assessment of the interplay between lawyers and communicators to the forefront, we can begin to mitigate the problematic interactions and habits that can greatly undermine a crisis response. An old adage says that everything that a person or an organization does or says is public relations, but we would humbly add that it would be done or said more effectively through collaboration.

References

American Bar Association. (n.d.) Rule 3.6: Trial publicity. https://www.americanbar.org/groups/professional_responsibility/publications/model_rules_of_professional_conduct/rule_3_6_trial_publicity/

Arthur W. Page Society. (2016, March). The new CCO: Transforming enterprises in a changing world. https://knowledge.page.org/wp-content/uploads/2018/12/The_New_CCO_-_Full_Report.pdf

Becker, J. (2003, September 30). Pepco to check outage tracking. *The Washington Post.* https://www.washingtonpost.com/archive/local/2003/09/30/pepco-to-check-outage-tracking/48fc1512-155d-44e7-ae99-1b40ed849549/

Cohen v. Cowles Media, 501 U.S. 663 (1991).

Eccles, R., Newquis, S., & Schatz, R. (2007, February). Reputation and its risks. *Harvard Business Review.* https://hbr.org/2007/02/reputation-and-its-risks

Ferdman, R., & Bhattarai, A. (2015, December 9). There's a crisis at chipotle. *The Washington Post.* https://www.washingtonpost.com/news/wonk/wp/2015/12/09/chipotle-food-outbreak-ecoli-reputation/

First National Bank of Boston v. Bellotti, 435 U.S. 765 (1978).

Food and Drug Administration. (2014). For industry: Using social media. https://www.fda.gov/about-fda/center-drug-evaluation-and-research-cder/industry-using-social-media

Food, Drug, and Cosmetic Act, 21 U.S.C. § 343(a) (2000).

Food, Drug, and Cosmetic Act, 21 U.S.C. § 321(m) (2000).

Gelles, D. (2019, October 28). Boeing 737 max: What's happened after the 2 deadly crashes. *The New York Times.* https://www.nytimes.com/interactive/2019/business/boeing-737-crashes.html

House of Representatives Report No. 1383, 73rd Congress, 2d Sess. 11 (1934).

Hsu, T. (2020, June 17). Aunt Jemima brand to change name and image over "Racial Stereotype." *The New York Times.* https://www.nytimes.com/2020/06/17/business/aunt-jemima-racial-stereotype.html

Latson, J. (2014, September 29). How poisoned Tylenol became a crisis-management teaching model. *Time.* https://time.com/3423136/tylenol-deaths-1982/

Lawyers for Civil Justice, Civil Justice Reform Group, U.S. Chamber Institute for Legal Reform. (2010). Litigation cost survey of major companies. https://www.uscourts.gov/sites/default/files/litigation_cost_survey_of_major_companies_0.pdf

Masson v. New Yorker, 501 U.S. 496 (1991).

Russoniello, S. (2010, June 14). *Penn and beyond.* University of Pennsylvania. https://ulife.vpul.upenn.edu/careerservices/blog/2010/06/14/it-takes-many-good-deeds-to-build-a-good-reputation-and-only-one-bad-one-to-lose-it-benjamin-franklin/

Report of investigation pursuant to section 21(a) of the securities exchange act of 1934: Netflix, Inc., and Reed Hastings, SEC, Release No. 69279, April 2, 2013.

Sidis v. F-R Publ'g Co., 113 F.2d 806 (2d Cir. 1940).

Virginia Bankshares, Inc. v. Sandberg, 501 U.S. 1083 (1991).

Virginia State Board of Pharmacy v. Virginia Citizens Consumer Council, Inc., 425 U.S. 748 (1976).

Part V

What Can Crisis Theories Do (Better) for Practice?

11 Situational Crisis Communication Theory (SCCT) and Application in Dealing with Complex, Challenging, and Recurring Crises

W. Timothy Coombs, Sherry J. Holladay, and Karen L. White

The focus of the 2019 Crisis Communication Think Tank was on sticky crises. Sticky crises are more complex and challenging than your typical crisis. The month of March in 2020 gave organizations around the world a taste of a sticky crisis with COVID-19. Organizations were confronted with new operating procedures if they were designated essential and allowed to continue to operate. Non-essential organizations shutdown if they could not switch operations to the digital environment. Suddenly anyone who could was working from home and restaurants became deliver or carry-out. COVID-19 was complex because it affected so many organizations simultaneously and was recurring because of the timeline created by epidemiologists. Organizations faced the challenge of communicating about COVID-19 with its stakeholders, especially with employees and customers. Professionals realized the crisis situation was different and many indicated they wished for a normal crisis.

Pandemics such as COVID-19 are rare but do illustrate the point that sticky crises are something different and more challenging for crisis communicators. However, simply because sticky crises are different from normal crises does not mean our existing knowledge base about crisis communication is invalid. Sticky crises and normal crises still share some features. What we need to do is to explore how existing crisis communication advice can be applied to sticky crises. This includes understanding what from existing advice still works, what requires modification, and where existing advice falls short. This chapter considers how advice generated by Situational Crisis Communication Theory (SCCT) can be applied to sticky crises. The chapter begins by detailing the development and evolution of SCCT followed by an explicating sticky crisis and tentative advice offered by the Crisis Communication Think Tank. The final section examines the way SCCT fits with and has any gap in addressing sticky crises.

Situational Crisis Communication Theory Development

SCCT stands as one of the first prescriptive theories of crisis communication. SCCT goes beyond just descriptive theories to provide predictions about how stakeholders will react to specific crisis response strategies in different crisis situations (Thaler, 2015). More specifically, SCCT is an evidence-based approach to communication taken from a cognitive perspective. Evidence-based approaches are used in a wide array of fields that seek to use interventions to change behaviors and attitudes. An evidence-based approach marries the best evidence about interventions with professional experience. The key question driving an evidence-based approach is whether or not a specific intervention has the desired effect. Hence, evidence of a cause-effect relationship is the strongest form of evidence (Bouffard & Reid, 2012). SCCT uses experiments to create evidence of the cause and effect relationship between crisis response strategies and common crisis outcomes, including post-crisis reputation, purchase intention, and negative word-of-mouth.

It is important to consider how the term "crisis" is used in SCCT because there are many different definitions of "crisis." A crisis is viewed as a violation of stakeholder expectations that can produce negative effects for stakeholders and the organization (Coombs, 2019). SCCT was designed to address organizational crises, not disasters or political crises. Organizational crises can be divided into operational crises and paracrises. Operational crises are those situations where there is actual or potential disruption to organizational operations. Industrial accidents, product harm incidents requiring product recalls, and removal of top executives for misconduct are all examples of disruptions to operations. Operational crises produce clear victims, those who are harmed by the crisis in some way.

Paracrises are situations where managers must publicly manage a crisis risk and face some type of challenge to their behavior (Coombs & Holladay, 2012). "Para" means like and paracrises look like crises but are really risk management efforts. Paracrises rarely escalate to the point of disrupting operations. Rather, the harm from a paracrisis is predominantly reputational. All crises inflict some reputational damage on an organization, but the primary threat from a paracrisis is the reputational damage. Stakeholders being offended by organizational messaging, misinformation circulating about an organization, an organization misusing social media, and stakeholders claiming organizational actions are irresponsible are examples of paracrises. Paracrises generally emerge in the digital environment, but unlike operational crises, they can be managed by one or a few people and do not require activation of the crisis management team (Coombs, 2019).

SCCT is a sociocognitive theory because it centers on attributions of crisis responsibility shared by stakeholders (Bundy & Pfarrer, 2015). How people attribute responsibility is a driving factor in SCCT. It is critical to understand how much responsibility for the crisis most stakeholders are attributing to the organization in crisis. The stronger the attributions of responsibility, the more damage an organization is likely to suffer from a crisis. In SCCT, assessment of the potential crisis responsibility attribution is a two-step process. The first step is to determine how the crisis is being framed. SCCT has identified various crisis types (operational crises) that are used to frame crises and are organized by the level of crisis responsibility associated with the crisis type. Textbox 11.1 provides an overview of the crisis types in SCCT. The second step is to consider the contextual modifiers that can alter how people perceived the level of crisis responsibility. Extant research has shown that a history of past crises and a negative prior reputation can all intensify attributions of crisis responsibility (Coombs, 2007). SCCT does not argue all stakeholders see a crisis in exactly the same way. Rather, SCCT focuses on how most stakeholders perceive or are likely to perceive crisis responsibility in a particular crisis situation. This is consistent with how other researchers discuss varying perceptions of negative organizational events (management).

Textbox 11.1: Crisis Types in SCCT

Victim: extremely low attributions of crisis responsibility and organization is considered one of the victims of the crisis

- Natural disasters: operational disruptions caused by natural disasters
- Malevolence: outside attack on the organization such as product tampering
- Workplace violence: employees attacked by current or former employee

Accidental: minimal attributions of crisis responsibility

- Technical-error product harm: technical failure results in a product becoming dangerous
- Technical-error accident/disruption: technical failure results in an accident or other disruption

Preventable: strong attributions of crisis responsibility

- Human-error product harm: mistake by a person results in a product becoming dangerous
- Human-error accident/disruption: mistake by a person results in an accident or other disruption
- Management misconduct: management acts in a way that places stakeholders at risk, is illegal, and/or is immoral
- Scansis: management seeks to exploit stakeholders resulting in strong perceptions of moral outrage

The level of crisis responsibility is assessed to help determine the optimal crisis response for the situation. An optimal crisis response allows a crisis manager to maximize the beneficial power of crisis response strategies for stakeholders and the organization. SCCT posits that any crisis response should begin with adjusting and instructing information (Sturges, 1994) or what is called the ethical base response. Instructing information helps stakeholders to protect themselves physically from a crisis. Product recall information, warnings to shelter-in-place, and reports of where to find shelter are all examples of instructing information. Adjusting information helps people to cope psychologically with a crisis and includes curative actions, corrective actions, expressions of sympathy, and details about the crisis event. Curative actions are those designed to prevent a repeat of the actions that caused the crisis, while corrective actions seek to repair the damage generated by the crisis. Adjusting information has been and remains an important aspect of the crisis communication practice (Jackson, 1996; Jackson & Peters, nd).

Once the ethical base response is provided, crisis managers can consider additional responses intended to lessen the crisis damage, especially the reputational damage. The optimal response is a function of crisis responsibility and acceptance of responsibility. Crisis response can be arrayed along a continuum ranging from defensive to accommodative. Defensive strategies focus on the needs of the organization, while the accommodative strategies address the concerns of victims (those injured in some way by the crisis). As attributions of crisis responsibility increase, the crisis response must increase in its level of accommodation. The more accommodative strategies also are perceived by stakeholders as accepting more responsibility for the crisis (Coombs, 2006). Textbox 11.2 provides a summary of the primary crisis response options in SCCT for operational crises.

The selection of the optimal crisis response strategies in SCCT uses perceptions of attributions of crisis responsibility as the guiding force. Moreover, the intentional crisis cluster has proven to be more complicated than originally conceptualized. Each of these findings has ramifications for the selection of optimal crisis response strategies. Originally, accidental crises were thought to match with moderately accommodative strategies. However, the moderate accommodative responses have little effect on the crisis outcomes. The ethical base response is actually the optimal response for accidental crises, a similarity it shares with the victim crises. Bolstering is a secondary strategy that can be used with any of the other crisis response strategies. Research tends to find limited benefits to using a bolstering strategy as part of the crisis response (Ye & Ki, 2017). Textbox 11.3 provides a summary of the crisis response recommendations for the victim and accidental crisis clusters.

A more recent development in SCCT has been the reconfiguration of the preventable crisis cluster resulting from the study of scansis (Coombs & Tachkova, 2019). Initially, SCCT used the label preventable for the third crisis cluster and that label was later changed to intentional. However, the recent research demands a return to the preventable label because it is a

Textbox 11.2: Crisis Response Strategies in SCCT

Ethical base response: initial response designed to protect people physically and to help people cope psychologically with a crisis.

- Instructing information: warns people about how to protect themselves physically from a crisis.
- Adjusting information: helps people to cope psychologically with a crisis

Denial: seeks to escape responsibility for the crisis

- Attack the accuser: aggressive response to those claiming a crisis exists
- Denial: claim no crisis exists
- Scapegoat: attempt to shift the blame to another entity

Diminish: seek to less attributions of organizational responsibility

- Excuse: seek to minimize organizational responsibility for the crisis through denial of intent or control over events
- Justification: seek to minimize perceived severity of the crisis

Rebuild: take positive actions to help crisis victims

- Apology: accept responsibility for the crisis and request forgiveness
- Compensation (punitive): provide money or gifts to victims

Bolster: seek to place organization in a more favorable light

- Remind: tell stakeholders about past good works
- Ingratiation: praise stakeholders for actions during the crisis
- Victimage: note how organization is a victim of the crisis too

Textbox 11.3: SCCT Crisis Response Recommendations for Victim and Accident Crises

1 The ethical base response should be the first crisis message.
2 Bolstering can be added but typically adds little to the response.
3 Provide compensation to offset costs of the crisis for victims (reimbursement).
4 When contextual modifiers indicate perceptions of crisis responsibility will strengthen, crisis managers can add an apology and/or punitive compensation to the response.
5 For victim crises, the message might imply the organization is a victim of the crisis but this should be a minor point.

more accurate representation of the crisis cluster. More specifically, while people view human-error crises as preventable, they do not view them as intentional. A scansis is the intersection of a crisis and scandal which is created when a crisis is also a scandal (Coombs et al., 2018). Scandal has too many varied definitions to be a useful term, which is why the term scansis was created. The term scandal simply means too many different things for people. The key to a scandal and scansis is the moral component. The scansis also must be a moral violation that triggers moral outrage. According to cognitive appraisal theory, moral outrage is a distinct emotion that is evoked when people perceive a situation to be an injustice and be motivated by greed (Antonetti & Maklan, 2016).

A scansis is socially constructed because people must perceive injustice and exploitation in order to feel moral outrage for a situation to be deemed a scansis. Entman's (2012) work on political scandals demonstrates the same actions are not always considered a scandal. What matters is that people come to frame the actions as a scandal. Until the moral violation is highlighted, the action is not a scandal. This means we cannot automatically classify an event as a scansis, we must determine if the situation evokes moral outrage (Coombs et al., 2018). However, crisis managers should consider that they are in a scansis if media reports indicate the action triggering the situation is a function of injustice and exploitation. Managers can evaluate the media discussion of the crisis and identify if the two scansis cues are emerging or not. Initially, scansis was added to the preventable crisis because most scansis crises begin as management misconduct crises that generated strong feelings of moral outrage (Coombs et al., 2018; Coombs & Tachkova, 2019).

The preventable crisis cluster now is composed of human-error accidents, human-error product harm, management misconduct (transgressions), and scansis. The problem was that while similar, you can also find differences between these different crisis types. The clearest distinction is with human-error crises. Human-error crises generate strong attributions of crisis responsibility but are not considered intentional. Human-error crises reflect the competence-based trust violation. A competence violation is a result of a failure to properly enact skills (Kim et al., 2004). For human-error crises, the crisis was caused by people not doing their jobs properly. This is different from intentional efforts that are the result of a moral failing. Moral violations involve a violation of accepted principles of conduct (Kim et al., 2004). Management misconduct and scansis are more intentional and reflect the idea of a moral-based trust violation (Coombs & Tachkova, 2019).

Research has shown that assessments of moral outrage can be used to create the formation of three distinctive sub-clusters for the preventable crisis cluster: (1) human-error crises, (2) management misconduct, and (3) scansis. Human-error crises produced the lowest moral outrage, scansis produces the highest, and management misconduct was in the middle. The discovery of these sub-clusters demanded refinements to SCCT, including the recommendations for the selection of optimal crisis response strategies.

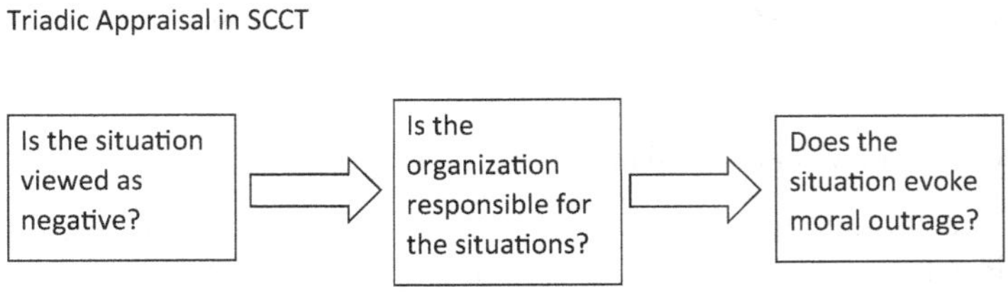

Figure 11.1 Triadic Appraisal in SCCT.

The addition of moral outrage indicated the value of a triadic appraisal in SCCT. SCCT has been premised on two cognitive appraisals. First, people decide if a situation is negative—a crisis. Second, people attribute responsibility for the crisis to the organization. Initially that was the end of the cognitive appraisals in SCCT. The new data indicate that it is instructive to consider a third appraisal, moral outrage. Moral outrage can significantly alter perceptions of the crisis and the ability of crisis response strategies to affect crisis outcomes. Figure 11.1 is a visual depiction of the triadic appraisal approach now recommended for SCCT.

Moral outrage also serves as a boundary condition for SCCT. Experiments have shown that the recommended crisis response strategies from SCCT can have a positive effect on post-crisis reputations for human-error crises but not for management misconduct or scansis crises (Coombs & Tachkova, 2019). When there is strong moral outrage, the communicative recommendations of SCCT no longer apply. However, the results do not imply that any crisis response can be used. Optimal crisis responses have a different effect on stakeholders in management misconduct and scansis. To understand this new effect, we need to explore the concept of organizational infamy.

A management misconduct or scansis crisis creates a potentially serious negative dynamic between an organization and its stakeholders. Stakeholders make a variety of social approval assessments about organizations that include reputation. Social approval represents the "more intuitive and affective perceptions inherent in social evaluations of an organization" (Bundy & Pfarrer, 2015, p. 348). Social approval assessments can create assets (favorable perceptions) or liabilities (unfavorable perceptions). Infamy is a social disapproval liability that is a result of value incongruence created by public attention to an organizational wrongdoing (deviant behavior that violates expectations). Infamy creates a negative affective response and promotes stakeholders' disidentification with the organization (Zavyalova et al., 2017). Both management misconduct and scansis are wrongdoings that attract media attention and create perceptions of value incongruence between the stakeholder and the organizations. Management misconduct and scansis are acts that lead stakeholders to conclude the organization is "not like me." Infamy is a social disapproval liability that is harmful to an organization. However, communication can be used to combat infamy.

Textbox 11.4: SCCT Crisis Response Recommendations for Preventable Crises

Human-Error Product Harm and Accident Crises

1 The ethical base response should be the first crisis message.
2 Bolstering can be added but typically adds little to the response.
3 Provide compensation to offset costs of the crisis for victims (reimbursement).
4 Add an apology and/or punitive compensation to the response.

Management Misconduct and Scansis Crises

1 The ethical base response should be the first crisis message.
2 Bolstering can be added but typically adds little to the response.
3 Provide compensation to offset costs of the crisis for victims (reimbursement).
4 Add an apology and/or punitive compensation to the response.
5 Acknowledge the moral violation has occurred and actions taken to prevent a repeat of the moral violation.

While people exposed to management misconduct and scansis crises did not see the typical positive effects from optimal crisis responses, there were some other positive effects. The optimal response involved acknowledging a violation of morals. Those exposed to the optimal crisis response in management misconduct and scansis crises did perceive the organization as more empathetic, a positive outcome related to forgiveness (Coombs & Tachkova, 2019). Moreover, a later study found the optimal crisis response did reduce value incongruence, an indicator that stakeholders were moving away from infamy (Coombs, 2019). For management misconduct and scansis, the purpose of the optimal response strategy is to combat infamy by promoting value congruence and empathy. The research generated studying scansis created a new set of optimal crisis response guidelines for the preventable crisis cluster. Textbox 11.4 presents the revised crisis response recommendations for SCCT and the preventable crisis cluster.

Scansis provides a connection between SCCT and the sticky crisis idea developed by the Crisis Communication Think Tank. Sticky crises are particularly challenging situations that move us beyond the common view of what constitutes a crisis. The stickiness is what creates greater challenges for crisis communicators. The next section highlights some of the key elements of sticky crises articulated by the Crisis Communication Think Tank

Sticky Crises: Insights for the Crisis Communication Think Tank

The 2019 Crisis Communication Think Tank wrestled with the concept of the sticky crisis. A sticky crisis is more challenging than the average crisis because it has elements that crisis managers do not typically encounter. Sticky crisis is an umbrella term for a number of different challenges created by crises. In this section, we will review a number of the key challenges that constitute sticky crises and some of the advice provided for managing them.

Context: The Digital Environment

The digital environment is a critical context for understanding sticky crises. We are not saying the digital environment created sticky crises but it does facilitate their development. The digital environment is the online world comprising various social media platforms and websites people can use to create and to share their ideas. Too often we think of these social media platforms as having a life of their own. Social media platforms only matter because people are willing to use them. Consider how a social media platform gets hot when users use it but can cool when users abandon it. The key is what has been termed digital naturals, people who are comfortable with and willing to use the various social media platforms and digital channels. The digital environment matters not because a social media platform exists but because digital naturals are willing to use them (Young & Akerstrom, 2015). One underlying theme in the Crisis Communication Think Tank discussion of sticky issues was the connection to the digital environment.

Variety of Challenges from Sticky Crises

Participants in the Crisis Communication Think Tank raised a number of factors that make a crisis sticky. Each of these factors presents a unique set of challenges for crisis managers. We will highlight seven factors that emerged from the discussion. Race was an early factor that was discussed. Race can be a component of a crisis and require the organization and stakeholders to engage in a serious discussion. A number of paracrises and crises have featured a racial component. Race can raise media attention to the situation, promote division, and evoke strong emotions. It is difficult to navigate a crisis or paracrisis that engenders division and powerful emotions. Social issues are very similar to race but more general. Social issues are divisive by nature because they are social concerns with at least two distinct sides. Social issues are about dissensus, not consensus. Social issues include same-sex marriage, gender equality, interracial marriage, and immigration. Emotion is a critical element in social issues too. Race and social issues share a concern with division and strong emotions. Organizations can be drawn into discussions of race or other social issues through the digital environment. Stakeholders can raise concerns about where the organization stands on race or other social issues or make claims that the organization is racist or violates their position on a social issue. Managers are then under pressure to respond to these public challenges (Coombs & Holladay, 2015).

Data privacy and breaches are important because organizations collect so much data about stakeholders. Stakeholders are concerned about how that data is used, shared, and the dangers of it being exposed. What is fascinating about data breaches is how stakeholders have quickly shifted from viewing those crises as victims to viewing them as preventable. People no longer see organizations as victims of hackers but as not properly defending their data. It does not help that many organizations have been slow to reveal data breaches and to move to help their stakeholders negatively affected by the breaches. The scansis is similar to data breaches because they are both preventable crises that evoke strong attributions of crisis responsibility. Scansis crises have proven too difficult to remediate effectively through typical crisis communication. Crisis communication has shown to have no effect on the common crisis outcomes of reputation, purchase intention, and negative word-of-mouth for a scansis (Coombs & Tachkova, 2019). Both data breaches and scansis require a strong focus on victim concerns due to the extreme reactions the crisis produces among stakeholders. The digital environment creates additional pressure by increasing awareness of the data breaches and scansis crises. Increased media attention helps to promote the moral outrage generated by scansis crises and increase stakeholder awareness of a breach and an organization's untimely disclosure of the breach.

Longitudinal crises are those that extend over a long period of time. We typically think of crises having a short duration, and one goal of crisis management is to shorten the duration of a crisis (Coombs, 2019). However, we now see crises that can linger for weeks and months. Consider the duration of Toyota's brake crisis for instance. This is a much different dynamic for crisis managers and the common crisis management tools may not be well suited for this new task. The digital environment can help to keep attention focused on a crisis even when traditional news media no longer cover the story. Another problematic dynamic is when a crisis becomes industry wide. Does the industry respond as a unified entity or does each organization fend for itself? The crisis communication becomes much more complicated when various organizations within the industry pursue different and often conflicting crisis communication strategies. The rhetorical arena theory (RAT) is among the few crisis communication theories to consider the challenges of an industry-wide crisis because RAT is sensitive to multiple crisis voices that may communicate with or against one another (Frandsen & Johansen, 2017). The digital environment is one forum in which organizations can conflict with their crisis communication messages.

Finally, we have the problem of disinformation. Whether deliberate or accidental, misinformation can circulate about an organization, its products, and/or its services. Disinformation focuses more on purposeful efforts but applies to accidental incidents as well. Organizations have always been confronted with disinformation, but the digital environment increases the likelihood of disinformation appearing and circulating. The digital environment increases the potential scope and speed of spread for disinformation. It is simply easier for disinformation to appear and to circulate in the digital environment. Procter and Gamble (P&G)'s disinformation about ties to devil worship is a great illustration. Prior to any Internet, P&G fought the disinformation that a top executive, on a television show, admitted a founder of the company made a pact with the devil for success and that money from P&G still supports devil worship. P&G managed this problem for years and seemed to be succeeding. Along comes the Internet and the devil worshiping disinformation explodes creating new headaches. At the core of the disinformation was the man-in-the-moon logo of P&G. The disinformation became so intense in the digital environment that P&G stopped using this iconic symbol.

Disinformation has been rising as a managerial risk globally. In 2019, the Global Risk Report from the World Economic Forum (2019) and risk consultancy Kroll's (2019) Global Fraud and Risk Report both identified disinformation as a serious threat. Both reports focus on purposeful efforts to use social media to spread disinformation that would harm an organization's reputation and even its stock price. Kroll's report, for instance, found that 84% of organizations consider disinformation a threat. We can ask the question, "How do organizations fight disinformation in this new digital environment?" The digital environment also provides tools for countering disinformation. The key is early detection and response to the disinformation. Consider the case of Starbucks and #borderfreecoffee. The disinformation effort claimed Starbucks would give a free Frappuccino to undocumented immigrants in the US. Starbucks deployed a rapid response to debunk the disinformation, including Twitter posts (Taylor, 2017. Research is still in the early stages of helping professionals understand what strategies are effective in fighting disinformation, but a quick response targeting the source and platforms for the disinformation seem to be the perfect starting point.

Counsel from the Crisis Communication Think Tank

Given the variety of ideas raised about sticky crises, there were not solutions for every specific concern. What did emerge were a number of ideas that could be applied to a variety of sticky crises. In this section, we will highlight four pieces of counsel that emerged from the discussions. We use the term counsel because it is not specific advice but rather important points to consider when encountering a sticky crisis.

Empathy was a common theme that emerged as advice for organizations facing sticky crises. Empathy centers on the need to focus on the concerns of victims by understanding their perspective on the crisis. Empathy is critical when you address divisive social issues. Crisis managers need to understand how people from the various sides, especially ones different from their own, feel about the issue. Managers also need to understand why a scansis crisis produces moral outrage and why stakeholders are so concerned about data breaches and data privacy. Empathy creates understanding and the ability to acknowledge how others are feeling and why they feel that way. Crisis managers must remember to consider empathy and to reflect empathy in their communication.

The concern with empathy relates directly to the second point of concern with emotions. Sticky crises will generate strong emotions. These emotions affect how people interpret the crisis and react to the organization's efforts to manage the crisis. Emotions complicate crisis communication, and crisis managers must be aware of the possible emotions they will encounter during the crisis.

Trust is the driving force in the organization-stakeholder relationship. Sticky crises are a threat to trust because there are trust violations. Scansis crises and data breaches are the clearest examples of how sticky crises violate trust. Part of crisis communication is understanding the need to rebuild trust and the potential actions that can be taken to rebuild trust.

Finally, there was a general sense of the need to engage with stakeholders over social issues (including race). The sticky crises driven by social issues are scary because managers must face divisive issues they would rather avoid. By taking a side on a social issue, managers know they will upset some of their stakeholders. Before hitting a social issue-related sticky crisis, managers must take the time to understand what values are important to the organization. Ideally, this is consistent with the values of your key stakeholders because the values are what drew them to your organization. If managers know their values, that provides the foundation for engaging with stakeholders on the social issues. The values inform the organization's position on and communication about the social issue.

Sticky Crises and SCCT: How Is the Fit?

We have detailed SCCT and explored what constitutes a sticky crisis, which leads us to consider how well SCCT fits with handling sticky crises. Given the variation within sticky crises, it is not surprising the answer is sometimes yes and sometimes no. In other words, it depends. SCCT works with sticky crises with those elements of sticky crises that fall within the parameters of SCCT. SCCT does not fit with elements of sticky crises that produce dynamics far removed from SCCT.

When There Is a Fit

SCCT fits well with scansis and data breaches. Recent re-conceptualizations of SCCT were developed to address scansis. Moral outrage was a boundary condition for the communicative recommendations of SCCT. SCCT was revised to help account for the effects or moral outrage. More specifically, SCCT found that a response that recognizes a moral violation (optimal response) is effective at realigning stakeholder and organizational values, creating a perception of empathy, and moving an organization away from infamy. This same advice should be useful when addressing data breaches because the response recognizes the emotions generated by the crisis and the need to express empathy for the crisis victims.

SCCT also can be applied to paracrises and crises that include racial and social issues. SCCT was extended a few years ago to include paracrises by providing guidance on factors to consider when responding to a paracrisis. This guidance can help crisis managers who find themselves drawn into a discussion of social issues, including race. Furthermore, SCCT's focus on empathy and appreciation of crisis emotions is useful when the racial or social issue does result in an actual crisis. Finally, SCCT conceptualizes reputation as trust—how much stakeholders trust the organization. Hence, SCCT does recognize the trust element that was identified as a key point in counsel for sticky crises.

When There Is Poor Fit

Disinformation is an evolving area that SCCT touches on minimally. SCCT treats disinformation as a paracrisis and has limited advice on the topic. The advice is similar to what we find among consultancies: respond quickly with messages designed to counter (debunk) the disinformation (Coombs, 2019). As research on disinformation increases, more precise advice can be developed for crisis managers facing the sticky crises driven by disinformation.

Industry-wide crises have the unique feature of multiple entities that might cooperate or might compete. RAT offers a better fit with its focus on a multi-vocal approach ability to map crisis voices (Frandsen & Johansen, 2017). SCCT can still apply as the entities select their crisis response but SCCT is not well equipped to handle the tracking of these different crisis voices. Longitudinal crises also have a unique dynamic that does not fit well with SCCT. SCCT was not designed to track crisis responses over time. Issues management actually has more appropriate tools for examining crisis response transpiring over an extended period of time (Crable & Faulkner, 1988). Again, SCCT can help with selecting isolated crisis responses at various points in the extended timeline but is not equipped to provide a more holistic analysis of that process. The regenerative crisis model can help to map the crisis communication process over time, but that is just a model, not a theory. The regenerative model argues that a crisis is composed of two phases, pre-crisis and post-crisis. A crisis is the dividing point and arises either as an event or the recognition of a problem. Moreover, turning points can occur that cause a redefinition/reframing of the crisis. A turning point creates a new marker for what is considered post-crisis and pre-crisis communication. Everything prior to the turning point becomes pre-crisis, while the time after is the post-crisis. The regenerative model attempts to capture the dynamic nature of crises by being more cyclical than linear (Coombs, 2017). More work needs to be done to develop tools to analyze the prolonged crisis. The chapter on corporate crisis communication provides a more detailed analysis of longitudinal crises.

Key Takeaways

Sticky crises impel us to reflect upon what we know about crisis communication because of the novel challenges they create for crisis managers. It becomes imperative to consider how well or poorly our existing theories and frameworks serve to redress sticky crises. This chapter has considered the fit between SCCT, a dominant theory used to guide crisis communication, and sticky crises. We first reviewed the essential elements of SCCT and characteristics of sticky crises. Broadly speaking, SCCT fits well with many of the ideas about sticky theories that emerged from the 2019 Crisis Communication Think Tank. SCCT has always considered trust as a central variable because SCCT defines reputation as trustworthiness. SCCT has recently been extended to include scansis and other crises that produce moral outrage and other extremely negative reactions from stakeholders. In addition, the recent revision includes a focus on the role of empathy in crisis communication. The paracrisis element of SCCT can help to provide guidance for racial and social issue risks that could manifest into crises. SCCT does not fit well with misinformation. Crisis managers and researchers need to monitor the misinformation research for ideas that can help sticky crises defined by misinformation. Nor does SCCT help to capture the complex elements of an industry-wide crisis. RAT provides an excellent framework for exploring and responding to industry-wide crises. Finally, longitudinal crises create unique challenges because those sticky crises are more akin to issues management than to traditional crisis management. Sticky crises remind us that crisis managers need to consider a range of theories and approaches. We must resist "best practices" that claim to have the one solution for all crises. A variety of crises, including sticky ones, will arise to test crisis managers. SCCT is one useful tool for addressing many crises but other perspectives must be part of the mix if crisis managers are to prepare to address the broad range of crises they might encounter.

References

Antonetti, P., & Maklan, S. (2016). An extended model of moral outrage at corporate social irresponsibility. *Journal of Business Ethics*, *135*(3), 429–444. http://dx.doi.org/10.1007/s10551-014-2487-y

Bouffard, M., & Reid, G. (2012). The good, the bad, and the ugly of evidence-based practicel. *Adapted Physical Activity Quarterly*, *29*(1), 1–24. http://dx.doi.org/10.1123/apaq.29.1.1

Bundy, J., & Pfarrer, M. D. (2015). A burden of responsibility: The role of social approval at the onset of a crisis. *Academy of Management Review*, *40*(3), 345–369. http://dx.doi.org/10.5465/amr.2013.0027

Coombs, W. T. (2006). The protective powers of crisis response strategies: Managing reputational assets during a crisis. *Journal of Promotion Management*, *12*(3–4), 241–260. http://dx.doi.org/10.1300/J057v12n03_13

Coombs, W. T. (2007). Protecting organization reputations during a crisis: The development and application of situational crisis communication theory. *Corporate Reputation Review*, *10*(3), 163–176. http://dx.doi.org/10.1057/palgrave.crr.1550049

Coombs, W. T. (2017). Digital naturals and the rise of paracrises: The shape of modern crisis communication. In S. Duhé (Ed.), *New media and public relations* (3rd ed., pp. 281–290). New York: Peter Lang.

Coombs, W. T. (2019). *Ongoing Crisis Communication: Planning, Managing, and Responding* (5th ed.). Sage Publications.

Coombs, W. T., & Holladay, J. S. (2012). The paracrisis: The challenges created by publicly managing crisis prevention. *Public Relations Review*, *38*(3), 408–415. http://dx.doi.org/10.1016/j.pubrev.2012.04.004

Coombs, W. T., & Holladay, S. J. (2015). CSR as crisis risk: Expanding how we conceptualize the relationship. *Corporate Communications: An International Journal*, *20*(2), 144–162. http://dx.doi.org/10.1108/CCIJ-10-2013-0078

Coombs, W. T., Holladay, S. J., & Tachkova, E. R. (2018). When a scandal and a crisis fuse: Exploring the communicative implications of scansis. In A. Haller, H. Michael, & M. Kraus (Eds.), *Scandology: An interdisciplinary field* (pp. 172–190). Köln: Herbert Von Verlag.

Coombs, W. T., & Tachkova, E. R. (2019). Scansis as a unique crisis type: Theoretical and practical implications. *Journal of Communication Management*, 23(1), 72–88. https://doi.org/10.1108/JCOM-08-2018-0078

Crable, R. E., & Faulkner, M. M. (1988). The issue development graph: A tool for research and analysis. *Communication Studies*, 39(2), 110–120.

Entman, R. M. (2012). *Scandal and silence: Media responses to presidential misconduct*. Malden, MA: Polity Press.

Frandsen, F., & Johansen, W. (2017). *Organizational crisis communication*. Sage.

Jackson, P. (1996, February 26). "Smoldering crises" account for 86% of business crises. *PR Reporter*, p. 4.

Jackson, P., & Peters, R. (nd). Issue anticipation/crisis management for beginning professionals. http://patrickjacksonpr.com/Theories%20&%20Models/Issues%20Anticipation-Crisis%20Management%20For%20Beginning%20Professionals%20for%20PRSSA.pdf.

Kim, P. H., Ferrin, D. L., Cooper, C. D., & Dirks, K. T. (2004). Removing the shadow of suspicion: the effects of apology versus denial for repairing competence-versus integrity-based trust violations. *Journal of Applied Psychology*, *89*(1), 104. http://dx.doi.org/10.1037/0021-9010.89.1.104

Kroll. (2019). Global fraud and risk report. https://www.kroll.com/en/insights/publications/global-fraud-and-risk-report-2019.

Sturges, D. L. (1994). Communicating through crisis: A strategy for organizational survival. *Management Communication Quarterly*, *7*(3), 297–316. http://dx.doi.org/10.1177/0893318994007003004

Taylor, K. (2017). Starbucks shoots down viral rumor that it's giving away free coffee to undocumented immigrants. https://www.businessinsider.com/fake-news-starbucks-free-coffee-to-undocumented-immigrants-2017-8

Thaler, R. H. (2015). *The making of behavioral economics: Misbehaving*. New York.

World Economic Forum (2019) Global risk report. http://www3.weforum.org/docs/WEF_Global_Risks_Report_2019.pdf.

Ye, L., & Ki, E. J. (2017). Organizational crisis communication on Facebook. *Corporate Communications: An International Journal*, *22*(1), 80–92. http://dx.doi.org/10.1108/CCIJ-07-2015-0045
Young, P., & Åkerström, M. (2015). Meet the digital naturals. In W. T. Coombs, J. Falkheimer, M. Heide, & P. Young (Eds.), *Strategic communication, social media and democracy: The challenge of the digital naturals* (pp. 1–10). Routledge.
Zavyalova, A., Pfarrer, M. D., & Reger, R. K. (2017). Celebrity and infamy? The consequences of media narratives about organizational identity. *Academy of Management Review*, *42*(3), 461–480. http://dx.doi.org/10.5465/amr.2014.0037

12 Managing Complexity

Insights from the Contingency Theory of Strategic Conflict Management

Yan Jin, Augustine Pang, Glen T. Cameron, Sungsu Kim, and Leonard (Len) A. Pagano, Jr.

Even as the first words are being written in this chapter, the world is engulfed in the COVID-19 pandemic, which challenges how organizations should effectively communicate about and respond to a complex crisis issue that threatens individuals, businesses, communities, and governments globally in unprecedented ways. With globalization and advancement in technology, interaction and intersection of people groups are almost instantaneous. A world without borders does not mean a simpler world. On the contrary, it has become more complex. Complex systems are generated from the interlocking and connections of people and situations (Ho, 2017). In a highly connected world, events that are seemingly simple, unanticipated, and unrelated can take on surprising forms, escalate, spread, and morph into complex crises – crises that are "harder than ever to contain" (PWC, n.d.). Boin (2009) also noted that crises can cross boundaries and they can cause "damage in an insidious way" crippling "critical infrastructures" as well as undermining "governance structures and processes" (p. 369).

Donald Rumsfeld, former United States (US) Defense Secretary, coined these famous words on the complexity of crises:

> As we know, there are known knowns; there are things we know we know. We also know there are known unknowns; that is to say we know there are some things we do not know. But there are also unknown unknowns—the ones we don't know we don't know.
>
> (Graham, 2014)

Amidst an increasingly porous international landscape, how do these affect the organization? One outcome is the idea of "cross-national conflict shifting" (Molleda et al., 2005), where in an increasingly permeable international landscape, a crisis that occurs in an organization in one country simultaneously impacts other countries. Molleda (2011) argued that because the lines between "national, regional, and international businesses" have diminished, there is little distinction between "domestic and foreign crises" (p. 49). These crises could affect the reputation of organizations in the home and host countries, thereby requiring more finesse in communication strategies (Molleda, 2011).

What this means for organizations, argued Pang et al. (2010c), is that organizations need to be:

- More responsive to ever-changing circumstances in the environment;
- More dynamic in their responses to their publics;
- More cognizant of the factors that undergird their decisions;
- More mindful in navigating through the minefields of complex crisis issues.

Complexity in Real-World Crises

Over a decade ago, public relations scholars called for a "complexity-based approach" to crisis management that "involved monitoring a full range of media to identify emergent patterns, and develop adaptive communication strategies before these patterns coalesced into crisis formations" (Gilpin & Murphy, 2010, p. 75). According to Gilpin and Murphy (2010), in the setting of crises, complex systems are made of multiple interacting agents (e.g., publics, organizations, media sources), the nature of which is dynamic, unstable, uncertain, and highly contextual. The key context types are history, culture, and media environment, which are "dynamic, interdependent, and mutually influential" (Gilpin & Murphy, 2010, p. 77).

Crisis complexity is thus manifested in stakeholders, strategic planning, and media environment (Gilpin & Murphy, 2010). From a practitioner's perspective, real-world crisis communication is an increasingly intricate and complex process. Imagine: How does one tell people what to do *during* a crisis, what is the difference in telling a baby boomer versus a millennial, what will *change* over the next ten years, and can one assume that educators—"communicators"—know *what* needs to be said?

Take disaster as an example: In Puerto Rico, people assume that there will be more hurricanes. The Safe America Foundation (SAF) seeks to educate youth on how to "deal with" issues in their homes and communities. But do they know how to advise their parents and teachers? Then, there's mainland America—and California—where the Los Angeles school system alone has more than 50 languages. Can people tell children (much less adults) what to do well?

Another example: Reports of gun violence have caused many to assume that there are many "mass shooters" out there. While the Federal Emergency Management Agency (FEMA) has advised people to "Run/Hide/Fight," the Metro Atlanta Police Commission has stated that "Police are NOT required to protect citizens." But do citizens have this perspective? This is unlikely, as people assume that law enforcement is "there to save our lives."

The challenge in both examples is: Who seems to think *they* are responsible to save themselves in disasters? Are people being *told* this today? The same issue is also a challenge when managing crisis complexity in business.

The SAF is aware that many businesses don't know how to rehearse for disasters.

As the world enters a new decade, it is imperative to have more people who are "prepared, not scared" (FEMA, 2019). Yet what will be the impetus for 40- or 65-year-olds to take on an active leadership role in times of disaster preparedness and responses? And how—and when—can millennials and "Selfie Gen" be expected to take an active part in community leadership? It comes down to these simple questions in managing crisis complexity:

- *Who* will be the *leader?*
- *What* do they perceive to *say?*
- And what *channel* (e.g., social media, traditional broadcasting, text messages) will they use?

An example of best practice and future potential for incorporating these factors is the SAF's 2010 campaign with Verizon—"Text First. Talk Second." The campaign urged people to use text technology as their first choice to contact loved ones during emergency situations. The Alert ID system helps make public safety information universally accessible in the country, allowing information to be immediately shared in a disaster and enabling individuals to plan and be prepared for such an event. The need for such a system is re-emerging, and 5G technology seems to be promising in enhancing the individual-empowered disaster information system. However, 5G is yet to be fully in place. There is a need for nationwide emergency communication via mass media—much like in the 1960s when television stations and networks would stage a "drill" on TV or Radio, based on the Federal Communication Commission's (FCC) guidelines. A new version of universal drills is urgently needed, which is why the SAF is working with the University of Georgia to grow a "Safety News Network" (SNN) emergency channel and a September "Drill Month." The SAF will also be working with AT&T, Walmart, Office Depot, and the International Association of Emergency Managers (IAEM) to promote a "9/11 Drill Down" Day (September 11).

Another idea the SAF envisions is to make the 366th day, as embedded in Leap Year every four years, a Safety Drill Day. This day could be further "embedded" in December—and become the 32nd day of the month. This concept—of establishing a December 32nd day every fourth year—may cause great "alarm" as people, by default, tend to regard February as having only 28 days *every* year. However, discussing the basic issues of *needing to be ready to resolve risks* could benefit from something "provocative" like growing December by one day every four years. How and what is said may help cultivate alignment among different companies, countries, and the global populations.

Such an idea could be pure fantasy, but creating a year-end day—every fourth Leap Year—could be a phenomenal way of raising the conversation on communicating risks more effectively. Strategic communication is essential in urgent storytelling, which can and will transform individual lives and community well-being. From the perspective of the SAF, there's no question of today's complexity in crisis communication. And, there is no doubt that crises will get more complex in the continuing evolution of society. How—and what—organizations like the SAF do to educate the next generation is critical to minimizing risks and saving lives.

Meeting the Challenges in Complexity: A Dynamic Approach

As Gilpin and Murphy (2010) noted, the complexity approach to crisis management emphasizes "the role of contingency, uncertainty, and accident; the unexpected confluence of unrelated events; and the destabilizing influence of rapidly changing circumstances" (p. 77). For public relations scholars and practitioners, the core to address crisis complexity lies with a systematic understanding of the situational, organizational, stakeholder, and media environment complexity comprehensively. Among existing public relations theories, the contingency theory by Cameron and his colleagues specifically tackles complex issues confronting practice (i.e., how to manage competition and conflicts), echoing the need to grasp "larger contextual patterns and relationships" advocated by Gilpin and Murphy (2010).

Since its origin in the 1990s, the contingency theory of strategic conflict management, as it is now known (Pang et al., 2010a), has emerged as an empirically tested grand theory that focuses on how public relations ought to be practiced in complex media environment and when confronted by complex issues. The contingency theory provides a theoretical framework that examines through a continuum whereby a variety of stances are practiced by organizations, depending on the complex circumstances, therefore functioning as a "sense-making effort to ground a theory of accommodation in practitioner experience..." (Yarbrough et al., 1998, p. 53).

Under the overarching "It Depends" philosophy, Cameron and his colleagues developed the contingency theory by using a continuum from pure advocacy to pure accommodation to represent the stance movement within an organization. The contingency theory focuses on the stance of the organization in dealing with a given public, not the outcomes of public relations practice, thus arguing that in a complex public relations situation (e.g., crisis or conflict), an organization's stance movements along the continuum would determine the position the organization undertakes "*at a given time* regarding *a given public*" (Cancel et al., 1999, p. 172; Yarbrough et al., 1998, p. 40). As a conflict management theory, the contingency theory has since been applied to crisis situations (e.g., Pang et al., 2010a; Shin et al., 2013). In complex crisis situations, the philosophical statement of the theory, "It Depends," helps guide the practice of identifying driving forces of stance movement and dissect the intertwined factors that jointly exert influences on both internal decision-making and external power negotiation.

"It Depends": Stance Movements

As a core construct of the contingency theory, *stance* is measured through a continuum, which has, at one end, advocacy—arguing for self—and, at the other end, accommodation—accepting the other party's proposal. The contingency theory argues that a realistic description of how public relations, conflict management, and/or crisis communication is practiced is through the examination of an organization's stance (Cancel et al., 1997). Stance is defined as the posture or position the organization assumes, which determines the strategies and tactics it might take next. In a complex crisis situation, it offers a perspective to examine how an organization relates to an affected public through the enactment of a given stance toward that public at a given point in time as the crisis cycle progresses and issues unravel.

Pure Advocacy Pure Accommodation
I---I

Between the two ends of a continuum are a wide range of operational stances and these entailed "different degrees of advocacy and accommodation" (Cancel et al., 1997, p. 37). The contingency theory seeks to understand the complex nature and the dynamics, in and out of the organization, which affect an organization's decision-making over time. It aims to "offer a structure for better understanding of the dynamics of accommodation as well as the efficacy and ethical implications of accommodation in public relations practice" (Yarbrough et al., 1998, p. 41). According to Cameron and his colleagues, stance moves along the continuum, representing an organization's willingness to make concessions or offer trade-offs at one end ("pure accommodation") and its willingness to plead its case at the other ("pure advocacy"). Stance changes, depending on the circumstances.

Circumstances Matter: Contingency Factors

According to the contingency theory, the stance an organization takes is entangled with different factors. Cameron and his colleagues identified a matrix of 87 contingent factors (see Textbox 12.1) based on public relations literature, excellence theory, observations, and grounded theory (Cameron, 1997). The contingency theory argues that any of the 87 factors can affect the location of an organization on the continuum "*at a given time* regarding *a given public*" (Cancel et al., 1999, p. 172; Yarbrough et al., 1998, p. 40).

Internal vs. External Variables. These factors were initially grouped into *internal variables* related to the characteristics of the organization (e.g., public relations department's characteristics, internal threats) and *external variables* regarding the environment and the characteristics of the publics (e.g., industry environment, issue under question).

Predisposing vs. Situational Factors. These variables were categorized into predisposing and situational factors. On one hand, *predisposing factors*

Textbox 12.1: Variables That Affect an Organization's Response

1 Organization characteristics
   - Open or closed culture
   - Dispersed widely geographically or centralized
   - Level of technology the organization uses to produce its product or service
   - Homogeneity or heterogeneity of officials involved
   - Age of the organization/value placed on tradition
   - Speed of growth in the knowledge level the organization uses
   - Economic stability of the organization
   - Existence or non-existence of issues management officials or program
   - Organization's past experiences with the public
   - Distribution of decision-making power
   - Formalization: Number of roles or codes defining and limiting the job
   - Stratification/hierarchy of positions
   - Existence or influence of legal department
   - Business exposure
   - Corporate culture

2 Public relations department characteristics
   - Number of practitioners total and number of college degrees
   - Type of past training: Trained in public relations (PR) or ex-journalists, marketing, etc.
   - Location of PR department in hierarchy: Independent or under marketing umbrella/experiencing encroachment of marketing/persuasive mentality
   - Representation in the Dominant Coalition
   - Experience level of PR practitioners in dealing with crisis
   - General communication competency of department
   - Autonomy of department
   - Physical placement of department in building (near CEO and other decision makers or not)
   - Staff trained in research methods
   - Amount of funding available for dealing with external publics
   - Amount of time allowed to use dealing with external publics
   - Gender: Percentage of female upper-level staff/managers
   - Potential of department to practice various models of public relations

3 Characteristics of dominant coalition (top management)
   - Political values: Conservative or liberal/open or closed to change
   - Management style: Domineering or laid-back

- General altruism level
- Support and understanding of PR
- Frequency of external contact with publics
- Departmental perception of the organization's external environment
- Calculation of potential rewards or losses using different strategies with external publics
- Degree of line manager involvement in external affairs

4 Internal threats (how much is at stake in the situation)
- Economic loss or gain from implementing various stances
- Marring of employees' or stockholder's perception of the company
- Marring of the personal reputations of the company decision makers

5 Individual characteristics (public relations practitioners, domestic coalition, and line managers)
- Training in diplomacy, marketing, journalism, engineering, etc.
- Personal ethics
- Tolerance or ability to deal with uncertainty
- Comfort level

6 Relationship characteristics
- Level of trust between organization and external public
- Dependency of parties involved
- Ideological barriers between organization and public

7 External threats
- Litigation
- Government regulation
- Potentially damaging publicity
- Scarring of company's reputation in business community and in the general public
- Legitimizing activists' claims

8 Industry environment
- Changing (dynamic) or static
- Number of competitors/level of competition
- Richness or leanness of resources in the environment

9 General political/social environment/external culture
- Degree of political support of business
- Degree of social support of business

10 The external public (e.g., group, individual)
- Size and/or number of members
- Degree of source credibility/powerful members or connections
- Past successes or failures of groups to evoke change
- Amount of advocacy practiced by the organization
- Level of commitment/involvement of members

- Whether the group has public relations counselors or not
- Public's perception of group: reasonable or radical
- Level of media coverage the public has received in the past
- Whether representatives of the public know or like representatives of the organization
- Whether representatives of the organization know or like representatives from the public
- Public's willingness to dilute its cause/request/claim
- Moves and countermoves
- Relative power of organization
- Relative power of public

11 Issue under question
- Size
- Stake
- Complexity

include the characteristics of dominant coalition, public relations' access to top management, organizational size and culture, and so forth. On the other hand, *situational factors* include characteristics of the external public, perceived urgency and threat, and feasibility of accommodation. Predisposing variables determine an organization's stance before it goes into a situation dealing with a given public, while the combination and variability of situational factors might shift the stance of the organization over time, depending on whether the situational factors are powerful enough to change the predisposing positioned stance on the continuum.

Proscriptive Factors. To understand why symmetrical or accommodation stances cannot be taken at some situations, Cameron et al. (2001) studied the following key *proscriptive factors*: (1) The morality of top management, (2) The position caught in-between two contending publics at the same time, and (3) Restriction from regulation. They were found to preclude an organization from accommodating or even communicating with a public. It is concluded that for those situations, even though an organization seems to take an excellence or "symmetrical" approach, their stance swiftly changes and moves on the continuum of accommodation based on the influence of those proscriptive factors.

Mapping Crisis Emotions

To extend the contingency model by shifting the focus from the organizational decisions and actions to publics' minds and hearts, Jin et al. (2012b) developed a systemic approach to understanding the responses of audiences to crisis situations—the Integrated Crisis Mapping (ICM) model. The ICM is based on a publics-based, emotion-driven perspective where responses to different crises are mapped on two continua, the organization's engagement in the crisis and primary publics' coping strategy. This multi-stage testing found that anxiety is the default emotion that publics feel in crises. The subsequent emotions felt by the publics vary in different quadrants involving different types of crises. As far as coping strategies were concerned, conative coping is more evident than cognitive coping across the four quadrants. Evidence also suggests strong merit that conative coping is the external manifestation of the internal cognitive processing that has already taken place. Cognitive coping is thus the *antecedent* of conative coping. Though both the publics and the organizations agreed that the crises were relevant to the organizations' goals, they differed on who should assume more responsibility.

As Jin et al. (2012b) advocated, publics' crisis receptions should increasingly dominate crisis research for the simple argument that organizational strategies would be ineffectual if these do not appeal to the hearts and minds of the publics the organizations are trying to reach. Thus, the ICM model is positioned to understand a crisis from the perspectives of the publics so that organizational strategies and responses can be more appropriately targeted and honed.

Adopting Ethics in Complex Situations

Pang et al. (2010b) also unearthed a set of new factors, grounded in corporate social responsibility (CSR) and conflict communication literature, called ethical variables that influence the organization's stance before it communicates with its stakeholders: (1) *the role of public relations practitioners*; (2) *the role of top management*; (3) *exposure of organizational business (e.g., different business environments in different countries) and to diversity of cultures (e.g., diverse internal and external cultures organizations are situated in)*; (4) *government influence and intervention*; (5) *nature of crisis*; and (6) *activism of the stakeholders.* These ethical factors may influence the organization's adoption of an ethical stance toward a given public at a given time from pure advocacy to pure accommodation.

These ethical factors were explored in both Singapore (Pang et al., 2016) and the US (Jin et al., 2018) contexts. Crisis managers interviewed defined an organization's ethical crisis communication as

> communicating with its prioritized publics with accurate and timely crisis information, during the entire crisis cycle, in a transparent, responsible and honest way, which contributes to the overall business strategy and reputational well-being of the organization in the long term.

They argued that organizations should develop a culture of ethics that permeates the organizations, which makes the consideration of ethical crisis communication much more straightforward and consistent with the values of the organization in an increasingly complex media environment with challenging issues rising constantly internally and externally.

New Frontier in Understanding Complexity in Crises

The contingency theory provides a broader framework that helps organizations manage complexity in the context of crisis occurrence. In this sense, the frontier that the contingency theory would take in the future is geared toward the publics' minds and perspectives, which is consistent with how scholars have attempted to develop the theory. As delineated in the previous sections, the contingency theory has been extended to include and discern publics' perspectives within the scope of the theory, with the help of empirical evidence, to ultimately guide organizations' crisis coping strategies and responses that appeal to publics most effectively (Jin et al., 2012b).

Organizational Confidence

In terms of adopting publics' perspectives in the contingency theory's framework, scholars suggested that developing and testing a new publics-centered continuum would be an essential starting point (Kim et al., 2017). The proposed continuum has two ends: total confidence and total doubt as represented below:

Total Confidence — Total Doubt
I---I

Between the two ends of the publics' continuum, how publics perceive organizations as capable of handling crises in relevant situations is manifested (Kim et al., 2017). Confidence is originally a concept that is based on "the belief, based on experience or evidence that certain future events will occur as expected" (Earle et al., 2007, p. 4). In this regard, organizational confidence from publics' view should examine whether they would believe the crisis is managed well or stopped by the organization confronting the crisis. According to previous literature about confidence, knowledge and information about past performance determines one's confidence level (Siegrist et al., 2007). Those who are confident of the organization's ability are likely to have prior experience to observe that it performs well. This should apply to publics' perception toward an organization in the context of crises.

Conceptually and quite naturally, crisis history acts as an indicator of past performance of an organization in terms of crisis management capability, which provides evidence or rationale for publics to have organizational confidence (Coombs, 2004). Because a repetition of similar crises is likely to be a consequence of the organization's poor past performance in crisis management, crisis history is a vital factor to influence publics' evaluation of the organization (Coombs, 2004; Hong & Len-Riós, 2015). On the confidence-doubt continuum, one's being closer to the end of total doubt should indicate that he/she may be aware of the past similar crises with which the organization was involved.

Conceptualization of organizational confidence is theoretically supported by an explication of crisis threat, which refers to "potentially negative situation involving publics" and has been explicated as a critical factor to determine organization's stances on the continuum of advocacy and accommodation (Cancel et al., 1997, 1999, p. 184; Jin et al., 2005, 2012a). Threat likely affects how accommodating the organization is, as "the greater threat a public presents to an organization, the faster the organization will respond to the public and the more accommodating the organization will be to the public" (Cancel et al., 1999, p. 184). Indeed, the threat appraisal model was developed to explicate public relations practitioners' decision on their organization's stances when conflicts with publics arise, based on threat dimensionality (i.e., threat duration, threat level, threat type) (Jin et al., 2005).

As an attempt to expand the contingency theory into the grand theory that includes the publics' minds in it, an extended notion of crisis threat was proposed (Kim, 2017). This novel approach regarded publics' perception of crisis threat as a variable to impact their evaluations of crisis and an organization (e.g., crisis responsibility, organizational reputation, crisis emotions, supportive behavioral intentions) (Kim, 2017).

This approach is benefited from adopting publics' viewpoints and is connected to the publics' continuum of confidence and doubt. Threat appraisal model listed threat's two components: situational demands (i.e., danger, uncertainty, and required effort) and resources (i.e., knowledge, skill, time, finances, and support from the dominant coalition) with the help of emotion appraisal theory (Jin et al., 2012a; Lazarus, 1991). Situational demands are perceived by primary appraisal and resources are by secondary appraisal (Jin et al., 2012a). According to Lazarus (1991), the primary appraisal entails individuals' evaluation of goal relevance, goal congruence or incongruence, and their involvement; the secondary appraisal is related to assessment of blame (or credit), coping potential, and future expectancy. Especially, the secondary appraisal of emotions, which centers on perception of the future, enables people to discern whether the coping would result in desirable outcomes (e.g., prevention of harms) (Lazarus, 1991).

Organizational confidence likely comes from the secondary appraisal of coping potential. Considering that the secondary appraisal of resources as a part of threat appraisal is centered on whether demands of encounter can be managed by coping actions (Lazarus, 1991), confidence about an organization's crisis coping ability should be a consequence of resource appraisal. Especially, in the secondary appraisal stage, publics likely evaluate coping potential which is tied to "whether and how the person can manage the demands of the encounter or actualize personal commitments" (Lazarus, 1991, p. 150). Even though coping potential is not an actual management action, it demonstrates an expectation of how the coping action would protect the person-environment relationship (Lazarus, 1991). This appraisal mechanism should be applied in threat appraisal and organizational confidence from the publics' perspectives. When the publics appraise threat in the context of crisis happening, they use two stages of appraisal (i.e., primary and secondary) and, especially, perceive coping potential of the organization in crisis, which is an essential part of the secondary appraisal of resources (Jin et al., 2012a; Lazarus, 1991). The confidence about an organization's crisis coping ability is, by nature, derived from the appraisal of coping potential because crisis is a demanding encounter the organization ought to handle.

Overall, the publics' stance on the confidence-doubt continuum is based on their perception of crisis threat. Coping potential should act as an antecedent of organizational confidence, which should ultimately affect other crisis responses (e.g., organizational reputation, crisis emotions). Future research may take this approach by examining how organizational confidence is formed and how it leads to the publics' perception of crisis and the organization.

Temporal Distance of Crisis Threat

Along with the public-centered continuum of confidence and doubt, consideration of time into the dimensionality of threat under the umbrella of the contingency theory was proposed (Kim, 2017). Temporal distance, derived from construal level theory, would extend the notion of crisis threat as an additional dimension and address the publics' minds in better understanding the audiences of crisis response messages (Kim, 2017). According to construal level theory, temporal distance makes a difference in individuals' psychological associations with an object (Trope & Liberman, 2010). Through a construal, which is "the processes that give rise to the representation of the event itself" (Trope & Liberman, 2010, p. 443), individuals perceive a temporally distal object as more abstract, high-level, and a temporally near event as concrete, low-level (Trope & Liberman, 2010). People's judgment, attitudes, and even behaviors are changed as a consequence of the construal process based on time (Eyal et al., 2008).

Looking into temporal distance from a crisis threat would be a systematic approach that helps understand publics' crisis responses (e.g., reputation, supportive behavioral intention, crisis attitudes) (Kim, 2017). It is expected that this novel approach beyond the traditional three-dimensionality of threat appraisal would provide beneficial implications that help develop effective crisis management strategies appealing to the publics. To this end, temporal distance from a crisis threat, along with organizational confidence, needs to be studied. The following section introduces an actual study that examined the notion of temporal distance and organizational confidence, which is a big step before the next phase of advancing the contingency theory of strategic conflict management.

An Actual Empirical Case for the Future Frontier of the Contingency Theory

In an experimental study (Kim, 2019), crisis history and temporal distance were explicated for empirically testing how organizational confidence and temporal distance from a crisis threat plays a role in crisis management. In this study, experiment participants were exposed to messages with different temporal distance from a crisis threat (i.e., proximal future vs. distant future) and crisis history (i.e., previous crisis history vs. no previous crisis history) in the context of drinking water contamination crisis of a fictitious company. The results indicated that crisis history significantly impacted organizational confidence, with those in "previous crisis history" condition reporting a lower level of organizational confidence than those in "no previous crisis history" condition. Additionally, the interaction effect of temporal distance and crisis history on organizational confidence was found. The mean difference between a proximal-future threat and a distant-future threat in "previous crisis history" condition was bigger than the difference between a proximal-future threat and a distant-future threat in "no previous crisis history" condition. This study demonstrates how crisis history and threat appraisal work in understanding publics' perception about the organization in crisis. In terms of embarking on the journey toward grand theory building, the directions proposed in this section need to be taken for future research of the contingency theory and more empirical testing ought to be conducted.

Key Takeaways

The dynamics and complexity of crises and crisis communication decision-making have presented challenges and opportunities for practitioners and scholars to co-assess the nature of crisis complexity and co-create mechanism to better (1) capture and explain ongoing issues and communication barriers, (2) predict communication outcomes and adapt timely challenges, and (3) advise organizations (either crisis-stricken or in charge of crisis response) on how, who, when, and with what channels to inform publics, help them cope with stresses and crisis emotions, and motivate them to respond to a crisis situation effectively, which contribute to public safety and well-being and help shield organizational reputation and ensure business continuity. The contingency theory of strategic conflict management provides a realistic roadmap for organizations to be mindful about (1) the set of complex and often-intertwining factors that are likely to co-influence the development and escalation of a crisis situation, and (2) the need to have strategic conflict positioning in order to navigate internal and external communication challenges and severe threats.

The tenet and key recommendations of the contingency theory of strategic conflict management help guide organizational stance movement and approaches to complex crisis issues and situation-specific demands, which provide insights for scholars and practitioners to continue co-addressing key questions in crisis communication in the 21st century, such as:

- What are the most complex crisis issues (and most important driving factors) confronting publics in the US and abroad, and how do organizations deal with them across industry and sector?
- What can be the "standard" crisis communications' channel or channel combinations that can be used when tailored message content is

disseminated to different publics with different temporal distance associated with a crisis situation?
- In the era of social media, how can mass communications elevate disaster "smartness"—like communicators did in the 1960s–1970s with the use of seat belts, thus strengthening its niche function in communicating to the general public about large-scale public emergencies?
- 2019 was the 75th anniversary of "Smokey the Bear" (NPR, 2019). Is an icon needed to help people recognize a wide spectrum of safety hazards they have in multiple areas? Examples of such areas are: (1) public health crises such as outbreaks, (2) transportation safety, (3) cyber security, (4) safety issues concerning community (venues) like stadiums, shopping malls, and churches, (5) pharmaceuticals that get "promoted'" as standard but are hazards (e.g., opioids), and (6) weather-related natural disasters as well as man-made disasters such as terrorist attacks.
- In the 1960s, airlines in the US had people 'hi-jack' planes to Cuba. In 2001, terrorists took planes into the Twin Towers. What will be the future with technology such as drones (as seen in Saudi Arabia, where they turned into catastrophic non-human air devices), and to what degree will technology provide internal and external threat/opportunity of managing conflicting issues and conflicted publics.

Answers to these questions need to be effectively used and shared with affected populations. With the increasingly diverse population in the US (e.g., Americans are becoming more bilingual or even trilingual) and the need for diverse voices globally when it comes to conflict management and crisis communication, the potential of images, with cross-cultural universal meaning associated with visual language and emotions, need to be unlocked so as to be effectively used or be used in conjunction with verbiage for more compelling truth telling. Furthermore, in the social media era, organizations need to collaborate with tech companies and social media platforms to co-research and co-create strategies and tactics, generating synergy of traditional mass media, social media, and interpersonal communion channels to align crisis information, public perception, crisis attribution, crisis distance assessment, and crisis stance as expected by publics and as positioned by organizations.

Future crisis communication research, built upon the roadmap and delineated key factors provided by the contingency theory of strategic conflict management, should investigate these interconnected issues and determine how these complex and important puzzles can be solved together by practitioners and scholars.

References

Boin, A. (2009). The new world of crises and crisis management: Implications for policymaking and research. *Review of Policy Research, 26*(4), 367–377. https://doi.org/10.1111/j.1541-1338.2009.00389.x

Cameron, G. T. (1997). The contingency theory of conflict management in public relations. *Proceedings of the Norwegian Information Service*. Oslo, Norway.

Cameron, G. T., Cropp, F., & Reber, B. H. (2001). Getting past platitudes: Factors limiting accommodation in public relations. *Journal of Communication Management, 5*(3), 242–261. https://doi.org/10.1108/13632540110806802

Cancel, A. E., Cameron, G. T., Sallot, L. M., & Mitrook, M. A. (1997). It depends: A contingency theory of accommodation in public relations. *Journal of Public Relations Research, 9*(1), 31–63. https://doi.org/10.1207/s1532754xjprr0901_02

Cancel, A. E., Mitrook, M. A., & Cameron, G. T. (1999). Testing the contingency theory of accommodation in public relations. *Public Relations Review, 25*(2), 171–197. https://doi.org/10.1016/S0363-8111(99)80161-1

Coombs, W. T. (2004). A theoretical frame for post-crisis communication: Situational crisis communication theory. In M. J. Martinko (Ed.), *Attribution theory in the organizational sciences: Theoretical and empirical contributions* (pp. 275–296). Information Age Publishing.

Earle, T. C., Siegrist, M., & Gutscher, H. (2007). Trust, risk perception and the TCC model of cooperation. In M. Siegrist, T. C. Earle, & H. Gutscher (Eds.), *Trust in cooperative risk management: Uncertainty and scepticism in the public mind* (pp. 1–50). Earthscan.

Eyal, T., Liberman, N., & Trope, Y. (2008). Judging near and distant virtue and vice. *Journal of Experimental Social Psychology, 44*(4), 1204–1209. https://doi.org/10.1016/j.jesp.2008.03.012

Federal Emergency Management Agency (FEMA) (2019). *Prepared, not scared* (written by D. Kaniewski). https://www.fema.gov/blog/2019-09-19/prepared-not-scared.

Gilpin, D. R., & Murphy, P. (2010). Implications of complexity for public relations: Beyond crisis. In R. L. Heath (Ed.), *Handbook of Public Relations* (2nd ed.). Sage Publications (pp. 71–83).

Graham, D. (2014, March 27). Rumsfeld's Knowns and Unknowns: The Intellectual History of a Quip. The Atlantic. https://www.theatlantic.com/politics/archive/2014/03/rumsfelds-knowns-and-unknowns-the-intellectual-history-of-a-quip/359719/.

Ho, P. (2017, April, 5). The Challenges of Governance in a Complex World. Lecture 1: Hunting Black Swans and Taming Black Elephants: Governance in a Complex World. IPS-Nathan Lectures.

Hong, S., & Len-Riós, M. E. (2015). Does race matter? Implicit and explicit measures of the effect of the PR spokesman's race on evaluations of spokesman source credibility and perceptions of a PR crisis' severity. *Journal of Public Relations Research, 27*(1), 63–80. https://doi.org/10.1080/1062726X.2014.929502

Jin, Y., Pang, A., & Cameron, G. T. (2005, May). *Explicating threats: Towards a conceptual understanding of the faces and fabric of threat in an organizational crisis*. Annual Conference of International Communication Association, New York, NY.

Jin, Y., Pang, A., & Cameron, G. T. (2012a). Pre-crisis threat assessment: A cognitive appraisal approach. In B. A. Olaniran, T. W. Coombs, & P. Augustine (Eds.), *Pre-crisis Planning, Communication, and Management: Preparing for the Inevitable* (pp. 125–146). Peter Lang Publishing.

Jin, Y., Pang, A., & Cameron, G. T. (2012b). Toward a publics-driven, emotion-based conceptualization in crisis communication: Unearthing dominant emotions in multi-staged testing of the integrated crisis mapping (ICM) model.

Journal of Public Relations Research, *24*(3), 266–298. https://doi.org/10.1080/1062726X.2012.676747

Jin, Y., Pang, A., & Smith, J. (2018). Crisis communication and ethics: The role of public relations. *Journal of Business Strategy, 39*(1), 43–52. https://doi.org/ 10.1108/JBS-09-2016-0095

Kim, S. (2019). *Unearthing Extended Threat Appraisal Model: The Role of Temporal Distance and Organizational Confidence (Unpublished doctoral dissertation).* The University of Georgia, Athens, Georgia, USA.

Kim, S. (2017). Applying the public's perception of temporal distance into crisis communication: An extended concept of threat. *Proceedings of International Public Relations Research Conference, 20,* 100–111.

Kim, S., Jin, Y., Reber, B. H., Pang, A., & Cameron, G. T. (2017, October). *The publics' response continuum in crisis communication: Extending the contingency theory of strategic conflict management.* Presented at the 5th International Crisis Communication Conference (Crisis5), Lisbon, Portugal.

Lazarus, R. S. (1991). *Emotion and adaptation: Vol. xiii.* Oxford University Press.

Molleda, J. C. (2011). Advancing the theory of cross-national conflict shifting: A case discussion and quantitative content analysis of a transnational crisis' newswire coverage. *International Journal of Strategic Communication*, 5(1), 49–70. https://doi.org/10.1080/1553118X.2011.537604

Molleda, J. C., Connolly-Ahern, C., & Quinn, C. (2005). Cross-national conflict shifting: Expanding a theory of global public relations management through quantitative content analysis. *Journalism Studies, 6*(1), 87–102. https://doi.org/10.1080/1461670052000328230

NPR.org. (2019, August 9). Careful with those birthday candles, Smokey: Beloved bear turns 75. https://www.npr.org/2019/08/09/748836909/careful-with-those-birthday-candles-smokey-beloved-bear-turns-75.

Pang, A., Jin, Y., & Cameron, G. T. (2010a). Contingency Theory of Strategic Conflict Management: Directions for the Practice of Crisis Communication from a Decade of Theory Development, Discovery and Dialogue. In W. Timothy Coombs & Shelley J. Holladay (eds.), *Handbook of Crisis Communication*, 527–549. Wiley-Blackwell.

Pang, A., Jin, Y., & Cameron, G. T. (2010b). Contingency theory of strategic conflict management: Unearthing factors that influence ethical elocution in crisis communication. *Proceedings of the 13th International Public Relations Research Conference*, 554–573.

Pang, A., Jin, Y., & Cameron, G. T. (2010c). Strategic Management of Communication: Insights from the Contingency Theory of Strategic Conflict Management. In R. L. Heath (Ed.). *Sage Handbook of Public Relations* (pp. 17–34). Sage.

Pang, A., Jin, Y., & Ho, B. (2016). How crisis managers define ethical crisis communication in Singapore: Identifying organizational factors that influence adoption of ethical stances. *Media Asia, 43*(3–4), 191–207.

PWC Global. (n.d.). The new reality of crisis – and crisis management. https://www.pwc.com/gx/en/services/advisory/forensics/global-crisis-survey/the-future-of-crisis.html.

Shin, J. H., Pang, A., & Cameron, G. T. (2013). Embracing the strategic management of conflict: A twenty-year review of contingency theory in public relations. In M. A. Yamanoğlu & B. P. Özdemir (Eds.), *Halkla İlişkilerin Kazancı Geçmiş Eğilimler Yeni Yönelimler* (pp. 145–160). DeKi Basim Yayim.

Siegrist, M., Gutscher, H., & Keller, C. (2007). Trust and confidence in crisis communication: Three case studies. In M. Siegrist, T. C. Earle, & H. Gutscher (Eds.), *Trust in cooperative risk management: Uncertainty and scepticism in the public mind* (pp. 267–286). Earthscan.

Trope, Y., & Liberman, N. (2010). Construal-level theory of psychological distance. *Psychological Review, 117*(2), 440–463. https://doi.org/10.1037/a0018963

Yarbrough, C. Richard, Cameron, Glen T., Sallot, Lynne M., & McWilliams, Allison. (1998). Tough calls to make: Contingency theory and the Centennial Olympic Games. *Journal of Communication Management, 3*(1), 39–56. https://doi.org/10.1108/eb023483

13 Calming Giants in the Earth

The Internalization, Distribution, Explanation, and Action (IDEA) Model as Strategic Communication in Crises with Competing Narratives

Timothy L. Sellnow, Deanna D. Sellnow, and Ciro Dias Reis

The relentless risk of deadly mudslides encountered by the more than 100,000 residents on Mount Elgon in the Bududa District of Uganda is reminiscent of Ole Edvart Rølvaag's (1927) classic book, *Giants in the Earth.* Rølvaag's novel chronicled the concurrent vitality and viciousness of the North American prairie as experienced by the first Scandinavian immigrants to settle there. The rich and fertile prairie soil produced abundant crops, but it also suffered from locust infestations, droughts, prairie fires, and deadly blizzards. The land that provided independence and livelihood beyond what the settlers had ever known also claimed the lives of many.

As was the case for the farmers on the North American prairie, farmers living on the steep slopes of Uganda's Mount Elgon are able to grow and trade a rotation of five different crops annually, nourished by rich volcanic soil and an equatorial climate. This same soil and climate also trigger life-threatening mudslides (Uganda landslide, 2018). During the rainy season, prolonged downpours loosen the soil embedded deep within the mountain. When the soil gives way, thousands of tons of earth and boulders plunge down the mountain, sweeping modest hut-like houses, schools, clinics, and other dwellings off their meager foundations and burying the residents alive. Over the course of the past decade, deadly mudslides have become more frequent, producing an urgent need to take protective action.

Recognizing this growing risk to residents, the country's Minister for Disaster Preparedness, Hilary Onek, met with the Uganda President, Yoweri Kaguta Museveni, to develop, fund, and implement a public relocation campaign for all of the Bududa District farmers living in these high-risk areas. To date, however, the national government's initiative has been largely unsuccessful.

Why would residents whose lives are clearly in danger due to recurring mudslides resist such an opportunity to relocate? The answer is due in large part to failed communication. More specifically, we argue that an effective strategic instructional risk narrative must, at its core, acknowledge and honor the cultural, psychological, and emotional norms and values of the communities while addressing the physical risks at hand. To do so, such communication campaigns must adequately address competing narratives of disparate publics involved. As our examination reveals, the self-protective instructions proposed to Bududa District residents by the Ugandan government have been unsuccessful largely because these officials failed to do so. In essence, the Bududa District case is ideal for exploring the sticky problem of instructing diverse publics to take actions necessary for self-protection in risk and crisis situations.

We begin the chapter with an explanation of instructional communication as not only important in the event of an acute crisis, but also as a pre-crisis and post-crisis strategy for stimulating self-protective actions. Specifically, we establish the internalization, distribution, explanation, and action (IDEA) model as a viable approach for engaging publics in effective self-protective actions. We then apply the IDEA model to the Bududa District case, focusing specifically on the narratives needed for guiding the audiences through the internalization and explanation processes in ways that motivate them to engage in the recommended actions. We end with conclusions for expanding strategic communication theory and implications for crisis communication practitioners.

The IDEA Model for Effective Strategic Instructional Risk and Crisis Communication

Instructional communication is relevant to both risk and crisis communication. Risk communication focuses on pre-crisis warnings and instructions for avoiding harm should a crisis occur. Crisis communication occurs after a risk is manifested into an observable crisis (Heath & O'Hair, 2009). Instructional messages, then, provide practical risk messages for avoiding crises. Once a crisis occurs, instructional messages focus on both self-protection and recovery. The IDEA model features instructional communication as a central feature in effective strategic risk and crisis communication (Sellnow & Sellnow, 2019). The model has demonstrated its utility across a variety of risk and crisis types when the ultimate goal is to engage in appropriate protective actions both prior to and in the event of a crisis event. This chapter explores how the IDEA model may also inform effective strategic communication in times of post-crisis.

IDEA is an acronym strategically designed for quick recall of the four essential components of an effective strategic instructional message: internalization, distribution, explanation, and action (Sellnow & Sellnow, 2019). Practitioners can construct effective risk and crisis messages by answering key questions related to each of these components:

- Internalization: How are target populations or those they care about affected? Answers may focus on potential impact, as well as breadth, depth, and personal relevance. For example, the risk or crisis could impose threats to health, safety, welfare, prosperity, happiness, and even life itself.

- Distribution: Which communication channels are most accessible to and relevant for reaching the intended publics? Moreover, convergent messages distributed through multiple channels ranging from face-to-face interactions to traditional and social media are most effective (Sellnow et al., 2019b).
- Explanation: What is happening and why, as well as what is being done to address the situation? Answers to this question need to come from credible sources and be explained both accurately and intelligibly.
- Action: What specific actions/steps ought to be taken (or not taken) for protection and reduced harm to oneself and others? Effective action step messages go beyond merely directing receivers to a website or other resources for more information (i.e., explanation) to indicate specific directives to be taken by receivers to mitigate harm to themselves and others.

The IDEA model argues that effective strategic instructional communication occurs when messages (a) motivate receivers to attend to them, (b) are explained in ways that are easily comprehended, and (c) provide precise protective actions to take. The model extends the foundational work of Mileti and Sorensen (1990) that identified strategies for alerts and warnings. These include an explanation of the hazard, guidance for self-protection, location of the area threatened by the disaster, amount of time available for engaging in protective action, and clarification about who is sending the message (Mileti & Peek, 2000). The IDEA model expands this work by providing an easy-to-understand and easy-to-apply model for designing effective instructional messages beyond alerts and warnings that address sticky risk and crisis events. Risk and crisis events become sticky when they are complex or multi-faceted. For example, some stakeholders may deny a risk exists or claim that a crisis is a hoax. In other cases, competing messages may advocate risk response strategies that are unsafe. For example, some sources still promote the triangle of life as an appropriate earthquake response despite overwhelming evidence that it is ineffective (Johnson et al., 2014). In other cases, the proposed solution may be perceived to create as many problems as it resolves. The IDEA model's combined focus on clarifying who is at risk, providing a basic scientific explanation why, and advocating protective action supported by available data is a potential means for maintaining a pragmatic focus when responding to sticky risks and crises.

Instructing information is a mainstay of crisis communication (Coombs, 2009; Sturges, 1994). From an instructional communication perspective, effective risk and crisis messages focus on what receivers learn and, consequently, are measured by the degree to which they produce three learning outcomes: cognitive, affective, and behavioral (Waldeck et al., 2010). Accordingly, for effective learning to occur, risk and crisis messages "must include not only elements of explanation, but also personal relevance and actionable directives" (Sellnow et al., 2015, p. 150). The model is unique in that it is intentionally easy to understand, as well as to recall and employ quickly when time is of the essence (Sellnow & Sellnow, 2019).

Strategic instructional risk messages have demonstrated their effectiveness in pre-crisis planning. For instance, in the case of Hurricane (a.k.a. Superstorm) Sandy, New York Mayor Michael Bloomberg and his team addressed the IDEA model elements when instructing residents to prepare. Before the storm ever made landfall, the team warned local residents that it could be the worst natural disaster ever (internalization) and asked them to prepare by storing food, water, and batteries (action). This team, perceived as credible and trustworthy, explained the forecasts simply and distributed their messages through a variety of channels ranging from websites to mainstream and social media (Spence et al., 2015). When some criticized him for offering these instructions, Mayor Bloomberg responded by saying we need to be prepared for the worst-case scenario. Effective pre-crisis IDEA model messages like these helped save lives when the storm eventually did devastate New York. Moreover, in the aftermath of the storm, officials formed a committee not only to identify infrastructural vulnerabilities (e.g., electricity, transportation, etc.), but also to understand stakeholder attitudes as a means to overcome apathy regarding risk preparedness in the future. They ultimately published a report, "Hurricane Sandy – After Action: Report and Recommendation to Mayor Michael R. Bloomberg," describing explicit risk preparedness instructions focused on internalization, explanation, and action (Gibbs & Holloway, 2013).

Unlike the case with Hurricane Sandy, a number of studies using the IDEA model have revealed a troubling trend by risk and crisis spokespersons to privilege explanation over the other components of the model (e.g., Frisby et al., 2014; Sellnow-Richmond et al., 2018). This trend is unfortunate because extant research offers compelling evidence that messages lacking any of these four components are unlikely to produce desired cognitive, behavioral, and affective learning outcomes (Mileti & Peek, 2000; Sellnow et al., 2012, 2015, 2017). Some research even suggests that messages lacking one or more of these components may reduce both receiver motivation and efficacy (e.g., Frisby et al., 2014; Kovoor-Misra & Olk, 2015; Roberto et al., 2009; Spence et al., 2008; Yang, 2015).

Moreover, when spokespersons announce plans instructing publics to take certain actions without also providing clear internalization elements to justify doing so can result in a refusal to enact the behavior at all, to cut corners, or even to engage in protests or riots (Sellnow et al., 2019b). This was, in fact, the case when the administration in São Paulo, Brazil, raised the price of public transportation by 20 cents in 2013 and when the federal government in Chile raised the price of metro fares by 20 pesos in 2019. No internalization or explanation elements were offered in either case and huge protests and demonstrations erupted.

In the case of Brazil, the protests came not because of the 20 cent increase but, rather, because of the government's failure to address public health, education, security, and corruption crises issues. As a result of massive protests erupting throughout the country, *S*ão Paulo administration cancelled the new price of the public transport ticket just days later, and the Federal administration was forced to respond to expectations regarding health and education coming from demonstrators (Milhares de pessoas lotam centro de Santiago em 1° protesto de 2020 no Chile, 2020).

In the case of Chile, the violent protests were again related to the government's failure to address general social conditions. The federal government declared a state of emergency and a curfew in an attempt to curb the violence. According to the National Institute of Human Rights, 26 protesters were killed and another 2,808 injured citizens were hospitalized. In addition, 2,210 riflemen and police were injured, and 188 police stations and 971 police vehicles were attacked. President Sebastián Piñera apologized five days after the demonstrations began. He claimed that he was unaware of the level of dissatisfaction among the Chilean population regarding general social issues. He said, "I recognize this lack of vision and I apologize to my countrymen." Still, his poor decisions resulted in an approval rating drop from 55% in December 2017 to 12% by the end of 2019 (Milhares de pessoas lotam centro de Santiago em 1° protesto de 2020 no Chile, 2020). In sum, these examples illustrate some of the potential consequences that can occur when each element of the IDEA model is not addressed.

Narrative as the Means for Moving from Internalization and Explanation to Action

As alluded to in the previous examples, one sticky problem for public relations practitioners is to fully implement each of the IDEA model elements when engaged in strategic instructional risk and crisis communication. Moreover, moving from explanation to action appears to be particularly difficult. However, as Bentele & Nothhaft (2015) explained, comprehending the relationships between "public communication and public action" is central to all strategic communication (p. 71).

Dewey's (2013/1938; 2016/1927) pragmatic perspective on communication provides insight on how to successfully link explanation and action. Grunig (1966) established a clear link between Dewey's volume of work, particularly with publics and the practice of public relations. To clarify, when faced with public problems, people attempt to identify and engage in innovative solutions (Dewey, 2013/1938). Self (2010) clarified further that "publics are (networks or) relationships of action assembled to solve problems" (p. 80). Moreover, human beings attempt to solve problems by thinking "through narratives and not through facts, numbers or equations, and the simpler the narrative, the better" (Harari, 2018, p. 3). From Dewey's perspective, then, publics are more likely to be motivated to take action through narratives that are introduced, contested, and adopted within the public sphere. As Coombs and Holladay (2015) summarized, narratives of self-protection are fitting with public relations because, "public safety is the number one priority of crisis managers" (p. 499).

Dewey (2013/1938) argued that narration serves as a means for moving from an "indeterminate problematic situation into a determinate resolved one" (p. 252). This transformation from indeterminate to determinate may be achieved through temporal and spatial representations offered in the narrative. Dewey explained, "But every narration has a background which if it were made explicit instead of being taken for granted, would be described; correspondingly, what is described exists within some temporal process of which 'narration' applies" (p. 348). In other words, two people might "see" the same event differently because one places higher priority on what is temporal than what is spatial. For example, someone who prioritizes the temporal in a crisis narrative asks questions about the events preceding, during, and following the crisis. By contrast, someone who prioritizes the spatial in a crisis narrative might ask questions about the physical conditions in the location where the crisis occurred. Making the narrative explicit, through both temporal and spatial observations, is key to creating plans for self-protective actions. In other words, in the case of strategic communication, narration initiates the transformation from problematic situations to resolved conditions.

For Dewey (2013/1938), the nature of this temporal-spatial coexistence leads to judgments based on direct experiences, indirect experiences, and historic accounts of past events. These judgments create propositions that provide a basis for moving fluidly among internalization, explanation, and action. Narration allows us to assign judgment to direct experiences that fall within our own "biography" (p. 352). Those experiencing events directly can offer explanations as a first-person narrative. Indirect experiences, by contrast, offer "no possibility of applying the doctrine of immediate or self-evident knowledge" (p. 359). Instead, these narratives rely on "inference as to what took place in the past" (p. 359). Such inference is based on the interpretation of observed particulars that serve as evidence. Finally, historical narration produces judgments that link the past and the present. Specifically, such judgments are based on narratives that describe sequences of outcomes from the past and speculate about the degree to which they provide insight about present and future events.

Competing Narratives

Combining the spatial and temporal foci and the varying perspectives of direct experience, indirect observations, and historical context creates the potential for what we call competing narratives. Crisis events are, by their nature, fraught with uncertainty (Hermann, 1963). The shock and anguish created by crises can, at least momentarily, cause affected publics to "question the viability of their world and self-view" (Park & Folkman, 1997, p. 123).

Initially, narratives are shared via dialogue among the publics and the agencies tasked with assisting in crisis recovery. These narratives consist of a variety of fragmented accounts—all of them seeking to re-establish an essence of order for those whose lives have been disrupted. These disparate narratives often conflict (diverge) before they slowly coalesce (converge) into a unifying grand narrative (a.k.a. metanarrative) of crisis resolution (Lyotard, 1979/1984; Seeger & Sellnow, 2016). Crises explained through a compelling and unified narrative tend to be resolved quickly. Crises explained through divergent narratives that compete with one another may take years to converge and some of them may never fully converge into a unified grand narrative.

We argue that Dewey's (2013/1938) perspective on spatial and temporal explanations based on direct, indirect, and historical judgments and shared through narratives may shed light onto why some crises foster conflicting narratives that are not easily resolved into a widely accepted grand narrative. These divergent narratives may focus on any aspect of the crisis ranging from interpretations of what it consists of and why it is important to agreeing upon the best instructions for resolution. Next, we summarize the case study used to exemplify the function of competing narratives in the IDEA model.

A Case Study of the Function of Competing Narratives: The Positive Results of Planning and the High Cost of Unpreparedness on Mount Elgon

"I quickly told my grandchildren to climb up onto the roof and hold onto the roofing poles. After ensuring that they were all holding themselves firm, I decided to hold onto the roofing poles of my house and that is how we survived" (Nyango, 2018, para. 3). This is part of the breathtaking story of Paul Saleh, a survivor of a sudden and disastrous 2018 mudslide in the Bududa District of Uganda. Saleh lifted his two grandchildren to the roof of his modest hut-like home and implored them to hold on for their lives as mud and water charged through his home and boulders rumbled through his village. Sadly, such mudslides are becoming the rule rather than the exception for the farming communities on Mount Elgon in Uganda's Bududa District.

The solution for protecting Mount Elgon farmers is not simple. To leave the mountain (as advocated by Ugandan government officials) involves great sacrifice. The villagers have lifelong ties to the land. Nearly all of them have been farming this land for generations. Moreover, replicating the prosperous quality of life they enjoy here is not likely anywhere else in Uganda. Thus, the residents are drawn to stay on the mountain for both cultural and financial reasons. The mountain is more than merely a place where they live and work. Rather, it is a fundamental part of their collective identity. Thus, the Bududa District case serves as an excellent case for examining the sticky problem of advancing successfully through the stages of the IDEA model to achieve a desired outcome.

Moving from an "indeterminate problematic situation into a determinate resolved one" (Dewey, 2013/1938, p. 252) often involves successfully moving from competing narratives to a unified grand narrative. To fully illuminate the intricacies of the competing narratives inherent in the Bududa situation, we have selected three distinct mudslide crises: a massive slide that occurred in 2010, a slide that devastated a trading center in 2018, and a deadly event that took place in 2019 and remains an immediate threat to residents.

March, 2010

Persistent heavy rains preceded an enormous mudslide in March of 2010. Huge boulders from high on the mountain rumbled through the villages of Nameti, Kubewo, and Nankobe, destroying an estimated 85 homes, a school, and a clinic. Blocked roads stalled the relief effort. Rescuers and rescue equipment were flown into the region using helicopters. "At least 300 people died and thousands were forced to flee after a landslide buried three villages" (At least 36 dead, 2018, para. 12).

Some of the bodies remain buried deep within the uprooted soil. A mass grave holds the bodies of many victims who died that tragic night. The site is marked now only by a weathered wooden cross in front of one of the massive boulders that rolled down the mountain during the slide. The unprecedented size and loss of life made the 2010 mudslide a major story that demanded a resolution. The Ugandan government instituted a plan to move residents to a new location far from Mount Elgon. Though some farmers initially accepted the government's offer, many eventually returned to the mountain, bitterly disappointed in the circumstances of their relocation.

October, 2018

The drizzling rain did not slow the bustling activity of the trading center linking the villages of Suume, Nyekhe, Malila, Lwanda, and Nanyinza. Visitors traded their crops, purchased items, and socialized with their neighbors as they always had. However, an unknown threat loomed further up the mountain where heavy rains had filled small lakes to overflowing. An earthen retaining wall became saturated, crumbled, and released water roaring down the mountain with such force it was as if a dam had burst. The water dislodged hundreds of huge boulders that also tumbled down the mountain. Residents had little or no warning as buildings were crushed or washed away. Today, the river that once flowed quietly through the trading center now meanders around boulders that were not there before the disaster. Only a few broken brick walls remain of the once bustling trading center. Sixty residents died that day (Bududa mudslide, 2018).

December, 2019

The mountain's slopes are particularly steep above the villages of Namasa and Naposhi in the Bushika Sub County of the Bududa District. The farmers living there are aware of the fact that their gardens and homes are located in a precarious part of Mount Elgon. Evidence of former mudslides is readily apparent, even to the casual observer. The December 2019 mudslide followed a similar pattern. In fact, persistent hard rains inspired some residents to leave their homes and walk down the mountain to a safer location. A massive shifting of earth spewed silt high into the air as the slide began. Some residents saw this "smoke" and ran for safety. Others were unaware of the landslide and remained in their homes. Twenty homes and gardens were swept down the mountain that night. An estimated 30 people died, with several still buried in the mudslide's residue (Over 30 feared dead, 2019).

Competing Narratives of Explanation and Action in the Bududa District

The primary action advocated in the narrative set forth by Hilary Onek, Uganda's Minister for Disasters Preparedness and Relief, was and still is to evacuate to one of two relocation sites provided by the government. The Ministry categorizes these Bududa District homes and farms into a single category of being at extreme risk. Following the colossal 2010 mudslide, hundreds of these at-risk farmers and their families did relocate. Disappointed by dramatically less productive soil at the relocation site and a keen sense of being disconnected from their identity, many returned to their homes in the Bududa District (Uganda landslide, 2018). The farmers' narrative of disappointment, loneliness, and loss of identity dwarfed the government's narrative of safety and risk reduction via relocation. Similarly, in the wake of the 2018 mudslide, Onek voiced frustration, "We had earlier predicted about a problem [landslides] in Bududa. We warned and advised those living in endangered areas to leave. But they ignored, resisted and insisted to stay. Now this tragedy has struck with devastating effects" (At least 36 dead, 2018, para. 9). Onek's bitter narrative is clearly competing with the villagers' story of disappointment in the relocation site and loss of cultural heritage/identity.

From Dewey's perspective, the impediment to moving from explanation to action in the government's relocation narrative is a tension between the temporal and spatial aspects of the Bududa District's distress (Littlefield & Sellnow, 2015). The Ministry of Disasters Preparedness narrative focuses primarily on spatial aspects. Farming on the mudslide-prone slopes of Mount Elgon is simply unreasonable. Consequently, the conclusion drawn is that to continue farming in the Bududa District is absurd.

In contrast, the primary narrative of the Bududa farmers is temporal in that it focuses on direct experience and historical context. Spatially, the farmers accept that mudslides are and have always been a threat on Mount Elgon. They also admit that some farms are now too unstable to support a family. Yet they see the relocation efforts of the government as unsatisfactory on multiple levels. The direct experiences of those who have accepted relocation and returned to the mountain tell a story of poor housing, limited options for crops, and broken promises. Historically, the farmers' narrative describes the pain they suffered at being relocated to an area hundreds of kilometers away from the people, customs, and communities that are core aspects of who they are. In short, relocating robbed many of these farmers and their families of their personal history and identity.

The appeals made by survivors of the 2018 and 2019 mudslides further complicate the temporal narrative of the victims of the 2010 mudslide. A survivor of the 2018 mudslide said, for example, "We are sad that every time the rains come we lose lives and property. Let people in mudslide prone areas be taken to safe areas" (Nyango, 2018, para. 7). Similarly, the Sub County Councilor, Simuya Mabuko, pleaded with the government, in the aftermath of the 2019 mudslide, to hasten efforts to relocate those residents at greatest danger. The residents feel the danger and are asking to be relocated (Over 30 feared dead, 2019). They tell a story of being forgotten by a government that has promised to relocate Bududa District victims to safer areas where the farming is comparable. The temporal tension created here, unlike that of the 2010 mudslide, is for government efforts to move more quickly to spare residents from further crises.

The narrative of the 2018 and 2019 mudslide victims who are eager to relocate seems to contradict that of the relocated farmers that returned to Mount Elgon. The farmers' emphasis on the temporal, again, provides insight. Residents of the more recent mudslides are understandably fearful. As time passes, however, these direct memories of chaos and loss may begin to fade. Another possible explanation may be that the time spent in a relocation area farming less fertile land and a nostalgic longing for home gradually diminishes the fears that originally motivated them to leave. From this temporal perspective, over time, the feelings of loss and longing may usurp the spatial perspective emphasized in the government's narrative.

Conclusions

Previous research applying the IDEA model has focused largely on reducing risk for publics threatened by potential crisis circumstances and during a crisis event. Less work has focused on the link between and among internalization, explanation, and action as they function post-crisis. This case study suggests that narratives serve a critical role in joining these elements in ways that ultimately achieve the goals of affective, cognitive, and behavioral learning (Waldeck, Plax, & Kearney, 2010). When competing narratives exist regarding the merits of engaging in a particular protective action, frustrated publics may choose not to comply. If managed effectively, however, divergent narratives may give voice to the voiceless in ways that enrich the marketplace of ideas into one grand narrative (Dewey, 2013/1938; Grunig, 1966; Self, 2010; Yuan, 2016). Unfortunately, these divergent narratives are sometimes not acknowledged until underrepresented populations share them in the form of demonstrations, protests, or riots. This appears to have been the case in both Brazil and Chile when the governments attempted to raise public transportation fees while ignoring public health and social service crisis issues (Milhares de pessoas lotam centro de Santiago em 1º protesto de 2020 no Chile, 2020).

The potential benefits of an expanded discussion of competing narratives prior to engaging in action do appear to have a point of diminishing returns. For victims of the 2010 and 2018 Bududa District mudslides, there is time to engage in dialogue before determining the best long-term solution. Conversely, 2019 mudslide survivors do not have the luxury of time to engage in dialogue about competing narratives. They realize their lives are in immediate danger as the rainy season begins. In this case, the short response time demands an expedient transition from a narrative of explanation to engaging in protective actions—in this case, relocation to a safer area. Perhaps time for discussing multiple narratives should occur post-crisis after removing residents from harm's way. This appears to have been the case during and after Hurricane Sandy. When residents criticized the Bloomberg team's preparedness action steps, they appeared to accept "prepare for a worst-case scenario" as a short-term response. Important to note, however, is that they did in fact reconvene to discuss competing narratives post-crisis and ultimately produce a report based on an agreed-upon grand narrative (Gibbs & Hollowa, 2013; Lyotard, 1979/1984).

This analysis of the Bududa District mudslide case highlights the tension produced by temporal relationships in narratives seeking to inspire action through explanation (Littlefield & Sellnow, 2015). Public dialogue is critical when proposing viable actions for reducing risk (National Research Council, 1989). When time is of the essence, however, dialogue must be compressed as direct self-protective actions must be quickly initiated (Sellnow & Sellnow, 2010). Nevertheless, competing narratives give voice to views that should be considered when making a long-term action plan. This analysis suggests that extended discussion about competing narratives as a means to converge into a grand narrative should happen not only post-crisis but also after potential victims are safe from imminent threats. In other words, generalizations about moving from explanation to action must consider the pressures of time introduced by the circumstances at hand.

The contrasting foci of competing narratives between spatial and temporal perspectives may also create challenges in moving from explanation to action. The question is not whether a spatial or temporal focus is superior. Both are relevant in managing crises such as the mudslide risk in the Bududa District. Rather, the sticky problem is based on the disparate foci on which each narrative is based. To clarify, the Ugandan government is rightly focused on their indirect analysis of physical evidence about the areas that are at greatest risk. Similarly, the residents are rightly focused on either a sense of urgency to leave based on their recent direct experiences or a historical reflection on their ancestral identity that is tied to the mountain. Ideally, decisions about the best actions for self-protection would consider both the spatial and temporal aspects of the crisis. By doing so, both residents and government agents would be positioned to achieve Dewey's vision where "publics are (networks or) relationships of action assembled to solve problems" (Self, 2010, p. 80). Resolving the situation in the Bududa District requires the two sides to acknowledge the simultaneous importance of both the spatial and temporal aspects of the competing narratives.

Dewey (2013/1938) explained that solid spatial-temporal reasoning is necessary for narratives to advance an "indeterminate problematic situation into a determinate resolved one" (p. 252). He further explained that "every narration has a background which if it were made explicit instead of being taken for granted, would be described" (p. 348). This analysis reveals the undescribed narrative biases of each side. In this case, moving from competing views to a shared narrative requires that both government agents and Bududa District residents acknowledge their predispositions and, in Dewey's terms, make them explicit. This process could aid both sides in building the network of relationships needed to form a shared narrative. Without a shared narrative, persuading residents to move from differing explanations to self-protective action is difficult. Similarly, those who feel the government agencies are too slow in responding to their needs may also benefit from comprehending the temporal constraints these agencies face in forming, financing, and implementing a relocation plan.

Practical Applications

The challenges the Bududa District residents and the Ugandan government face are not unique to this crisis. Practitioners tasked with crafting messages advocating self-protective actions in response to any risk situation or crisis event are likely to encounter competing narratives. For example, crisis communicators must overcome challenges in persuading at-risk or crisis-stricken publics to evacuate during natural disasters such as floods, fires, or hurricanes. In these cases, however, those asked to evacuate may be focused on a spatial narrative (e.g., wanting to protect their homes and possessions), while government agencies may be focused on a temporal narrative (e.g., seeing the urgency created by the impending disaster). Like the Bududa District case, however, such practitioners would be wise to make explicit the subtleties of both narratives. Doing so would require a message acknowledging the fears residents have about leaving their homes and valuables unattended. Messages reassuring residents that their homes will be protected from looting and that whatever steps possible to protect their homes from damage will be taken might be the first step in reaching the level of dialogue described by Dewey (Self, 2010).

Practitioners may also benefit from simply acknowledging the fact that the uncertainty inherent in crises makes multiple narratives a recurring consequence. Thus, practitioners should not be shocked or become frustrated when confronted by the sticky problem of competing narrative explanations that result in resistance to engaging in protective actions they advocate. Allowing for narrative explanations that include a balance of spatial and temporal reasoning is likely a way forward in many crisis communication situations.

Finally, the practical applications mentioned above are secondary to situations where time is of the absolute essence. When shifting winds make wildfires an instantaneous threat for residents, for example, we fully recognize that time for dialogue is not available (Sellnow & Sellnow, 2010). In these cases, explanation is limited to a statement that the fire is minutes away and remaining in your home will result in certain death. Similarly, residents who insist on remaining in homes on coasts where hurricanes at advanced levels are certain to hit should be told that they have no chance for survival if they stay. The form of dialogic relationship we advocate in this chapter is reserved for cases where a reasonable amount of time is available for discussing the merits of recommended actions.

Key Takeaways

Narratives attempting to make sense of uncertainty created by crises occur regardless of context. Dewey described this uncertainty as a natural part of life when he wrote, "Man [*sic*] lives in a world of surmise, of mystery, of uncertainties" (1934/1980, p. 34). The threats imposed by crises, however, make moving from explanation to protective actions essential and, in some cases, urgent. The ultimate goal for practitioners is to create a unifying grand narrative proposing protective actions that honors the cultural norms and values of the publics they are attempting to engage. The IDEA model offers a step-by-step explanation of how this crisis communication process can effectively move from internalizing and explaining risk to taking the steps needed for self-protection. Focusing on narratives and their potential to divide and unify publics may equip crisis communicators with strategies for empowering the publics they serve. Without a unifying narrative that endorses a tailored series of fitting actions, there is little hope for Mount Elgon residents to tame the giants stirring in the earth beneath them.

References

At least 36 dead in Uganda landslides as school disappears beneath mud. (2018, October 12). *The Guardian*. https://www.theguardian.com/global-development/2018/oct/12/uganda-landslides-36-dead-school-disappears-beneath-mud-bududa

Bentele, G., & Nothhaft, H. (2015). Strategic communication and the public sphere from a European perspective. In D. Holtzhausen & A. Zerfass (Eds.), *The Routledge handbook of strategic communication* (pp. 53–73). Routledge.

Coombs, W. T. (2009). Conceptualizing crisis communication. In R. L. Heath & H. D. O'Hair (Eds.), *Handbook of risk and crisis communication* (pp. 99–118). Routledge.

Coombs, W. T., & Holladay, S., J. (2015). Strategic intent and crisis communication: The emergence of a field. In D. Holtzhausen & A. Zerfass (Eds.), *The Routledge handbook of strategic communication* (pp. 497–507). Routledge.

Dewey, J. (1980). *Art as experience.* Penguin Books. (Originally published in 1934).

Dewey, J. (2013). *Logic: The theory of inquiry.* Read Books, Ltd. (Original work published in 1938).

Dewey, J. (2016). *The public and its problems.* In M. L. Rogers (Ed.), *The public and its problems: An essay in political inquiry* (pp. 144–170). Ohio University Press. (Original work published 1927).

Frisby, B. N., Veil, S. R., & Sellnow, T. L. (2014). Instructional messages during health-related crises: Essential content for self-protection. *Health Communication, 29*, 347–354. https://doi.org/10.1080/10410236.2012.755604

Gibbs, L. I., & Holloway, C. F. (Eds.). (2013, May). *Hurricane Sandy—After Action. Report and recommendations to Mayor Michael R. Bloomberg.* https://www1.nyc.gov/assets/housingrecovery/downloads/pdf/2017/sandy_aar_5-2-13.pdf

Grunig, J. E. (1966). The role of information in economic decision making. *Journalism Monographs*, No. 3.

Harari, Y. N. (2018). *21 lessons for the 21st century.* Penguin Random House.

Heath, R. L., & O'Hair, H. D. (2009) Significance of crisis and risk communication. In R. L. Heath & H. D. O'Hair (Eds.), *Handbook of risk and crisis communication* (pp. 5–30). Routledge.

Hermann, C. F. (1963). Some consequences of crisis which limit the viability of organizations. *Administrative Science Quarterly, 8*, 61–82.

Johnson, V. A., Johnston, D. M., Ronan, K. R., & Peace, R. (2014). Evaluating children's learning of adaptive response capacities from ShakeOut, an earthquake and tsunami drill in two Washington State school districts. *Journal of Homeland Security and Emergency Management, 11*(3), 347–373. http://doi.org/10.1515/jhsem-2014-0012

Kovoor-Misra, S., & Olk, P. (2015). Leader culpability, hopelessness, and learning during organizational crises. *Journal of Leadership Organizational Development, 36*, 990–1011. https://doi.org/10.1108/LODJ-04-2014-0070

Littlefield, R. S., & Sellnow, T. L. (Eds.). (2015). *Risk and crisis communication: Navigating the tensions between organizations and the public.* Lexington Books.

Lyotard, J-F. (1979). *The postmodern condition: A report on knowledge* (G. Bennington & B. Massumi, trans., 1984). University of Minnesota Press.

Mileti, D. S., & Peek, L. (2000). The social psychology of public response to warnings of a nuclear power plant accident. *Journal of Hazardous Materials, 75*, 181–194. https://doi.org/10.1016/S0304-3894(00)00179-5

Mileti, D. S., & Sorensen, J. H. (1990). *Communication of emergency public warnings: A social science perspective and state-of-the-art assessment* (No. ORNL-6609). Oak Ridge National Lab., TN (USA).

Milhares de pessoas lotam centro de Santiago em 1° protesto de 2020 no Chile. (2020, March 1). *Conheca seu Futuro.* https://www.efe.com/efe/brasil/mundo/milhares-de-pessoas-lotam-centro-santiago-em-1-protesto-2020-no-chile/50000243-4143707

National Research Council. (1989). *Improving risk communication.* National Academy Press.

Nyango, Y. (2018, October 13). Bududa deadly mudslides: Survivor's tale. *News Vision.* https://www.newvision.co.ug/new_vision/news/1487550/bududa-deadly-mudslides-survivor-tale

Park, C. L., & Folkman, S. (1997). Meaning in the context of stress and coping. *Review of General Psychology, 1*(2), 115–144. https://doi.org/10.1037/1089-2680.1.2.115

Rølvaag, O. E. (1927). *Giants in the earth.* Harper & Brothers.

Roberto, A. J., Goodall, C. E., & Witte, K. (2009). Raising the alarm and calming fears: Perceived threat and efficacy during risk and crisis. In R. L. Heath and H. D. O'Hair (Eds.). *Handbook of Risk and Crisis Communication.* (pp. 287–303). Routledge.

Seeger, M. W., & Sellnow, T. L. (2016). *Narratives of crisis: Telling the stories of ruin and renewal.* Stanford University Press.

Self, C. C. (2010). Hegel, Habermas, and community: The public in the new media era. *International Journal of Strategic Communication, 4*(2), 78–92. https://doi.org/10.1080/15531181003704651

Sellnow, D. D., Lane, D., Littlefield, R. S., Sellnow, T. L., Wilson, B., Beauchamp, K., & Venette, S. (2015). A receiver-based approach to effective instructional crisis communication. *Journal of Contingencies and Crisis Management, 23*(3), 149–158. https://doi.org/10.1111/1468-5973.12066

Sellnow, D. D., Lane, D. R., Sellnow, T. L., & Littlefield, R. S. (2017). The IDEA model as a best practice for effective instructional risk and crisis communication. *Communication Studies, 68*(5), 552–567. https://doi.org/10.1080/10510974.2017.1375535

Sellnow, D. D., & Sellnow, T. L. (2019). The IDEA model for effective instructional risk and crisis communication by emergency managers and other key spokespersons. *Journal of Emergency Management, 17*(1), 67–78. http://doi.org/10.5055/jem.2019.0399

Sellnow, T. L., Sellnow, D. D., Helsel, E. M., Martin, J. M., & Parker, J. S. (2019a). Risk and crisis communication narratives in response to rapidly emerging diseases. *Journal of Risk Research, 22*(7), 897–908. https://doi.org/10.1080/13669877.2017.1422787

Sellnow, D. D., Sellnow, T. L., & Martin, J. M. (2019b). Strategic message convergence in communicating biosecurity: The case of the 2013 porcine epidemic diarrhea virus. *Communication Reports, 32*(3), 125–136. https://doi.org/10.1080/08934215.2019.1634747

Sellnow, T. L., & Sellnow, D. D. (2010). The instructional dynamic of risk and crisis communication: Distinguishing instructional messages from dialogue. *The Review of Communication, 10*(2), 111–125. https://doi.org/10.1080/15358590903402200

Sellnow, T. L., Sellnow, D. D., Lane, D. R., & Littlefield, R. S. (2012). The value of instructional communication in crisis situations: Restoring order to chaos. *Risk Analysis: An International Journal, 32*(4), 633–643. https://doi.org/10.1111/j.1539-6924.2011.01634.x

Sellnow-Richmond, D. D., George, A. M., & Sellnow, D. D. (2018). An IDEA model analysis of instructional risk communication in the time of Ebola. *Journal of International Crisis and Risk Communication Research, 1*, 135–165. 10.30658/jicrcr.1.1.7

Spence, P. R., Lachlan, K. A., & Burke, J. M. (2008). Crisis preparation, media use, and information seeking: Patterns across Katrina evacuees and lessons learned for crisis management. *Journal of Emergency Management, 6*, 11–23. https://doi.org/10.5055/jem.2008.0009

Spence, P. R., Lachlan, K. A., Lin, X., & del Greco, M. (2015). Variability in Twitter content across the stages of a natural disaster: Implications for crisis communication. *Communication Quarterly, 63*(2), 171–186. https://doi.org/10.1080/01463373.2015.1012219

Sturges, D. L. (1994). Communicating through crisis: A strategy for organizational survival. *Management Communication Quarterly, 7*, 297–316. https://doi.org/10.1177/0893318994007003004

Uganda landslide near Mount Elgon kills more than 40. (2018, October 12). *BBC News*. Retrieved from https://www.bbc.com/news/world-africa-45836381108

URN. Bududa mudslide death toll reaches 60. (2018 October 19). *The Observer*. https://observer.ug/news/headlines/58970-bududa-mudslide-death-toll-reaches-60

URN. Over 30 feared dead in fresh Bududa mudslide. (2019 December 4). *Daily Monitor*. https://www.monitor.co.ug/News/National/Over-30-people-feared-dead-in-fresh-Bududa-mudslide/688334-5372426-9kko4t/index.html

Waldeck, J. H., Plax, T. G., & Kearney, P. (2010). Philosophical and methodological foundations of instructional communication. *The SAGE Handbook of Communication and Instruction*, 161–179.

Yang, Z. J. (2015). Altruism during Ebola: Risk perception, issue salience, cultural cognition, and information processing. *Risk Analysis*, *36*, 1079–1089. https://doi.org/10.1111/risa.12526

Yuan, C. (2016). *Giving a voice to the voiceless*. Wipf & Stock.

14 The Social-Mediated Crisis Communication (SMCC) Model

Identifying the Next Frontier

Brooke Fisher Liu, Yan Jin, Lucinda Austin, Erica Kuligowski, and Camila Espina Young

***Disclaimer: Certain commercial entities, equipment, or materials may be identified in this document in order to describe an experimental procedure or concept adequately. Such identification is not intended to imply recommendation or endorsement by the National Institute of Standards and Technology, nor is it intended to imply that the entities, materials, or equipment are necessarily the best available for the purpose.*

In 2009, governments experimented with using social media to respond to a global crisis: the H1N1 pandemic (Smith, 2009). Research demonstrated that these early social media efforts displayed areas for improvement, including government agencies communicating inconsistent information via social and traditional media and releasing social media posts with sentences cut off because of Twitter's 140 character limit at that time (Kim & Liu, 2012; Liu & Kim, 2011).

Since then, social media have become integral to many governments' crisis responses. For example, after the 2013 Boston Marathon bombing, the mayor sent messages via Twitter to initiate community healing, such as through sharing resources and employing humanistic communication (Williams et al., 2017). Likewise, after Hurricane Harvey in 2017, government leaders employed social media to praise their partners, express solidarity, and improve community morale (W. Liu et al., 2018). In some cases, power outages have precluded the use of social media during disasters, as was the case in 2017 Hurricane Maria (Andrade et al., 2020). In other cases, social media have perpetuated misinformation, such as the rumor that genetically modified mosquitoes caused the spread of Zika during the height of the 2016 outbreak (Annenberg Public Policy Center, 2016).

Understanding the role of social media in governments' disaster responses remains a critical priority for protecting life and property. Communications is one of 16 critical infrastructure sectors that are vital to the United States and "their incapacitation or destruction would have a debilitating effect on security, national economic security, national public health or safety, or any combination thereof" (Department of Homeland Security, 2019, para. 1). Indeed, the majority of US adults use social media channels such as YouTube and Facebook (Perrin & Anderson, 2019). With the proliferation of smartphones, social media channels are increasingly used by organizations and citizens to share information about how to prepare for and respond to imminent threats and how to recover from disasters (Niles et al., 2019). Research over the past decade has demonstrated how governments can effectively use social media. Yet there remain critical information gaps, such as distinguishing the effects of different social media channels and broadening the research focus beyond the US (Eriksson, 2018).

In this chapter, we begin with a review of why social media matter during disasters, integrating perspectives from practitioners and academics. We then review the past decade of research on the social-mediated crisis communication (SMCC) model, which was the first theoretical model to explore the role of social media in crisis communication and public relations (Duhé, 2015), and other related research. We conclude with key takeaways for scholars and practitioners about the role of social media in disasters, including promising areas for future research.

Why Social Media Matter during Crises

This section provides a discussion focused on how emergency management officials leverage social media to support critical functions for preparing for and responding to crises, including reaching at-risk publics, obtaining situational awareness, and engaging with the populations they serve. In turn, this section ends with a brief overview of current limitations of integrating social media into formal emergency management.

Social media provide several advantages to emergency management officials before, during, and after crises. First, these platforms can be used to facilitate communication with at-risk publics. Emergency managers rely on multiple channels to provide at-risk publics with the information necessary to better prepare for, respond to, and recover from disasters (Army Corps of Engineers, 2019). Up until recently, news media organizations have played a primary role in disseminating warning messages and other critical information to at-risk publics. However, with declining viewership of local broadcast television news and readership of print newspapers (Barthel, 2019), emergency managers must consider alternative ways to reach at-risk publics.

Reaching At-risk Publics

Research findings provide compelling support for the use of social media to reach at-risk populations during disasters. A 2018 Pew Research Center report found that an increasing number of Americans prefer to obtain their news through social media (Barthel, 2019). During crises, audiences have shown a preference for using social media and text messaging to find and share crisis-related information with friends and family (Austin et al., 2012). Studies have also demonstrated that affordances, like multimodal capabilities, render social media platforms an effective solution for providing people with disabilities and their caretakers with accessible information (Rotondi et al., 2019). Similarly, social media can be leveraged to reach linguistically diverse populations during disasters, provided that the main barriers of trust, as well as message tailoring and translation, are addressed (Ogie et al., 2018). Taken together, these findings suggest that emergency managers can capitalize on news preference trends and social media features to meet some of the needs of at-risk publics in disasters.

Obtaining Crisis-related Situational Awareness

Social media platforms can also be used to obtain situational awareness of current disaster conditions via user-generated content. Recent studies illustrate that social media data have the potential to inform disaster planning, logistics, coordination, and assessments in a variety of ways. For example, social media content can provide keen insight on the temporal progress of a disaster (Fang et al., 2019) and evacuation patterns of at-risk populations (Kumar & Ukkusuri, 2018; Martín et al., 2017), which have been shown to complement physical sources of disaster information, such as rainstorm and flood precipitation data (Fang et al., 2019), official flood inundation maps (Martín et al., 2017), and satellite imagery from the National Aeronautics and Space Administration (NASA) (Kibanov et al., 2017).

Engaging Stakeholders in Emergency Management and Preparedness Efforts

Social media further contribute to emergency management by advancing the Federal Emergency Management Agency's (FEMA) Whole Community effort, a philosophical framework that seeks to engage all stakeholders in preventing, preparing for, responding to, and recovering from all threats and emergencies (FEMA, 2011). Table 14.1 illustrates the three principles and six strategic themes included in the approach:

Emergency managers have long acknowledged that social media can help embody the principles and strategic themes outlined in the Whole Community approach (FEMA, 2011). Recent research findings further support the role that

Table 14.1 FEMA's Whole Community Principles and Strategic Themes

Principles	*Strategic Themes*
Understand and meet the actual needs of the whole community	Understand community complexity Recognize community capabilities and needs
Engage and empower all parts of the community	Foster relationships with community leaders Build and maintain partnerships
Strengthen what works well in communities on a daily basis	Empower local action Leverage and strengthen social infrastructure, networks, and assets

Source: FEMA (2011, p. 5).

social media play in fostering a multi-faction collaborative approach to emergency management, such as using social media to disseminate information on resource needs and supply sources (Dutt et al., 2019), link rescue requests and available volunteers (Nguyen et al., 2018), and motivate publics to engage in prosocial behaviors like donating or volunteering (Boulianne et al., 2018).

Current Areas of Improvement

Despite the benefits of social media during disasters, there are limitations. For example, some emergency management officials are still reticent about using social media as a source of information for situational awareness. This is due to perceptions of information overload (Plotnick et al., 2015), lack of personnel and resources (Bergstrand & Stenmark, 2016), as well as concerns about the trustworthiness of the content (Lazreg et al., 2018).

Additionally, most of the research related to crisis communication is based on two social media platforms: Facebook and Twitter (Cheng, 2018; Wang & Dong, 2017). In addition, there is a need for more knowledge about device portability. Indeed, social media coupled with mobile devices can shape emergency communication practices and outcomes in significant ways (Centers for Disease Control and Prevention, 2014), including enabling citizens to use live-streaming capabilities to provide emergency managers with real-time updates (Banikalef et al., 2018).

Finally, there is a need for better understanding of how to address crisis misinformation given the proliferation of news sources and user-generated content flooded by misinformation (Southwell et al., 2018). From an organizational perspective, **van der Meer** and Jin (2019) argued that organizations should use different misinformation debunking strategies (e.g., simple rebuttal or factual elaboration) to correct crisis misinformation spread on social media. Coombs (2015) suggested four strategies in response to challenges or paracrises (i.e., refutation, repression, reform, and repentance) along with recommendations when to use or not use strategies (see Table 14.2). However, from the perspective of the publics, little is known about how they may verify or vet crisis misinformation online.

Table 14.2 Summary of Four Strategies in Response to Challenges on Social Media (based on Coombs, 2015)

Strategies	*Responses to Challenges*
Refutation	Invalidate the challenge and provide evidence to demonstrate that the organization is actually meeting stakeholder expectations
Repression	Prevent stakeholders from making others aware of their challenge
Repentance	Admit claims were exaggerated and work to meet the expectations the organization had already claimed to be meeting
Reform	Acknowledge there is a violation of expectations and explain how the organization is trying to meet those expectations
	Legitimize stakeholder expectations, seeking to alter the organization's behaviors to reflect these expectations

Theorizing Social Media and Crisis Communication: Overview

Research on social media and crisis communication has grown tremendously with a fast-shifting focus (i.e., variety of social media platforms) (Cheng & Cameron, 2017) and tremendous increase in volume (Rasmussen & Ihlen, 2017). According to Austin and Jin (2017), research on crisis communication in social media has focused on a variety of different practice areas and industries, including corporate, nonprofit/philanthropic, political/governmental, health, disaster, and sports. The majority of this research has focused on corporations, followed by governmental organizations; fewer studies have focused on nonprofit or philanthropic organizations (Cheng, 2018; Eriksson, 2018).

In a summary of trends and themes of current crisis communication research emphasizing social media, Eriksson (2018) reported that social media, when used effectively, can aid crisis communication in building dialogue and tailoring messages, sources, and timing. However, theorizing on social media and crisis communication is still relatively nascent. Here, we summarize dominant theoretical perspectives (see Table 14.3).

Table 14.3 Main Theoretical Approaches to Social Media Crisis Research

Theoretical Approaches	*Leading Scholars and Exemplar Citations*
Situational Crisis Communication Theory (SCCT): Recommends most effective organizational crisis communication response(s) according to different crisis attributions in different situations.	Coombs and Holladay (e.g., Coombs, 2007, 2014)
Image Repair and Restoration Theory: Recommends how organizations and their leaders can improve crisis-damaged images and restore reputation using different crisis discourse(s).	Benoit (e.g., Benoit, 2004)
Social-mediated crisis communication (SMCC) model: Explains the flow of information and relationships between different types of media, online and offline communication, organizations, and influential publics during crises.	Liu et al. (e.g., Liu, Jin, Austin, et al., 2012; Jin et al., 2014)
The risk amplification through media spread (RAMS) model: Explains how infectious disease outbreak information spreads and amplifies via social media and news media among the health community and at-risk publics.	Vijaykumar et al. (e.g., Vijaykumar et al., 2015)
The misinformation and crisis information vetting model: Identifies the misinformation vetting process and recommending corrective communication strategies to combat crisis misinformation.	**van der Meer** et al. (e.g., **van der Meer** & Jin, 2019; Lu & Jin, 2020)

Among existing theories applicable to social media and crisis communication research, scholarly reviews of research identified Situational Crisis Communication Theory (SCCT) (Coombs, 2007) and image repair and restoration (Benoit, 2004) as the most commonly used theories to study social media and crisis communication from the perspective of public relations (Cheng & Cameron, 2017; Wang & Dong, 2017), followed by the model of crisis communication content (Cheng, 2018). Since a decade ago, new theoretical models have emerged and have been utilized to examine crisis communication specifically within the social media context, most prominently the SMCC model (Austin & Jin, 2016; Liu, Jin, Austin, et al., 2012). Below we summarize research on this model.

Theorizing Social Media and Crisis Communication: The SMCC Model

The SMCC model was proposed to explain the flow of information and relationships between different types of media, online and offline communication, organizations, and influential publics during crises (see Figure 14.1). The SMCC framework grew out of the blog-mediated communication model (BMCC), which provided guidance for how crisis communicators might respond to influential blogs at different stages of crises (Jin & Liu, 2010). Shortly after its development, and influenced by exploratory research testing the BMCC model (Briones et al., 2011; Liu et al., 2012), the model and its principles related to blogs were adapted more broadly to social media and micro-blogging through social media platforms to create a renamed, more comprehensive model: the SMCC model (Liu, Jin, Austin et al., 2012; Liu, Jin, Briones et al., 2012). The new SMCC model also included the importance of social media influencers and platforms in crisis interactions, in addition to bloggers, offline word-of-mouth communication, and more traditional media.

The SMCC model includes several key components (see Figure 14.1): organizations, key publics (described as influential social media creators, followers, and inactives), forms of communication (i.e., traditional media, social media, and offline word-of-mouth communication), and the flow of information (e.g., information processing, seeking, and sharing as indicated in the model by direct and indirect relationships). Also considered in the model are organizational considerations, which include factors about the crisis itself (e.g., crisis origin and crisis type), characteristics of the organization (e.g., organizational infrastructure), and messaging recommendations (e.g., message strategy and message form) (Austin & Jin, 2016).

SMCC model research has tested model propositions through interviews, surveys, experiments, content analysis, and large data analysis. Through a series of interviews and experiments, early research explored the impact of crisis information form (i.e., traditional/social media and offline) and source (i.e., organization or third party) on publics' information seeking,

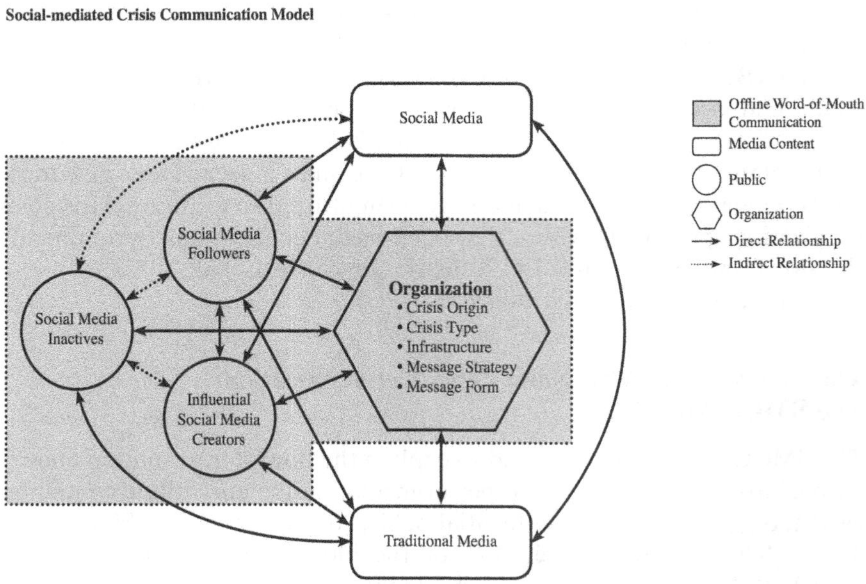

Figure 14.1 Social-Mediated Crisis Communication Model (Liu et al., 2012).

information sharing, emotional responses, and acceptance of crisis messages (Austin et al., 2012; Jin et al., 2014; Liu et al., 2011, 2013). In these studies, both source and form affected crisis communication outcomes.

In terms of information seeking, publics sought different forms of information for different informational needs (e.g., social media were used to obtain eye-witness information, whereas traditional media were sought more for educational needs), and traditional media forms and third-party sources were seen as more credible sources of information (Austin et al., 2012). For information sharing, hearing about a crisis from an organization via traditional media resulted in more positive information sharing, whereas receiving offline word-of-mouth communication resulted in more negative sharing of information (Liu et al., 2013).

SMCC model research has also revealed different uses and motivations for information seeking and sharing via different forms of media (Austin et al., 2012; Liu et al., 2013). For example, Fraustino et al. (2017) found that individuals use social media during disaster response to seek additional information, receive timely and unfiltered information, learn about the magnitude of the disaster, check on family/friends, mobilize, connect with a community, and foster emotional support/healing.

Emerging research on the SMCC model is further expanding theoretical connections. For example, Liu et al. (2019) explored how the SMCC model could be combined with the situational theory of problem solving (STOPS)

(Kim & Grunig, 2011) to examine active and passive communication in response to tornadoes. Findings from this research suggest that the SMCC model's unique way to assess communicative engagement through different media channels can better help to predict protective action taking in a tornado context—compared to STOPS measures for communicative action. Additional research (Zhao et al., 2019) examines how social media influencers and followers adopt different and distinctive communication functions during crises. In this research, influential social media creators shared information and facilitated the exchange of support, while followers used platforms for opinion expression and emotional needs, such as coping.

Recently, Lu and Jin (2020) called for a SMCC model update, adding information vetting as one key component of publics' crisis coping. Lu and Jin (2020) defined crisis information vetting as individuals' psychological process of judging (1) the accuracy of crisis information in terms of content correctness and source credibility, and (2) the validity of one's own judgment in terms of the perceived correctness of their attitude toward a crisis. Lu and Jin posited that, in social-mediated crisis and risk communication, publics' information processing (i.e., information seeking and sharing) is motivated by their desire to make correct judgments and can be prohibited by their confidence in their ability to make correct judgments. This recent extension of the SMCC model provides a conceptual foundation for empirical studies to examine how individual differences, crisis features, and message characteristics influence publics' motivation for and their ability to vet information, the findings of which will generate insights for tailoring social-mediated informational interventions during misinformation triggered or aggravated crises.

Measuring Effectiveness of Social Media in Crisis Communication

When it comes to measuring the effectiveness of using social media in crisis management, limited research has focused on this topic (Jiang & Luo, 2017; Jin & Liu, 2010). As summarized in the prior section, recent SMCC model research has begun to uncover what distinguishes influential social media content creators from followers during crises (Zhao et al., 2019). Other research has focused on the interactivity of social media and crisis communication effectiveness (e.g., Ki & Nekmat, 2014; Yang et al., 2010). For instance, in examining Fortune 500 companies' use of Facebook during crises, Ki and Nekmat's (2014) found that interacting with online users at a certain level was associated with users' positive response to the target organizations and their crisis responses. Following up on this finding, Jiang and Luo (2017) proposed a preliminary measurement model to assess the effectiveness of social media management in crisis communication along four dimensions: (1) *crisis involvement*: providing timely and accurate information and cultivating offline involvement and awareness; (2) *crisis interaction*: requesting real-time information, sharing credible sources, and creating credible media content; (3) *crisis intimacy*: expressing empathy and attending to the emotional needs of the affected publics; and (4) *crisis influence*: including constant multimedia-enhanced conversations, content forwarding, and a multi-directional communication network. Jiang and Luo (2017)'s social media management model reinforces *engagement* as a critical metric in social media measurement and the need for demonstrating both the online and offline emotional needs of affected communities.

From an applied perspective, guidelines recommend the use of key performance indicators to assess the effectiveness of social media programs within emergency management (Department of Homeland Security Science and Technology Directorate, 2019). According to the Department of Homeland Security Science and Technology Directorate (2018), some of the more common social media metrics include numbers of the following: people that visit an organization's social media profile/page/group, views per post or video, users that follow the account, sharing/forwarding of social media content, public comments on content, and clicks that links receive. Other post-engagement metrics include the number of comments, mentions, likes, shares, and impressions. Resources like the Social Media Plan Guide (USDHS S&T, 2019) provide more detail about the different metrics that organizations can use to assess the effectiveness of social media engagement across different platforms like Facebook, Twitter, Instagram, Snapchat, Nextdoor, and LinkedIn. Concerning benchmarks or thresholds for effective social media engagement, guidelines highlight that "a best practice for measurement is to start small and develop more focused metrics over time" (USDHS S&T, 2018, p. 8). In turn, when key performance indicators cannot convey the effectiveness of social media engagement, best practices highlight the value of case studies and lessons learned.

Identifying the Next Frontier

In this chapter, we have reviewed why social media matters for crisis communication, current dominant theorizing about social media and crisis communication, and current perspectives on measuring effectiveness of crisis communication via social media. We now conclude with our thoughts on the next frontier for research and practice.

Social Media Forms and Messages

SMCC model researchers (Liu et al., 2011, 2013) and other scholars (e.g., Eriksson, 2018) have called for further examination of the impact of different social media forms on crisis communication outcomes. Notably, the majority of prior research examines two crisis communication forms when it comes to social media: Facebook and Twitter (Cheng, 2018; Wang & Dong, 2017). A large body of scholarship investigates affordances, which are the "multifaceted relational structure between an object/technology and the user that enables or constrains potential behavioral outcomes in a particular context" (Evans et al., 2017, p. 36). Following this rich body of scholarship, crisis communication scholars have just begun to delve into the different enabling and constraining features of unique social media (Banikalef et al., 2018) and much more research is needed. Likewise, practitioners should consider what crisis messages might be best suited for which channels and which messages should be distributed via all channels.

One important enabling feature of social media is visuals, which are more prominent in some social media channels (e.g., Instagram) than others. Scholars have just begun to examine visual crisis communication. For example, Jin et al. (2017) proposed the concept of strategic crisis visuals, which are defined as "images, in the form of photographs, graphics, and infographics alone or in combination with text or other image(s), that are selected and incorporated strategically by an organization to be disseminated to and/or shared with primary publics as relevant crisis information, serving the function of making crisis information content more concrete, coherent, or comprehensible" (p. 301). Jin et al. (2017) further identified different types of strategic crisis visuals, which should be tailored for different types of visual social media (VSM), according to different publics and specific crisis threats at hand. Illustrating this concept, research has shown that tailored maps of a wildfire scenario compared with text-based messages can increase comprehension and elevate risk perceptions, suggesting that such visuals could in turn prompt safe and efficient response of at-risk publics during disasters (Cao et al., 2016). More research is needed to understand how visuals can be strategically paired with words for desired crisis communication outcomes such as public safety.

As noted previously, there is a need for more knowledge about device portability. Currently, the research record does not distinguish between social media consumed via mobile devices versus computers or tablets. Government agencies such as the Centers for Disease Control (2014) recommend integrating the use of mobile devices into crisis communication plans. A National Academies (2018) report concluded there is insufficient knowledge about what information should be included in emergency messages for portable devices. The report also concluded that there is a need for more disaster and alerting education for the public and, overall, a better understanding of how to engage at-risk publics with disaster information via portable and non-portable devices.

Influence, Evaluation, and Misinformation Management

Research and practice have begun to identify how to measure social media influence during crises and, overall, how to measure the impact of social media use for crises. Proposed measures include crisis involvement, crisis intimacy, crisis influence, and engagement metrics such as comments, mentions, likes, and shares (Department of Homeland Security Science and Technology Directorate, 2019; Jiang & Luo, 2017; Jin & Liu, 2010). Importantly, there is a need to better understand how to measure influence by platform type. How organizations and publics establish and sustain influence during crises is an open, empirical question, which scholars have just begun to address (e.g., Zhao et al., 2019). Considering these challenges, there is a need for more public-private partnerships to develop solutions.

For example, in the US, Purdue University's Center for Visualization and Data Analytics (CVADA), funded by the Department of Homeland Security, unveiled the Social Media Analytics and Reporting Toolkit (SMART). This toolkit was developed by researchers in collaboration with emergency managers to analyze and visualize aggregated social media data most useful for decision-making during disasters (Department of Homeland Security Science and Technology Center of Excellence, 2016). This example illustrates that emergency practitioners and researchers, together, can develop the insight and resources needed to fully capitalize on opportunities provided by social media for effective disaster mitigation, protection, response, and recovery.

Combating misinformation is important so that individuals and organizations can establish and evaluate their influence online during crises is to combat misinformation. Crises are, by their nature, uncertain events that create conditions for rumors or misinformation spreading (Seeger et al., 1998; Starbird et al., 2014). The question is, however, what is the best way to respond? As previously discussed, scholars have begun to propose response strategy options (Coombs, 2015; **van der Meer** & Jin, 2019). However, more theoretical development and empirical testing are needed before these response options can confidently be put into practice.

The Crisis Life Cycle

Coombs (2015) outlined the effects of social media and what organizations should consider throughout the crisis life cycle: (1) Discern real crisis versus paracrisis at the *precrisis* stage; (2) Be proactive on social media channels and follow social media rules in communicating with stakeholders at the *crisis response* stage; and (3) Deliver updates and address specific follow-up questions on proper social media channels at the *postcrisis* stage. Yet the vast majority of research examines the role of social media in crisis responses. When examining social media and crisis preparedness, scholars have found that humor can greatly extend message reach and how familiar members of at-risk publics are with government agencies who frequently communicate about risks (Fraustino & Ma, 2015; Liu et al., 2020). Additional attention to the role of social media in crisis preparedness and recovery could help government agencies and their publics be more resilient to disasters.

Key Takeaways

Social media are integral to organizational crisis planning, response, and recovery efforts. Over the years, social media have been increasingly used by government agencies, organizations, and the general public to share information on preparedness and response to and recovery from crises. This chapter provides a review of why social media matter for crisis communication, the current dominant theories in the field, perspectives on measuring social media effectiveness, and thoughts on future research and practice. While much has been done to understand the appropriate use of social media in disaster contexts and how to best measure effectiveness, more work is needed to better engage practitioners in its use and develop research programs that further explore misinformation management, visual communication, device portability, different social media forms, public-private partnerships, and social media usage throughout the disaster timeline. Social media technology and usage will only continue to grow over time. The theories, research, and ideas presented in this chapter support and enhance social media use in the protection of life and property in future crises. As social media platforms and their use by publics continue to evolve and adapt, so too will research in this area need to progress.

References

Andrade, E. L., Barrett, N. D., Edberg, M. C., Rivera, M. I., Latinovic, L., & Seeger, M. W. (2020). Mortality reporting and rumor generation: An assessment of crisis and emergency risk communication following Hurricane María in Puerto Rico. *Journal of International Crisis and Risk Communication Research, 3*, 14–48. https://doi.org/10.30658/jicrcr.3.1.2

Annenberg Public Policy Center. (2016, February). *Half of Americans concerned Zika will spread to their neighborhoods*. https://www.annenbergpublicpolicycenter.org/half-of-americans-concerned-zika-will-spread-to-their-neighborhoods/

Army Corps of Engineers. (2019). *A guide to public alerts and warnings for dam and levee emergencies*. Washington, DC: Department of the Army. https://www.publications.usace.army.mil/Portals/76/Users/182/86/2486/EP%201110-2-17.pdf?ver=2019-06-20-152050-550.

Austin, L. L., & Jin, Y. (2016). Social media and crisis communication: Explicating the social-mediated crisis communication model. In A. Dudo & L. A. Kahlor (Eds.), *Strategic communication: New agendas in communication* (pp. 163–186). Routledge.

Austin, L. L., & Jin, Y. (2017). *Social media and crisis communication*. Routledge.

Austin, L. L., Liu, B. F., & Jin, Y. (2012). How audiences seek out crisis information: Exploring the social-mediated crisis communication model. *Journal of Applied Communication Research, 40*, 188–207. https://doi.org/10.1080/00909882.2012.654498

Banikalef, A., Bataineh, K. A., & Atoum, M. (2018). Exploring Facebook affordances in natural disaster: Case study of the 2018 dead sea flash floods in Jordan. *International Journal of Engineering & Technology, 7*, 5001–5006. https://doi.org/doi: 10.14419/ijet.v7i4.25862

Barthel, M. (2019, July). *5 key takeaways about the state of the news media in 2018*. PEW. https://www.pewresearch.org/fact-tank/2019/07/23/key-takeaways-state-of-the-news-media-2018/

Benoit, W. L. (2004). Image restoration discourse and crisis communication. In D. P. Millar, & R. L. Heath (Eds.), *Responding to crisis: A rhetorical approach to crisis communication* (pp. 263–280). Lawrence Erlbaum.

Bergstrand, F., & Stenmark, D. (2016, January). Leveraging bystander reports in emergency response work: framing emergency managers social media use. In *2016 49th Hawaii International Conference on System Sciences* (HICSS) (pp. 162–171). https://ieeexplore.ieee.org/document/7427203

Boulianne, S., Minaker, J., & Haney, T. J. (2018). Does compassion go viral? Social media, caring, and the Fort McMurray wildfire. *Information, Communication & Society, 21*, 697–711. https://doi.org/10.1080/1369118X.2018.142865

Briones, R. L., Kuch, B., Liu, B. F., & Jin, Y. (2011). Keeping up with the digital age: How the American Red Cross uses social media to build relationships. *Public Relations Review, 37*, 37–43. https://doi.org/10.1016/j.pubrev.2010.12.006

Cao, Y., Boruff, B. J., & McNeill, I. M. (2016). Is a picture worth a thousand words? Evaluating the effectiveness of maps for delivering wildfire warning information. *International Journal of Disaster Risk Reduction, 19*, 179–196. https://doi.org/10.1016/j.ijdrr.2016.08.012

Centers for Disease Control and Prevention (CDC). (2014). *CERC: Social media and mobile media devices.* https://emergency.cdc.gov/cerc/ppt/CERC_Social%20Media%20and%20Mobile%20Mia%20Devices.pdf

Cheng, Y. (2018). How social media is changing crisis communication strategies: Evidence from the updated literature. *Journal of Contingencies and Crisis Management, 26*, 58–68. https://doi.org/10.1111/1468-5973.12130

Cheng, Y., & Cameron, G. (2017). The status of social-mediated crisis communication (SMCC) research. In L. Austin & Y. Jin (Eds.), *Social media and crisis communication* (pp. 9–20). Routledge.

Coombs, W. T. (2007). Protecting organization reputations during a crisis: The development and application of situational crisis communication theory. *Corporate Reputation Review, 10*(3), 163–176. doi:10.1057/palgrave.crr.1550049

Coombs, W. T. (2014). State of crisis communication: Evidence and the bleeding edge. *Institute of Public Relations.* http://www.instituteforpr.org/state-crisis-communication-evidence-bleeding-edge/

Coombs, W. T. (2015). *Ongoing crisis communication: Planning, managing, and responding* (4th ed.). Sage.

Department of Homeland Security (DHS) Science and Technology Directorate (S&T). (2018). *Social media business case guide.* https://www.dhs.gov/sites/default/files/ publications/1024_IAS_HSHQDC-17-C-B0013_Social-Media-Business-Case-Guide_181003-508.pdf

Department of Homeland Security (DHS) Science and Technology Directorate (S&T). (2019). *Social media plan guide.* https://www.dhs.gov/sites/default/files/publications/social_media_plan_guide_09_20_2019.pdf

Department of Homeland Security (DHS) Science and Technology (S&T) Center of Excellence (COE). (2016). *Improving disaster response and recovery: Social media analytics and reporting toolkit.* https://www.dhs.gov/sites/default/files/publications/cvada_social-media_coe-factsheet_1604-508.pdf

Duhé, S. (2015). An overview of new media research in public relations journals from 1981 to 2014. *Public Relations Review, 41*, 153–169. https://doi.org/10.1016/j.pubrev.2014.11.002

Dutt, R., Basu, M., Ghosh, K., & Ghosh, S. (2019). Utilizing microblogs for assisting post-disaster relief operations via matching resource needs and availabilities. *Information Processing & Management, 56*, 1680–1697. https://doi.org/10.1016/j.ipm.2019.05.010

Eriksson, M. (2018). Lessons for crisis communication on social media: A systematic review of what research tells the practice. *International Journal of Strategic Communication, 12*, 526–551. https://doi.org/10.1080/1553118X.2018.1510405

Evans, S. K., Pearce, K. E., Vitak, J., & Treem, J. W. (2017). Explicating affordances: A conceptual framework for understanding affordances in communication research. *Journal of Computer-Mediated Communication, 22*, 35–52. https://doi.org/10.1111/jcc4.12180

Fang, J., Hu, J., Shi, X., & Zhao, L. (2019). Assessing disaster impacts and response using social media data in China: A case study of 2016 Wuhan rainstorm. *International Journal of Disaster Risk Reduction, 34*, 275–282. https://doi.org/10.1016/j.ijdrr.2018.11.027

Federal Emergency Management Agency (FEMA). (2011). *A whole community approach to emergency management: Principles, themes, and pathways for action.* https://www.fema.gov/media-library-data/20130726-1813-25045-0649/whole_community_dec2011__2_.pdf

Fraustino, J. D., Liu, B. F., & Jin, Y. (2017). Social media during disasters: A research synthesis and road map. In L. Austin & Y. Jin (Eds.), *Social media and crisis communication* (pp. 283–295). Routledge.

Fraustino, J. D., & Ma, L. (2015). CDC's use of social media and humor in a risk campaign-"preparedness 101: Zombie apocalypse." *Journal of Applied Communication Research, 43*, 222–241. https://doi.org/10.1080/00909882.2015.1019544

Jiang, H., & Luo, Y. (2017). Social media engagement for crisis communication: A preliminary measurement model. In L. Austin & Y. Jin (Eds.), *Social media and crisis communication* (pp. 401–422). Routledge.

Jin, Y., & Liu, B. F. (2010). The blog-mediated crisis communication model: Recommendations for responding to influential external blogs. *Journal of Public Relations Research, 22*, 429–455. https://doi.org/10.1080/10627261003801420.

Jin, Y., Liu, B. F., Anagondahalli, D., & Austin, L. (2014). Scale development for measuring publics' emotions in organizational crises. *Public Relations Review, 40*, 509–518. https://doi.org/10.1016/j.pubrev.2014.04.007

Jin, Y., Liu, B. F., & Austin, L. (2014). Examining the role of social media in effective crisis management: The effects of crisis origin, information form, and source on publics' crisis responses. *Communication Research, 41*, 74–94. https://doi.org/10.1177%2F0093650211423918

Ki, E-J., & Nekmat, E. (2014). Situational crisis communication and interactivity: Usage and effectiveness of Facebook for crisis management. *Public Relations Review, 35*, 140–147. https://doi.org/10.1016/j.chb.2014.02.039

Kibanov, M., Stumme, G., Amin, I., & Lee, J. G. (2017). Mining social media to inform peatland fire and haze disaster management. *Social Network Analysis and Mining, 7*, 30. http://dx.doi.org/10.1007/s13278-017-0446-1

Kim, J.-N., & Grunig, J. E. (2011). Problem solving and communicative action: A situational theory of problem solving. *The Journal of Communication, 61*, 120–149. https://doi.org/10.1111/j.1460-2466.2010.01529.x.

Kim, S., & Liu, B. F. (2012). Are all crises opportunities? A comparison of how corporate and government organizations responded to the 2009 flu pandemic. *Journal of Public Relations Research, 24*, 69–85. https://doi.org/10.1080/1062726X.2012.626136

Kumar, D., & Ukkusuri, S. V. (2018, April). Utilizing geo-tagged tweets to understand evacuation dynamics during emergencies: A case study of Hurricane Sandy.

In *Companion of the Web Conference 2018 on the Web Conference 2018* (pp. 1613–1620). International World Wide Web Conferences Steering Committee.

Lazreg, B. M., Chakraborty, N. R., Stieglitz, S., Potthoff, T., Ross, B., & Majchrzak, T. A. (2018, August). Social media analysis in crisis situations: Can social media be a reliable information source for emergency management services? In *Proceedings of the 27th International Conference on Information Systems Development (ISD2018)*. Lund, Sweden.

Liu, B. F., Austin, L. L., & Jin, Y. (2011). How publics respond to crisis communication strategies: The interplay of information form and source. *Public Relations Review, 37*, 345–353. https://doi.org/10.1016/j.pubrev.2011.08.004

Liu, B. F., Jin, Y., & Austin, L. L. (2013). The tendency to tell: Understanding publics' communicative responses to crisis information form and source. *Journal of Public Relations Research, 25*, 51–67. https://doi.org/10.1080/1062726X.2013.739101

Liu, B. F., Jin, Y., Austin, L. L., & Janoske, M. (2012). The social-mediated crisis communication model: Guidelines for effective crisis management in a changing media landscape. In S. C. Duhé (Ed.), *New media and public relations* (2nd ed., pp. 257–266). Peter Lang.

Liu, B. F., Jin, Y., Briones, R., & Kuch, B. (2012). Managing turbulence in the Blogosphere: Evaluating the blog-mediated crisis communication model with the American Red Cross. *Journal of Public Relations Research*, *24*, 353–370. https:// doi.org/ 10.1080/1062726X.2012.689901

Liu, B. F., & Kim, S. (2011). How organizations framed the 2009 H1N1 pandemic via social and traditional media: Implications for U.S. health communicators. *Public Relations Review, 37*, 233–234. https://doi.org/10.1016/j.pubrev.2011.03.005

Liu, B. F., Seate, A. A., Iles, I., & Herovic, E. (2020). #TornadoWarning: Understanding the national weather service's tornado communication strategies. *Public Relations Review.* Advance online publication. https://doi.org/10.1016/j.pubrev.2019.101879

Liu, B. F., Xu, S., Lim, J. R., & Egnoto, M. (2019). How publics' active and passive communicative behaviors affect their tornado responses: An integration of STOPS and SMCC. *Public Relations Review.* Advance online publication. https://doi.org/doi:10.1016/j.pubrev.2019.101831

Liu, W., Lai, C-H, & Xu, W. (2018). Tweeting about emergency: A semantic network analysis of government organizations' social media messaging during Hurricane Harvey. *Public Relations Review, 44*, 807–819. https://doi.org/doi:10.1016/j.pubrev.2018.10.009

Lu, X., & Jin, Y. (2020). Information vetting as a key component in social-mediated crisis communication: An exploratory study to examine the initial conceptualization. *Public Relations Review.* https://doi.org/10.1016/j.pubrev.2020.101891

Martín, Y., Li, Z., & Cutter, S. L. (2017). Leveraging Twitter to gauge evacuation compliance: Spatiotemporal analysis of Hurricane Matthew. *PLoS One, 12*, 1–22. https://doi.org/10.1371/journal.pone.0181701

National Academies of Sciences, Engineering, and Medicine. (2018). *Emergency alerts and warning systems: Current knowledge and future research directions.* The National Academies Press. https://www.nap.edu/catalog/24935/emergency-alert-and-warning-systems-current-knowledge-and-future-research

Nguyen, L., Yang, Z., Zhu, J., Li, J., & Jin, F. (2018). Coordinating disaster emergency response with heuristic reinforcement learning. *arXiv preprint arXiv:1811.05010.*

Niles, M. T., Emery, B. F., Reagan, A. J., Dodds, P. S., & Danforth, C. M. (2019). Social media usage patterns during natural disasters. *PLoS One, 15*, 1–6. https://doi.org/doi:10.1371/journal.pone.0210484

Ogie, R., Rho, J. C., Clarke, R. J., & Moore, A. (2018). Disaster risk communication in culturally and linguistically diverse communities: The role of technology. *Proceedings, 2*, 1–7. https://doi.org/10.3390/proceedings2191256

Perrin, A., & Anderson, M. (2019, April). Share of U.S. adults using social media, including Facebook, is mostly unchanged since 2019. *Pew Research Center.* https://www.pewresearch.org/fact-tank/2019/04/10/share-of-u-s-adults-using-social-media-including-facebook-is-mostly-unchanged-since-2018/

Plotnick, L., Hiltz, S. R., Kushma, J. A., & Tapia, A. H. (2015, May). Red tape: Attitudes and issues related to use of social media by US county-level emergency managers. In L. A. Palen, T. Comes, M. Buscher, A. L. Hughes, & L. A. Palen (Eds.), *Proceedings of the ISCRAM 2015 Conference: 12th International Conference on Information Systems for Crisis Response and Management.* http://www.scopus.com/inward/record.url?scp=84947774210&partnerID=8YFLogxK

Rasmussen, J., & Ihlen, Ø. (2017). Risk, crisis, and social media: A systematic review of seven years' research. *Nordicom Review, 38*, 1–17. https://doi.org/doi:10.1515/nor-2017-0393

Rotondi, L., Zuddas, M., Marsella, P., & Rosati, P. (2019). A Facebook page created soon after the Amatrice earthquake for deaf adults and children, families, and caregivers provides an easy communication tool and social satisfaction in maxi-emergencies. *Prehospital and Disaster Medicine, 34*, 137–141. https://doi.org/10.1017/S1049023X19000086

Seeger, M. W., Sellnow, T., & Ulmer, R. (1998). Communication, organization, and crisis. *Annals of the International Communication Association, 21*, 281–274. https://doi.org/10.1080/23808985.1998.11678952

Smith, S. (2009, December 11). New media spread the word on H1N1: Twitter, YouTube messages aimed at public. *Boston Globe.* http://archive.boston.com/news/health/articles/2009/12/11/new_media_spread_the_word_on_h1n1/

Southwell, B. G., Thorson, E. A., & Sheble, L. (2018). Misinformation among mass audiences as a focus for inquiry. In B. G. Southwell, E. A. Thorson, & L. Sheble (Eds.), *Misinformation and mass audiences* (pp. 1–14). University of Texas Press.

Starbird, K., Maddock, J., Orand, M., Achterman, P., & Mason, R. M. (2014, March). Rumors, false flags, and digital vigilantes: Misinformation on Twitter after the 2013 Boston Marathon bombing. In *Proceedings from the 2014 iConference* (pp. 654–662). https://doi.org/10.9776/14308

van der Meer, T. G. L. A., & Jin, Y. (2019). Seeking formula for misinformation treatment in public health crises: The effects of corrective information type and source. *Health Communication.* Advanced online publication. https://doi.org/10.1080/ 10410236.2019.1573295

Vijaykumar, S., Jin, Y., & Nowak, G. (2015). Social media and the virality of risk: The risk amplification through media spread (RAMS) model. *Journal of Homeland Security and Emergency Management, 12*, 653–677. https://doi.org/10.1515/jhsem-2014-0072

Wang, Y., & Dong, C. (2017). Applying social media in crisis communication: A quantitative review of social media-related crisis communication research from 2009 to 2017. *International Journal of Crisis Communication, 1*, 29–37. http://www.lifescienceglobal.com/pms/index.php/IJCC/article/view/4834/2743

Williams, G. A., Woods, C. L., & Staricek, N. (2017). Restorative rhetoric and social media: An examination of the Boston Marathon Bombing. *Communication Studies*, *68*, 385–402. https://doi-org.proxy-um.researchport.umd.edu/10.1080/10510974.2017.1340901

Yang, S.-U., Kang, M., & Johnson, P. (2010). Effects of narratives, openness to dialogic communication, and credibility on engagement in crisis communication through organizational blogs. *Communication Research*, *37*, 473–497. https://doi.org/10.1177%2F0093650210362682

Zhao, X., Zhan, M., & Liu, B. F. (2019). Understanding motivated publics during disasters: Examining message functions, frames, and styles of social media influentials and followers. *Journal of Contingencies and Crisis Management.* Advanced online publication. https://doi.org/10.1111/1468-5973.12279

Part VI

Looking Ahead and Trekking Forward Together

15 The Future of Collaborative Crisis Research

Yan Jin, Matthew O'Connor, Bryan H. Reber, and Glen Nowak

> A business man once stated that there is nothing so practical as a good theory.
>
> Kurt Lewin (1951a, p. 169)

The Quest for Good (and Practical) Crisis Research

This maxim of Kurt Lewin, founder of social psychology and a pioneer in studying group dynamics in organizational psychology, sheds some light on our journey here, in this final chapter, or rather, how this book project got started.

We teach theory in undergraduate and graduate programs. Critical thinking and problem solving—the core attributes of learning and advancing any theory—are among the most important skills higher education is meant to impart to learners, scholars, and future professionals. In labs or in fields, scientists study complex phenomena (natural or social) and attempt to describe, explain, predict, and ultimately recommend solutions on critical issues based on good theories and evidence-based measurement tools that have been proved to be valid and reliable.

When it comes to the business of crisis communication, we have good news and bad news. The good news is straightforward: we have a lot of good theories to offer professionals (Ha & Boynton, 2014). The bad news, pretty simply, is that a gap still exists between crisis research and its implementation in practice, despite ongoing efforts from both communities. As Sha (2016) observed, "both anecdotal evidence and scholarly research tell us that public relations practitioners do not always follow theory-based guidelines, a problem that some have called the scholar-practitioner divide or the 'rigor-relevance gap'" (p. 214–215). What causes this lingering bad news (i.e., the gap) is complicated. First, not every organization or business recognizes the fact that there are good and practical crisis theories. Second, not every theory-based academic study (peer-reviewed and published by a reputable outlet) is adequately translated for a business/practitioner audience. Third, "research," in its general sense, is not something novel or unique to academia. Firms and government agencies conduct research and use research findings to guide business decisions and policy making, which is a no-brainer common practice. Every organization or business conducts its own research (formal or informal, informative or evaluative) via in-house experts, outsourcing to research firms, or a combination of both. So, why are crisis theory and academic research even needed by practitioners? Conversely, why should scholars work with practitioners if the existing academic research and publication machinery works just fine in our safe and productive ivory tower? One of the reasons why practitioners are not using academic research lies in their impression that "practically relevant research is not undertaken by academics" (Claeys & Opgenhaffen, 2016, p. 233).

Therefore, the unique contribution of crisis theory and academic research in advancing crisis communication effectiveness needs to be first more precisely defined and then sustainably supported. Instead, we make general statements, such as "crisis research can inform practice," which have saturated academic and professional conferences and publications. To bridge any gap, we must first be clear where the gap is. To begin with, we want to know what crisis insights are essential to organizations across industry types and sectors and which ones are unlikely to be obtained by any organization alone or based on a single study. It is at this level of "big" research questions, confronting crisis communication practice, that crisis theory and academic research are uniquely positioned to generate and disseminate knowledge that advances the overall practice.

Our book is therefore created as an initial effort in the quest for good theory and meaningful academic research that are practical and bring unique value to crisis communication practice. To do so, we bring crisis scholars together with practicing professionals to integrate academic theories and research with the knowledge and lessons learned on the frontlines of crisis communication and management. This volume, co-created by scholars and practitioners, starts with identifying *complex and challenging issues*, both *currently* (Chapter 1) and *historically* (Chapter 2), in crisis communication plans and efforts. From there, our crisis scholar and practitioner contributors share insights and observations in managing some of the most challenging *organizational crises* (Chapters 3, 4, and 5), *public crises* (Chapters 6 and 7), and *crises amplified by media and aggravated by misinformation* (Chapters 8, 9, and 10) when it comes to choosing and implementing crisis communication strategies, plans, and coordination.

Next, emphasizing how crisis practice benefits when academic perspectives are connected with practitioner experiences, we feature a set of crisis theories, models, and frameworks and how they have been or can be applied to help practice: the *Situational Crisis Communication Theory* (SCCT) (Chapter 11), the *Contingency Theory of Strategic Conflict Management* (Chapter 12), the *Internalization, Distribution, Explanation, and Action (IDEA) Model* (Chapter 13), and the *Social-Mediated Crisis Communication (SMCC) Model* (Chapter 14).

Together, these chapters illustrate (1) how academic theories and research can inform crisis management and response and (2) how practitioners can use, inform, and strengthen academic theories and research. In light of topic areas (with examples and applications) covered, we believe a strong case is made that public relations scholarship, integrated with practice, can advance crisis communication effectiveness. In this concluding chapter, we look ahead and recommend a more concerted approach for scholars and practitioners to work together, in a sustainable manner, to make a more impactful and timely contribution to the field of crisis communication. The approach we advocate, the essence of this book, is *collaborative crisis research.*

Collaborative Research: Definitions and Current Practice in Public Relations

Defining Research Collaboration

Research collaboration is critical in supporting scientific and technological innovation, social development, and economic growth (Acs et al., 2009; Mensah & Enu-Kwesi, 2018; Schumpeter, 1983). It involves interactions among individuals, groups, and/or entities of diverse interests to (1) embark upon research and (2) use the research findings for pre-determined purposes such as advancing knowledge in a scientific field (Baba et al., 2009; Teirlinck & Spithoven, 2013).

According to Mensah and Enu-Kwesi (2018), the forms of research collaboration range from business-business research collaboration (Teirlinck & Spithoven. 2013), university-industry research collaboration (Cunningham & Link, 2015), international research collaboration (Melber, 2015), and research collaboration among researchers in the same, or from different, academic disciplines, universities, or national research institutes (Bellotti et al., 2016). University and industry are particularly identified as two major infrastructures of national innovation systems in all leading scientific and industrial settings (Rad et al., 2015). Grounded in these two infrastructures, *university-industry research collaboration* emphasizes academic engagement and university-industry interactions. It contributes to a knowledge-related *collaboration* by academic researchers with non-academic organizations (Bozeman et al., 2013). It can be manifested in informal activities (e.g., meetings and conferences) and/or formal activities such as collaborative research (Mensah & Enu-Kwesi, 2018).

Research collaboration, as a type of formal academia-industry interactions, has two main forms (Capaldo et al., 2016): research services and collaborative research. First, *research services*, referring to activities that firms request from universities, are regulated by specific contracts establishing objectives, deliverables, and available financial resources, including *research contracts* (research directly commercially relevant to firms and therefore usually ineligible for public support) and consulting activities (research or advisory services provided by individual academic researchers to their industry clients) (Perkmann & Walsh, 2008). In contrast to consulting activities, in which researchers employ their existing expertise to solve well-known problems, research contracts allow firms to commission academic researchers to explore "specific, previously un-researched aspects of a problem (Perkmann & Walsh, 2007)" (Capaldo et al., 2016, p. 275). Second, *collaborative* (or joint) *research* (e.g., research partnership) is based on formal collaborative arrangements among organizations aimed at co-operating on research and development activities (Hall et al., 2001).

As the most widespread mode of knowledge transfer (Meyer-Krahmer & Schmoch, 1998), *collaborative research*, in the form of joint research or research partnership between scholars from university and practitioners from industry, is the essential mode our book advocates for advancing crisis communication knowledge for both academia and industry.

Research Collaboration in Public Relations and Crisis Communications

Zooming in to the field of public relations, the social scientific community has suggested two concrete ways for scholars and practitioners to work together (Claeys & Opgenhaffen, 2016): (1) *one-way approach*, evidenced in (a) books written by scholars and practitioners, and/or (b) articles jointly reviewed or written by scholars and practitioners, and (2) *two-way collaborative research*, evidenced in (a) research conducted together by scholars and practitioners, and/or (b) information disseminated in academia and industry.

So far, the gap-bridging efforts taken by public relations scholars and practitioners mostly take the one-way approach (i.e., hoping the other side would use their research output for practice or research/teaching). Additional examples of a one-way approach include: academic conferences inviting practitioners to participate as audiences or speakers; professional associations having special membership categories or divisions for educators; universities hiring practitioners to teach undergraduate crisis courses either as part-time faculty or full-time faculty of practice; journal editors' special collections of articles made available to practitioners on specific crisis topics (e.g., crisis and risk communication collections for COVID-19 response), encouraging practitioners to use topic-specific published academic research. However, these efforts contribute mostly to research dissemination and classroom teaching, less significantly to collaborative research itself (e.g., generating new knowledge). One of the few exceptions, in the United States, is the annual International Crisis and Risk Communication Conference (ICRCC) hosted at the University of Central Florida (UCF) by T. Sellnow and D. Sellnow. ICRCC encourages scholars and practitioners to present and discuss research findings. It also provides networking opportunities for scholars and practitioners to brainstorm potential collaboration ideas. Its official peer-reviewed, open-access journal, *Journal of International Crisis and Risk Communication Research*, has become one of the leading outlets for crisis and risk research that matters to practice.

The two-way collaborative approach is what we advocate for as the future direction of collaborative crisis research: true collaborative crisis research.

Specifically, we define *collaborative crisis research as (1) conceptualized and conducted by scholars and practitioners together, (2) aimed at generating knowledge for both theory and practice advancement, and (3) used by scholars (in teaching and academic research) and practitioners (in practice).* The unique challenges to this two-way approach are well documented in frustrating experiences (e.g., communication difficulties and the lack of collaboration facilities) (Claeys & Opgenhaffen, 2016). Therefore, it is critical for practitioners and scholars to address communication difficulties together and develop specific programs that foster and facilitate collaborative knowledge generation and dissemination that benefit practice.

We recommend future collaborative research tackling these two primary challenges by the following: first, the software upgrade, which focuses on fostering mutual understanding and appreciation between academia and industry, especially the unique contribution and value theories and academic research can bring to the table for high-level strategic decisions along the life cycle of crisis management; and, second, the hardware support, which builds sustainable infrastructures or collaborative models that help overcome challenges inhibiting practitioners' engagement in ongoing collaborations (e.g., considerations related to timing, circumstance, legal context, and cultural context; see Claeys & Opgenhaffen, 2016).

Unique Contribution of Theory and Academic Research to Crisis Practice: Gaining Crisis Knowledge at a Higher Ground

Crisis research is a type of social scientific research. According to Shoemaker et al. (2003), science is a particular way of knowing. It is different from other ways of knowing (i.e., authority, intuition, or tenacity) as it applies logic to approaching a question. Social science specifically deals with knowledge of society and the social world, focusing on the study of socially constructed phenomena, how they relate to each other, structure of society, and the activity of its members. Accordingly, crisis communication research examines crisis-related phenomena; how crisis issues, crisis-stricken entities, and crisis-affected publics are related to each other; as well as the short-term and long-term impacts on business continuity and community well-being. Not all research has a theory component, thus we have theory-based research (mostly done in academia) and research not based on or not aimed at development or testing a theory (mostly done in industry).

Crisis Theories

Complex and challenging crisis issues (see Chapter 1) confront practitioners with not only how to deal with a crisis issue at hand but also how to predict its mutations and be prepared for uncertainties in the future. This type of crisis knowledge is to be generated by scholar-practitioner collaborative research, integrating theory and practical insights (see Chapter 2 through

Chapter 14). As Stacks and Salwen (2008) defined, theory is the rationale we extend to understand the world around us (e.g., crisis, risk, disaster). Research provides ways to test or make sense of that rationale (theory) from different approaches (e.g., quantitative or qualitative) (Stacks & Salwen, 2008). Based on these general definitions of theory and research, we further define a *crisis theory* as a theory that explains crisis phenomena and engenders the creation of new theories in crisis communication and management. Aiming to advance crisis theory and conduct crisis research that matters to practice, a collaborative crisis research program can contribute to crisis knowledge by (1) creating new crisis theories or (2) enhancing existing crisis theories (e.g., applying an existing crisis theory to a new situation, industry, context, or culture). Scholars and practitioners can enrich each other in the entire process of theorizing and research. Here are some social-scientific recommendations:

First, any research process starts with asking "good" research questions (Stacks & Salwen, 2008). Quality research questions are derived from different sources, deductively or inductively, often involving a systematic study of an area of communication interest (i.e., literature review of both scholarly literature and trade publications). Often a practitioner's timely comment on an ongoing crisis issue or an in-depth panel discussion at a professional conference panel sparks research ideas among scholars, and vice versa, leading to meaningful questions about a focal concept, how it relates to other crisis factors, the value of certain communication strategies and its impact on policies, etc.

Second, theory-based research is essential for advancing crisis communication. Outputs from theory-based research are useful in summarizing knowledge, providing practical applications, and guiding research itself (Stacks & Salwen, 2008). The four theories we highlight in this book—the *Situational Crisis Communication Theory* (SCCT) (Chapter 11), the *Contingency Theory of Strategic Conflict Management* (Chapter 12), the *Internalization, Distribution, Explanation, and Action (IDEA) Model* (Chapter 13), and the *Social-Mediated Crisis Communication (SMCC) Model* (Chapter 14)—are examples of established theories and models in crisis communication. Besides advancing existing theories in public relations and mass communication, new crisis theories can be built collectively by scholars and practitioners.

Third, practice inspires and drives crisis theory building. In general, Stacks and Salwen (2008) posited that theory building is driven by the desire to explain something, a theoretical problem, and/or problems (intellectual, practical, or both) a researcher would like to address. In collaborative crisis research, crisis theory building is most likely to be driven by a desire to explain a crisis communication issue or challenge, concerning/intriguing both practitioners and scholars, which they both want to make sense of and provide possible solutions. Although practitioners are likely to bring the issue or topic to the attention of scholars (e.g., inspire overarching questions), the scholars are likely to lead the specific procedures of theory building, which starts with explicating focal concepts, forming hypotheses or further narrowed down research questions, and refining them after deep dive in literature review. Furthermore, for any collaborative crisis research project, practitioners can contribute throughout the multiple steps of theory building (see Shoemaker et al., 2003) and the linkages between ideas, evidence, conclusions as well as the overall validity and reliability of the research itself (Chaffee, 1991).

Best Practices and Gap Studies

Another knowledge gaining benefit for practitioners is "best practices" research, although there are disagreements among practitioners as well as scholars whether the term "best practice" is proper for any crisis research at all (see Chapter 10). As of May 2020, in the database of "Communication & Mass Media Complete," the search keywords "best practices of crisis communication" generated 63 articles written about best practices from either crisis scholars or practitioners' perspectives. The academic journals that published the most crisis communication best practices pieces are *Journal of Applied Communication Research* (n=7), *Public Relations Review* (n=6), and *Journal of Communication Management* (n=5). Some of them are more practice area specific (e.g., *Health Communication, Journal of Communication & Religion*). Knowing which academic journal outlets value and publish applied crisis communication research sheds light on where to strategically promote outputs generated from collaborative crisis research.

Opposite, yet complementary to best practices research, are gap studies. For example, uncertainty, defined as an individual's probabilistic beliefs (Dowling, 1986; Peter & Tarpey, 1975), is a well-studied concept in psychology. However, communicating crisis uncertainty is a key knowledge gap scholars have identified in crisis literature (Liu et al., 2016). Through the lens of practitioners, Beeson (2020) referred to health crisis communication as navigating "ever-changing" waters with enormous uncertainty and rapid changes, emphasizing the importance of understanding and communicating about uncertainty in times of crisis. Advice from Nowak (one of the editors of this book, a leading scholar in our field and a top practitioner who led the CDC's communication activities for years before returning to the academia), was cited extensively in Beeson's article: (1) "...through my experience in research that a lot of what we do in health communications is setting, guiding and managing people's expectations"; (2) "when you have a brand new infectious disease [COVID-19], you know very little... You need to let people know that the recommendations you give today may be different tomorrow, when more information is known"; and therefore (3) "... when you're in an environment where there is so much uncertainty, you have to be cautious when you're making statements of certainty." Both Liu et al.(2016) and Nowak (in Beeson's article) make observations that shed light on the need for developing new (and expanding existing) crisis theories, as well as learning from both best practices and knowledge gaps identified by practitioners and scholars.

Critical Areas for Future Collaborative Crisis Research: Practitioner's Viewpoint

Crisis situations are so dynamic with so many variables that communications practitioners must primarily rely on preparation and practice to navigate through a storm of news media inquiries and social media commentary while simultaneously investigating and verifying factual information. The complexity of crisis communication responses is compounded by the nuances of each situation. Two similar types of incidents can quickly evolve in vastly different ways, rendering previously tried-and-true messaging open to harsh criticism and potential backlash from audiences that can include consumers, employees, investors, and regulators, with subsets of socioeconomic background and lifestyle interests. Therefore, case studies that analyze situations in hindsight are beneficial, but seldom offer in-depth understandings that skilled communications practitioners can apply in the moment when they are navigating a crisis, whether it is reputation-oriented or a matter of health and well-being.

While the mainstream news media tend to be even-handed in their reporting of events across print, broadcast, and online channels, consumers who post and comment on social media can quickly complicate the situation by relying on speculation, misinformation, and bias. Consumer sentiment on social media is ripe to go viral during crisis situations and can therefore pose a threat to an organization's or person's brand reputation if messaging is not quickly and thoughtfully injected into the conversation and as early as the holding statement. Because newsrooms often scan social media for trending topics, viral social media topics can influence reporting by bona fide news media outlets (Ferrer-Conill & Tandoc, Jr., 2018).

This dynamic is compounded by news outlets' desire to quickly file stories online, incorporating videos of first-person witness accounts that are posted to social media channels and comments made by first responders before official statements by those authorities are issued, while facts are still being investigated and verified. Such an example is the April 2018 tragedy when Southwest Airlines Flight 1380 experienced a catastrophic engine failure which caused a passenger window to break at an altitude of 30,000 feet, resulting in a passenger fatality. The incident was instantly covered by national news media, which initially relied heavily on passengers' social media posts for their reporting. Southwest Airlines and its public relations team received accolades for its response to the situation for quickly responding with empathy and transparency, yet the incident remains a clear example of how practitioners are put in the unenviable position of responding to news and social media inquiries while facts about the incident are still being gathered and verified. Additional challenges arise if there is a loss of life and the victims' identities have not been verified or their next of kin have not yet been notified.

Further complicating these challenging circumstances is the nature of how consumers congregate on social media, gathering with like-minded people who openly share their opinions on the situation, including how the impacted organization or people respond during the crisis through their behavior and comments (Austin et al., 2012). This intersection of crisis communications messaging and consumer sentiment, especially impassioned consumers with strongly held views are actively engaged, is the fertile soil for more collaborative efforts between practitioners and academic researchers. Although practitioners are best positioned to respond to their organizations' crises, it is the academic researchers who are better positioned to help identify best practices from other industries and messaging that resonates with, and offends, numerous types of relevant audiences. These insights, which can be identified well before different types of crises occur, potentially have the greatest opportunity to impact a practitioner's performance in the midst of a crisis.

Further, while historically used primarily for marketing communications messaging, A/B testing and other forms of message testing can be researched across diverse audiences well in advance of a crisis. Such topics should include sensitive issues among broad national or international audiences such as gun control and lesbian, gay, bisexual, transgender and queer or questioning (LGBTQ) rights, as well as industry-specific issues that could include addressing consumer safety concerns, rectifying gender pay gaps, and improving environmental sustainability standards. For example, the topic of gun control versus the right to own firearms was addressed in 2018 and 2019 by national retailers—including Dick's Sporting Goods, Kroger, and Walmart—as a result of national sentiment concerning public safety. Walmart had previously tightened its policies on selling firearms and ammunition before two shootings occurred at two of the retailer's locations in one week in 2019. In response, the company again changed its approach to selling firearms and ammunition (e.g., "Walmart ends all handgun ammunition sales and asks customers not to carry guns into stores," 2019). The updated company policy, and how the change was communicated, was implemented in a way to satisfy the majority of the retailer's customers, employees, and the public at large while being respectful to those with strong viewpoints on both sides of the issue.

Just as proactive marketing communications messaging is carefully crafted for target audiences in order to advance an organization's business priorities, an equal amount of rigor should be incorporated into crisis communications practices. Enhanced practice needs to be informed by not only industry reports but also academic research guided by theory and empirically supported according to social and behavioral sciences. To accomplish this, a feasible and sustainable platform for scholars and practitioners to actually collaborate is essential. In the next section, we explore existing and emerging collaboration models, which provide promising ways for collaborative crisis research infrastructure building.

Infrastructure for Knowledge-based Collaborative Crisis Research

As defined earlier in this chapter, collaborative crisis research (1) is conceptualized and conducted by scholars and practitioners together, (2) aims at generating knowledge for both theory and practice advancement, and (3) is used by scholars (in teaching and academic research) and practitioners (in practice). In the center of our definition is the concept and practice of collaboration. According to McNamara (2012), collaboration is an interaction between individuals or entities working together to pursue complex goals (e.g., complex crisis issues and communication challenges) based on shared interests (e.g., crisis communication) and a collective responsibility for interconnected tasks (e.g., gaining evidence-based insights to advance crisis communication effectiveness), which cannot be accomplished individually.

Triple Helix (TH) Approach and Crisis Helixes

Crisis scholars Johansen and Frandsen (2018) presented a triple helix (TH) model comprised of public crisis communication, political crisis communication, and corporate crisis communication, which shed initial light on the potential of applying the TH theory from innovation and collaboration research to the specific context of collaborative crisis research. According to Zhou (2014), a TH model emphasizes a TH of university-industry-government relations, which creates a shared sphere among the three parties and functions as a social organization highly conducive to innovation.

Research also showed that the three helixes of universities, industries, and governments are pivotal in strengthening local, national, and global knowledge economy (Galvao et al., 2019) and the capitalization of knowledge (Viale & Etzkowitz, 2010), via four clusters of collaborative research (Galvao et al., 2019): (1) innovation and knowledge policies; (2) entrepreneurial universities; (3) business innovation strategy; and (4) TH stakeholders in innovation, knowledge, and regional development. Several scholarly publications (books and *Triple Helix*,[1] a journal of university-industry-government innovation and entrepreneurship) have specifically dedicated themselves to understanding the university-business partnership through the TH approach, exploring how government, industry, and academia interact as universities increasingly adopt new economic roles in different parts of the world (Etzkowitz & Leydesdorff, 1997; Muravska & Prause, 2012).

In the overall collaborative crisis research infrastructure we are exploring, universities and industries (including both public and private sectors, e.g., government health agencies, corporations, and public relations agencies) are the two helixes that function as the pillars. One promising approach yet to be fully tapped into for collaborative crisis research is the university research group (URG) model, in which an URG interacts with outside businesses or organizations, systematically fostering academic-industry idea exchange (Voges et al., 2020).

University Research Group (URG) Model

The URG approach is grounded in the theoretical foundation of: (1) transaction cost economy (e.g., Argyers & Zenger, 2012; Gancarczyk, 2017) and (2) social network analysis (e.g., Freeman, 2004; Sommerfeldt & Kent, 2015). Despite the challenges for sustainable partnership building, successful URG-industry collaboration models can be mutually beneficial, which has been evidenced in successful models and outcomes in strategic communication areas, contributing to: (1) industry-wide problem solving and (2) organization support (e.g., research funding, professional networks) that enhances the URGs' ability to conduct research. Key observations and recommendations for URG-based collaborative communication research (Voges et al., 2020) include (a) strong network of personal relationships with industry/university partners; (b) projects relevant to more than one organization; (c) strong URG brand; and (d) mutually beneficial university-industry relationships based on shared interests.

These URG findings (Voges et al., 2020) echo what Mensah and Enu-Kwesi (2018) reported to be essential for research collaborations: funding and trust building between academia and industry. We further extract a few key ingredients (i.e., three criteria) for successful small-scale, university-based two-way collaborative model (in contrast to large-size professional association led collaboration, which inevitably tends to be one-way):

- People: Crisis scholars and practitioners who share the research interest and are willing to engage in interactive research activities;
- Resource: Research funding (direct and indirect, if needed) to support the proposed activities;
- Collaborative System: A sustainable infrastructure that supports and incentivizes impactful research that advances crisis communication theory and practice, addressing individual and shared needs for both academia and industry.

However, here is the practical challenge: Although there are university-based research centers/institutes/labs that serve as models for current/best practices in sciences, arts and humanities, and multidisciplinary fields, these centers are often supported by large government research grants (e.g., the National Institutes of Health [NIH] and National Science Foundation [NSF]), there is a lack of established infrastructure or two-way model suitable for university-based collaborative research dedicated for advancing the effectiveness of crisis communication, meeting all three criteria (i.e., people, resource, and system).

Crisis Communication Think Tank (CCTT)

Similar to the URG approach that focuses on URG-organizational relationship and mutual understanding, the potential for increased funding for research; and the URG-business relationship insight co-dissemination, a think tank approach has been taken by the three editors of the book (Jin, Reber, & Nowak) at the University of Georgia.

The Crisis Communication Think Tank (CCTT) invites a select group of crisis communication thought leaders in both the academy and industry to create and foster two-way crisis research collaboration at the URG-business level. One of many features that make the CCTT different from existing scholar-practitioner collaboration models is that: The CCTT brings communication pros together with crisis communication scholars, in one shared physical space and throughout an entire day on an annual basis, to discuss issues of mutual interest and develop year-long research programs with practical applications. In other words, the CCTT is a program designed to foster and facilitate collaborative knowledge production and dissemination, capitalizing upon the established network and collaborative relationship via the think tank members. Its goal is to: (1) curate and highlight the CCTT pros and academics' research projects; (2) disseminate research findings and practical insights to both academia and industry across sectors and around the world; and (3) serve as a scholarly flagship that is leading the ongoing and future research force in bridging the chasm between crisis research and practice, where both sides have so many insights to offer and an ever stronger urge and capacity to enrich each other.

The co-existing opportunities and challenges are in the area of establishing a collaborative crisis research URG mechanism that will: (1) strengthen CCTT trust and relationships among scholar and practitioner members, and (2) create and sustain project-generated funding revenues that will allow scholars (faculty and graduate researchers) to design and conduct research as well as translate the insights to practitioners in a timely manner.

The Horizon of Collaborative Crisis Research: Capturing the Best of Both Worlds

When this book was conceptualized in the fall of 2018, we focused on three major domains of crisis communication research and practice: organizational crisis, public crisis, and new media and technology that disrupt crisis management. Overall, we advocate a multi-agency crisis management system to overcome complex crisis threats and mitigate their severe impact on public safety and societal well-being (Coombs, 2015) besides organizational reputation.

Recent crisis histories (e.g., 2008 financial crisis) and the 2020 COVID-19 pandemic have vividly illustrated Johnson, Connolly, and Carter's (2011) argument that the management of a large-scale crisis mandates collaboration between private (e.g., corporations) and public sectors (e.g., government agencies). As Johnson et al. posited, "[t]he failures of governments in emergency-management-related activities have highlighted the importance of how corporations engage in the response, recovery, planning, and mitigation of disasters" (p. 352). As scholars know, despite academic research's intention to help predict and offer insights for crisis preparation, the practical value of crisis theories and academic research at large tends to be more fully recognized by practitioners only after a crisis has already occurred—a delayed "A-Ha!" moment, so to speak.

For example, back in 2015, Vijaykumar, Jin, and Nowak published the risk amplification through media spread (RAMS) model, a public health crisis communication framework specifically designed for infectious disease outbreak communications grounded in the authors' prior studies and professional insights. In March 2020, as the world was threatened by the COVID-19 pandemic, the authors were approached by a strategic and risk communication expert from Lebanon, who was keen on using the table from the original RAMS paper for training healthcare workers responding to COVID-19. Quickly responding to the practitioner's request for a visual representation of the original table, a visual summary (see Figure 15.1) was created and sent to the practitioner as well as disseminated by CCTT to its social channels. Now, it has been used by practitioners at various organizations and shared via their professional networks.

Furthermore, as MacGregor and Carleton (2012) emphasized, different collaboration models (e.g., TH, URG, and CCTT as outlined in this chapter) can help sustain innovation in a complex ecosystem (e.g., complex crisis issues and increasingly challenging media environment) by systematically and continuously generating values via collaboration between different groups (e.g., crisis scholars and practitioners). Such current and future collaboration can overcome multiple challenges (e.g., academic-industry divide, competing agendas and priorities, the effectiveness of translational research) and work together productively over a long term (MacGregor & Carleton, 2012). In the unique domain of crisis communication, this book, with a collection of chapters co-contributed by both scholars and practitioners, provides the intellectual outcome of our CCTT members and affiliates and their collaboration. It covers a shared definition of crises, jointly articulated problems and evidence-based (potential) solutions, and a co-created vision on how to tackle crisis issues in corporate communications, public health, and risk communications, and the battle against misinformation and conflicting information on various media channels and different industry landscapes. In sum, our book conceptualizes, contextualizes, and actualizes answers not only to "what" and "why" questions but also translates such knowledge to inform "so what" and "how" decisions.

To conclude, we would like to cite what Lewin (1951b) stated, echoing his maxim statement that the innate nature of a good theory is its usefulness (1951a), "[one] should view the present situation–the status quo–as being maintained

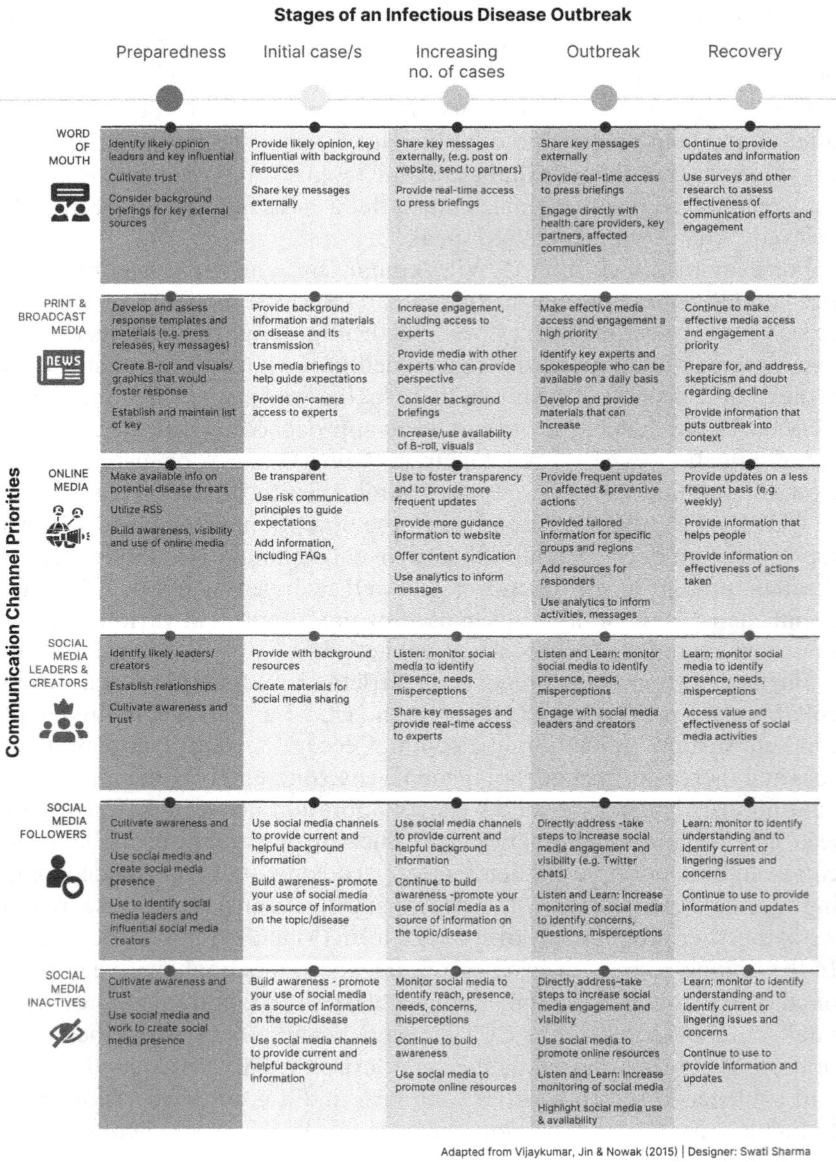

Figure 15.1 Visual Summary of the Risk Amplification through Media Spread (RAMS) Framework (based on Vijaykumar et al., 2015).

Credit: Santosh Vijakumar and Swati Sharma (designer).

by certain conditions or forces" (p. 172). Theory and academic research allow us to investigate and make sense of these uncertain and complex (often interacting) conditions or forces (for example, see Chapter 12). The non-linear process of building a *good* theory (that is, *practical* for business) "is difficult because it requires both great discipline and great creativity, and although a person may possess one of these attributes, few people seem to possess both" and requires "an ability to see things that others have not been able to see, to synthesize disaggregated parts into a new whole" (Shoemaker et al., 2003, p. 10).

The ability and passion to "see things that others have not been able to see" brings back vivid memories of one of the editors' (i.e., Jin) graduate school experience. On the second floor of the Walter Williams Hall at the Missouri School of Journalism, Dr. Keith Sanders was lecturing on factor analysis. In the midst of note-taking and mind-wandering, Jin recalled hearing Dr. Sanders say [likely not the exact words but the essence of what was articulated]:

> Remember the last time you were under a starry night, trying to identify different constellations formed by infinite and seemingly-random stars? Then you might recall the existence of constellations, each formed by a cluster of invisibly connected star-dots, some bearing a divine name from Greek mythology... Soon you started to see the patterns, as our ancestors did, and how the constellations start to emerge from the dark dome to reveal their formations to you, the stargazer, the phenomenon-observer, and the pattern identifier... Well, that's what factor analysis does for us [researchers], to 'see' the hidden patterns in data, to make sense of their connections meaningfully, and ultimately devise some good guide for yourself and your fellow night travelers.

For Jin, that was an "A-Ha!" moment.

This time, in this book, scholars are traveling with practitioners, side by side, providing each other inspiration, support, and guide. And our journey, under infinite starry night, has just begun.

Note

1 Leiden, Netherlands: Brill 2014–2018.

References

Acs, Z. J., Braunerhjelm, P., Audretsch, B. D., & Carlsson, B. (2009). The knowledge spillover theory of entrepreneurship. *Small Business Economics*, *32*, 15–30. https://doi.org/10.1007/s11187-008-9157-3

Argyers, N., & Zenger, T. (2012). Capabilities, transaction costs, and firm boundaries. *Organization Science*, *23*(6), 1643–1657. https://www.jstor.org/stable/23362018

Austin, L. L., Liu, B. F., & Jin, Y. (2012). How audiences seek out crisis information: Exploring the social-mediated crisis communication model. *Journal of Applied Communication Research*, *40*, 188–207. https://doi.org/10.1080/00909882.2012.654498

Baba, Y., Shichijo, N., & Sedita, S. R. (2009). How do collaborations with universities affect firm's innovative performance? The role of "Pasteur scientists" in the advanced materials fields. *Research Policy, 38*, 756–764. https://doi.org/10.1016/j.respol.2009.01.006

Beeson, L. (2020). *Health communications in a crisis.* The University of Georgia. https://greatcommitments.uga.edu/story/health-communications-in-a-crisis/

Bellotti, E., Kronegger. L., & Guadalupi, L. (2016). The evolution of research collaboration within and across disciplines in Italian Academia. *Scientometrics, 109*(2), 783–811. https://doi.org/10.1007/s11192-016-2068-1

Bozeman, B., Fay, D., & Slade, C. P. (2013). Research collaboration in universities and academic entrepreneurship: The-state-of-the-art. *The Journal of Technology Transfer, 38*(1), 1–67. https://doi.org/10.1007/s10961-012-9281-8

Capaldo, G., Costantino, N., Pellegrino, R., & Rippa, P. (2016). Factors affecting the diffusion and success of collaborative interactions between university and industry: The case of research services. *Journal of Science and Technology Policy Management, 7*(3), 273–288. https://doi.org/10.1108/JSTPM-12-2015-0038

Chaffee, S. H. (1991). *Explication.* Sage.

Claeys, A.-S., & Opgenhaffen, M. (2016). Why practitioners do (not) apply crisis communication theory in practice. *Journal of Public Relations Research, 28*(5–6), 232–247. https://doi.org/10.1080/1062726X.2016.1261703

Coombs, W. T. (2015). *Ongoing crisis communication: Planning, managing, and responding* (4th ed.). Sage Publications, Inc.

Cunningham, J. A., Link, A. N. (2015). Fostering university-industry R & D collaborations in European Union countries. *International Entrepreneurship and Management Journal, 11*(4), 849–860. https://doi.org/10.1007/s11365-014-0317-4

Dowling, G. R. (1986). Perceived risk: The concept and its measurement. *Psychology & Marketing, 3*(3), 193–210. https://doi.org/10.1002/mar.4220030307

Etzkowitz, H., & Leydesdorff, L. (1997). *Universities and the global knowledge economy: A triple helix of university-industry-government relations.* Pinter.

Ferrer-Conill, R., & Tandoc Jr., E. C. (2018). The audience-oriented editor: Making sense of the audience in the newsroom. *Digital Journalism, 6*(4), 436–453. https://doi.org/10.1080/21670811.2018.1440972

Freeman, L. C. (2004). *The development of social network analysis: A study in the sociology of science.* BookSurge, LLC.

Galvao, A., Mascarenhas, C., Marques, C., Ferreira, J., & Ratten, V. (2019). Triple helix and its evolution: a systematic literature review. *Journal of Science and Technology Policy Management, 10*(3), 812–833. https://doi.org/10.1108/JSTPM-10-2018-0103

Gancarczyk, M. (2017). *The process of SME growth: Integrating the resource-based and transaction cost approaches.* Jagiellonian University Press.

Ha, J. H., & Boynton, L. (2014). Has crisis communication been studied using an interdisciplinary approach? A 20-year content analysis of communication journals. *International Journal of Strategic Communication, 8*, 29–44. https://doi.org/10.1080/1553118X.2013.850694

Hall, B. H., Link, A. N., & Scott, J. T. (2001). Barriers inhibiting industry from partnering with universities: Evidence from the advanced technology program. *Journal of Technology Transfer, 26*(1), 87–98. https://doi.org/10.1023/A:1007888312792

Johansen, W., & Frandsen, F. (2018, October–November). *Public crisis communication, political crisis communication, and corporate crisis communication: A new triple helix model?* Presentation at the 7th European Communication Conference (ECC), Lugano, Switzerland.

Johnson, B. R., Connolly, E., & Carter, T. S. (2011). Corporate social responsibility: The role of Fortune 100 companies in domestic and international natural disasters. *Corporate Social Responsibility and Environmental Management*, *18*, 352–369. https://doi.org/10.1002/csr.253

Lewin, K. (1951a). Problems of research in social psychology. In D. Cartwright (Ed.), *Field theory in social science: Selected theoretical papers* (pp. 155–169). Harper & Row.

Lewin, K. (1951b). Psychological ecology. In D. Cartwright (Ed.), *Field theory in social science: Selected theoretical papers* (pp. 170–187). Harper & Row.

Liu, B. F., Bartz, L., & Duke, N. (2016). Communicating crisis uncertainty: A review of the knowledge gaps. *Public Relations Review*, *42*(3), 479–487. https://doi.org/10.1016/j.pubrev.2016.03.003

MacGregor, S. P., & Carleton, T. (2012). *Sustaining innovation: Collaboration models for a complex world*. Springer.

McNamara, M. (2012). Starting to untangle the web of cooperation, coordination, and collaboration: A framework for public managers. *International Journal of Public Administration*, 35(6), 389–401. https://doi.org/10.1080/01900692.2012.655527

Melber, H. (2015). Knowledge is power and power affects knowledge: Challenges for research collaboration in and with Africa. *Africa Development*, *4*, 21–42.

Mensah, M. S. B., & Enu-Kwesi, F. (2018). Research collaboration for a knowledge-based economy: Towards a conceptual framework. *Triple Helix*, *5*(1). https://doi.org/10.1186/s40604-018-0049-5

Meyer-Krahmer, F., & Schmoch, U. (1998). Science-based technologies: University-industry interactions in four fields. *Research Policy*, *27*(8), 835–851. https://doi.org/10.1016/S0048-7333(98)00094-8

Muravska, T., & Prause, G. (2012). *European integration and Baltic Sea region studies: University-business partnership through the triple helix approach*. BWV Berliner Wissenschafts-Verlag.

Perkmann, M., & Walsh, K. (2008). Engaging the scholar: Three forms of academic consulting and their impact on universities and industry. *Research Policy*, *37*, 1884–1891. https://doi.org/10.1016/j.respol.2008.07.009

Perkmann, M., & Walsh, K. (2007). University–industry relationship and open innovation: Towards a research agenda. *International Journal of Management Review*, *9*(4), 259–280. https://doi.org/10.1111/j.1468-2370.2007.00225.x

Peter, J. P., & Tarpey Sr, L. X. (1975). A comparative analysis of three consumer decision strategies. *Journal of Consumer Research*, *2*(1), 29–37. https://doi.org/10.1086/208613

Rad, M. F., Seyedesfahani, M. M., & Jalilvand, M. R. (2015). An effective collaboration model between industry and university based on the theory of self organization: A system dynamics model. *Journal of Science & Technology Policy Management*, *6*(1), 2–24. https://doi.org/10.1108/JSTPM-08-2014-0035

Schumpeter, J. A. (1983). *The theory of economic development*. Transaction publishers. German edition: Schumpeter, J. A. (1983) Theorie der wirtschaftlichen entwicklung (trans: Opie R, New Intro: Elliott JE). Harvard University.

Sha, B.-L. (2016). Editor's essay. *Journal of Public Relations Research*, *28*(5–6), 213–216. https://doi.org/10.1080/1062726X.2016.1262151

Shoemaker, P. J., Tankard, J. W., & Lasorsa, D. L. (2003). *How to build social science theories*. Sage.

Sommerfeldt, E. J., & Kent, M. L. (2015). Civil society, networks, and relationship management: Beyond the organization–public Dyad. *International Journal of Strategic Communication*, *9*(3), 235–252. https://doi.org/10.1080/1553118X.2015.1025405

Stacks, D. W., & Salwen, M. B. (2008) (Eds). *An integrated approach to communication theory and research* (2nd ed.). Routledge.

Teirlinck, P., & Spithoven, A. (2013). Research collaboration and R & D outsourcing: Different R & D personnel requirements in SMEs. *Technovation*, *33*(4), 142–153. https://doi.org/10.1016/j.technovation.2012.11.005

Viale, R., & Etzkowitz, H. (2010). *The capitalization of knowledge: A triple helix of university-industry-government*. Edward Elgar.

Vijaykumar, S., Jin, Y., & Nowak, G. (2015). Social media and the virality of risk: The risk amplification through media spread (RAMS) model. *Journal of Homeland Security and Emergency Management*, *12*, 653–677. https://doi.org/10.1515/jhsem-2014-0072

Voges, T. S., Guthrie, W. S., Jin, Y., & Reber, B. H. (2020, September). *Best practices for corporate communication research collaboration between university research groups and industry businesses and organizations: A structure and function analysis*. Presentation at the International CCI International Virtual Conference on Corporate Communication.

Zhou, C. (2014). Four dimensions to observe a Triple Helix: invention of “cored model” and differentiation of institutional and functional spheres. *Triple Helix*, *1*(11). https://doi.org/10.1186/s40604-014-0011-0

Contributors

Editorial Assistants

Caitlin Oh (BA, University of Georgia) was the 2019–2020 University of Georgia (UGA) Crisis Communication Think Tank Intern. She assisted with think tank strategic planning and event programming, as well as coordination between the book editors and chapter contributors. She graduated from UGA in 2020 with bachelor's degrees in public relations and psychology (with an emphasis in neuroscience). She currently studies at Emory University School of Law for her JD degree.

Taylor S. Voges (MS, Texas Christian University) is a doctoral student and graduate assistant at the Grady College of Journalism and Mass Communication, University of Georgia. She studies public relations and ethics—with an interest in conflicts and legal issues. She has published in *Public Relations Review* and presented at national and international research conferences. In 2020, she received a Top Student Paper Award from the Cultural and Critical Studies Division of the Association for Education in Journalism and Mass Communication (AEJMC).

Foreword

C. Richard Yarbrough (BA, University of Georgia) is a graduate of the Grady College of Journalism and Mass Communications at the University of Georgia. He retired as vice president—public relations at BellSouth Corporation and was named managing director—communications and government relations for the Atlanta Committee for the 1996 Centennial Olympic Games. He was recognized by PRWeek Magazine as one of the 100 Most Influential Public Relations Practitioners of the 20th Century. Yarbrough has created the C. Richard Yarbrough Professorship in Crisis Communications Leadership at his alma mater.

Chapter 1: Complex and Challenging Crises: A Call for Solutions

Yan Jin (PhD, University of Missouri) is the Georgia Athletic Association Professor and a professor of public relations at the Grady College of

Journalism and Mass Communication, University of Georgia (UGA). She is also the Assistant Department Head of Advertising and Public Relations and Associate Director of the Center for Health & Risk Communication at UGA. Dr. Jin's work serves as a framework for crisis and risk communication in a rapidly evolving media landscape and amidst emotionally charged conflict situations, ranging from organizational crises to disasters and public health emergencies. She is a co-founder of UGA's Crisis Communication Think Tank.

Glen Nowak (PhD, University of Wisconsin-Madison) is a Professor of Advertising and Public Relations at the University of Georgia College of Journalism and Mass Communication and Director of its Center for Health and Risk Communication. Dr. Nowak spent 14 years at the US Centers for Disease Control and Prevention, including six years as the Communications Director for the National Immunization Program and six years as the agency's Director of Media Relations.

Bryan H. Reber (PhD, University of Missouri) is C. Richard Yarbrough Professor in Crisis Communication Leadership and Head of the Department of Advertising and Public Relations at the College of Journalism and Mass Communication, University of Georgia. Dr. Reber has published over 50 journal articles, book chapters, and encyclopedia entries. He is co-author of the book *Gaining Influence in Public Relations: The Role of Resistance in Practice*, and three top-selling public relations textbooks. Dr. Reber is a member of the Arthur W. Page Society and serves as Research Director of the Plank Center for Leadership in Public Relations.

C. Richard Yarbrough (BA, University of Georgia) is a graduate of the Grady College of Journalism and Mass Communications at the University of Georgia. He retired as vice president—public relations at BellSouth Corporation and was named managing director—communications and government relations for the Atlanta Committee for the 1996 Centennial Olympic Games. He was recognized by PRWeek Magazine as one of the 100 Most Influential Public Relations Practitioners of the 20th Century. Yarbrough has created the C. Richard Yarbrough Professorship in Crisis Communications Leadership at his alma mater.

Chapter 2: The Evolving Complexity of Crisis Issues: The Role of Crisis History

LaShonda L. Eaddy (PhD, University of Georgia) is an assistant professor of public relations and strategic communication in the Division of Corporate Communication and Public Affairs at Southern Methodist University. Dr. Eaddy is a crisis history expert and investigates ways that crisis history can inform crisis communications scholarship and crisis communication strategy. The self-proclaimed "practitioner scholar" is passionate about public relations research as well as practice. She is accredited in public relations (APR) and has spent time as a public relations professional primarily in the healthcare industry.

Shelley Spector, (MS, Newhouse School, Syracuse University) is founder/director of the Museum of Public Relations, the world's only museum serving the public relations field and founder/director of Spector & Associates, an award-winning public relations firm in NYC. An adjunct professor at NYU and Baruch College/CUNY, Spector speaks to PR classes on public relations history. Spector has contributed chapters to PR history books, co-authored the book *Public Relations for the Public Good,* and co-edited the book *Diverse Voices,* published with the PRSA Foundation.

Chapter 3: Corporate Crises: Sticky Crises and Corporations

W. Timothy Coombs (PhD, Purdue University) is the George T and Glady H Abell Professor in Liberal Arts in Department of Communication at Texas A&M University, has been an honorary professor at Aarhus University, a 2013 Fulbright Scholar in Estonia, and was the NEMO Professor at Lund University, Helsingborg Campus. His primary research area is crisis communication, including the award-winning book Ongoing Crisis Communication. Dr. Coombs has been researching, consulting, and training in crisis communication for the past 20 years. He has provided crisis training in Belgium, Sweden, Estonia, Norway, Indonesia, Singapore, South Korea, and China.

Sherry J. Holladay (PhD, Purdue University) is Professor of Communication at Texas A&M University in College Station, Texas, US. Her research addresses strategic communication in (para)crisis communication, issues management, corporate social responsibility and irresponsibility, and activism. Her work has appeared in *Public Relations Review, Management Communication Quarterly, Journal of Communication Management, and International Journal of Strategic Communication.* She is co-editor of the *Handbook of Crisis Communication* and co-author of *It's Not Just PR: Public Relations in Society, Public Relations Strategies and Applications: Managing Influence,* and *Managing Corporate Social Responsibility.*

Rick White (BA, University of North Carolina-Chapel Hill) has provided leadership and counsel to organizations and industries operating in challenging business, regulatory, political, and media environments for over four decades. His experience in military public affairs, telecommunications, energy, and higher education includes more than 25 years as a Fortune 500 chief communications officer. He is a member of the adjunct faculty of the School of Journalism and Media at The University of North Carolina at Chapel Hill.

Chapter 4: Connected in Crisis: How Nonprofit Organizations Can Respond and Refocus

Mark McMullen (MA, University of Phoenix) is Senior Vice President of Membership & Marketing for the Knights of Columbus. In his role, he leads the membership and program efforts of the nearly 2,000,000 Knights of Columbus worldwide.

Hilary Fussell Sisco (PhD, University of South Carolina) is a Professor of Strategic Communication at Quinnipiac University. Dr. Fussell Sisco is also the founding Chair of the Strategic Communication Department at Quinnipiac. Dr. Fussell Sisco is the Editor-in-Chief of *Public Relations Journal*. She is accredited in public relations (APR).

Chapter 5: Media Relations for Government/Public Affairs Crises: Ethical and Unethical Components of Scandal and Spin

David E. Clementson (PhD, Ohio State University) is Assistant Professor of Public Relations at the University of Georgia. He runs experiments testing the effects of public figures dodging questions. His research has been published in *Journal of Communication, Presidential Studies Quarterly, Public Relations Review*, and *Political Psychology*, among others. His research has been featured in *Politico* magazine, *Newsweek, Psychology Today, Scientific American, the New York Post, New York* magazine, NBC news, the *Daily Mail*, and NPR. He has worked as a journalist covering government and politics, and as a campaign manager and consultant for successful Democratic and Republican candidates.

Michael Greenwell (BA, University of Missouri-Kansas City) is Vice President of Business Development at ICF International, a global consulting services company. He has experience across multiple sectors, including health and risk communications. He served for 14 years as the communications director for two large centers within the CDC. He serves on numerous boards, including the American Heart Association and the Sudden Cardiac Arrest Association, and has served as a senior consultant to the Arthritis Foundation, Chronic Fatigue and Immune Deficiency Syndrome Association, and the Interstitial Cystitis Association.

Joseph Watson, Jr. (JD, Harvard University) is the Carolyn Caudell Tieger Professor of Public Affairs Communications at the University of Georgia. He directs the first-in-the-nation Public Affairs Communications Program, providing undergraduate students with practical training in the strategy and practice of public affairs communications focused on government, public policy, and politics. Watson has over 20 years' experience in campaigns and communications. He served as an appointee in the Administration of President George W. Bush, as a senior aide to former US Senator Peter G. Fitzgerald, and established and led the public advocacy group for a Fortune 100 company.

Chapter 6: A Promising but Difficult Domain: Complex Health-related Crises and Academic-Professional Collaboration

Michael Greenwell (BA, University of Missouri-Kansas City) is Vice President of Business Development at ICF International, a global consulting services company. He has experience across multiple sectors, including health and risk communications. He served for 14 years as the communications director for two large centers within the CDC. He serves on numerous boards, including the American Heart Association and the Sudden Cardiac Arrest Association, and has served as a senior consultant to the Arthritis Foundation, Chronic Fatigue and Immune Deficiency Syndrome Association, and the Interstitial Cystitis Association.

Glen Nowak (PhD, University of Wisconsin-Madison) is a Professor of Advertising and Public Relations at the University of Georgia College of Journalism and Mass Communication and Director of its Center for Health and Risk Communication. Dr. Nowak spent 14 years at the US Centers for Disease Control and Prevention, including six years as the Communications Director for the National Immunization Program and six years as the agency's Director of Media Relations.

Chapter 7: Disaster and Emergency Crisis Management Communication

Chris Glazier (BA, University of Florida) is an Account Manager at Porter Novelli and has over a decade of experience in public relations and journalism. He specializes in developing and executing comprehensive traditional and digital media outreach across a variety of industries, including nonprofit, healthcare, retail, and tech. He currently leads the agency's work with the CDC diabetes campaign, National 4-H Council, and Navicent Health. He has experience in crisis and issues management, working with the Georgia Emergency Management Agency and developing crisis playbooks for major organizations. Chris started his career as a magazine editor before transitioning to PR.

Greg Guest (BA, University of Georgia) is senior director of corporate communications for Georgia-Pacific (GP), responsible for corporate reputation and storytelling and employee communications. Greg joined GP in 1994 supporting communications for the timberland operations. He has held positions focused on communicating to internal and external audiences, including leading GP's financial communications and media relations function, and serving in investor relations when GP was publicly held. Previously, Greg was in communications with Savannah Electric and worked as a journalist with newspapers in Augusta and Savannah, Georgia.

Robert L. Heath (PhD, University of Illinois) is professor emeritus at the University of Houston. He has published extensively in journals, book chapters, and books on topics such as emergency management communication, crisis communication, issues management, public relations, strategic communication, corporate social responsibility, and organizational rhetoric.

J. Suzanne Horsley (PhD, University of North Carolina-Chapel Hill) is an associate professor of public relations and Assistant Dean of the College of Communication and Information Sciences at The University of Alabama. She previously spent a decade in the public relations industry, primarily with state government agencies in Virginia, and has volunteered as a disaster public affairs spokesperson and media trainer with the American Red Cross since 2009.

Chapter 8: Managing Misinformation and Conflicting Information: A Framework for Understanding Misinformation and Rumor

Lucinda Austin (PhD, University of Maryland) is an assistant professor of public relations and PhD program director in the Hussman School of Journalism and Media at the University of North Carolina at Chapel Hill. Her research examines pressing problems in public relations and public interest, primarily addressing social media, crisis, and health communication, and publics' perspectives in corporate social responsibility and advocacy. She is co-editor of the Routledge book *Social Media and Crisis Communication.*

Yen-I Lee (PhD, University of Georgia) is an Assistant Professor of Strategic Communication in the Edward R. Murrow College of Communication at Washington State University. Her primary research is in the areas of health communication and strategic communication, focusing on the role of messaging content, technology use, visual attention, and emotions in the context of health crisis and risk communication.

Jim Spangler (BS, University of Illinois at Urbana-Champaign) is Chief Communications Officer at Markel Corporation, where he leads global communications for insurance operations. Spangler and his team are responsible for developing and executing strategic internal and external communications designed to drive business performance and enhance the company's reputation with key stakeholders. Critical areas of focus include internal communications, media relations, executive communications, issues management, and crisis communications.

Toni G. L. A. van der Meer (PhD, University of Amsterdam School of Communication Research) is an assistant professor in Corporate Communication at the Amsterdam School of Communication Research (ASCoR) at the University van Amsterdam. Besides crisis communication, his current research primarily focuses on the process of media and public framing of issues, mediatization, and biases in news media.

Chapter 9: Technology and Social Media: Challenges and Opportunities for Effective Crisis and Risk Communication

Lucinda Austin (PhD, University of Maryland) is an assistant professor of public relations and PhD program director in the Hussman School of Journalism and Media at the University of North Carolina at Chapel Hill. Her research examines pressing problems in public relations and public interest, primarily addressing social media, crisis, and health communication, and publics' perspectives in corporate social responsibility and advocacy. She is co-editor of the Routledge book *Social Media and Crisis Communication.*

Ciro Dias Reis studied Literature and Journalism at Universidade São Paulo (USP) in São Paulo, Brazil. Founder and CEO of Brazilian PR & Public Affairs firm Imagem Corporativa, he became Global Chair of PROI Worldwide in June 2020. He is also a board member of the International Communications Consultancy Organization (ICCO) and member of the Advisory Council of the Grady College of Journalism and Mass Communication, University of Georgia. Ciro Dias Reis was president of the Brazilian association of PR companies (Abracom) for two terms and is a council member of the organization.

Deanna D. Sellnow (PhD, University of North Dakota) is a professor of strategic communication and Assistant Director of the Nicholson School of Communication and Media at the University of Central Florida. Her research focuses on strategic instructional communication in a variety of contexts, including risk, crisis, and health. She has conducted numerous funded research projects with agencies such as the CDC, USDA, WHO, and USGA, and has published in national and international journals.

Chapter 10: Law and (Lack of) Order in Complex Crises

James D. Firth (MBA, University of New Hampshire) is a strategic communications and public affairs executive. He served as a senior vice president at Exelon Corporation, a Fortune 100 energy company. Firth led the company's communications organization and oversaw corporate communications, internal communications, public advocacy, and corporate giving. He also served as an officer at a New England electric utility company and established a public affairs consultancy. Firth serves on the board of WTTW/WFMT and Chicago's public television and radio stations, and the corporate board of Chicago's Boys and Girls Clubs, and is an Arthur W. Page Society member.

Jonathan Peters (PhD, University of Missouri, JD, Ohio State University) is a media law professor at the University of Georgia, with appointments in the College of Journalism and Mass Communication and the School of Law. He is the press freedom correspondent for the *Columbia Journalism Review* and a coauthor of the textbook *The Law of Public Communication*, now in its eleventh edition.

Joseph Watson, Jr. (JD, Harvard University) is the Carolyn Caudell Tieger Professor of Public Affairs Communications at the University of Georgia. He directs the first-in-the-nation Public Affairs Communications Program, providing undergraduate students with practical training in the strategy and practice of public affairs communications focused on government, public policy, and politics. Watson has over 20 years of experience in campaigns and communications. He served as an appointee in the Administration of President George W. Bush, as a senior aide to former US Senator Peter G. Fitzgerald, and established and led the public advocacy group for a Fortune 100 company.

Chapter 11: Situational Crisis Communication Theory (SCCT) and Application in Dealing with Complex, Challenging, and Recurring Crises

W. Timothy Coombs (PhD, Purdue University) is the George T and Glady H Abell Professor in Liberal Arts in Department of Communication at Texas A&M University, has been an honorary professor at Aarhus University, a 2013 Fulbright Scholar in Estonia, and was the NEMO Professor at Lund University, Helsingborg Campus. His primary research area is crisis communication, including the award-winning book *Ongoing Crisis Communication.* Dr. Coombs has been researching, consulting, and training in crisis communication for the past 20 years. He has provided crisis training in Belgium, Sweden, Estonia, Norway, Indonesia, Singapore, South Korea, and China.

Sherry J. Holladay (PhD, Purdue University) is Professor of Communication at Texas A&M University in College Station, Texas, US. Her research addresses strategic communication in (para)crisis communication, issues management, corporate social responsibility and irresponsibility, and activism. Her work has appeared in *Public Relations Review, Management Communication Quarterly, Journal of Communication Management, and International Journal of Strategic Communication.* She is co-editor of the *Handbook of Crisis Communication* and *co-author of It's Not Just PR: Public Relations in Society, Public Relations Strategies and Applications: Managing Influence,* and *Managing Corporate Social Responsibility.*

Karen L. White (BA, University of Georgia) is Executive Director, Corporate Affairs at Amgen, Inc., a global biotechnology company. Over her 30-year career in corporate public relations in the healthcare industry, she has led communication efforts in a variety of crisis situations, including natural disasters, regulatory issues, and restructuring. She earned a Bachelor of Arts in Journalism/Public Relations at the University of Georgia.

Chapter 12: Managing Complexity: Insights from the Contingency Theory of Strategic Conflict Management

Glen T. Cameron (PhD, University of Texas at Austin) is a professor emeritus and the Maxine Wilson Gregory Chair in Journalism Research at the Missouri School of Journalism. He also is founder and co-director of the Health Communication Research Center at the University of Missouri. Cameron has a joint appointment in Family and Community Medicine to study patient-centered outcomes research.

Yan Jin (PhD, University of Missouri) is the Georgia Athletic Association Professor and a professor of public relations at the Grady College of Journalism and Mass Communication, University of Georgia (UGA). She is also the Assistant Department Head of Advertising and Public Relations and Associate Director of the Center for Health & Risk Communication at UGA. Dr. Jin's work serves as a framework for crisis and risk communication in a rapidly evolving media landscape and amidst emotionally charged conflict situations, ranging from organizational crises to disasters and public health emergencies. She is a co-founder of UGA's Crisis Communication Think Tank.

Sungsu Kim (PhD, University of Georgia) is an Assistant Professor of Advertising and Public Relations in the School of Communication at Kookmin University, South Korea. His research areas include public relations, crisis communication, strategic health communication, campaign message effects, and social media interaction. He focuses on exploring the role of crisis distance in determining how publics perceive and react to crisis in different contexts ranging from organizational crisis to health crisis and disasters. His research has appeared in journals such as *Health Communication*, *International Journal of Communication*, *American Journal of Health Behavior*, *Journal of Communication Management*, and *Communication Studies*.

Leonard (Len) A. Pagano, Jr. (ABJ, University of Georgia) is the founder and CEO of the Safe America Foundation. Headquartered in Atlanta, the nonprofit has worked for over 25 years in being the 'voice of safety,' providing guidance to health and safety to both individuals as well as companies. Originally, Len's work was in broadcasting (with NBC Television affiliates). After his work in news, Len ran chambers of commerce in Atlanta and Miami, winning 17 national marketing awards. He also engineered Atlanta's hosting the Democratic Party Convention in 1988.

Augustine Pang (PhD, University of Missouri) is Professor of Communication Management (Practice) at the Lee Kong Chian School of Business, Singapore Management University. At SMU, he is the Academic Director, MSc in Communication Management. In 2019, he was made Fellow, SMU Academy. He is an Honorary Fellow at Hong Kong Polytechnic University; a member of the Arthur W. Page Society (US); and Vice-Chair of the Asia-Pacific PR Research and Education Network. In 2016, he won the Kitty O Locker Outstanding Researcher Award from the Association for Business Communication (US) for his body of work in crisis communication and management.

Chapter 13: Calming Giants in the Earth: The Internalization, Distribution, Explanation, and Action (IDEA) Model as Strategic Communication in Crises with Competing Narratives

Ciro Dias Reis studied Literature and Journalism at Universidade São Paulo (USP) in São Paulo, Brazil. Founder and CEO of Brazilian PR & Public Affairs firm Imagem Corporativa, he became Global Chair of PROI Worldwide in June 2020. He is also a board member of the International Communications Consultancy Organization (ICCO) and member of the Advisory Council of the Grady College of Journalism and Mass Communication, University of Georgia. Ciro Dias Reis was president of the Brazilian association of PR companies (Abracom) for two terms and is a council member of the organization.

Deanna D. Sellnow (PhD, University of North Dakota) is a professor of strategic communication and Assistant Director of the Nicholson School of Communication and Media at the University of Central Florida. Her research focuses on strategic instructional communication in a variety of contexts, including risk, crisis, and health. She has conducted numerous funded research projects with agencies such as the CDC, USDA, WHO, and USGA, and has published in national and international journals.

Timothy L. Sellnow (PhD, Wayne State University) is a professor of strategic communication in the Nicholson School of Communication at the University of Central Florida. Dr. Sellnow researches biosecurity, pre-crisis planning, and strategic communication for risk management and mitigation in government, organizational, and health settings. He has conducted funded research for the Department of Homeland Security, the Department of Agriculture, the Centers for Disease Control and Prevention, the Environmental Protection Agency, the United States Geological Survey, and the World Health Organization. He has served as an advisor for the National Academy of Sciences and the Food and Drug Administration.

Chapter 14: The Social-Mediated Crisis Communication (SMCC) Model: Identifying the Next Frontier

Lucinda Austin (PhD, University of Maryland) is an assistant professor of public relations and PhD program director in the Hussman School of Journalism and Media at the University of North Carolina at Chapel Hill. Her research examines pressing problems in public relations and public interest, primarily addressing social media, crisis, and health communication, and publics' perspectives in corporate social responsibility and advocacy. She is co-editor of the Routledge book *Social Media and Crisis Communication*.

Yan Jin (PhD, University of Missouri) is the Georgia Athletic Association Professor and a professor of public relations at the Grady College of Journalism and Mass Communication, University of Georgia (UGA). She is also the Assistant Department Head of Advertising and Public Relations and Associate Director of the Center for Health & Risk Communication at UGA. Dr. Jin's work serves as a framework for crisis and risk communication in a rapidly evolving media landscape and amidst emotionally charged conflict situations, ranging from organizational crises to disasters and public health emergencies. She is a co-founder of UGA's Crisis Communication Think Tank.

Erica Kuligowski (PhD, University of Colorado at Boulder) is a Sociologist and Fire Protection Engineer with 18 years of experience working as a Research Social Scientist and Engineer in the Engineering Laboratory at the US National Institute of Standards and Technology (NIST). Her research on evacuation and sheltering behavior and emergency communications in disaster events has received prestigious awards from the US Department of Commerce and international fire engineering organizations. Her work has led to the development of new or improved building codes and community standards and decision-making tools for disaster response.

Brooke Fisher Liu (PhD, University of North Carolina) is a professor of communication at the University of Maryland (UMD) and Associate Dean of Academic Standards and Policies within the UMD Graduate School. Her research examines how government messages, media, and interpersonal communication can motivate people to successfully respond and recover from disasters. From 2018–2020, she served as the editor of the *Journal of International Crisis and Risk Communication Research*.

Camila Espina Young (PhD, University of Georgia) is a Research Social Scientist in the Structures Group of the Materials and Structural Systems Division (MSSD) of the Engineering Laboratory (EL) at the National Institute of Standards and Technology (NIST). At NIST, she is currently part of the Hurricane Maria Program, specifically working on the National Construction Safety Team (NCST) Act project characterizing the performance of critical facilities, such as hospitals, schools, and shelters. Her research interests include media effects, risk communication effectiveness, and social media use before, during, and after disasters.

Chapter 15: The Future of Collaborative Crisis Research

Yan Jin (PhD, University of Missouri) is the Georgia Athletic Association Professor and a professor of public relations at the Grady College of Journalism and Mass Communication, University of Georgia (UGA). She is also the Assistant Department Head of Advertising and Public Relations and Associate Director of the Center for Health & Risk Communication at UGA. Dr. Jin's work serves as a framework for crisis and risk communication in a rapidly evolving media landscape and amidst emotionally charged conflict situations, ranging from organizational crises to disasters and public health emergencies. She is a co-founder of UGA's Crisis Communication Think Tank.

Glen Nowak (PhD, University of Wisconsin-Madison) is a Professor of Advertising and Public Relations at the University of Georgia College of Journalism and Mass Communication and Director of its Center for Health and Risk Communication. Dr. Nowak spent 14 years at the US Centers for Disease Control and Prevention, including six years as the Communications Director for the National Immunization Program and six years as the agency's Director of Media Relations.

Matthew O'Connor (BS, University of Kentucky) is Senior Manager of Public Relations at UPS where he is responsible for urgent and crisis communications, issues management, and local market public relations. A veteran of small, medium, and large agencies and corporations, he specializes in reputation management, integrated marketing communications, and customer engagement.

Bryan H. Reber (PhD, University of Missouri) is C. Richard Yarbrough Professor in Crisis Communication Leadership and Head of the Department of Advertising and Public Relations at the College of Journalism and Mass Communication, University of Georgia. Dr. Reber has published over 50 journal articles, book chapters, and encyclopedia entries. He is co-author of the book *Gaining Influence in Public Relations: The Role of Resistance in Practice* and three top-selling public relations textbooks. Dr. Reber is a member of the Arthur W. Page Society and serves as Research Director of the Plank Center for Leadership in Public Relations.

Index

Note: **Bold** page numbers refer to **tables** and *italic* page numbers refer to figures.